CONTENTS

List of Tables and Figures   *vii*

Acknowledgements   *ix*

Foreword   *xi*

Introduction   1

SECTION ONE – PRACTICE AND LIVED EXPERIENCE

1   Young Person's Story: There's No Place Like Home   10

2   Worker's Story: The Impossible Task?   26

SECTION TWO – RESIDENTIAL CHILD CARE

3   Myths Surrounding Residential Child Care   60

4   Residential Child Care in the Republic of Ireland   73

SECTION THREE – THEORY AND APPROACHES

5   Attachment Theory, Resilience, Focal Theory
and Listening   119

6   Social Pedagogy, Relationship-Based Practice
and Mentoring   164

SECTION FOUR – CHILDREN'S RIGHTS AND POLICY

7   Children's Rights   181

8   Social Policy   203

SECTION FIVE – RESEARCH

9 Research in Care and Aftercare   218

10 An Alternative Research Construct   240

SECTION SIX – RETHINKING RESIDENTIAL CARE, LEAVING CARE AND AFTERCARE

11 The Profession, the Professional and Professionalisation 247

12 The Socio-Political and Socio-Economic Context   269

Conclusion   325

Appendix: The Economic Case for Statutory Aftercare in the Republic of Ireland   330

Bibliography   339

Index   393

LIST OF TABLES AND FIGURES

List of Tables

Table 1: Key Issues Arising from Keith's Story   28

Table 2. Percentage of Children in Care in Residential
Placements by Country   74

Table 3: Summary of HIQA Findings for Special Care Units   79

Table 4: Summary of HIQA Findings for Detention Schools   80

Table 5: Cost of Special Care Units   81

Table 6: Cost of High Support Units   81

Table 7: The Data for the Period 2006-2014 used to Inform
Figures 5 and 6 and Includes Data for Children in Special Care
Placements and Out-of-State Placements   100

Table 8: Care Placements, 2006-2008   101

Table 9: The Total Number of Children in Care within July
2014 and the Breakdown of Placements within the Residential
Care Sector   102

Table 10: The Number of Care Leavers in Receipt of
an Aftercare Service over the Period 2006-2014   208

Table 11: Cost Comparison Northern Ireland and
the Republic of Ireland   311

Table 12: Lifetime Costs per Person Leaving Care
in Australia   336

List of Figures

Figure 1: Bronfenbrenner's Ecological Model (1979) 2

Figure 2: The Total Number of Children in Care in the
Republic of Ireland, 1970 and 2006 96

Figure 3: The Number of Children in Foster Care Placements
in the Republic of Ireland, 1970-2006 97

Figure 4: The Number of Children in Residential Care
Placements in the Republic of Ireland, 1970-2006 97

Figure 5: The Number of Children in Care and Admitted into
Care and the Number of Children in Foster Care, 2006-2014 98

Figure 6: The Number of Children in Residential Care
Placements, Private Foster Care Placements, Private Residential
Care Placements and High Support Placements, 2006-2014 98

Figure 7: The Number of Private Residential Care Centres and
HSE/Tusla (statutory) Centres over the Period 2006-2015 104

Figure 8: The Idealised Model of Developmental Relationship 129

Figure 9: The Diamond Model 168

ACKNOWLEDGEMENTS

First and foremost, I must acknowledge the support and love of my wife and children. Their patience, love and support was and is immense.

Others who warrant mention for their role in either contributing to my ability to write this book or directly to the book are: Simon Bradford, Finbar Markey, Gabriel Eichsteller, Stefan Kleipoedszus, Victor, Paul Boucher, Patricia Mulligan, Ray Roger, Sinead Lynch, Alan Hendricks, Deirdre Coyle, Patrick Tomlinson, Eamonn Murphy, John Pinkerton and David Givens from The Liffey Press.

I owe much for the encouragement of Noel Howard, Sr. Stan and Ray Arthur who read early drafts and gave priceless positive feedback. Versions of my chapter and Keith's chapter appeared in the book *Social Care: Learning form Practice* published by Gill and Macmillan in 2014 and edited by Noel Howard and Denise Lyons. I am grateful to Noel, Denise and Gill and Macmillan for permission to reproduce adaptations of these chapters in this book, and highly recommend their book for the many other excellent chapters therein affording insight into social care practice in a wide range of settings. Also Eoin O'Sullivan, Jessica Breen and Social Work Now for permission to reproduce data on children's services from 1970–2006.

Finally, I am deeply grateful to Keith King for permission to use his story in this book. He, and so many other young people I met over my time working in residential care, continue to fill me with hope and determination and this book is mostly written for them.

FOREWORD

John Pinkerton

This book by Maurice Fenton is a timely and challenging contribution to the leaving and aftercare literature from a much needed vantage point – that of a critically reflective practitioner who has worked at all levels in residential care, trainee to director, within the statutory, voluntary and private sectors, and who is spurred on by experience, research and reflection to constantly ask why and why not?

Over the last decade in a growing number of countries, including the Republic of Ireland, there has been an increasing interest in the experiences of young people transitioning from out of home care into adulthood. In part this interest has been fuelled by a sense of failure. Internationally, the received wisdom is that care experienced young people are generally ill prepared and coping poorly with the challenge of contemporary youth transitions when compared to their contemporaries. The tendency towards aftercare outcomes that paint a bleak picture and bode ill for future life are emphasised – housing insecurity, low educational attainment, unemployment, loneliness, young parenthood, dependence on state benefits, trouble with the law, involvement with psychiatric services, vulnerability to sexual exploitation.

Even in those countries with the resources and welfare systems to take seriously the leaving and aftercare responsibilities of corporate parenting, the multidimensional life stage transition into adulthood seems to be becoming more difficult for care experienced young people. They are faced with finding ways to make the transition from out of home care, which have been disorientated by austerity programmes, into uncertain, complex and shifting aftercare arrangements which uneasily combine elements of family, civil society, market and state.

But there is another, positive cause for the growing international engagement with leaving and aftercare. There now exists a momentum for change – albeit uneven in its impact and uncertain in its direction. There is an optimism fuelled by experience and understanding of where and how advances can be made: assertive advocacy, not least by care experienced young people themselves; legislative reform and policy development underpinned by the UN Convention on the Rights of the Child; improvement in service design and practice delivery that differentiates between the various needs requiring attention; and improvements in information and research allowing for individual and systemic monitoring and evaluation. All of this means that law and policy-makers, service designers, managers and practitioners and all those working alongside young people coping with leaving and aftercare are better prepared for the task than they have ever been.

Both those perspectives are reflected in the wealth of material purposefully marshalled in the six sections that make up this book. In the ensuing discussion of difficult and disputed issues, an evidence-based and theory-informed approach is used to ensure even-handed consideration. That does not mean shying away from taking a position on what is impeding and what is promoting the young person-centred and relationship-based practice Maurice is concerned to better understand in order to better advance. It is no accident that the first chapter is a young person's story followed then by a worker's story – both in their way Maurice's own story. He uses the power of testimony to capture the poignancy and contradictions of the lived experience of residential care, leaving care and aftercare as human relationships. As his attention to the skilled managing of professional, personal and private relationships and boundaries makes clear, social inclusion through appropriate interdependence, not social exclusion dressed up as independence, is both the goal and the method.

Having established the lived experience of relationship-based practice as his core concern, Maurice then constructs a framework for critical reflection based on a detailed description of legal and institutional arrangements in Ireland, emphasising the residualisation of residential care, along with a review of key theory (including a particularly useful account of focal theory) and up to date research, including his own. Anyone who has attempted to teach critical reflection knows how hard it is to capture and convey it in a tangible way. This book is a splendid expression of it – not least its contentious and unfinished nature.

As the contents of this book makes clear, if care experienced young people in Ireland, and elsewhere, are to achieve social inclusion, attention must be focused on finding ways of meeting their material needs: maintaining good health, finding accommodation, getting an income, continuing or entering education, training or employment. At the same time, they have to be helped to become sufficiently secure in their own identity and to have the self-confidence and social competence to cope with the emotional and relationship challenges that they will face. For those working alongside them it is necessary to be constantly considering both the material and the psycho-social dimensions to their lives and how the two are interacting. It is also necessary to locate that dynamic in the context of their changing personal, socio-economic and political circumstances.

As with any socially excluded group, it is the expectations, judgements and actions of care experienced young people themselves, individually and collectively, that is their core resource for achieving their well-being and protection and optimising their life chances. The challenge to those responsible for helping them to realise their potential, whether through law reform, policy development, service design or skilled social care practice, is to find ways together to provide supportive scaffolding and to dismantle disabling barriers. That requires constant critical reflection based on active engagement, information, understanding and a constant curiosity – precisely the ingredients that give this book its strength.

John Pinkerton
Professor of Child & Family Social Work
Queen's University Belfast

The Stolen Child

W.B. Yeats

Come away, O human child!
To the waters and the wild
With a faery, hand in hand,
For the world's more full of weeping
Than you can understand.

Introduction

There has been a notable paucity of published works addressing the integration of residential care, leaving care and aftercare as connected elements in a system of care. A system of care (Anglin, 2004) comprises the different forms of services available within a wider care system. These can include kinship care, semi-independent living and supported independent living arrangements, short-term foster care, mainstream residential care, special care and secure care. A care system involves a wide variety of stakeholders in a child's life including, but not limited to, policymakers, service providers, including those within the disability and mental health sectors, administrators, judiciary and legal professionals, politicians and government departments, researchers and family.

Such a perspective recognises that to consider aftercare it is necessary to understand the in-care experience, as well as the wider forces that shape that experience. Adopting such a perspective requires the recognition of the care experience for both the young person and the carer, as the two are dyadic elements. Quality social care is delivered by properly resourced and valued staff who are able to synthesise the wider dynamics at play which influence both their profession and those they seek to support. This book will employ an ecological framework approach which "provides a systemic framework in which to consider various psychological and sociological theories in respect of human behaviour and events" (de Róiste, 2013:81) and consequently will be located within psychological and sociological paradigms.

Figure 1: *Bronfenbrenner's Ecological Model (1979).*

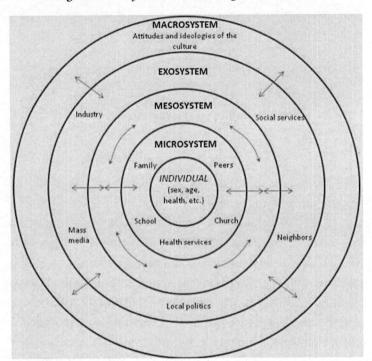

There will be a focus of the role that dominant paradigms in practice, theory, policy, research and the socio-political environment play in influencing practice. As research informs both theory and policy development, which in turn inform practice, each of these areas will be examined in addition to the human experiences of both young people in care and workers in the social professions. A balanced evaluation of these factors by the worker, using their professional judgement which necessitates the interrogation of commonly held assumptions, will be advocated. The objective is to identify which theoretical approach or model of practice, or combination of theories or approaches, is most appropriate for the individual young person or group they are supporting. Critical reflection will be promoted by the strategic inclusion of certain key concepts and reflective questions throughout the book. This objective is in line with the recommendation of the Munro Report (2011), which advocated moving away from a culture of compliance towards one of reliance on professional judgement, which it identified as:

> ... requires social workers to be in possession of the right knowledge and be capable of clear reasoning. Children need and deserve a high level of expertise from their social workers who make such crucial decisions about what is in their best interests. This expertise should include being skilled in relationships where care and control often need to be combined, able to make critical use of best evidence from research to inform the complex judgements and decisions needed and to help children and families to solve problems and to change. (Munro, 2011:84)

In addressing social policy it is recognised that:

> Social policy is political in its aims and social effects, both intended and unintended and develops out of a system of power and control in a society. With cultural and economic factors, it contributes to a macrosystem and provides the context for the microsystem (see Bronfenbrenner, above)... (Petrie, 2011:75)

This, then, requires the inclusion of psychosocial, socio-political and socio-economic factors, including structural inequalities and social policy responses. Consequently, issues such as social justice and the professionalisation agenda currently unfolding in the UK and the Republic of Ireland will also be investigated. Neither residential care nor aftercare occur in isolation; they are interconnected within wider systems.

Coupled with this deficit in published material there is also an absence of formal modules on either undergraduate or postgraduate courses covering the area of leaving care and aftercare in both the Republic of Ireland and the UK. Neither are there any Continuous Professional Development (CPD) modules available in either jurisdiction. This book is intended to address these gaps and to stimulate further research within the professions of social care and social work, and the sub-domains of residential care and aftercare.

This book will examine the areas of residential care, and the two components of throughcare, namely, preparation for leaving care and aftercare, with a specific focus on the Republic of Ireland. For the purposes of this book I am selecting the model of throughcare defined within the *Pathways Handbook* published by the Scottish Throughcare and Aftercare Forum:

> Throughcare is the ongoing preparation and support for young people who have been looked after and who may soon be making the transition to live more independently.

There is much in common in terms of welfare and social service provision between the Republic of Ireland and the UK (Stein and Munro, 2008; Pinkerton, 2012). This, together with the fact that much of the cited research is internationally located, affords a comparative aspect to this book. Indeed, the 2008 research paper by Collins and Pinkerton, "The policy context of leaving care services: A case study of Northern Ireland", was based on just such a premise with the case study of one state, Northern Ireland, affording comparative insight into developments in the USA and elsewhere.

This analysis will be facilitated by an examination of key components in this area using academic texts as well as practice knowledge and lived experience. Consequently, this book will be both subjective, by calling on practice experience largely in the beginning and ending, and objective, by following more formal academic conventions within the main body of the text. This merging of the personal with the professional is deliberate as the dualistic conception of social care practice, where either the personal or the professional aspects to a worker's persona is recognised, has caused untold difficulty for workers in forming meaningful relationships with young people. I have witnessed many social care workers struggle with the issues associated with boundaries within this either/or approach.

The European approach of social pedagogy has much to offer practice in the Republic of Ireland and the UK, not least within this boundaries area. The 3 P's acknowledged within social pedagogy of the personal, private and professional aspects of the worker's persona allow for the professional as well as the personal to be brought into practice, and this affords a much improved approach. The professional self is informed by learning, which assists to understand the child's behaviour. The personal self is about revealing who we really are, our strengths but also our weaknesses, to the child. Revealing our flaws can make us more real and thereby allow children to be themselves and, at times, to make mistakes as well. Thus by using our personality we promote a more genuine relationship with the young person.

Relationship-based practice is inherently both personal and professional. The denial or suppression of the personal does not meet the needs of the child, and for the worker can create cognitive dissonance and stress which can be antecedents to burnout (Briner, 1999; Grandey, 2000; Talyor, 2007). This has clear negative implications for the well-being of the young people in care.

Professionalisation and professionalism are key issues within social care in the Republic of Ireland and the UK and will be considered as well. Social justice underpins the work of social work and social care, and consequently this will be explored with regard to residential care and aftercare provision. Together, these components, considered from both a psychological and sociological perspective, will afford a nuanced consideration of residential care, leaving care and aftercare today.

Throughout this book reference is made to the social care and social work professions. Whilst social work is relatively established, and therefore, arguably, better understood, some readers may be less familiar with what social care work entails. "Social care is difficult to define" (Lalor and Share, 2013:1). Therefore, I offer definitions of these terms to promote clarity and preclude assumption. For this book I have selected a definition of social care offered by the Joint Committee on Social Care Professionals (2002:8):

> Social care is the professional provision of care, protection, support, welfare and advocacy for vulnerable or dependent clients, individuals or in groups. This is achieved through the planning and evaluation of individualised and group programmes of care, which are based on needs, identified

in consultation with the clients, and delivered through day-to-day shared experiences. All interventions are based on established best practice and in-depth knowledge of life span development.

The global definition of social work offered by the International Federation of Social Workers (2014) is:

> Social work is a practice-based profession and an academic discipline that promotes social change and development, social cohesion, and the empowerment and liberation of people. Principles of social justice, human rights, collective responsibility and respect for diversities are central to social work. Underpinned by theories of social work, social sciences, humanities and indigenous knowledge, social work engages people and structures to address life challenges and enhance wellbeing.

The term social professions may be unfamiliar to many in the English-speaking world, an issue identified by Sarah Banks:

> The term 'the social professions' includes a number of related occupational groups involved in care, social control, informal education and advocacy with a range of vulnerable, troublesome or 'disadvantaged' group. The configuration of occupational groups and tasks varies in different European countries, but includes social workers, social pedagogues, special educators, youth workers and community workers. Although not yet in widespread usage in the English-speaking world, this term is beginning to be used in a European context (for example Siebel and Lorenz 1998), and reflects a concern with commonalities in the work, as well as a tendency towards a blurring of the boundaries between different occupational groups. (Banks, 2007:328)

Section 1 looks at the experiences of children in care and care leavers, workers and also professional practice. Chapter 1 is a biographical account of a former young person in care, now a qualified social worker, affording a unique insight into the lived experience prior to entering care, within residential care and thereafter in aftercare from the young person's perspective. Chapter 2 is the author's account of working with this young person in the role of key worker some twenty years ago. This affords insight into the author's experiences as a worker and also on professional practice, both at that time and in the intervening years to date.

Section 2 examines residential child care and its place within the care system, starting with a consideration of the myths surrounding it. We then consider the current status of residential child care in the Republic of Ireland, examine Special Care and High Support and briefly address fostering, secure care and other care placements.

Section 3 considers theory and approaches to care relevant to this area. Attachment, resilience and focal theory will be critically evaluated, together with the role theory has in informing practice. As communication is key to the task of social care, theory relevant to the skill of listening will also be addressed. This is followed by a consideration of two approaches to care: social pedagogy and relationship-based practice. Both have much to offer the development of an integrated approach to social care and out-of-home care. Finally, the role of mentoring for care leavers will be explored.

Section 4 considers issues associated with children's rights and childhood. It includes an interrogation of the Irish National Policy for Leaving and Aftercare (2011) from a children's rights perspective, using the United Nations Convention on the Rights of the Child (UNCRC). It then considers social policy relevant to this area.

Section 5 considers the role of research in regard to aftercare and policy formation with specific focus on qualitative research. It offers an alternative research construct for this area.

Section 6 is an overview of the preceding chapters within the socio-political and socio-economic context of the twenty-first century. There is an examination of the issues of professionalism and professionalisation. The chapter identifies the failings and highlights the strengths within a range of relevant areas. Within this section issues of language and terminology are addressed. The term "care leavers" is identified as inaccurate use of language with "support seekers" identified as more accurate. However, for the sake of economy and consistency within the text the term care leavers will be used throughout the book. This section frames the case for change to a legislative basis providing statutory entitlement to aftercare support in the Republic of Ireland.

Appendix contains a cost/benefit analysis for a statutorily prescribed aftercare service in the Republic of Ireland. It employs a tripartite framework to achieve this which firstly identifies the amount currently being spent on aftercare annually in the Republic of Ireland; then the amount it would cost to provide a statutorily prescribed aftercare service; and finally the benefits of such a change.

SECTION ONE –
PRACTICE AND LIVED EXPERIENCE

Introduction

The following two chapters are accounts of the experiences of a former young person in care and a worker, the author, who acted as his key worker whilst he was in residential care. The young person's name has been changed, as have the names of all young people referenced in this book, to preserve anonymity. These narratives were written independently in 2014 as their recollections of events some 20 years earlier when the young person, Keith, was in care. Keith offers an honest and frank account of his life pre-care, in-care and post-care, in his own words, for which I am deeply grateful. I have addressed some of the issues arising from Keith's story in the following chapter, as well as including some of my own reflections on my experiences in residential care at that time and in the intervening years. I am sure, however, that the reader will also take their own learning from his story. Keith speaks very positively of me at times, but these are his words and this is his story so I have to accept this. However, I know that in truth much of what he writes is more a reflection of his own remarkable capacity for forgiveness of others' failings without judgement or recrimination than an accurate reflection of my skill as a care worker.

These biographical chapters are intended to frame the remainder of the book which is theory-based but also includes learning from my practice experience. Keith's story affords us this connection between theory and practice which it is hoped will remain relevant to the reader throughout the book.

Chapter 1:

Young Person's Story:
There's No Place Like Home

This is a quote taken from the story *The Wizard of Oz*. While the film portrayed a young girl caught between the realms of reality and a dream world, my experience was that of reality, not a fictitious dream or film script with second takes.

I was born into a large family that suffered physically, socially and psychologically through domestic violence and alcoholism. Growing up in an unstable home environment had many consequences that affected me directly and indirectly within my family and social systems. My role was supposed to be that of a child sheltered from abuse and offered love and security from both parents. However, due to the nature of alcoholism this was not the case as the roles of child and parent became skewered and reversed, and I felt suppressed as a child, having to mature and develop rapidly before my time.

I recall finding myself doing the parents' jobs quite often as one or both parents would be out socialising or too intoxicated to function. I also took on this role in terms of meal preparation for younger siblings, house cleaning, advising and assisting younger siblings, as well as protecting them from violence and danger in the world around them.

Even though it was not an ideal childhood of nurturing and security, and although times within the family were difficult and harsh, we were raised with good family morals and values that have benefitted me to this day.

Individuals may have a realistic or unrealistic view of what it is like to grow up in a chaotic environment that was entrenched in social disorder, violence and alcohol abuse. However, although this may be the case, one has to remember that parents do not usually desire to hurt or punish a child unduly or unfairly. Unfortunately, addicts with a disease that consumes their very being are left with a distorted view of reality and behaviour that is reflected on the members within the home environment. I must state this part clearly: although my parents were, as I know now, functioning alcoholics, they were extremely loving when alcohol was not involved. However, sadly, alcohol use was quite prevalent within the home, which altered normal adult functioning, therefore impacting on social order and normal development within the home.

The negative impact of alcoholism on me as a child took many directions. One major impact was that I never knew my identity nor could I decide who I was due to the implications of domestic violence and alcoholism. Why? I can only speak for myself. I remember attending primary school and always wondering at around 2.30 what I was going home to today. Was the alcoholic going to be drunk, sober, asleep, happy, sad or unconscious on the ground? Would the dinner be burnt again? This was the reality of my growing up. You learn to exist more than live; you don't allow your emotions or feelings to flow naturally – my mood always reflected that of the alcoholic on arriving home. It got to the stage as I got older that I could anticipate my parents' mood or mental state by observing how they dressed, stood, or even to how my mother had her hair brushed. This is a state of mind where one is hypersensitive to the environment and the individuals in it.

A recommendation I make to individuals who wish to engage on a professional level with children who come from chaotic backgrounds is to be very aware of this. As children who have lived through these experiences we become extremely attuned to observing people's body language. By body language I mean tiny, minuscule actions the worker may not even be aware of, such as frowning, rolling eyes and avoidance.

As a child living within this situation I would have to make choices, some good and some bad, to meet my needs and the needs of others. I wish to expand on this further.

When working with children who are labelled as deviant or aloof, be mindful as to why they may be that way. For example, as I entered secondary school, one parent had deserted the family as had an older sibling; the other parent had been admitted to hospital which occurred, to my recollection, on a number of occasions. These events left five underage children fending for themselves at home without any financial support or adult guidance. During these times I would have to resort to stealing food and milk on a regular basis to provide for myself and other family members. This in turn led to me getting a reputation within the school and community as a thief and someone not to be trusted in friends' houses. I recall a couple of incidents in school where teachers and members of the community accused me of anti-social behaviour. Although the criminal damage had nothing to do with me, I suffered from prejudice in school and the community due to previous behaviours. My teenage years made me feel worthless and damaged due to living within an unstable home environment with no sanctuary, and feeling shunned by the community.

So what happened? When did my life change? I took up employment at 15 years of age in the city centre. At this stage I was the eldest child in the home as my two eldest siblings had already left home and were in state care. As I was the eldest it was now my responsibility and duty to offer support to younger siblings as well as doing domestic chores. At this stage the alcoholism was still rife with either or both parents absent at varying times. If anything, it was getting worse, as was the violence and the alienation from peers. When I refer to alienation I mean I was too embarrassed to bring friends to my house or too afraid that the alcoholic parent would start arguments with them.

As the drinking became progressively worse I knew that I had to leave the environment as it was affecting my quality of life. I had also befriended an undesirable group in the community who I felt comfortable with as I was accepted by them and not judged on my status.

So I left home and moved into the city centre with the plan of maintaining my full-time job and obtaining a small bed-sit. However, this did not happen as I ended up losing my job as I had no stable accommodation and was couch-surfing with friends. After a period of time, contact was initiated with the social services to source appropriate accommodation. At first I was put into a B&B on Talbot Street in Dublin for approximately a week until more suitable accommodation was sourced. Eventually, I was sourced emergency accommodation in a residential centre in Dublin city centre.

People have often asked me what my experience within the care system was like. I am aware that most young people who enter appear unhappy, due to the stereotype of being in care, the shame associated with it and the loneliness and segregation from their family, friends and community. My experience ticked all the boxes in relation to the above feelings.

Trust, or lack of it sometimes, became a key element in my experience of the care system. When you are young and vulnerable and placed into new surroundings with other children and adults, you don't know who to trust. Also, from previous social learning, all unfamiliar adults in authority can come across as untrustworthy.

When I first entered this particular care centre most of my fears slowly trickled away. I recall prior to entering I had to attend a drop-in coffee shop in the city centre to get assessed and meet with professionals.

I remember sitting in the café for hours and observing everyone in the place. However, one person caught my attention. I recall seeing a middle-aged man playing with a child. My first reaction was that of jealousy and envy as I felt this is what fathers were supposed to do with their children – giving them attention and generally interacting with them in a playful manner – while here I was, alone, afraid and feeling I had no one. I assumed this middle-aged man was the father of that child. However, I soon found out this was not the case because when I arrived at the care centre, possibly within the next couple of days, the same man from the café was there. For some reason I immediately felt safe around this person as I had seen him previously and noticed how he appeared to be a loving and caring person. I was told that this man would be my key worker.

I remember my first day in care at the age of 16. I arrived at the centre that evening just before dinner time. I recall having the role of key worker explained to me and then I was brought to the kitchen for dinner. This moment I remember most. I remember dishes of food being placed on the table and everyone tucking into it. However, I was painfully shy and took a small piece of food, probably not even enough to feed a budgie. It wasn't shyness that prevented me from taking more food, even though I was starving – it was more the fear of taking too much food and getting into trouble or depriving someone else of some food. One must remember that coming from a disadvantaged home where food portions would have been basic and limited, you dared not try to take extra or the repercussions could have been harrowing.

As my time in state care progressed so did my confidence, social life, self-esteem, self-development and, most importantly, a sense of my identity began to emerge. This is why I always say that living in state care had a very positive impact on me as a person.

As I mentioned above, I was truly blessed in having the gentlest of men and the best key worker possible who made a massive impression on my life. In discussing this with him some 20 years later he was very reluctant in taking credit for his part in my success, but I do believe he contributed greatly in my developing a moral code and sense of values.

Although we may have only been together for a relatively short period of time (five months) he – Maurice – made a massive impression on my life. During my time in care he was always there to offer advice and I knew I could trust him completely. He earned my trust because of what my observations of him told me. My trust in him grew because he always stood up and advocated for me. I remember him taking time with me to go for walks into town just to spend time with me and discuss events in my life. This simple reality would have been taboo for me previously at home.

It is ironic how small memories have stay with me throughout my life. Over the intervening years I often wondered does Maurice remember the time we went into the city centre for a chat. On this particular occasion we were walking through town and went into Clery's department store on O'Connell Street. While in Clery's there were two game consoles on display and we played a racing car game for a short period of time. At that time it was just great to be a child again and have fun with an adult without questioning their motives. This was my first experience of an adult man showing a genuine interest in me as a child.

While in care during the early 1990s one could not lounge around the centre in the way that seems to happen today. It was mandatory to be enrolled in an educational course of some sort to maintain your bed. I enlisted in a Youthreach programme in computers even though I had no interest in them as they were not a part of life like today. I recall probably spending more time out of the course walking around the city centre than attending. One evening I returned to the centre and was called into the office by the centre manager. I remember Maurice being there also. Well, I can tell you I got the riot act thrown at me for not attending my course. I remember the manager being furious with me and I think she was threatening that if my attendance did not improve in the course I would lose my bed in the centre. I recall the tears welling up in my eyes and the lump in my throat forming. I was petrified. It revived memories of being screamed at by an adult without having any say in the matter. Even if I was given a chance to speak I would probably not have been able to as I was so upset and on the verge of sobbing.

The following morning I attended the course without hesitation due to the flea in my ear still ringing. Upon returning to the centre that evening the centre manager called me into her office and sat me down. This time she could not apologise to me enough for how she spoke to me the previous day. I accepted her apology graciously as I had never before experienced an adult apologising for their behaviour towards me. However, it was later when speaking to Maurice I realised he had challenged the manager for the way she spoke to me the previous day. After this, I knew this man would always advocate for me and have my best interest at heart.

15

During the remainder of my time in this centre I felt secure and most of all I could discover who I was as a person. While at home I never knew who I was as I was always living in the shadow of violence and being associated as "one of those"; in other words, while at home or in the community I was never known as Keith. It was always, "he's one of that lot". I was tarnished with a preconceived notion that I must be the same as other family members.

Being in care had its perks and privileges for a number of reasons. However, these privileges would eventually have had a bittersweet ending for me. As a child who came from poverty, I soon found being treated like how a child should be was phenomenal. I was given pocket money for the first time in my life and a clothing grant of eighty pounds to buy clothes for Christmas. Every Saturday and Wednesday evening we were taken on pleasurable activities which consisted of go-karting, the cinema and trips to the beach or the mountains. This was true heaven for me as I had no worries, thus feeling safe and secure, plus I had the chance to enjoy being a child. For the first time in my life I longed to go home to the care unit after my computer course and spend time with some adults without worrying about it. This of course depended on which care staff were on duty. Although all the care staff had good qualities and attributes, some I found to be more nurturing than others, thus allowing for positive relationships to form.

The bittersweetness, however, came after five months. My time to exit this centre approached swiftly as it was only a six-month transitional centre. I was now getting ready to move into semi-independent living (aftercare). I recall being uncertain about aftercare as I did not know what to expect. I remember prior to Christmas going up to this new residence to meet the new staff team and have aftercare explained to me and what semi-independent living was. Maurice always accompanied me to these meetings so I felt safe as I trusted him in his actions and decision making on my behalf. I knew he always had my best interests at heart. I don't think I took these meetings too seriously, as it was prior to Christmas and I knew the move wouldn't be till February. The reason I know these meetings happened prior to Christmas is that I had a pair of runners that were falling off my feet. They were so bad my toes

16

were talking to me. I remember people being more focused on my runners than me, which made me feel uncomfortable. However, I had a new pair of runners back in the residential centre (Maurice having pointed out to the staff that I needed them), but I didn't want to wear them until Christmas.

That Christmas came and it was the most difficult Christmas ever. Though extremely anxious about going home, I was also excited to see the family. I ended up returning to the centre that night because, like every Christmas at home, too much alcohol was consumed and fighting followed. I remember feeling so bad leaving the home that night, not for myself but for the younger siblings who begged me to stay. I couldn't as I had to protect myself and think of my needs.

When I returned to the centre Maurice was on duty. I always remember that Christmas night and the gist of the conversation we had, and every Christmas since I have recalled this memory.

I told Maurice I just wanted to have a Christmas where no alcohol or violence was involved. Although I had no power to change this situation at the time, I remember Maurice giving me a glimmer of hope and a dream to hold on to. He told me that although things are difficult now, in time, when I had children and a family of my own I could give them all the Christmas wishes they and I desire.

The time came to leave the residential centre and move into aftercare. I was devastated and so sad to say goodbye to particular staff members and the friends I had met. I knew I wasn't going far but it was more the loss of familiarity and the trusting relationships that had been formed. It felt like they were gone forever.

Although I was eased into aftercare by doing a stay overnight once a week, I was still unsure and most of all completely unprepared for what lay ahead. I spoke earlier about living in residential care and it being a great experience, allowing me to be a child again and to develop. However, moving to aftercare at sixteen did not make me an adult. No matter how mature I thought I was, or how I thought I knew it all, I was still only a child.

In residential care there was a chef who made lovely homemade meals every Monday to Friday and the carers made the meals at the weekend. We had a cleaner who would clean the centre. I had pocket money, activities and a care team constantly around me as well as recreational areas where I and friends could play pool or watch television, etc. We were nurtured and treated like children, as we should have been. But now the downside to care came crashing in. Now, in aftercare, all these luxuries had gone – and I mean gone completely!

If anything, I fell more into poverty and almost starved to death, at least that's how it felt to me sometimes. As I was in a Youthreach course I earned £28 a week if I completed a full week. Out of that I would have to pay rent and save an allocated amount on a weekly basis. A budget was set aside for shopping – if I produced a shopping receipt for my weekly shop I would be reimbursed £10 per week. So, basically, I had to feed myself for one week on £10, and this is without taking into account things like light bulbs and toiletries.

How unrealistic was this? I had £1.50 a day to live on. My diet had now turned from a homely made dinner every day to a packet of noodles and a couple of slices of bread per day and maybe a treat of a biscuit. This is no exaggeration. This was the reality.

I recall starting to build bridges with my parents and I had to walk twelve miles from the city centre to visit them, hoping that they or a friend could lend me the bus fare back into the city. I do believe what pushed me to building bridges with my family was the longing for a meal if I went to visit.

Unfortunately, and strangely, back then the rules of leaving care were that once I entered aftercare I was not allowed re-enter the residential centre for support or advice. However, Maurice was allowed to continue visiting me on a couple of occasions. Even though I had a new key worker in aftercare I just did not feel I connected with her as I did with Maurice.

I enjoyed these visits so much as I had a great relationship with him. The biggest struggle I had in aftercare was the loneliness, something which affected me into my adult life until my late twenties. When I moved into aftercare I was given a little bedsit at the top of the house. It had a bed, two-ringed cooker, small fridge, sink, a table with one chair and a wardrobe. I will never forget the loneliness and the four walls. All I had for company during the night was a white Morphy Richards alarm clock radio with a lamp attached to it that Maurice and I bought as a going away present. Every night I would listen to Atlantic 252 for comfort and companionship. I remember feeling so lonely as I hadn't even a television to watch. All I had were my thoughts.

Although there were other residents within the building we were like passing ships as we had no common recreational area, and some of these lads had reputations and were older than me. So for a long time I just avoided the place and wandered the city centre and adjacent areas with casual friends.

I stayed in this aftercare centre for one year until an event occurred that caused my placement there to break down. The centre was broken into and all the residents' savings and petty cash were stolen. I was disgusted to be accused of this crime, but the staff didn't believe me. They were so adamant that I had robbed the premises that a meeting was called with my social worker. I will always remember feeling so alone in that meeting and my voice being lost again over adults' voices and accusations.

I remained in the unit for a period of time after this accusation but my relationship with the staff had deteriorated, especially with my key worker – she was adamant I was involved. Maurice would always believe me and advocate on my behalf, but unfortunately I hadn't got a Maurice anymore.

Social Workers

I remember one meeting in particular while in residential care. I was informed that my mother and the social worker would be attending a meeting in the hostel and I would have to be present. I remember wishing for the ground to open up and swallow me; the fear was so intense I can still remember it today.

Maurice assured me he would be there, so that eased my tensions, but still I wasn't sure why I was to be there as the social worker had no contact with me to discuss this meeting or what was expected. The morning of the meeting came and this is how I remember it.

I was called into the room in the centre and my mother, the social worker and Maurice were there. I don't remember if anyone else was in attendance.

I remember basically being asked was my mother an alcoholic. I remember the fear, the sadness of this question. I felt I was put in an impossible and traumatising situation. Yes, my mother was an alcoholic; yes, I hated her drunken behaviour but I loved her deeply. I never wanted to go against my mother, nor did I want to embarrass her in front of these people. Plus I didn't know whether my statement might result in my younger siblings being taken into care. The weight of that question was so heavy for me as a child I would say it crushed me completely. I gave the social worker the answer he wanted and I remember my mother looking at me in disbelief, as much as to say, "How could you?", while at the same time giving excuses for her drinking.

More or less immediately after the magical question was asked and answered, the meeting ended. The social worker got up and left without saying anything else to me, and soon after so did my mother. I recall her leaving the building without even saying good-bye. I was left feeling so alone in that room after that meeting as I cried my eyes out. I cried because I knew I had hurt my mother for the sake of the social worker. I understand that the social worker had a job to do. However, the burden placed on my shoulders that day scarred me forever. Why? The social worker had been working with my family for years. He knew what was going on in the house since the eldest child left years earlier, with little or no intervention, yet he put me through that shame and torture for a reason I have yet to understand to this day.

My only grace for that moment in time was Maurice. I do remember him sitting with me afterwards until I stopped sobbing while every other adult disappeared. I suppose the reason that memory is etched into my mind is that I always had a close relationship with my mother, through thick and thin, while understanding she had a disease. I hurt her so much that day when I sided with the social worker and my mother never let me forget that scene all through my adult life up until she passed away.

I suppose what I am trying to say here is that when we work with vulnerable people it is part of our job and discipline to ask questions and investigate abuse in the family. However, when asking questions one must be mindful on how the question or answer is going to impact upon the individual at hand. Will there be repercussions for the individual? Does the question serve a purpose, and if so, for whom – the child, the family, or the social (care) worker? Most of all, is the person supported afterwards? Although it was a terrible time for me, at the time I was lucky in the sense I had a good reliable key worker whom I trusted and knew would ensure my well-being.

How Did Key Working Assist Me Throughout My Life?

While in care, early on I could have fallen into abusing drugs and alcohol and loitering around the city, which was the culture of children in care who had no adult guidance or support. I do believe that it was the relationship with my key worker and family morals that helped me avoid these pitfalls. Maurice was there for me to talk to when I needed assistance and, more important, he took the time to get to know the real me. More often than not he knew when I needed guidance, even if I did not. It was Maurice who encouraged me to attend a course and take up counselling at an early age to discuss issues that had previously happened in my life. Although I did not wish to attend the computer course or counselling, I did this for him because I trusted him and knew he wanted the best for me.

Just after my first Christmas in care – my first away from home – a family member who had left home years earlier returned to my social circle. With his return he brought a new trend – drugs. I remember vividly the effects alcoholism had on my family and I watched this addiction consume friends and siblings. Although I did not get involved in the drug scene I felt I had no choice but to remain in this social circle for several reasons. They were my friends and family and I felt safe in this group, plus I had a sense of belonging. Remaining in this circle did cause me a lot of stress as I ended up becoming known to the guards due to my association with these people.

This was a crossroads in my life; but when I look back, to be honest it was Maurice who possibly saved me and my future. I do truly believe it was Maurice who changed my destiny – I could have easily decided to bow to peer-pressure. Most important, my relationship with Maurice was more sacred to me as this man had nurtured me in the most difficult times in my life and believed in me. He also took the time to be honest with me, no matter how difficult the topics were that required addressing. He advised me about my brother and how associating with him and his peers was derailing me. It was probably easy for Maurice to have these tough conversations with me due to the fact we had a strong relationship.

From my subsequent experience of working with teenagers I find we often do not want to approach tough subjects with them. But sometimes we need to be honest and direct and not beat around the bush with concerns we have regarding individuals who are in crisis.

Basically, what I am trying to say here is that family and friends were important for me, while also having an extremely negative side effect on me. It was Maurice who pointed this out even though I knew this all along in my own head. However, listening to some-one else telling me confirmed my opinion. Maurice encouraged me and advised me to step back away from my older brother, as he feared he would pull me down with him. I took this advice and did step away from my social circle. It was fortunate for me that I had a great key worker and took his harsh but correct advice as many of my friends ended up in prison, deceased, addicted to drink and drugs, and/or with a range of diseases from hepatitis to HIV.

Adult Life/Career

I always say as children we have no control over the family, culture or community we are born into. One could assume that as children we have no control over our own destiny as our very existence as children is governed by society and our parent's views and ideologies. For instance, our parents decide which neighbourhood we grow up in, what religion we should follow, what school we go to, and which friends we socialise with. Within a "normal" home it can be difficult for a child to challenge the belief, norms and values of the family; however it can be even more difficult in a dysfunctional home of violence and alcoholism to challenge family morals out of fear.

As a child growing up in a chaotic environment I was aware from a young age that the family system was fractured due to violence and alcohol abuse. Although I was aware of the abnormalities within the family I would not speak to adults or peers in the community about my family dysfunctions out of embarrassment and fear of repercussions.

As I entered adult life I progressed as best I could, however the demons and past life struggles followed me into my late teens and early twenties. At this period of my life it felt like Pandora's Box had opened in my mind. It was during this life period that all the demons from the past re-emerged and I was trying to make sense of it all. I became angry and resentful of my life at this point as I watched all my childhood friends finish schooling and college and entering good jobs and go travelling. Although I always maintained full-time employment, I was never satisfied with my life or employment choices. I always knew I was capable to do more in my life and career. However due to growing up in a dysfunctional family and having to leave home early I felt I was never given the appropriate chance to fulfil my dreams and education and this had serious implications on my education status, thus my social life, self-esteem and confidence. These feelings of past resentments also affected my personal relationships with partners. As a child I never allowed anyone get too close or find the real me, which was also due to the fact I did not know the real me. From my experience of growing up in domestic violence I learned to always depend on myself as it was easier to rely on yourself, that way other individuals are not given the chance to hurt you or let you down. I felt it was this psychological self-isolation that opened Pandora's Box, as I always felt I could take on anything the world had to throw at me, alone, and in silence. Even though I kept myself in a psychological prison I had a very good peer group with many friends whom I always assisted when I could. I found I always had time to listen to other people's problems and offer them solutions, but could never find solutions for my own demons.

Eventually, I opened up with personal friends, partner(s) and even parents about my resentment, anger and anxiety. This was the best step forward in my life I could have chosen, as now I felt I could release myself from the past psychological prison as, most importantly, I made peace with my mother. Even though I can not entirely escape the past, I was glad of this. Why? As I stated earlier as a child I had no control over my upbringing, plus I always felt I had more to offer this world and more importantly myself. I decided that although the past could not be rectified I could use it to my advantage. As a youth I enjoyed sport and saw the benefit of sport as a valve to release stress and anxiety, whilst as an adult I enjoyed offering advice and support to friends. From this I decided to use my past experiences and skills to benefit my future, so I returned to education at 28 to complete the equivalent to the leaving certificate. Before I go any further I must say this was the biggest challenge of my life in terms of confidence and financial reliance. I decided to give up full-time work as I wanted to progress in life, plus I always desired to have children and a family of my own. I didn't want a job that I had to work sixty hours-a-week to make a decent living, thus jeopardising time with a family. In returning to college I must acknowledge the efforts and support I got from friends, and especially previous partners.

For the past six years I have worked with young people and families both in community settings and residential care. Although one could say that I had a chequered past in terms of social learning, I believe with self-development and a multitude of academic learning I feel I have succeeded in working professionally and appropriately with clients in crisis. By interlinking my personal life experiences and academic knowledge I have the skills and competence to assist individuals who are in distress. While working with teenagers I always treat them with a non-judgemental attitude and listen to them when they decide to open up.

From a professional perspective, I have always maintained a silent and patient approach to working with teenagers. The reason for this is that teenagers and individuals who are in crisis, or who have just entered residential care, are likely scared and unsure of whom they can trust and rely upon. While key working clients I always listen to them and advocate on their behalf without hesitation. This was due to the fact I recall when I was in care acknowledging my key worker and how we built a trusting relationship developed on his patience, trust and openness.

I am still in contact with many of these friends from when I was in care. It is unfortunate, perhaps, that I am the only one who appears to have succeeded in life so far. Why is this? I do believe a key part was down to Maurice having faith in me, believing in me and taking notice of my life inside and outside the walls of the residential unit.

I wish to conclude with a final piece of advice to future practitioners in social care: take the time to get to know your client. Always show an interest in what is going on in their social circles. Have the tough conversations with them, if required, as you won't say anything to them that they are not already aware of or about which they have some understanding.

Chapter 2:

Worker's Story: The Impossible Task?

Keith's is a remarkable story and I genuinely feel privileged and grateful to know him. He says I played a major role in his story but at the time, I just did the best that I could in working with him and other young people in care. Interestingly, at that time, I was relatively inexperienced in social care and unqualified. I have subsequently immersed myself in academia but my work with Keith had no benefit from academic learning or lengthy experience, just a desire to make a difference. This desire to make a difference is the one prerequisite of relational practice, which I believe underpins best-practice in social care. It is also an essential element of what it means to be professional within the social professions, an issue we will address in greater detail in later sections. Experience, knowledge and qualifications enhance this fundamental motivation. These factors may erroneously be considered as the sole requirements for a claim to professional status within the social professions in the twenty-first century. However, as we shall see in greater detail in forthcoming sections, the desire to make a difference – the vocational element motivating entry into the social professions – is also a constituent part of what it means to be a professional. However, this is often overlooked in professionalisation agendas currently unfolding in the social professions both in the Republic of Ireland and the UK. There is more than one way to be professional and we would do well to embrace this realisation – as Mark Smith has said, "Actually being professional is about getting the job done, competently and ethically" (Smith, 2009:136). Keith's story confirms that young people can differentiate those staff for whom this desire to make a difference is the primary motivation and I hope that I have held onto this motivation throughout my career.

Keith's story encompasses many issues that are pertinent to young people in care, and I will address some of these in more detail. In discussion with Keith about how he is making a success of his life he describes how he chose to take responsibility for his own life and not blame others. This, I suspect, is a key factor in Keith's success as he focused on himself rather than others, and in taking responsibility for his own life he also claimed the agency and ability to change his life. Whether consciously or not, Keith appears to have recognised that he can change himself but not others. He developed a strong internal locus-of-control, that is a "belief that forces shaping one's life are largely within one's own control" (Luthar, 1991:610). He would appear to have actualised this potential circa age 28. Residential care, and to some extent my part therein, aided him in this, but he had a caring nature and good moral compass prior to my meeting him. Also, and fortunately, I met him at a turning point in his life (Rutter, 1994, 2006; Gilligan, 2009).

Keith has focused on the positive in his life rather than the negative, distinguishing the love from the harm, that is, distinguishing his mother from her behaviours which were brought about due to her alcoholism. Similarly, we as social care workers are challenged to separate the child from their behaviour when working with young people who have experienced trauma. We need to constantly see the behaviours as a communication of a need and a symptom of an underlying trauma. We are tasked with seeking to understand the causes of the behaviour to better assist the young people we work with.

I choose to believe that human beings want to be liked and that given the right circumstances people will choose to do the right thing. This belief aligns with Carl Rogers' "actualising tendency", a central tenet of the humanistic approach. This approach posits that given the correct socio-environmental conditions human beings have a universal motivation that results in growth, development and autonomy of the individual (Rogers, 1961, 1963). One of our core challenges, if not the core challenge, as social care professionals is to aid in the creation of the right circumstances for those in our care to access the resources they require to meet their needs and thereby enabling each to make progress towards reaching their full potential. We need to achieve this despite their, at times, refusal or inability to accept our support. When I think of Keith's story I am reminded of the story of an old Cherokee teaching his grandson about life. The Cherokee tells his grandson:

"A fight is going on inside me. It's a terrible fight between two wolves. One is evil – he is anger, envy, sorrow, regret, greed, arrogance, self-pity, guilt, resentment, inferiority, lies, false pride, superiority and ego. The other is good – he is joy, peace, love, hope, serenity, humility, kindness, benevolence, empathy, generosity truth, compassion and faith. The same fight is going on inside you – and inside every other person too."

The grandson thinks about this for a minute and then asked his grandfather: "Which wolf will win?"

The old Cherokee simply replied: "The one you feed."

Some of the key issues arising from Keith's story with regard to practice, theory and research can be illustrated in Table 1.

Table 1: *Key Issues Arising from Keith's Story.*

Trauma	Hyper-sensitivity, hyper-vigilance, coping, re-experiencing and re-enactment of trauma, and developmental implications
Social Exclusion	Prejudice, stigma, poverty, injustice, social isolation, labelling
Relationships	Key working, family, professionals, peers, attachment theory, importance of relationship
Power	Powerlessness, vulnerability, lack of voice, choice and responsibility
Residential care	The benefits, transitions, levels and types of support
Hope	Belief, trust, unconditional positive regard

Identity	Development, belonging; confidence and self-esteem
Aftercare	Loneliness, transitions and levels of support.

Trauma

Keith's descriptions of growing up within a dysfunctional family, and the need to act in socially unacceptable ways to survive, give valuable insight into how trauma affects a child's development and what underpins some of their behaviours. This affords us an understanding of why children in care may exhibit a range of complex and challenging behaviours that, at times, appear to bear little relationship to their present surroundings. This is because what is happening for them internally can be associated to past trauma, or developmental delay caused by this trauma, and not what is actually going on in their present life space. We must recognise that to care for these young people therapeutically we need to allow time and understanding for what is going on for them internally to catch up with what is going on externally. There is much research addressing the effects of trauma on children's development (Anglin, 2002; Abramovitz and Bloom, 2003; Hughes, 2006; Perry, 2009) and we now know from neuroscience that children's brain development is altered physiologically following prolonged exposure to trauma (Teicher *et al.*, 2002; van de Kolk, 2003; Twardosz and Lutzker, 2010). We also know that neuroplasticity enables the brain to adapt in later life and neurological connections can be formed ameliorating some of the early life experiences inflicted by trauma (Chamberlain, 2008; Kegan and Lahey, 2009).

> ... a child's earlier experiences can be overcome if therapeutic intervention takes place and emotional stability and security is provided (Clarke and Clarke, 1999, Messer, 1999). (Mennen and O'Keefe, 2005:581)

Keith describes how hyper-sensitive he became to issues of trust and threat and how confused his identity formation had become. These are some of the symptoms of "attachment trauma" which Jon Allen (2008) identifies as an interpersonal trauma most conspicuously associated with childhood maltreatment.

> ... attachment trauma entails fear of emotional dependence. Perhaps most significantly, attachment trauma is associated with anticipation of betrayal in attachment relationships (Freyd, 1996). (Allen, 2008:11)

His descriptions of the incident where the manager "read him the riot act" and how this evoked fearful and painful feelings within him clearly illustrates the importance of being aware of a child's past and being sensitive to the effects of trauma. Allen (2008) further identifies the concept of the 90:10 reaction with regard to emotional responses of traumatised individuals in situations which, often, may appear as innocuous to observers yet evoke memories of past trauma, thereby inducing a re-experiencing of this trauma for the person. In such situations there is "90 per cent of the emotion coming from the past and 10 per cent from the present" (Allen, 2008:177). For my part, I know this manager had no intention to cause him this harm and was acting out of concern for him to maintain his placement, but she communicated this too strongly to him. To her credit, once she was made aware of this, she apologised genuinely, which had a significantly beneficial effect on Keith. Keith describes this as the first time an adult ever apologised to him for their actions, and thus exposed him to adults acting in nurturing and responsible ways, challenging his previously held perception. It has been my experience in care that we all, at times, make mistakes attempting to care for traumatised young people. As Einstein (1879-1955) said, "Anyone who has never made a mistake has never tried anything new."

We have the opportunity to aid young people in evaluating their truths/narratives/biographies. In this (re)evaluation young people can re-author some of these truths to more positive worldviews and expectations and/or less traumatic memories. This episode illustrates the sobering reality of the power which each worker carries in their daily interactions with children in care. We, individually, have the potential to enhance their lives or diminish them on a daily basis, and we can do this unbeknown to ourselves if we are not self-aware and know the histories of the children we care for. This manager made a mistake but redeemed herself. She utilised reflective practice (Ruch, 2007; Jude and Regan, 2010) in her work and was open to constructive criticism. I respected her for this, as professional respect is earned not given by title or role. The young people in our care have earned our respect by virtue of the trauma and hardship they have suffered yet strive to overcome. We must always respect the fact that we are only there to aid them in professional roles framed within the paramountcy of the child principle which, by definition, demands that we show them respect at all times. If we wish for them to show respect for themselves and others we must first model this in our interactions with them and also between ourselves. By treating young people with respect they are more apt to return this respect and, in so doing, many potential difficulties are eliminated whilst trust is built. This is a simple yet highly effective concept which is none too surprising when we consider how society marginalises and excludes many of these young people, thereby affording them little or no respect.

With regard to the above manager I think it fair to say she neither knew the harm she caused when she "read the riot act" nor the extent of the good her apology accomplished. This episode also makes clear the power of an apology. This requires a willingness to work competently with power by exposing a degree of vulnerability in accepting a personal or professional failing with the possibility that the apology may be rejected. Furthermore, this episode encapsulates the accomplishment of another of the core challenges of social care work, what metaphorically can be represented as the completion of Bruno Bettleheim's (1903-1990) impossible task set within the fairytale battleground where hero children must prevail over villains such as the "big bad wolf". She turned a poor beginning into a positive outcome and every child in residential care came into care due to a poor beginning (Kendrick, 2012; Hiles *et al.*, 2013). But, thankfully, she was not alone in this accomplishment as Keith also accomplished the impossible task of vanquishing his villainous foes – foes which, regrettably, still blight the lives of many young people who have left care into their adult lives. He achieved this with the aid of people such as this manager and nurturing care workers who showed him how caring adults deport themselves. He himself fed his good inner wolf, that wolf we as workers must also nurture, both in ourselves and in the children we support, to better aid them with their inner struggle. At times, our task in residential care appears to be impossible, so great has the trauma been to the children and so difficult can be the systems we must work within. Yet we persevere and sometimes we play key roles in aiding them to overcome apparently intractable adversity, occasionally unbeknown to ourselves and perhaps years after we have parted company from them. The seeds we have sown bear fruit, proving that ours is not an impossible task; rather, it is a highly complex task filled with uncertainty, but also possibility. The promise of the possibility is our good inner wolf.

Vulnerability

The willingness to show vulnerability and appropriately admit mistakes takes strength, confidence and self-awareness.

> The capacity to be in touch with the client's feelings is related to the worker's ability to acknowledge his or her own. Before a worker can understand the power of emotion in the life of the client, it is necessary to discover its importance in the worker's own experience. (Shulman, 1999:156)

If we hope for the children in our care to trust us and in so doing expose their vulnerability we must be prepared to do likewise, which therefore means that self-awareness is critical to ensure that we can understand and manage our own feelings and vulnerabilities. Vulnerability must not be seen as weakness or confused with fear, an issue which Furedi explores in some depth.

> The identity of vulnerability is the flipside of the autonomisation of fear. (Furdei, 2007:8)

Two incidents illustrating the impact of the expression of vulnerability stand out in my mind from my practice within more recent times than in Keith's case. My role was no longer that of direct worker as I had moved into senior management and I was overseeing residential managers. I did have a role in the lives of the young people within the residential centres, though much altered from former years. As a director of services I likened my role to what Donald Winnicott (1896-1971) might have termed a distant father figure – permanent but intermittently present and vested with power and, I would like to think, mostly benign.

Sue

The first was a teenage girl, Sue, who was having some difficulties in her life and was engaged with her residential manager in petitioning to be given some specific item or allowance that was important to her in this difficult time. I happened to be in the house and whilst passing through the room where this discussion was occurring Sue called me over, I suspected to see if she could get from me that which she was unsuccessfully seeking from the manager. I had only occasional interactions with her previously so I would say our relationship was not very deep at that time, though appropriate for my role. She proceeded to voice her frustration to the manager, and now me, about whatever the issue that was causing her difficulty. After a few minutes her frustration began to overwhelm her and she broke into tears. I stood close to her, the manager and she were sitting on a sofa, and I made no comment. I let my gaze stay on her face with, I hoped, a sympathetic or at least a neutral expression. I felt a range of feelings and emotions, including sorrow for her upset, embarrassment for her, helplessness, discomfort, a desire to fix things and uncertainty. I thought to say something to reassure her but didn't as I felt I might inadvertently demean or invalidate her feelings, so I just stood and was fully present during this time. The manager also sat with her without comment, offering her presence as support. We held her distress between us as she expressed her feelings for several minutes. Silence can be worth a thousand words and sometimes all one needs is our time and attention and not to be judged. We must remember that the process of listening is *in itself* helpful, and this process alone can change someone's life (Acott, 2015). The manager and I aided her in regulating her emotions by remaining in control of our own and thereby enabling her to regain her emotional balance

33

with our responses acting as containment for hers. We enacted what is termed emotional co-regulation (Butler, 2013).

When she ceased crying and began to compose herself I made a closing comment to the effect that I understood how hard things were for her at this time. I added that I, and the manager and staff, would try to do all we could to help her with the specific issue she was struggling with, and that I hoped things would get better for her soon. I left and on my journey home thought to myself how sad for this young lady to have to show this vulnerability to me who she didn't know very well. Simultaneously, my understanding of how hard life was for her was much deeper than before the episode and I felt that I knew her better. Without thinking about it my con-nection with her had deepened, our relationship had grown as the experience had invoked an empathetic response on my part which I believe she sensed and responded to. Thereafter, whenever I met her we had amicable exchanges and our relationship continued without much overt change from before this incident. There was, however, a better connection between us and I sensed we were more at ease in each other's presence.

It was only when I was leaving that post and saying goodbye that I realised what an impact that series of moments we had shared had on our relationship. She made a point of giving me a hug, the first one ever, and wishing me well. I knew in that moment that this genuine expression of feeling on her part was directly connected to the incident on the sofa when spontaneously we had made a real connection. Within these moments of vulnerability, if we are correctly attuned within a dyadic relationship with the young per-son, we can enter periods of real and meaningful intersubjectivity. Intersubjectivity is a complex psychoanalytically-based theory of "the bidirectional and reciprocal impact of one mind on another in the clinical dyad" (Shill, 2011:2). Or as Andrew *et al.* (2013:6) state:

> Intersubjectivity is about joining a child or adult in his ex-perience, experiencing it with him, matching his affective state and exploring the experience of it with him to make better sense of it.

These intersubjective moments can be very powerful in relationship formation, personal development and the building of bonds of trust (Siegel, 2000; Livingston, 2001; Hinshelwood, 2012).

On reflection, I can now see that I also, somewhat unwittingly, practiced collaborative meaning-making by maintaining a silence during her distress. In so doing I did not jump in to try to fix the problem, as I may have interpreted it to be, before giving her the time to tell us in her own words what was happening for her.

> The people involved, workers as well as service users, each have different perspectives upon situations and a consensus about what the problem is, or even whether there is a problem at all, has to be explored and negotiated to reach agreement. (Cooper, 2011:20)

Before moving on from Sue's story it is important to consider in more depth two critical issues arising from it – the importance of self-awareness and self-care on the part of the worker. Bearing witness to another's vulnerability can be an uncomfortable and challenging experience, which can evoke our own vulnerability, emotions, feelings and past experiences, some of which I experienced whilst being present with Sue and then on my journey home. We can also experience some of the other's pain if we connect to and "therapeutically hold" them (Winnicott, 1975), or "hold the child in mind" (Ruch, 2005), during these times of distress. By recognising that we "hold" something it can be seen that some degree of possession is implied on the part of the carer. This means we also can become affected by their pain and we can experience vicarious trauma, what Hatfield *et al.* (1994) describe as a form of emotional contagion that causes the carer to "catch the emotions" of those they care for. Vicarious trauma can also be referred to as compassion fatigue (Figley, 2002) which, although with different causation, is sometimes associated with secondary traumatic stress (Pryce *et al.*, 2007), which in turn is more closely associated with post-traumatic stress except that the stress is experienced through another person rather than first hand, that is, vicariously. It is important to recognise that these concepts are contested (Sabin-Farrell and Turpin, 2003) and that "the actual causes of vicarious traumatization have not yet been established" (Bloom, 2003:459). Consequently, there is no certainty regarding which workers will, if any, or to what degree, experience these conditions. However, what is incontestable is that working with others does have an impact on the worker and that this needs to be acknowledged and managed.

In my experience following such incidents as this one with Sue vicarious vulnerability might be an appropriate terminology to use. Trauma implies harm, which in turn could be said to imply that the young person has caused harm to the worker, even if un-intentionally. Equally, compassion fatigue could be seen to imply that the needy or demanding young person invokes fatigue on the part of the worker, thus casting the young person as the cause of this fatigue. This, then, could lead to the young person becoming perceived as the cause of the harm, the problem, when clearly they are not. It is the harm that has been caused to them by others that is the cause of the problem.

During, and after, the incident with Sue I was not traumatised or fatigued but I did connect with and re-experience some of my own vulnerability as well as hers. Connecting with another's vulnerability through identification with our own is fundamen-tal to empathy. This concept of vicarious vulnerability allows for recognition of the worker's own pre-existing vulnerability to be recognised as part of this condition, and thus the young person is not solely responsible for the worker's experiences. This vulner-ability stayed with me for some time after the episode with Sue, as evidenced by my reflections whilst driving home. This reflective process is part of my self-care regime which, together with super-vision and talking to trusted colleagues, enables me to process the feelings arising from such encounters.

Carl Jung (1875-1961) theorised that many carers and helpers are motivated to enter caring professions as a result of their own "wounds" from prior life experiences. He coined the term "wound-ed healers". Jackson (2001) identifies the "wounded healer" not as a flawed professional but rather one whose past experiences can be utilised to better attune them to caring for others. She cites Gothe (1749-1832), "Our own pain teaches us to share in the suffering of others" (2001:17), and makes explicit that the "wounded healer" is not a victim of burnout, rather the healer's own suffering and vulnerability. She identifies how both Freud and Jung were themselves "wounded healers". Research by Maeder (1998), Regehr *et al.* (2001) and Rizq and Target (2010) identified that high percentages of workers in social work, counselling and psychotherapy professions had experienced prior "wounding" experiences which motivated them to enter these professions. From this research we can see the magnitude of the potential for workers' having pre-existing vulnerabilities that may be effected by children's and young people's vulnerabilities, but that correctly managed this need not be a negative phenomenon. This, then, confirms the absolute imperative for workers to be aware of their own vulnerabilities and to manage them.

In the event that the worker does experience vicarious trauma, it "is important to recognise that neither clients nor the negligent helpers are responsible for VT. Rather it is an occupational hazard, a cost of doing the work" (Pearlman and Caringi in Courtois and Ford, 2009:205).

It is also important to recognise that none of these conditions – vicarious trauma, compassion fatigue or secondary traumatic stress – are the same as burnout. However, they can be antecedents to burnout and may develop into burnout if not dealt with appropriately.

The potential for the evoking of our own vulnerability and past experiences, as well as potentially experiencing vicarious trauma or compassion fatigue, makes clear the imperative for workers not just to be self-aware but also to have good self-care practices (Newell and MacNeil, 2010; Cuskelly, 2013) to process their emotional responses, not only to take care of themselves but also to be more effective in caring for the distressed young person.

> We propose here that helpers' personal distress and emphatic responses, if processed adequately, can result in growth for both client and helper. (Pearlman and Caringi in Courtois and Ford, 2009:205)

It is important to recognise that vicarious trauma and compassion fatigue are very treatable conditions and can be resolved successfully with self-care practices and/or professional support should the worker experience them. The role of supervision is critical within this area.

However, these vicarious processes all present with varying degrees of negative implications for workers. Whilst I have experienced many, if not all, of the symptoms of these processes over the years, I have also had many positive experiences with young people in care. Vicarious resilience (VR) has only relatively recently been acknowledged by academia with Hernández *et al.* (2007) first identifying the concept with reference to psychotherapists working with traumatised clients. They argue that "this process is a common and natural phenomenon illuminating further the complex potential of therapeutic work to both to fatigue and to heal" (2007:237). They also highlight that vicarious resilience offers a mechanism to counterbalance vicarious trauma and, crucially, that practitioners' awareness of it boosts its potential benefits.

> Both processes can be managed: VT can be identified and decreased, and VR can be identified and increased, by developing awareness, purposefully cultivating and expanding it. (2007:239)

Silveira and Boyer (2015) found that in addition to experiencing vicarious resilience counsellors of traumatised children were also imbued with increased levels of optimism, which they attribute to the vicarious mechanisms of engaging with children overcoming trauma. They also identify how professionals who are familiar with vicarious resilience can look for it within young people and share findings with the children's families, thus affording the families opportunities for experiencing vicarious resilience and enhanced optimism also. This, they point out, could potentially transform family dynamics in positive ways "and contribute to better therapeutic outcomes for clients" (2015:523). They recommend, and I concur, that vicarious resilience be brought into discussions within supervision and professional development workshops.

With regard to the concept of compassion and trauma, there is also a positive construct identified as self-compassion (Thompson and Waltz, 2008) that warrants inclusion from a self-care perspective. Self-compassion has been gaining purchase in recent years for its potential to enhance practitioners' mental health within a framework that avoids the self-evaluation and self-judgement that is inherent in many other models. This, then, enables the person to be less judgemental of others. Kristin Neff (2003) identifies how people are apt to be much harsher towards themselves than they are to others they care about, or even strangers.

> Self-compassion entails seeing one's own experiences in light of the common human experience, acknowledging that failure, suffering and inadequacies are part of the human condition, and that all people – oneself included – are worthy of compassion. (Neff, 2003:87)

Neff identifies the three elements of self-compassion as:

> (a) self-kindness – extending kindness and understanding to oneself rather than harsh judgements and self-criticism, (b) common humanity – seeing one's experiences as part of the larger human experience rather than seeing them as separating and isolating, (c) mindfulness – holding one's painful thoughts and feelings in balanced awareness rather than over-identifying with them. (Neff, 2003:89)

Consequently, awareness of vicarious resilience, coupled with the practice of self-compassion, can improve practitioners' well-being. Self-care is a critical component of professional competence in social care.

· ·

To have the capacity and capability to care for others we must first take care of ourselves.

· ·

Paul

The second incident where the expression of vulnerability was significant in my practice was when I was asked to come to a residential centre to intervene with a teenage boy, Paul, who was allegedly intimidating other young people. Paul was over six feet tall and heavily built and had a history of multiple placement breakdowns. When I arrived I engaged with him casually and we chatted about how he was getting on in general. The conversation moved to a hallway where there was a large mirror on the wall and we stood discussing why I was there and the impact he was having on others in the house. I was non-confrontational and tried to explain to him how fearful others were of him when he became agitated or demanding as they experienced him as threatening. I was careful to state clearly that I did not necessarily believe this was his intent. He listened and didn't become agitated, though he didn't appear to be fully understanding or agreeing with what I was trying to convey. By chance, I noticed that we were in front of the mirror and whilst looking into it I thought to myself how large he looked by comparison to me, as I am no more than five feet ten inches tall.

Spontaneously, I said that right then I was conscious that he was clearly larger than me and capable of putting me "through the wall with a punch" if he chose to do so. Therefore, I explained that I was experiencing him as potentially threatening due to my sense of vulnerability. We looked at each other in the mirror for a short while and I reiterated, "look how much bigger than me you are", still trying to get my point across. In truth, I was not experiencing fear, as I had no expectation that he would hit me, and if I had such a concern I certainly would not have voiced it. However, rationally I was vulnerable should he have chosen to do so. To my immense surprise, whilst still looking in the mirror he said, "but that's not how I feel inside, inside I feel only like this size" (here he put his hand to his midriff). We then moved back into the house, sat at a table and shortly thereafter he said to me, "I am this way because I have to be". I knew he was revealing an insight into his inner self as, given his background and what he had been exposed to, he had been forced to fend for himself in the most effective way he could just to survive.

I took heart from these revelations as I knew he was showing a vulnerable side of himself which his prior life experiences had led him to suppress. I made no comment on either revelation as I was frankly too surprised to think of appropriate responses and, in truth, didn't at the time grasp the full significance of the mirror incident. Perhaps no comment was actually the right choice. Our discussion continued about what his life could become if he grasped the opportunities now being offered to him in this placement, including a possible move-on option based on him fulfilling what I believed to be his potential. I knew enough to know that he was communicating honestly and at a deep level which augured well for the future.

It was only through effective supervision that I came to see the significance of showing him my vulnerability in the mirror, which enabled him to then show me his in return. This learning clearly reinforced the value of good supervision. Once I recognised this for what it was through critically reflective processes, I became able to replicate it in similar situations, making me wonder if this is a way in which empirical knowledge might be generated?

As with the residential manager in Keith's case, I didn't know the good that I did until later which, in my experience, is often the case in social care. Each day working with young people is made up of a series of moments where we have the opportunity to meet their current needs. I believe there is such a thing as a "law of opportunity" which holds that opportunity can come in a multitude of guises and forms – moments of opportunity – which are around us at numerous unscheduled and largely unknown times. It is those who can seize these moments of opportunity, and then utilise them to the best effect, who are successful within social care. I call it a law because this reinforces the existence of such opportunity even at times when we may be at low ebb and least able to anticipate positive experiences. To capitalise on this law, attunement (Winnicott, 1960; Siegel, 2007), which is enhanced with a positive outlook, is invaluable. We are more likely to find something we are looking for than stumble across something unanticipated, and here the words of Winston Churchill are worthy of reflection:

> The pessimist sees the difficulty in every opportunity whilst the optimist sees the opportunity in every difficulty.

I am glad to say that both Sue and Paul remained within their placements for their full durations and moved on successfully in planned and supported transitions. The impact on me of these moments has been profound as evidenced by my vivid recollections. These were some of my moments of validation over many years of practice, and I have learnt over the years that we must take our validation when, and where, it can be found. It can be scarce but critical to our well-being and for me is a vital part of my self-care.

Relationship is the Key

Our epistemological position (typologies of knowledge – what we know and how we know it) is a valuable insight for each practitioner to be aware of as it is we ourselves that are our most valuable tool in working with young people. Therefore self-awareness is paramount.

> An approach that is grounded in the belief that "I already know" is one that is immobilised and is oblivious to context and perspective, which in turn pigeonholes experiences, behaviours, objects and other people into existing categories. In other words an individual's way of knowing predisposes a way of being and may obstruct learning. (Bellefeuille and Ricks, 2010:1237)

Relationships and key working are central to Keith's story. If we accept that each carer is their own most valuable tool, their most empowering factor, then it is self-evident that the medium which most facilitates the use of self is the relationship between carer and worker.

Keith talks of the hope that I gave him that Christmas night so many years ago and clearly this had a profound effect on him. I believe that hope is integral to change (Yalom, 1995; Phillips, 2008) and that "to instil hope in others one must have a sense of their own hope" yet "there's a general lack of information and literature on hope or hope theory in the social work field" (McCarter, 2007:119/120). Weingarten (2010) and Nelson and St. Cyr (2015) have theorised the construct of "reasonable hope", hope that is both "sensible and moderate", and the link between hope and resilience for professionals working with victims of trauma. Weingarten (2010) identified five characteristics of reasonable hope that aid professionals in the caring professions to nurture authentic hope in the face of challenging circumstances, uncertainty and even despair. These are the recognition that hope is: relational; something that can be practiced; sees the future as open, uncertain and influenceable; seeks goals and pathways; and accommodates doubt, contradictions and despair.

> Reasonable hope softens the polarity between hope and despair, hope and hopelessness (Flaskas, 2007b) and allows (more) people to place themselves in the category of the hopeful. Reasonable hope refers to actions that one takes not, as hope does, feelings one may or may not be able to summon. (Weingarten, 2010:7)

Winnicott (1956, 1973) saw the lack of hope as the basic feature of the deprived child and, therefore, he theorised that delinquency and challenging behaviour are in fact signs of hope. He saw these apparently anti-social behaviours as the child's desire to regain what has been lost, the non-available mother figure. This desire and attendant anti-social behaviours are, in Winicott's opinion, an expression of moments of hope and should be recognised as such by professionals working with these children rather than suppressed as purely negative behaviours. Tomlinson (2008) also addresses the issue of hope with regard to children. He promulgates an attachment perspective and attributes the formation of hope as learning achieved by an infant whose feelings of distress are safely contained by its parents. Thus, he posits, children who have internalised good experiences can tolerate prolonged difficult situations as they have internal reservoirs to draw on affording them an expectation that better times will follow. However, a child who has not experienced this positive parenting may not develop a sense of hope. Tomlinson cites Dunne (2007):

> They may not be able to wait for a "better time" as they do not know what a "better time" is. A child who has experienced distress, followed by hopefulness, only to have those hopes obliterated can soon descend into a hopelessness where it is too risky to expect a "better time". (Tomlinson, 2008:23)

Affording children in care hope can significantly strengthen their resilience. We must be mindful that for children and young people

> ... those with unrecognised trauma and those with un-relenting trauma are both often unable to feel hopeful. Trauma clamps down on hopefulness; fear trumps hope. (Weingarten, 2010:12)

For workers caring for traumatised children it is important to remember that

> ... sometimes trauma sufferers must depend on others for hope: feeling hopeless, they must rely on borrowed hope, hope that others hold out for them. (Allen, 2008:292)

Whilst not endorsed as a truth, there is much to reflect on in the saying, "Man without hope is an animal". I see a correlation between an inquiring stance, where many outcomes are possible, and hope, as opposed to a position of certainty where only limited outcomes are possible (Pozatek, 1994).

Curiosity is an invaluable asset to our work as we must always seek the why of the situations we encounter – the cause, rather than merely dealing with the effect. Not dealing with the cause will consign us to the role of "fire-fighters" constantly dealing with the same recurring issues. Addressing the causes will render us "edu-cators" where lasting life-changing growth is nurtured. Dismiss-ing or blaming may cause harm to the child and thereby render us "abusers" in our work with traumatised children by reinforcing maladaptive learning and making their problems worse. No matter how many times we have encountered certain behaviours, each person is unique and thus the causation may be different and bears diligent investigation in each case. We cannot claim to value each person as an individual with inalienable worth if we do not afford them such curiosity. The propensity to slide into judgmentalism is something we must guard against. I have found critical reflection (self-curiosity) and supervision invaluable when, at times, I have fallen short of the mark in this regard in my practice. Although not offered as an incontrovertible truth, there is cause for reflection and a stimulus for debate in Bukowski's famous quip:

> The problem with the world is that the intelligent people are
> full of doubts whilst the stupid ones are full of confidence.

This is proffered with the understanding that we cannot become paralysed with self-doubt whilst also recognising that, at times, a certain amount of irreverence coupled with a sense of humour is also appropriate in our work, especially with adolescents and young adults. Humour, in its various forms, can be highly therapeutic. This is one area where shared meaning (collaborative meaning-making) can naturally occur in everyday interactions which can be a strong factor in relationship development and a powerful tool in pre-empting difficulties (Edmond, 2004; Boeckel, 2013; Smith *et al.*, 2013).

Trust and belief were fundamental to my key working relationship with Keith. One incident which I have long wondered about occurred during his time in the residential centre whilst I was his key worker. Keith was accused of some misdemeanour and this came up for discussion at a team meeting. I advocated his innocence as he had told me he didn't do it before the meeting. Sometime later, after he had left the centre, he told me he had in fact committed this misdemeanour and I sensed that there was something important about this to him, but until I read his story I didn't fully know why.

I believed him and he was able to manipulate me because of this belief, just as children often do with their parents. We act *in loco parentis* to children in care and whilst I extend unconditional love to my own children doing likewise in residential care might not be deemed appropriate or indeed possible. Yet we know children cannot thrive without love, and even though we are acting as substitute parents, sometimes precisely because parents cannot supply these children with love, we are conflicted about this core issue to parenting and child development. As Daniels and Livingstone (2011) ask, how will children in care know they are lovable if they do not receive love while in care?

Similarly, with regard to children's experiencing of being cared for, Nel Noddings (1996) makes the point that care needs to be experienced by the child for care to be actually happening. She maintains that if the child does not feel the care that the carers claim to be affording them then they are being treated as an object and not a person (Stevens, 2008).

Trust is a key factor within positive relationship formation (Cameron, 2013). Within my key working relationships I always tried to extend what Carl Rogers termed "unconditional positive regard" to everyone I work with. However, we all fall short of the mark sometimes and, as with my own children, failings represent opportunities for learning and trust needs to be re-established as quickly as possible. Sometimes we have to *fake it till we make it* and encourage them to do likewise as nothing succeeds like success.

Social care staff are generally very good at identifying when children in care behave in ways that breach the expectations of living within the residential centre or social and legal norms. These deficits can be readily identified as they often come with a known history. Less obvious are the reasons for such deficits and the protective factors that sometimes may underpin these behaviours.

Adopting a "risk and resilience" perspective, which we shall consider further in the section on resilience, to some of these behaviours affords insights into what drives them. Within this perspective, if mindful of the pitfalls of a deficit-based approach where "labelling a child a 'psychiatric case' can be more harmful than the disorder itself" (Buchanan, cited in Houston, 2010:358), and the potential for self-fulfilling prophecies (Heath *et al.*, 1994; Rhule, 2005) and learned helplessness (Seligman, 1975), we can see justification for:

1. Why the young person is behaving in this way;

2. A rationale for filtering or prioritising which issues to address and letting some issues slide.

Clearly the crux here is identifying what issues are appropriate to let slide and which have to be addressed. In my practice with young people I have, at times, casually let them know I am aware of an issue but that I am taking no further action on the matter. Obviously, if they can completely fool me too easily this could equally have a negative effect on our relationship. Rhythm and wavelengths as outlined by Garfat (1998) are, in my experience, important within residential child care. I have always tried to develop relationships where reciprocity is a strong feature as I sought to find this balance with the young people in my care. This I have found to be very effective in developing trust. Once on a wavelength, like surfing a wave, life goes smoother. This is a process of reflexive (re)negotiation and is a practical, if not essential, life skill. This can be analysed and evaluated from perspectives such as transactional analysis developed by Eric Berne (1964) or considered within Pierre Bourdieu's (1994:9) construct of "feel for the game" as forms of social capital, both of which afford insight into the dynamics at play in such processes.

Such an approach affords a mechanism for addressing multiple issues in a phased and progressively managed manner rather than all at once. Relationships are dynamic in their nature and as trust develops so does the ability to address issues. Rome was not built in a day and trust is dynamic and involves elements of risk (Fu, 2004). Also, with the benefit of ongoing professional development, I can now see self-protective dimensions to some of these non-conforming behaviours by young people in care which further supports the adoption of this approach. These behaviours may have enabled them to survive the abuses and trauma perpetrated on them. Trust, which formerly was broken, is essential to enable them to move on from such behaviours (Ungar, 2004). Whilst we endeavour to separate the child from their behaviour, it can be beneficial to separate our cognitive functioning from our emotional responses. Additionally, this separation of the child from the behaviour can be aided by reframing what is often seen negatively as "attention-seeking behaviour" (Mellor, 2005) to a more positive concept with clearer meaning of "attachment-needing behaviour". It is all too easy to see the problem rather than the child. In deciding which issue to address there are often so many factors at play that no singular rule can apply. I have witnessed some excellent practice in this area over the years where colleagues have built trust with hard-to-reach young people yet maintained team consistency. This is a classic "grey area" where so much relational work occurs.

All agree that it is normal adolescent development to test boundaries, including relationship and trust boundaries. Reframing this as the negotiation of boundaries affords a normalised and strengths-based perspective. If we replace the ubiquitous social care term "challenging" with "negotiation", we may see more strengths-based processes at play in our daily interactions. For example, in place of challenging behaviour we would have negotiational behaviour. Where will young people in care get this opportunity to negotiate boundaries if not within the key working relationship and with individual social care workers?

Working from a strengths-based perspective has much to offer our work, both for ourselves and the people we support.

> Identifying and expanding our clients strengths will isomorphically identify and expand our own. (Pozatek, 1994:402)

I now see from reading Keith's story the significance of my belief and faith in him. Whatever the misdemeanour it was trivial compared to the effect my belief in him had. I saw the positive in him and kept the focus on that whilst always remembering this personal mantra when working with young people:

> Be prepared to lose battles every day in caring for young people; it's the war we want to win.

I am glad I unknowingly lost the battle over this misdemeanour as it may have played a small part in aiding Keith to go on and win the war.

The Role of the Key Worker

Key working is so central to both mine and Keith's dyadic story that it merits further examination.

> Within the fields of policy and practice related to residential care services for young people, the recognition of "key working" as a core concept associated with good practice with young people across a number of different sectors is firmly embedded. (Holt and Kirwan, 2012:372)

There is no clear definition of what constitutes key working, or indeed evidence supporting the above quotation. Holt and Kirwan undertook a review of international literature on the subject which is worthy of readers' attention. They make the point that without clarity of purpose and function of key working, "it is possible, if not likely, that key working as a concept and as a practice means different things to different people" (Holt and Kirwan, 2012:373).

> The authors (Holt and Kirwan) conclude that relationships are not only integral to key working but are also inextricably linked to successful transitions. (Coyle and Pinkerton, 2012:305)

Keith's story authenticates this finding. Clearly my key working role in his placement had a significant effect which he articulates very well. But, as pointed out earlier, I had very little experience and no qualification at that time. Although I had a desire to make a difference, this alone would not have ensured that our key working relationship would have been so effective. There was a team supporting me in my work, and indeed at a wider level there was an agency which, at that time, espoused values that placed the young person at the centre of all services. I had a mentor who guided my practice in my induction. This practice has been recognised to have beneficial effects on practice competence development (Collins, 1994). I also remember following the examples of good practice I witnessed by some of my colleagues. This methodology has remained for me a mechanism for positive practice development and one that I regard, informed by DiMaggio and Powell (1983), as "mimetic practice isomorphism". That is the process of (re)production based on (self) absorption or, simply put, a form of imitation. This has close association with the psychoanalytical process of "mirroring" (Caldwell, 2011; Ruch, 2011). Complementing this developmental process I was empowered to develop my own style of key working. This facilitated the expression of my personality rather than a prescribed model of key working which allowed me to connect with Keith with more authenticity. I believe this played a key role in fostering his trust in me, as young people in care, by harsh necessity, have learnt to discern authenticity and intent in adults.

I am also conscious that my relationship with Keith was reciprocal in its nature. For example, I developed into the role of residential care worker and key worker partly through the experience of our relationship. I found my professional identity whilst Keith began the process of discovering his "true identify" (Winnicott, 1960). Keith has identified in his story how confused he was about his identity growing up in a dysfunctional home where he had to "morph" his behaviour to match conditions within the family home depending on his parent's state of intoxication, thereby masking and distorting his true identify. Winnicott identified such identity confusion as "false identity" (Winnicott, 1960).

We both made mistakes and we both learnt from these mistakes. In fact, I would say that I have learnt, at a minimum, as much from my relationship with Keith as he may have from me, and this continues to this day. I was deeply affected on reading his story for the first time to see the real extent to which he suffered from loneliness and poverty on moving into the aftercare placement, and how I had not seen this at the time when I was the one person who could have helped him. Cognitively, I know that I was not fully responsible for this, but emotionally I still felt the deep distress of not having been there for him when he so badly needed support. All I can do with this feeling is to accept it and learn from it so that if ever a similar situation arises I respond differently, whilst also highlighting this issue so that others may also learn from it. Officially, my duty may have ended when he was discharged from my care, but morally and on an interpersonal level it did not and I feel that, in this crucial regard, I failed him.

Keith has also caused me to consider the protectionist nature of my relationships with young people by virtue of my relationship with him beyond care. My tendency was still to consider him from a protectionist stance, despite his being an adult, and this caused me to re-evaluate my stance with young people in care. In this evaluation I shifted my position on the protectionist continuum more towards liberation. I have become aware of how easy it is for the professional to adopt a protectionist stance, often with benign and laudable motivations. When we consider that social care is dominated by protectionist paradigms, such as child protection, then this propensity becomes apparent. Because of this the professional must constantly re-evaluate, through processes of critical reflection and critical thinking (Gambrill, 2012, 2013), whether their stance is appropriate to the young people they are supporting.

A final point on key working is an excellent recommendation from Holt and Kirwan (*ibid*) that young people have a voice in the selection of their key worker.

Loneliness

Clearly, the loneliness Keith experienced on his transition to the aftercare service was severe. Whilst this was twenty years ago and today there would be two staff on duty, and therefore more available to him, the same service still operates and caters for young people of his age. Keith was just weeks short of his seventeenth birthday when he made this transition. Current practice in preparation for leaving care does not always address this area of young peoples' lives, their psychosocial and emotional well-being (Stein and Wade, 2000; Dixon, 2008; Barry, 2010; Gaskell, 2010 Hannon *et al.*, 2010).

Research by Iglehart and Becerra (2002) supports this assertion with the finding that young people themselves stated how critical relationships with adults were to them in their preparation for leaving care. The young people in this study placed such relationships above the skills development aspects of independent living programmes in importance to their well-being. Over the intervening years I have witnessed much suffering for many young people who have left care where hardship, lost accommodation and crisis stem from loneliness. Loneliness can have serious consequences for mental, physical and emotional health (Hawkley and Cacioppo, 2007), casting a malignant, far-reaching shadow which clouds the lives of care leavers. Loneliness was formerly acknowledged as vulnerability associated with old age, but research by Hawkley and Cacioppo (2010), amongst others, has identified adolescents' vulnerability to loneliness. However, this area remains under-researched within the Republic of Ireland and the UK (Murphy and Shelvin, 2012). I have too often witnessed some of the consequences of this loneliness poignantly captured by Meg Lindsay in her beautifully composed, yet pain-laden, line, recounting the experience of a care leaver named "Mary":

> Her loneliness couldn't close the door on "friends," who spent her cash for her, and alienated her new neighbours. (Lindsay, 2000:59)

Transition

Research by Dima and Skehill (2011) and Anghel (2011), utilising the Bridges (2004) model, has identified that transition is composed of two distinct processes – the physical and the psychological – and with three distinct stages – endings, neutral zone and new beginnings.

The significance of transitions to successful outcomes for children in care is made explicit within the influential Demos *In Loco Parentis report*, wherein they state:

> A strong body of evidence and our own primary research shows the most positive experiences of care, and the best outcomes for looked-after children, to be associated with the following three factors:
>
> 1. early intervention and minimum delay;
>
> 2. stability during care;
>
> 3. supported transitions to independence. (Hannon *et al.*, 2010:9)

When young people move from one service to another the levels of support ideally should be kept the same in the new placement to allow them the time and space to process the change. This can be conceptualised with an analogy of using doors between rooms at different levels. Building regulations require that when you go though a doorway you cross the door saddle onto a step at the same height so that both feet are at the same level. If you stepped through a door to a lower level it is quite possible that you might fall so building regulations, and common sense, prohibit this. Similarly, when moving between placements only when this step encompassing the first two stages of transition has been accomplished can the levels of support be reduced, as appropriate to the new setting in the new beginnings stage. This is especially important when dealing with Step-Down type services. There is more than one step within the transition and the one least allowed for in leaving care is the neutral stage, where the opportunity to "space out" within what anthropologists term the "liminal state" provides a time for freedom, exploration, reflection, risk-taking and identity search (Stein, 2008a, 2012).

Whilst the transition process can allow for co-existence of the beginning and ending states, for example, we all have the inner child co-existing with our adult selves, we cannot exist in both states simultaneously. We may retain the potential for both but there are strong elements of separation, loss and acquisition inherent within the transition process.

> What we call the beginning is often the end
> and to make an end is to make a beginning.
> The end is where we start from.
> (T.S. Eliot, 'Little Gidding')

Poverty and Independence

Keith's description of living in poverty within care highlights an issue that is unacceptable, then or now. We cannot dismiss this as being an issue from 1994 as, sadly, today care leavers can still be marginalised and socially excluded (Raffo, 2000; MacDonald, 2007; Harder *et al.*, 2011; Stein, 2012). Increasingly, the focus of aftercare support services are shifting to models of independence (mainstreaming into adult services with a focus on certain skills or competencies needed to function autonomously) rather than interdependence (the nurturing of autonomy within webs of dependence and facilitating the use of specialist services allowing for developmental work) (Mendes and Moslehuddin, 2006; Samuels and Pryce, 2008; Propp *et al.*, 2003; Antle *et al.*, 2009). As a direct result of this, increasing numbers of care leavers are experiencing poverty and homelessness (EPIC, 2012; Focus Ireland, 2014).

> ... interdependence models saw leaving care more as a psychosocial transition, a high priority placed on interpersonal skills, developing self-esteem and confidence, and receiving ongoing support after a young person leavers care (Stein and Carey, 1986). (Stein, 2012:31)

Indeed, the idea of independence itself can be confusing and it benefits from qualification as to its intended meaning.

. . . .

> *What is the individual becoming independent from? Is it the residential or foster home – in which case the appropriate qualification might be independent living arrangements or independent accommodation? Or is it independent from the HSE/Child and Family Agency (Tusla) and/or the state that is the goal, and here the broadest and unqualified interpretation of independence might be seen to support such a position.*

. . . .

The definition of independence as listed in Cambridge Dictionaries Online tends to lend support to this latter interpretation:

> Freedom from being governed or ruled by another country;
>
> The *ability* to *live* your life without being *helped* or influenced by other people.

. . . .

> *Does anybody become truly independent of their family if they move out of the family home to live in independent accommodation, as so few actually have the means to do so before their mid- to late twenties?*

. . . .

In most Member States in the EU28, more young people were living with their parents in 2011 than in 2007, the proportion of 18–29 year-olds doing so rising from 44 per cent to 48 per cent ... this increase is significant for both the younger age group (those aged 18–24 years) and the older group (aged 25–29), for both men and women. Young men are more likely to live with their parents than young women, and, as expected, those aged below 25 are significantly more likely to live with their parents than those aged between 25 and 29. (Eurofound, 2014:6)

The American terminology is notable with regard to care leaving. Here the leaving care process is referred to as the emancipation of young people. This has specific connotations of freedom with arguably an implicit validation for the separation between oppression (from state care and therefore ongoing state support) and the newfound freedom. The use of language can be of profound importance in social care and social policy. In this respect the Ryan Report (2009) can be commended in referring to aftercare as a vital service to assist care leavers in the transition to *independent living* rather than merely stating independence. However, the addition of the word *arrangements*, thereby encompassing the interdependent dimensions implicit in such settings, might have been more appropriate. Bullock *et al.* (2006:17) make the well-founded point that:

The withdrawal of support, and sometimes the loss of a home, produce a new set of problems for young people that are often glossed over in euphemistic talk about independent living.

Clearly, living in independent accommodation is a different thing from being totally independent of whatever support may be needed to aid the person to sustain themselves. There is a pressing need for clarity across multiple domains pertaining to aftercare provision in the Republic of Ireland.

So, to bring my chapter to a conclusion, it is appropriate for me to give a brief overview of my experience of working with Keith and others over my years of practice in residential care. This experience has taught me that the most appropriate approach is one where tolerance of risk and uncertainty, use of self and collaborative meaning-making are fundamental to practice. This approach I now regard as "care on the edge" – on the edge because often I was unsure of which way events would unfold with the ever present possibility for things to go either positively or negatively with very fine and shifting lines demarking one from the other. This, at times, induced stress and anxiety on my part, that growing feeling of impending doom in the pit of my stomach, whilst attempting to outwardly portray a façade of calm and confidence. All the while I would be forestalling the rising temptation to act decisively to alleviate the uncertainty, as such action might be motivated by fear and anxiety and could have made things worse. This was not inaction to avoid conflict, rather inaction to avoid an unpredictable reaction. Yet by tolerating the uncertainty and managing the risk things tended to work out well in the end. I have also learned that:

> Each child is unique and so their needs will be best met at unique and shifting locations along these continuums (of care and need) and so we must be prepared to shift along these continuums with them. (Fenton, 2015)

Many children in care, especially those in residential care, live "on the edge" – the edge of social and educational exclusion, the system of care within the placement of last resort, the judicial system, crisis and mental ill health, to name but a few. Consequently, the worker moving to the edge with them facilitates closer connection and thereby better understanding of their realities. This can then aid in predicting their responses, individually and as a group, and thereby chart the best course of action. There is also the enhanced potential for co-regulation, though in my experience this can be an exhausting space to inhabit due to the reality of the stress and anxiety these young people must live with for prolonged periods of time. That "feeling of doom" in the pit of my stomach, the foreboding that things were about to go very badly wrong, and the feeling of exhaustion at the end of a tense shift, can be ever-present for these young people for prolonged periods of time. Understanding and appreciating this makes their willingness to try to cope, with varying degrees of success, therefore all the more remarkable.

In sharing experiences with other workers it is abundantly clear that the vast majority also have experienced the "on the edge" dynamic in their work. However, these can be turned to advantage with time, reflection, good supervision and support. In my own case, as the years went by the feelings of anxiety reduced as I became more at ease with risk and uncertainty. I like to think I became less uncomfortable and fearful at the edge as I became more certain that this was the right place to be, but I retained the connection to the feelings I had previously experienced.

With regard to the care system I have witnessed many changes over the years. Many have been for the better but some have detracted from its ability to function in an integrated and congruent way (Anglin, 2002). A congruent system of care optimally meets the needs of young people and supports practitioners to practice with authenticity, what Hepworth *et al.* (1997:120) define as "the sharing of self by relating in a natural, sincere, spontaneous, open and genuine manner". Keith's story is one of hardship, pain, loneliness, love and ultimately great positivity. However, there is also for me, just as there was for Keith on leaving the residential centre, a bittersweet reality. When I reflect on that time, the memories of those young people I worked with but who tragically died before reaching adulthood live side-by-side with the positive memories. I attended my first funeral for a child in care at that time. Twenty years later legislation underpinning aftercare is still inadequate. Consequently, there is a lack of clarity as to what aftercare constitutes, who is eligible for it and under what circumstances. As a result, young people continue to leave care underprepared and without adequate support. This was unacceptable when Keith left care and it is even more so now. We have failed to learn from the lessons of the past.

Summary

These two chapters offered insight into the experiences of both a child in care and the worker caring for that child. The honesty with which Keith recounts his story of family life where violence and alcohol, as well as love, were present, and his positive experiences in residential care and hardship within aftercare, affords a poignant insight into the realities faced by many children in care. The dyadic nature of the relationship between worker and child emerged throughout with both of us benefiting.

Keith identified many issues that affected him, such as trauma, loneliness, poverty, relationships, prejudice, stigma, vulnerability, trust and hope. Some of these were addressed in my chapter and others will feature throughout the rest of the book. Ultimately, theory, research, policy and the socio-political environment all inform practice which represents the actual expression of care young people receive when in care and when they have left.

Section Two – Residential Child Care

Introduction

This section addresses the area of residential care and the misunderstandings, myths and assumptions surrounding this form of out-of-home care. Keith's story offers an insider perspective to some of the benefits of residential care which challenges many of the misconceptions associated with residential care in the twenty-first century.

Kahan (1994:4) observed that the usage of residential child care has "waxed and waned and waxed again depending on the fluctuations of professional and political theories and fashions and changing pressures on national resources". This observation still resonates today and these issues are explored in the forthcoming two chapters and throughout the book.

The history of the service is examined and comparisons are made with trends internationally, both in residential care and foster care, as well as a consideration of the factors that may be driving these trends, and how these trends may impact on children in care and on the care system. There is a detailed examination of out-of-home care provision in the Republic of Ireland.

Chapter 3

Myths Surrounding Residential Child Care

Keith clearly identifies the benefit that residential child care afforded him. This is significant because in my time working in residential care I have witnessed an increasingly negative perception of residential care develop, which I believe does a disservice to young people requiring specific forms of care (Kendrick, 2013). Residential care is compared unfavourably with foster care and non-residential care (Kahn, 1984; Bates *et al.*, 1997; Melton *et al.*, 1998; Iwaniec, 2006). It is seen as too expensive relative to the outcomes achieved, many of which are considered poor. It is perceived as not facilitating attachment formation and providing unrealistic standards of living to children that they won't retain on leaving care. It is associated with scenes of past abuses and a confused theoretical base (Berridge and Brodie, 1996; Jones and Landsverk, 2006; McLeigh and Briddell, 2011). It is seen as oppressive by those advocating the tenets of normalisation, deinstitutionalisation, mainstreaming, minimal intervention and the use of the least restrictive environment (Fulcher, 2009).

This has been exacerbated by two factors:

1. Residential care has been used as a placement of last resort and not used for children most likely to benefit from it – the residualisation of residential care (Corby *et al.*, 2001; Edmond, 2004; Foltz, 2004; Stevens, 2008; O'Sullivan, 2009; Smith, 2009). Rather, it is used for young people who cannot receive the support and/or safety they need from their own families or foster families, or who pose a danger to others. (Berridge *et al.*, 2003; Whittaker, 2004; Little *et al.*, 2005)

60

The picture today of residential childcare is one of inexo-
rable decline, with a surviving residue of institutional activity now focused almost exclusively on children and young
people seen as very hard to serve and a population deemed
beyond the capacity of more community-based options.
(Gilligan, 2009a:275)

2.   There is a tendency for the problem under review to be associ-
     ated with the child being in care rather than consideration of
     the factors that resulted in the child being admitted to care in
     the first place. (McSherry *et al.*, 2008)

Several noted publications critical of the merit of residential
child care have had lasting impact since the mid-twentieth century. John Bowlby, the noted attachment theorist, was critical of
substitute care and very critical of institutional care for children.
It must be noted, however, that the institutional care he was critical of bears little resemblance to today's small group homes. His
focus was firmly on the relationship between the infant and the
mother with his famous refrain, "Better a bad home than a good
substitute" (Bowlby in Issroff, 2005:88). He did, however, relent
somewhat from this position in later years and acknowledged that:

Therapeutic residential child care of disturbed children
had a role, if not something intrinsically desirable, at least
as a practical necessity for the foreseeable future. (Bowlby
in Issroff, 2005:89)

However, within this debate the distinction between therapeutic residential child care and institutional care, both physically and
culturally, is seldom made clear.

As its name implies, a group home strives to offer a home-
like environment not attainable within an institutional setting while removing the intimacy and intensity of a family
environment. (Anglin, 2004:178)

Despite his retraction of his earlier unequivocal rejection of
substitute care, and acknowledgement of the merit of residential
care, Bowlby's condemnation of institutional care for children has

61

had long-term impact. It still reverberates today in the debate on the pros and cons of residential child care and foster care.

> Indeed, attachment theory – and in particular Bowlby's 1951 Monograph for the World Health Organisation – lies at the heart of the English preference for foster care. (Petrie, 2007:77)

Goffman's (1968) influential book *Asylums,* which developed an understanding of the impact of institutionalisation on human development, was another notable publication that was hostile to residential child care, as was Wolfenberger's (1972) theory of normalisation (Milligan and Stevens, 2006a; Smith, 2012).

Anglin and Knorth cite the following from another influential publication, *The Stockholm Declaration*:

> - There is indisputable evidence that institutional (i.e. residential) care has negative consequences for both individual children and for society at large.

> - It is alleged that the UN Convention on the Rights of the Child includes an obligation of "resorting to institutional care only as a last resort and as a temporary response. (Stockholm Declaration on Children and Residential Care, May 2003, cited in Anglin and Knorth, 2004a:141)

A meta-analysis by Knorth *et al.* (2008) challenges many of these erroneous assumptions, now widely taken as unequivocal, and particularly the Stockholm declaration statements as outlined above. In contrast, they find that residential care in fact improves the children's psychosocial functioning and they conclude:

> ... the "indisputable evidence" that this form of care has (mainly) negative consequences for individual children and for the society at large, as stated in the Stockholm Declaration, has not been supported. (2008:133)

Indeed, since the turn of this century there has been an increasing body of research validating the place of residential care in the system of care (Anglin, 2002, 2004; Hair, 2005; Hillan, 2005; Little *et al.*, 2005; del Valle *et al.*, 2008; Bettmann and Jasperson,

2009; Lee *et al.*, 2011; De Swart *et al.*, 2012; Kendrick, 2012, 2013). Children have expressed a preference for residential care over foster care, as evidenced within a study by Sinclair and Gibbs (1998). This study found that one in three children whom they interviewed expressed a preference to be placed in residential care over foster care.

In a European context del Valle *et al.* find:

> The general dismissal of residential care, observed in many countries, has had the consequence of removing this type of provision from the political agendas of priorities in child care. At the same time, the population requiring child care is more and more problematic, and foster care services are finding it difficult to achieve stability and positive results. The data indicate that residential care can make highly positive contributions, but for this there is a need to define its role (Utting, 1997) and its functions within the child care system. (del Valle *et al.*, 2008:22)

Within the UK Kendrick makes the point that:

> A number of national enquiries have concluded that residential care is a 'positive choice' for some children and young people (Kent, 1997; Utting, 1997; Shaw, 2007). (Kendrick, 2013:77)

With regard to the misinterpretation of the Stockholm Agreement, Ainsworth and Thoburn (2014) identify the role language may play:

> However, while in the English language 'institution', 'children's home', 'group care facility' or 'residential treatment unit' may all be in use (sometimes synonymously but more often to denote different types of care regime), in many languages (Armenian as but one example) differentiation between 'institution' and 'children's home' translate as 'children's home'. (Ainsworth and Thoburn, 2014:16)

Ainsworth and Thoburn also identify that the research carried out in the latter half of the twentieth century which led to these alleged negative effects of institutional care becoming identified as prevalent were of a design that would not be acceptable by today's research standards. They find that therefore "the conclusions drawn from the research should be viewed with some caution" (2014:16).

A further major factor underpinning the residualisation of residential child care arising from the Stockholm Declaration is the identification of the "least restrictive" placement option as the preferred choice. This has led to child welfare professionals placing children in residential care, which is perceived as a restrictive placement, only after the young person has been placed in a number of less restrictive options, such as kinship or foster care, and only after these have broken down (Hannon *et al.*, 2010; Jones *et al.*, 2011). Stuck *et al.*, (2000) identified a "systemic bias" amongst child welfare professional towards the least restrictive option:

> The linear model creates a crisis driven system in which movement along the continuum frequently only occurs after placement disruption. (Stuck *et al.*, cited in Owens, 2008:20)

In addition to the above-cited growing body of research that challenges assumptions created by the Stockholm Declaration, in his review of residential child care treatment, costs, placement stability and outcomes, Sansei (2005) found that:

> ... when the appropriate level of care is selected at the outset, the majority of residents will exit the residential care system and return home or go to home-like settings. (2005:62)

This, according to Sansei, resulted in a cost saving for the state over repeated failures within less expensive placements which re-currently break down.

✗   It has been my experience that some children prefer residential care over foster care, a point made by Milligan and Stevens (2006) and Kendrick (2013). Furthermore, residential care and social care can be seen to be dominated by social work and legislative paradigms. The latter were introduced via the multiple inquiries into abuse within residential care which occurred in the 1970s and 1980s with the legislature remaining *in situ* ever since (Howe, 1998). It has also been my experience that our profession has become increasingly litigious over this time with insurance requirements increasingly encroaching into practice. For example, a manager might be forbidden to apologise to a staff member who may have been injured at work as this is deemed as an admission of liability by insurers and as prejudicial to the case. This can inflame staff and management relations and foster adversarial practice.

The transition from institutional care to community-based lower-occupancy residential centres was decreed internationally within the Stockholm and Malmo Declarations (Angling and North, 2004), and in the Republic of Ireland in the Kennedy Report (1970) and the Task Force Report on Child Care Services (1980). The Task Force Report recommended that community-based homes catering for between seven to nine children be established in well populated areas to replace reformatories and industrial schools. However, given that both social work and justice (legislative paradigms) look primarily at the individual, as opposed to the community dimension, this prompts three questions:

. . . .

1. *Current residential centres and residents are often not truly integrated into the local community whilst retaining the hallmarks of institutions and commercial buildings – internal signage, emergency green lighting, self-closing doors, etc. Have we merely moved large institutions into community settings with lower numbers of residents, in essence creating micro-managed mini-institutions?*

2. *Given the incremental reduction in occupancy levels in residential centres over recent years, with many now registered for three placements, what empirical evidence is there that this reduction is producing better outcomes?*

3. *Have the aspirations of normalcy identified by Goffman's and Wolfenberger's work been achieved in the move to community-based settings, or has the preoccupation with risk and proceduralism which dominate current practice negated many of the benefits in this transition?*

. . . .

We shall return to the first question in the next chapter and consider in more detail the issue of the location of children's residential homes. There is, however, little doubt that the move away from large institutions played a key role in eliminating the abuses that formerly occurred in these institutions. The location within more public community-based settings was an important factor in achieving this essential outcome. Here, greater visibility of the operation of these centres, and therefore protection to the children, was an important factor. The absence of mechanisms for children to voice what was happening to them in the former institutional settings was identified as a significant factor in facilitating the abuses that occurred. The promotion of children's rights, with robust complaints procedures now enshrined in all residential centres, has also addressed this issue, though ongoing vigilance is essential to ensure implementation. However, these abuses were not universal occurrences within residential care (Smith, 2009) and we need to be wary of universalising what is (or was) the particular (Bourdieu, 2000). Many of these shocking abuses were not associated with the residential or group care model; rather, they were associated with the management, staffing, location, structure, practices, cultures, oversight and regulation of these institutions. Consequently, the move to smaller occupancy centres was but one strand of multiple processes which jointly resulted in the elimination of abuses. Effective recruitment, vetting and training of staff with double-cover staffing becoming the norm, where each staff acts as an observer of the other's practice, combined with robust management, child protection structures, culture improvements and inspection and monitoring regimes remain key factors.

• •

What impact have the State's responses to the systemic abuses within the former institutions and the role of Religious Orders in this abuse had on the development of residential children's services in the Republic of Ireland?

Have these responses contributed to the current imbalance in the tension between a child protection or child welfare orientation to social policy and social services (Spratt, 2001; Hayes and Spratt, 2014)?

If so, now that this systemic abuse has been eliminated is it time to re-evaluate this relationship given that there is a growing body of data highlighting the negative potential of policies more orientated towards child protection than child welfare (Lonne et al., 2009, Munro, 2011, Featherstone et al., 2014 cited in Smith, 2014)?

. . . .

A recent research report by Biehal *et al.* (2014) investigated the issue of abuse and neglect of children in care in the UK.

> Encouragingly, recent studies of children's homes in the UK have not evidenced abuse by staff, although these studies did not have a particular focus on allegations (Bridge *et al.*, 2008; 2011; 2012). (Biehal *et al.*, 2014:123)

Notably, this research found no incidence of sexual abuse within residential care reported to the researchers from the sample group of 211 Local Authorities in the UK during the period 2009-2012.

The research identified that there were between 1,100 and 2,500 allegations of abuse or neglect within residential care each year with 21 to 23 per cent of these confirmed as abuse or neglect. This means that there was an estimated 250 to 300 confirmed cases per year during the period under investigation. It is noteworthy that more than half of the cases concerning residential staff were categorised as either physical abuse or use of excessive physical restraint. These cases were similar in nature, generally involving staff reacting inappropriately to episodes of challenging behaviour by young people. The fact that this does not include abuse by peers or those outside of the centres is noteworthy. Additionally, many of the cases reported occurred in secure settings where restraint may be more frequently employed, and challenging behaviour more frequently exhibited, and there is no way of determining how many of these case related to general residential care.

In foster care they found that there were on average 2,000 to 2,500 allegations of abuse or neglect each year with 22 to 23 per cent confirmed. This means that there was an estimated 450 to 550 cases confirmed per year. The abuse confirmed within a sub-group of 118 confirmed cases comprised 37 per cent physical, 30 per cent emotional, 17 per cent neglect and 11 per cent sexual (another 15 were reported to concern poor standards of care falling short of abuse). The lack of oversight in foster placement was cited as a likely factor for the actual number of cases being higher than that recorded. The frequency of social worker visits and time spent alone with the foster child were also identified as significant factors in facilitating disclosure of abuse by foster children. In addition, foster children in long-term placements were identified as requiring ongoing opportunity to make disclosures. Almost half of the foster carers involved in cases that were substantiated had been the subject of previous allegations.

There are many variables that require factoring in before making determinations based on these findings. For example, children placed in residential care, especially residualised residential care, may present with different propensities for making allegations than those in long-term foster care. However, this report does contribute valuable knowledge to an under-researched area and highlights where further research might be needed.

> From the limited evidence currently available, it is not possible to tell whether the apparently higher rates of allegations or confirmed abuse or neglect in foster care reflect a real difference in the extent of actual abuse in different settings, or simply differences between settings in the level of reporting of abuse or neglect. (Biehal *et al.*, 2014:31)

The failings of foster care are being identified on an ongoing basis within the Republic of Ireland (Children's Rights Alliance, 2010a; EPIC, 2011a; HIQA, 2013, 2014) and internationally (Doyle, 2007; Smith *et al.*, 2013).

> We have known for some time that many foster carers have not been subject to adequate checks and that large numbers have not been trained. This has proven a risk to the safety

of children and recent proceedings in the high court have established that the risk is in fact a reality. (IFCA, 2012)

Alarmingly, a HIQA Follow-up Inspection on the Implementation of National Recommendations to Health Service Executive Foster Care Services (2011a) found that of the twelve overarching recommendations made in 2010 only one was fully met. A further nine were partially met and two continued to fail to meet the required standard. Of the 58 sub-recommendations made in 2010, 33 remained not met with 21 partially met in 2011. The conclusion of this report states:

> The inspection process highlighted continuing deficiencies in the HSE foster care service that may compromise the safety of some children and effectiveness of service delivery. Therefore, considerable improvement is required in the implementation of many of the recommendations of this report, including:
>
> • the implementation of Children First: Guidelines for the Protection and Welfare of Children;
>
> • the development of national registers of children in foster care and their foster carers;
>
> • assigning every child and foster carer a social worker;
>
> • assessing and vetting of all foster carers;
>
> • assessing the needs of children with disabilities in foster care;
>
> • developing a care plan for all children in foster care.

Internationally, Jones and Landsverk (2006:1153) make the point:

> The empirical literature on foster care has not demonstrated that the presumed problems with residential care have been solved by foster care.

The reality is that for some young people residential care is the best option, and this has proven to be the case internationally where, just as within the Republic of Ireland, there has been a concerted drive to minimise, if not eliminate, residential care (Iwaniec, 2006). Through my practice experience I have known young people who struggled in foster care settings but thrived in residential care. For some, as with Keith, they remained emotionally connected to their parent(s) and/or family who, for whatever reasons, could not adequately care for them. These young people may not be able to tolerate adults who they perceive as attempting to recreate or replace their parents or family. For them, residential care is appropriate as multiple adult carers best meet their needs (Ombudsman for Children, 2013). It may be that the levels of intimacy are more tolerable for these young people in residential care with its often unappreciated "'extrafamilial home' dimensions" (Anglin, 2004:178). For some:

> ... residential care can allow a space for insight into previous experiences that can emanate from family frustrations which a repetition of family based placements does not allow. (ICHA, 2014:12)

There are also young people with complex needs where the availability of resources within residential care, with qualified staff rotating every 24 hours and thus continuously refreshed, is preferable. Anglin (2004) identifies the personal ownership of property implicit within foster care, as opposed to the organisational ownership implicit in residential care, and the impact this has on carers' ability to tolerate property damage. He also identifies supervision of residential staff, which foster parents do not receive, as another significant factor. Additionally, children placed in foster care are often expected to fit within the family routines which, for some, can be problematic. In residential care the routines of the centre are adapted to fit the needs of the child.

A Save the Children study in Scotland by Monica Barry (2001) substantiates many of these points:

> Most of the sample had experience of both foster and residential care, whether as respite, short-term or long-term placements. Many respondents felt that they could not relax

in foster homes, partly because it was someone else's house but mainly because they were wary of carers usurping the role their own parents should have been taking. They often felt that the carers own children were given preferential treatment, leaving them feeling alienated. Foster care was seen to have more rules and idiosyncrasies than residential care, with carers often being older people with limited training in childcare or counselling. There also seemed to be a higher incidence of neglect or physical abuse in foster care than in residential care.

Residential care, on the other hand, was seen to be less intense. One could blend into the background more easily in a unit than in a family – and there were always other young people around and a wealth of different adult personalities and perspectives. (Barry, 2001:13)

Therefore, minimising the usage of residential care based on erroneous assumptions and fiduciary agendas has the potential to deprive some young people of being appropriately placed. This weakens the entire care system, causing further and unnecessary harm. Australia is one such example where residential care was so reduced that, when needed, appropriate placements were no longer available for some children, as identified by Ainsworth and Hanson:

Australian children and young people who might well have been placed by child care and protective services in residential programmes are in desperate circumstances when foster care fails, as no other alternative exists. (2009:147)

The place of residential care within the system of care is of major importance when considering the outcomes of care leavers. Stable placements and meaningful relationships in care are indicators of positive outcomes (Clough *et al.*, 2006) and residential care has a key role to play in meeting the complex needs of many children requiring out-of-home care. The residualisation of residential care needs to be redressed and the service utilised as placement of choice for those children who will benefit from such placements

71

(Anglin, 2002; del Valle, 2008; Kendrick, 2012; Ombudsman for Children, 2013).

> Residential care cannot be seen as a last resort as this is a grossly unfair message to young people. It indicates that it is their fault that they are in care and residential care and does not provide a sense that residential care is a positive option for them, a decision they made in the interest of their life chances. (Hillan, 2005:4)

Chapter 4

Residential Child Care in the Republic of Ireland

The usage of residential child care in the Republic of Ireland has declined steadily since the 1970s. At the time of the Kennedy Report in 1970 there were approximately 2,200 children in residential care (O'Sullivan and Breen, 2008:31; O'Sullivan, 2009) compared to 388, representing 7.3 per cent of the total number of children in residential care, in 2007 (HSE, Analysis of Child Care Dataset, 2007:7). In 2011 this figure was 7.2 per cent (HSE Review of Adequacy Report, 2011).

This decrease shows no sign of abating with recent data showing a further projected decline to 5 per cent or less for residential child care. This is clearly stated in Section 8.3.4, Placement Type for Children in Care, of the Review of Adequacy of HSE Children and Family Services, 2010, published in April 2012:

> Performance indicators in the HSE National Service Plan 2010 included targets that at least 61 per cent of children in care would be placed in general foster care, 28 per cent in relative foster care, and no more than 7 per cent in residential care. These targets were met in 2010 for foster care and relative care, with 60.6 per cent (n=3,612/5,965) of placements in Foster Care General and a further 29.2 per cent (n=1,742) of children in Relative Foster Care (figure 12). Around 7.4 per cent (n=440) of placements were in residential care, a rise from 6.8 per cent (n=383) in December 2009. The HSE Corporate long term plan is for children in residential care to be 5 per cent or less: on a total care

population of 5,965, this would equate to *298* i.e. 142 fewer children in residential care than in 2010.

Within the context of the above, and with specific regard to the previously referenced Australian experience as set out by Ainsworth and Hanson, the following table compiled by Eurochild (2010) and taken from Ainsworth's and Thoburn's (2014:16) paper bears the readers full attention.

Table 2. *Percentage of Children in Care in Residential Placements by Country.*

Country	Percentage
Australia, Ireland	0-10
Englans, USA	11-20
Hungary, Scotland, Spain, Sweden	21-30
France, Romania	31-40
Denmark, Italy, Poland Russian Federation	41-50
Germany, Lithuania, Ukraine	51-60
Armenia, Czech Republic, Israel, Japan	70-95+

It must be noted that the numbers in residential care in Northern Ireland, England and Scotland had also declined to below 10 per cent in 2013. In Northern Ireland the figure was 8 per cent (DHSSPNI, 2013), and in England and Scotland the figure was 9 per cent (Department of Education, 2013; Scottish Government, 2014). Germany, which can be considered as the ideal type of conservative welfare state regime (Esping-Adnderson, 1990), maintains its higher usage of residential care than foster care. There is a strong socio-pedagogical approach to care which stresses the upbringing and education of children and young people where they have a legally defined right to such support until the age of 21, coupled with counselling of their parents (Köngeter *et al.*, 2013; Stein, 2014).

It is timely that in December 2013 the Irish Ombudsman for Children published a Meta-Analysis of Repetitive Root Cause Issues Regarding the Provision of Services for Children in Care. Within this report the issue of sufficient availability of residential care is identified as one of the seven root cause issues arising for children in care. The report states:

> Residential care should be considered as having the potential to offer an effective early intervention and support to and for some young children, young people and their families...These cases illustrate the inadequacies in the range of residential accommodation for children and young people in terms of their availability and suitability. (pp. 16-17)

Within the recommendation section of the Ombudsman's report the following preamble and recommendation is made:

> There is a pressing need to identify the place that residential child care should occupy in the range of services for children in the care of the State, in order to open up its potential for a more creative and effective role in responding to the needs of children and young people.

and

> It is recommended that the Health Service Executive/ Child and Family Agency urgently develops a strategic development plan for residential child care services which would shape the future direction of services, plan for the provision of sufficient services in locations throughout the country and ensure that the needs of children and young people are met. (pp. 30-31)

However, just as with the Stockholm Declaration, there are already different interpretations of this Meta-Analysis. Some have chosen to interpret this report as an indictment of our residential child care services. They apparently conceive of residential child care services as an autonomous segment of the system of care services rather than acknowledging the macro picture, as intended by the authors, which indicts the HSE for the residualisation of residential child care services. In the UK, a similar misinterpretation was identified as a finding of a House of Commons Education Committee Review of Residential Care Report 2014 which found that:

> One of the messages from the evidence we received was the importance of looking at residential care within the overall context of provision for looked after children, and not as a discrete entity. (House of Commons, 2014)

The reality is that residential care, whether within the private, statutory or voluntary sectors, is delivered within parameters, including both quality and quantity, determined by Tusla management with compliance from providers ensured by funding mechanisms, contracts and Service Level Agreements. Additionally, the Health Information and Quality Authority (HIQA) and Tusla Registration and Inspection and Monitoring Services play a powerful role in shaping practices within residential care via inspection and monitoring regimes. Clearly, critiques of residential care require encompassing these agencies for their role in determining how the service is delivered and configured. No residential child care centre can operate without licence from HIQA/Registration and Inspection and Monitoring Service and placements therein being sanctioned, ideally, via Service Level Agreements from Tusla.

Yet neither the Ombudsman's Report nor this research can claim to be the first to highlight such residualisation of children's residential child care. As far back as 1970 the Association of Resident Managers of Reformatories and Industrial Schools issued the following response to the Kennedy Report, which prompts reflection as to why we are still questioning this issue today:

> Substitute Care 4.8
>
> Residential care should be regarded in itself as a particular service. For children who require this service residential care is essential in many areas, and is often superior to broken family life, it should not be regarded as a last resort. However, the Association stresses that it should be

resorted to when nothing more can be done for the family at home. (Cited in O'Sullivan, 2009:Appendix 2)

The report makes the following point in regard to aftercare and once again induces reflection as to what progress has been made in the intervening 45 years given that today we still have young people leaving care poorly prepared and without adequate support (Carr, 2014):

Aftercare 8.6

Aftercare is in dire need of attention. The lack of proper aftercare is perhaps responsible for the many failures in our system to-date. This matter deserves strong government financial support. (Cited in O'Sullivan, 2009: Appendix 2)

Current residential care services are being denigrated by many without being given the opportunity to function as they optimally can. Children whose needs can only be met within specialist placements requiring enhanced levels of support, compared to children whose needs can be met within mainstream residential care services, are mixed together thus weakening the efficacy of these centres. By operating as a placement of last resort it is thereby ensured that few children within these services will actually benefit. In this regard the efficacy of these centres is compromised which leads to the generation of additional hostile evidence as to their usage. This, then acts as a form of self-fulfilling prophecy of failure as advocated by those calling or scripting for its minimisation or even elimination.

Special Care, High Support and Secure Care

This situation where children with different levels of need are being placed in the same centres has been exacerbated with the closure in 2014 of the last of the former 13 High Support Units and the elimination of this High Support Service. In 2005, the High Support Service provided 93 specialist beds nationally (O'Sullivan, 2009, Point 4.3). Of the final two High Support Units, Rath na nÓg closed in 2013 and Crannóg Nua closed in May 2014 (Dáil Debates, 2013, Written Answers, 47701/13). This has been compounded by the fact that there are only three Special Care Units currently operating with all three under ongoing critique from HIQA, the media (*Irish Independent*, 2014) and children's representative organisations (EPIC, 2011c, 2012a).

The HSE define Special Care and High Support as:

> Special care refers to a type of care that is provided to children and young people who are in need of special care or protection by the HSE and would usually be placed in a 'special care unit' (SCU). These units are purpose built secure locked facilities, managed by HSE Children and Families Services (there is one in Dublin, one in Limerick and one in Cork). This means that children/young people placed in a special care unit by order of the High Court cannot leave of their own accord.

and

> High support units offer a residential service to children and young people who are in need of specialised targeted intervention: they are 'open' in that the young person is not detained. High support units aim to assist young people in developing internal controls of behaviour, to enhance self-esteem, facilitate personal abilities and strengths, and to build a capacity for constructive choice, resilience and responsibility. There are high supports units that are managed locally and two high support units that are managed nationally. (HSE, 2012:58-59)

The published HIQA Inspection Reports for 2013 for these three Special Care Units – Coovagh House in County Limerick, Ballydowd in County Dublin and Gleann Álainn in County Cork – highlighted ongoing issues of either partially met standards of practice or previous recommendations or, in some instances, practices that failed to meet the required standards. A summary of the findings highlighting the number of residents within each unit and the standards either partially met or failed within these reports (HIQA, 2013a) is as follows:

Table 3: *Summary of HIQA Findings for Special Care Units.*

Special Care Unit	Year	Residents	Partially Met Standard	Failed to Meet Standard
Ballydowd, Dublin	2013	8	7	2
Ballydowd, Dublin	2012	9	10	1
Ballydowd, Dublin	2011	9	12	2
Ballydowd, Dublin	2010	4	18	15
Ballydowd, Dublin	2009	12	20	14
Coovagh House, Limerick	2013	3	10	-
Coovagh House, Limerick	2012	2	9	-
Coovagh House, Limerick	2011	Closed 7/2011-6/2012		
Coovagh House, Limerick	2010	2	18	2
Coovagh House, Limerick	2009	2	15	-
Gleann Álainn, Cork	2013	4	8	-
Gleann Álainn, Cork	2012	5	11	1
Gleann Álainn, Cork	2011	7	*	3
Gleann Álainn, Cork	2010	6	16	-
Gleann Álainn, Cork	2009	3	17	-

* Unclear from report exact number of partially met practice standards due to non-standardisation of Inspection Reports and narrative format of this particular report.

The Children's Detention Schools located at Oberstown, Lusk, County Dublin, comprising Trinity House School and Oberstown Girls and Boys Centres, achieved the following inspection findings (HIQA, 2013b):

Table 4: *Summary of HIQA Findings for Detention Schools.*

	Year	Residents	Partially Met	Failed to Meet
Oberstown Campus	2013	36	7	1
Oberstown Campus	2012	-	5	-
Oberstown Campus	2011*	41	21	

* *"Of the standards reviewed in the course of this inspection there were no practices that fully met the required standard." (HIQA, 2011:8)*

Coupled with the closure of High Support Units (HSUs), the fact that the newly commissioned detention centre at Oberstown, with extra capacity for Special Care, are not projected to come fully on-stream until at least late 2015 means that, other than for the 17 beds occupied in Special Care, there are only mainstream residential care centres for the welfare needs of some of the State's most traumatised children. This places these centres under serious operational pressure, if not in some cases crisis.

> EPIC is also concerned about the impact of the closure of high support units for children with high levels needs who do not need placement in special care. These children's needs cannot be adequately met in mainstream residential services. (EPIC, 2014)

The concern voiced by EPIC of the unsuitability of placement is not without precedence. Kelleher *et al.* (2000) found that 25 per cent of all young people within their study were considered to have been inappropriately placed (Doyle *et al.*, 2012), whilst in 2011 a HSE-commissioned review identified that 252 young people were unsuitably placed nationally. This review of 600 placements found that 65 per cent were fully suitable, 24 per cent were partially suitable and 9 per cent were unsuitable (*Irish Times*, 2014b).

The cost of running these Special Care Units and HSUs has been the subject of scrutiny for some time. Operational costs for the Special Care Units in 2012 were identified in the *Irish Examiner* (2013) as:

Table 5: *Cost of Special Care Units.*

Ballydowd	€5.4 million	€11,538 per-child, per-week
Coovagh House	€2 million	€19,230 per-child, per-week
Gleann Álainn	€2.4 million	€9,230 per-child, per-week

The two remaining HSUs in 2013, Crannóg Nua and Rath na nÓg, had a cost in 2012 of:

Table 6: *Cost of High Support Units.*

Crannóg Nua	€3.9 million caring for six children	€12,500 per-child, per-week
Rath na nÓg	€3 million caring for four children	€14,423 per-child, per-week

However, the above referenced costs do not present a truly accurate cost per centre. The educational components within these centres operate under the Department of Education and Skills with associated costs, including salaries, funded by this Department as opposed to the Department of Health and Children. Neither do the cited figures take account of significant legal costs. Thus the real cost-per-centre and cost-per-placement is actually considerably higher than the above-cited figures. It is notable that the Department of Education and Skills website references High Support as a secure environment.

> High Support and Special Care Units provide residential care for children legally termed "out of control". This term refers to children who are at risk and in need of care and protection and who require the provision and delivery of an education service in a secure and therapeutic environ-

ment. The age profile of these children is 12-17 years... The Department of Education and Skills has responsibility to provide education services for these young people, and to ensure that it is adequate and meets their needs, and does so in the 'High Support Special Schools' which are an integral part of the High Support and Special Care Units. (Department of Education and Skills, 2014)

Private Provision in the Republic of Ireland

. . . .

Six per cent of children in care in the Republic of Ireland are placed in private provision.

. . . .

On the 31st August 2014; 413 (6 per cent/6,489) of children in care were in a private care placement. Of the children in a private placement 60.0 per cent (248/413) were in foster care general; 36.8 per cent (152/413) residential general; 1.7 per cent (7/413 other care placement and 1.5 per cent (6/413) in a residential out of state secure placement. (Tusla, 2014d:5)

Private Provision of Residential Child Care

During the period 2006-2014, the utilisation of private companies to provide children's residential services increased significantly. Such provision is subject to the budgetary-defined levels of usage, with short-term placements and ongoing placement reviews by HSE/Tusla. The identified cost of placement within the private sector now averages between €4,500-€5,000 per-child, per-week (Dáil Debates, 2014, Written Answers, 5126/14; *Irish Times*, 2014a).

These costs have been significantly reduced from what they were pre-2011 when prices were "capped" by the HSE at €5,000 per-child, per-week.[4]

In early 2012 Children and Family Services undertook a tendering campaign to secure eighty places at a cost of €18.7m per annum or €4,500 per place purchased for a 2-year period (extendible for a further two years if required). This process is now complete and currently being awarded for 2014. It is estimated that the procurement arrangements utilised will reduce the spend in this area by €3.9m in 2014. (Joint Committee on Health and Children, 2013, Question 4)

There are clear implications for significant cost savings by utilising the private sector to cater for those children formerly in HSUs. The lack of available data on children in care, and more particularly accurate budgetary data for children's residential services, makes accurate financial comparisons problematic (Darmody *et al.*, 2013). Indeed, all evaluation of children's residential services is problematic due to the lack of available data and the poor quality in terms of compatible formatting and inaccuracies contained within what data are available (O'Sullivan and Breen, 2008; Burns and MacCarthy, 2012). However, in 2006 John Smith, on behalf of the HSE, responded to questions posed by Judge Conal Gibbons regarding children's services in the Republic of Ireland. Within this response the annual expenditure on High Support in 2003 was listed by Mr Smith as €25,421,000 for 66 recipients, with an annual cost per recipient of €385,178. This yields a weekly cost per-child of €7,407 (Gibbons, 2007:7). However, the only recent data we have is for the last two remaining HSUs in 2013, Crannóg Nua and Rath na nÓg. If we aggregate the cost of placement between Crannóg Nua (€12,500) and Rath na nÓg (€14,423) we obtain an average cost per-child, per-week of €13,461 or €699,972 per annum (not including Department of Education or legal costs). The difference between the published weekly cost of placement of €7,407 per week in 2003, and €13,461 per week 2012, is considerable. Although some of this may be accounted for in terms of different structure and operations within Crannóg Nua and Rath na nÓg, as these were purpose-built as HSUs, this disparity would tend to indicate that the running costs for the years preceding 2012 were, pro rata, significantly higher than the figure cited for 2003.

We have an approximate figure for private provision in 2013 of €50 million for the 65 private centres, which may include children placed out-of-state (Joint Committee on Health and Children, 2013, Question 4). Minister Flanagan most recently identified expenditure in 2012 as €49,323 million, and in 2013 as €48,972 million (Dáil Debates, 2014, Written Answers, 27288/14). If we accept the figure put forward by both Tusla and the Minister for Children of €5,000 per-week as the average cost of private placement, we can calculate a figure for the annual expenditure on private provision of children's residential services in 2014 based on 152 identified placements of €39,520,000 (Tusla, 2014). However, this would appear to be significantly at variance with the identified costs for 2012, when there were 142 children in private placements, and for 2013, when there were 127 children in private placements. In fact, the figures for 2012 and 2013 do not tally with the declared criteria of costings of an average of €5,000 per week. What is clear, however, is that the young people formerly placed in the 93 placements originally available in HSUs, in the cases of the last two remaining HSUs at an average cost of €13,461 per week, may now be placed in the private sector at an identified average cost of circa €5,000 per week.

In the absence of any other residential services, other than the identified 17 beds in Special Care, it would appear that, in fact, there is nowhere else other than the children's residential centres and out-of-state placements where these children can be accommodated. The ecology of residential care placements has been diminished. It is notable that in June 2014 usage of private residential provision increased by 34 per cent from that in June 2013 (Tusla, 2014c).

It is worthwhile to consider the cost of private residential services in other jurisdictions such as England, where there is a longer history of usage of private providers for children's residential services, in order to give context to the service in the Republic of Ireland. In England, where in 2011 of 1,810 children's homes registered with OFSTED, 439 were local authority run and 1,317 were in the private or voluntary sector (Department of Education, 2012), the cost of weekly placement can range from €3,000-€11,500 per week, depending on the level of need (Stanley and Rome, 2013). Curtis (2012) calculated the average cost in England in 2012 as €4,717 per week. It is also noteworthy that the cost of operations in England and the Republic of Ireland are different, most notably because the qualification requirements in England are lower and therefore attract a lower salary than in the Republic of Ireland. In the Republic of Ireland the requirement is for an ordinary degree in Applied Social Studies, or acceptable equivalent, as a minimum requirement, whilst in England the minimum requirements are less well defined with, in fact, no clear requirement (College of Social Work, 2012).

Regardless of the efficacy of the service by the very act of identifying the need for 93 beds in HSUs in 2005, there was implicit recognition that a robust system of care required this level of service to function optimally. Children placed therein were assessed to have a high level of need and therefore likely to attract a higher cost within the English system. This poses many questions, including whether the needs of this cohort of children can be appropriately met for €5,000 per week in the Republic of Ireland (EPIC, 2014), and also what provision is to be put in place to care for these children during the period between the closure of all HSUs and the opening of Special Care beds at the Oberstown campus? Also, are children's residential centres suitable structures to care for these children with higher levels of need?

This is a pertinent question given that part of the rationale for closing the nine HSUs between 2005 and 2013, where only the purpose-built centres of Crannóg Nua and Rath na nÓg remained, was that these centres had been adapted from buildings that had often formerly been residential children's centres, and that these buildings were therefore not-fit-for purpose as HSUs. HSUs were not solely about having higher staff-to-child ratios, though, as they also provided on-site educational facilities, access to therapeutic services, and recreation and leisure facilities. Whilst the private centres may be able to put in place higher staff-to-child ratios, they may not be able to replicate these other criteria formerly provided within the HSUs.

It is noteworthy and deeply worrying within the context of the structure and design of children's residential centres that the 2012 HIQA Overview of Findings of Inspection Activity in Children's Residential Services within the statutory sector found:

> Over 27 per cent of centres did not meet the fire safety Standard while over 42 per cent met the Standard in part (Figure 10). This was of concern to inspectors... Other deficits which required action were identified. Some premises were identified as being unsuitable for use as a residential centre and not all were in a good state of repair. There was a lack communal space for visitors and not all services had created a homely atmosphere. There were also gaps in safety statements. A robust process of risk assessments was required in order to provide a safe and suitable environment. (HIQA, 2013:17)

. . . .

> *The question arises as to how and why these centres are allowed to continue to care for vulnerable young people when they are not compliant with fire and safety standards? It also calls into question the high-profile media attention with regard to non-compliant fire safety procedures within the last two remaining High Support Units, Rath na nÓg and Crannóg Nua, which were closed following the publication of HIQA Inspections Reports, ID:577 and ID:655 respectively (RTE, 2013; Irish Examiner, 2014b; Irish Independent, 2014).*

. . . .

The usage of private companies to deliver residential child care services is a contentious arena with divided opinion as to the merits and flaws. However, the paucity of research in this area renders factual assessment problematic.

> There have been some assessments about the differences in public versus at least nonprofit service delivery but very little empirical proof has been offered... In sum, there is no definitive answer as to which sector, public, non-profit or for-profit, provides better or "best" social services... There

is a paucity of research examining whether welfare clients fare better in public, non-profit or for profit-agencies. (Riccucci and Meyers, 2008:1443,1445,1451)

One commonly voiced criticism is that for these companies profit is the primary motive which is incompatible with a paramountcy of the child principle. The implied assumption is that the mandate to make profit will take precedence over the needs of the children. This was an argument put forward by Rees (2010). However, within this study Rees makes some questionable assertions regarding private companies, whilst also making some insightful points. Amongst the former is the assertion that:

> State financing of alternative care services for children in the independent sector raises, of course, a number of very real ethical issues. In subcontracting out the care of children the corporate parent has taken on a more distant role and is arguably less able to safeguard the well being and rights of the children. (2010:327)

This is a questionable assertion when we consider the proven poor track record of the state in caring for children in residential care settings. The fact is that the abuse that occurred within the statutory and voluntary sector in the twentieth century was, thankfully, not recorded within several recent studies in the UK as identified by Biehal *et al.* (2014:123). Here, it must be acknowledged that the private sector has since become the largest provider of residential child care in both the UK and the Republic of Ireland. Therefore, whilst there have also been other factors, as previously identified, that contributed to this very promising finding by Biehal *et al.* (*ibid*), it is possible to argue that the evidence suggests that the private sector is, at a minimum, as safe as the other sectors, if not safer. Rees would seem to be implying that these children would be less "safe" or well cared for in the independent sector, when clearly the evidence does not support such a claim.

Rees does make some interesting points, including that he acknowledges that the independent sector is not homogeneous. He identifies that some of the not-for-profit companies operate similarly to the for-profit companies:

> Interestingly, though, Le Grand (2007) argues that even independent not-for-profit organizations do actually make profits but choose to describe them as "surpluses". (Rees, 2010:322)

Consequently, the lack of clarity and objectivity with regard to the use of independent companies to care for children prompts several questions:

. . . .

1. *What evidence is there that the quality of care is diminished within private provision?*

2. *Given that outcomes for care leavers from residential care have been identified as poor prior to private providers entering the sector, is it reasonable to blame private providers for current poor outcomes? Or are private providers being held accountable for an entire sector, residential child care, without being afforded the opportunity to improve it? The real responsibility rests with those within the statutory sector who monitor, commission, evaluate and develop policies relating to the usage of residential child care, as well as the political system, as we shall see further along.*

3. *Are all private companies operating under the same principles and with the same values? Or are small and large companies being conflated as one group with the high-profile flaws of one segment, the large, sometimes multinational companies with shareholders including private equity, being associated with the smaller operators? These large companies may have a defined mandate to pursue profit on behalf of the shareholders that smaller companies with only owner shareholding do not necessarily have.*

. . . .

There is also the moral argument that "it is wrong to make a profit out of children" (Sharpe, 2008:46). Here several questions must be posed:

. . . .

1. *If the private sector can provide better quality care and produce better outcomes for specific cohorts of children than the statutory or voluntary sectors and, in this process make a profit, is this not beneficial to children in care?*

2. *Are we intellectualising our moral dilemmas, most often from positions within academia, the statutory or voluntary sectors, and soothing our consciences (or perhaps professional pride) by expressing our moral distaste at the expense, in terms of placement options, of the very children at the centre of the controversy?*

3. *Have children in care been consulted to illicit their opinion on this issue, and thereby empower them with the agency we claim to afford them whilst also, in the process, making service providers accountable to those using the service?*

. . . .

According to Tusla, *2.35 per cent of the 6,489* children in care on 31 August 2014 were in private residential placement in the Republic of Ireland (Tusla, 2014d).

Private Provision of Fostering

Various forms of foster care have developed since 2005, including enhanced, short-term and emergency fostering, which now provides a National Out-of-Hours service, to name but a few. Recently it has emerged that since 1995 at any given time up to 50 European children can be placed in Irish fostering placements by European agencies. One such recent case involved a European teenager who went missing for 48 hours without being reported by the foster family, which had not been Garda vetted (*Irish Independent*, 2013).

In 2012 the HSE paid €19.1 million to four private fostering companies for the care of 347 children, which equates to a weekly cost of €1,052 (*Irish Examiner*, 2013b). Similarly to private residential child care, the cost of placement was reduced in 2011 to the lower cost of €1,000 per-child, per-week (Dáil Debates, Written Answer, 40720/12). However, as with much of the data regarding children in care emanating from the HSE, the quantity and quality of data on children in private foster care are poor. Minister Fitzgerald in July 2012 within Written Answer 33324/12 to Dáil Debates gave the following information:

> The HSE has advised me that 249 children were placed in private foster care at a cost of €6,727,698 in 2009, 304 children were placed in private foster care at a cost of €9,581,360 in 2010 and 360 children were placed in private foster care at a cost of €12,893,243 in 2011. The information requested for 2007 and 2006 is not available at this time.

> While the HSE was unable to provide details of precise costings to date in 2012, it has advised me that there are currently 251 children in private foster care at a weekly cost of €342,265…The HSE generally utilise private foster care companies where children have a higher level of need including stepping down from high support placements.

According to the data offered to the Dáil by Minister Fitzgerald, the cost of placement per week over the period 2009-2012 was as follows:

- 2009: €519
- 2010: €606
- 2011: €688
- 2012: €1,363.

This is curious as costs were reduced in 2011/12 to on average €1,000 per week, having been €1,200 and €1,350 per week for the two largest private fostering organisations prior to this reduction. Minister Fitzgerald herself made this very point in Written Answer 40720/12 of 26/11/2012 wherein she stated:

> I am advised by the HSE that placement charges have been reduced significantly as a result of a review of services and costs of both residential and foster care provided by the private sector.

Again, according to Tusla, *3.85 per cent of the 6,489* children in care were in private foster placement on 31 August 2014 in the Republic of Ireland (Tusla, 2014d).

Out-of-State Care

The cost of placement out-of-state in St. Andrew's in Northampton, one of the most frequently used out-of-state placements with six children placed there in 2012, is €10,000 to €12,000 per week (Dáil Debates, Written Answers, 25805/13; 56768/12). Between January and July 2014 there were nine children placed in Northampton (Dáil Debates, Written Answers, 36473/14). In 2011 four adult patients died at the charity-managed St. Andrew's facility within a seven-month period. All were on the same ward and allegedly on anti-psychotic medication with calls for an independent inquiry (*Guardian*, 2013).

Children placed in care in other jurisdictions become subject to the laws of those jurisdictions, which can have serious implications for the consequences of their actions, as opposed to the consequences for similar actions within the Irish justice and care systems.

Length of placement is another serious factor with out-of-state placements. Placements in a foreign country away from family and community for lengthy periods can have significant impact of the cultural, psychological and psychosocial development of an adolescent. This makes reintegration into Irish society a difficult process. Such prolonged placements within specialist settings can be seen to have the potential to institutionalise the child. In 2014 a child was returned to the Republic of Ireland following four years in a "non-secure detention" placement in Boys Town in the USA. He experienced serious problems within six months of his return and required a secure placement, however no secure place could be found after five court hearings. Another child was identified in the same report as being forced to remain in a psychiatric secure detention unit in another jurisdiction as there were no services available to meet his needs in the Republic of Ireland. He had been in this out-of-state placement for three years at the time of this report (Child Care Law Reporting Project, 2015).

There is also the issue of aftercare for these children on their return to the Republic of Ireland. Continuing robust aftercare support is all the more essential to afford these young people the opportunity to leave care successfully. However, it must be borne in mind that these facilities utilised for out of-state placements are a mixture of general residential placements, secure and private residential placements as well as foster placements. Preparation for leaving care is not the primary remit of these centres, let alone to leave care in a foreign jurisdiction.

Without adequate preparation for leaving care and ongoing appropriately resourced aftercare, there is the potential for exporting one problem only to import another, with these young people entering the homeless services in the Republic of Ireland upon turning 18.

Unaccompanied Minors

> Internationally, research suggests that separated young people are a vulnerable group, with many suffering psychological and emotional problems (Sourander, 1998; Bean et al., 2007). In Ireland, the available literature also points to this vulnerability (Abunimah and Blower, 2010; Rea, 2001). (Ní Raghallaigh, 2013:5)

Prior to 2010, unaccompanied minors, children aged under 18, were accommodated in hostels. This was widely criticised (Commissioner for Human Rights, 2008; Corbett, 2008; Charles, 2009; Irish Refuge Council *et al.*, 2011) as exposing these vulnerable children to harm. Poor supervision with untrained childcare staff, sometimes with only security staff on duty caring for large numbers of minors, were identified as amongst numerous serious deficiencies. Many children "went missing" from these placements. Between 2000 and 2008, 463 were reported as missing with only 53 subsequently identified as traced (ESRI, 2009:xiv). The inherent tension between welfare policy and immigration policy has also been identified as an issue, as has been the the absence of statutory age assessments to determine eligibility for entry into care and appropriate placement once admitted (Horgan, 2011).

Subsequent to 2010, unaccompanied minors aged twelve and over are generally placed initially in short-term residential care and thereafter in foster care or supported lodgings. This is an interesting reversal of the situation where residential care was used as a placement of last resort for children in care in the Republic of Ireland (Ní Raghallaigh, 2013).

A 2014 ESRI report, which updated the above-cited 2009 report, found that although there has been a marked improvement in this sector underpinned by the move away from hostel provision, key challenges still remain. These include:

- There is no targeted national strategy for unaccompanied minors. National oversight of care provision to this group is limited and variations in care are in evidence.

- Several different sections of the Child Care Act 1991 are used to take unaccompanied minors into Tusla care. The decision on which section to apply is taken locally and may impact on the minor's legal guardianship.

- Key data and information gaps persist, for example, in the total number of unaccompanied minors in care in the State, although progress towards national-level data is underway.

- Social workers reported practical difficulties arising from the lack of a clear immigration status for many unaccompanied minors, including difficulties accessing a Personal Public Service Number or travelling outside the State, for example on a school trip.

- Some ambiguity exists as to who has the statutory responsibility for determining the age of unaccompanied minors, although a high level of cooperation on age assessment is reported by the agencies involved.

- The experience of unaccompanied minors reaching 18 years of age varies; those who have made an asylum application may enter the Direct Provision system. Regional disparities exist in aftercare provision, which depends on local resources and practices.

Unaccompanied minors are first and foremost children and consequently are impacted by the same issues affecting all children in today's society, in addition to those issues known to negatively impact children in care (Dixon, 2008). However, for unaccompanied minors, these issues are multiplied as they live in a country not of their birth and therefore with major cultural challenges to overcome. Then, on turning 18 they may enter Direct Provision services and face a range of specific difficulties (Frazer and Devlin, 2011), including uncertainty regarding aftercare support (Ní Raghallaigh, 2013).

With regard to Direct Provision it must be acknowledged that children growing up in such an environment is unacceptable. Over one-third of residents in Direct Provision are children. The impact on a child's development of growing up in a hostel where they cannot witness their parents acting as role models and working, or in many centres even cooking, is appalling to contemplate. These centres are often unhygienic and children must share communal bathrooms with other adult residents. Children are exposed to a range of risks on an ongoing basis that other children rarely encounter (Holohan, 2011; Arnold, 2012). In 2015, an Oireachtas Report found that the Direct Provision service was not fit for purpose by causing unnecessary complications and delays in processing asylum applications in a system that was designed and resourced to be a short-term solution. The average length of stay in Direct Provision is five years, with one in five residents there for seven years or more and the longest being there for eleven years (Joint Committee on Public Services Oversight and Commissions, 2015).

Supported Lodgings

The fact that in 2012 136 children were placed in "other placements" which include supported lodgings (HSE, 2012), despite there being limited data accessible regarding such placements, warrants attention. This number reduced to 108 in 2013 but rose again to 124 in January 2014.

The HSE 2011 Review of Adequacy for Children and Family Services offers the following information regarding supported lodgings – notably one of the few accessible HSE or Tusla reports to do so – and identifies that there were 147 such providers of supported lodgings in 2011:

> Supported lodgings is the provision of accommodation, support and a family setting to young people who cannot live at home, but are not ready to live independently. Supported lodgings should only be considered for young people, aged 16 and above, who are deemed, through a thorough assessment process capable of living independently without a full range of supports. Children under 16 are not to be accommodated in supported lodgings. (HSE, 2011:47)

The HSE 2010 Review of Adequacy for Children and Family Services identified the following findings from a National Audit of Supported Lodgings (2010) undertaken at the behest of HIQA:

> Some 140 service providers were identified, of whom 98 per cent (n=137) were vetted, 90 per cent (n=120) were assessed and 94 per cent (n=132) were approved. A total of 125 children and young people were identified as being place in supported lodgings, 74 per cent of whom had a care plan... Of 127 children in supported lodgings, four were under 12 years, five were aged 12-14, 23 were aged between 14-16... While most LHOs indicated that safety and quality was monitored by link workers and allocated social workers, only two stipulated that National Foster Care Standards and Regulations were applied. (HSE, 2010:65/66)

Why four children aged under 12, five aged between 12 and 14 and 23 aged between 14 and 16 were placed in a service catering for young people aged 16 to 18 is unclear.

Following this National Audit of Supported Lodgings in 2010 the HSE drafted a Policy on Supported Lodgings (2012) which was intended to address these deficiencies. The Office of The Ombudsman for Children made the following observation with regard to this policy:

> Of note some of the other documentation within the policy, namely the letter to GP's and guidance for persons providing a reference, refer to the age of 15 years, as does the FCC

document. This creates potential for confusion and varied application of the policy. (OCO, 2012:14)

In September 2014 there were *35 children* placed in supported lodgings (Tusla, 2014e).

Trends, 1970-2014

O'Sullivan and Breen (2008) conducted a review of children in care from 1970-2006 with Figures, 2, 3 and 4 below showing the trends over that timeframe. I propose to expand on this research to address the period 2006-2014, and to encompass trends within different formats of service provision within the private and statutory sectors. The data to inform the period 2006-2014 has been extrapolated from HSE Data Sets, Reviews of Adequacy for HSE Children and Family Services (Figures 4 and 12), Tusla Monthly National Performance Activity Reports, and Dáil Debates Written Answers, DCYA website (2014).

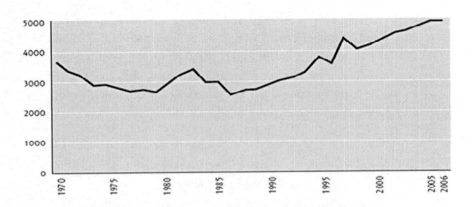

Figure 2: *The Total Number of Children in Care in the Republic of Ireland, 1970 and 2006 (O'Sullivan and Breen, 2008:29).*

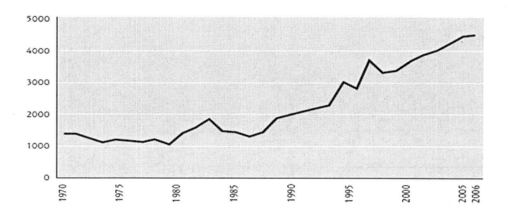

Figure 3: *The Number of Children in Foster Care Placements in the Republic of Ireland, 1970-2006 (O'Sullivan and Breen, 2008:32).*

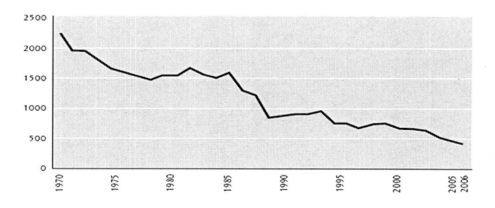

Figure 4: *The Number of Children in Residential Care Placements in the Republic of Ireland, 1970-2006 (O'Sullivan and Breen, 2008:31).*

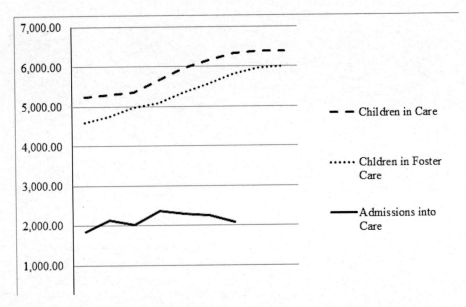

Figure 5: *The Number of Children in Care and Admitted into Care and the Number of Children in Foster Care, 2006-2014.*

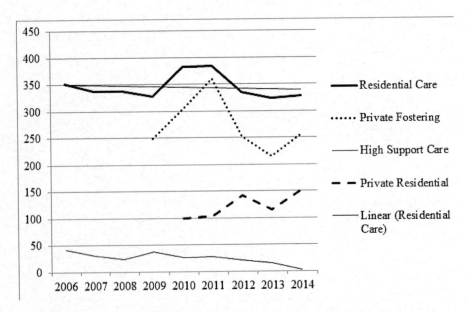

Figure 6: *The Number of Children in Residential Care Placements, Private Foster Care Placements, Private Residential Care Placements and High Support Placements, 2006-2014.*

Consideration of Trends

The fall in the number of admissions into care since 2009, whilst there has been an increase in child protection and welfare referrals during the same period, is curious.

However, it must be acknowledged that the HSE Child and Family Services were subject to imperatives whereby "more for less" was the operational directive in force from 2009 onwards (Doyle *et al.*, 2012). Residential child care provision may be located within this context of more for less and the fact that the budget allocation does not reflect this increase in demand:

> ... of around 91 per cent since 2006 (n=40,187/21,040) and an increase in children in care over the same period of 20.7 per cent (n=6,332/5,247) while the 0-17 population has also grown in the same period by 11.6 per cent (n=1,160,200/1,039,500) and the number of births by 10.4 per cent (n=72,225/65,425). (HSE, 2012:3)

This shows the success in achieving this imperative of increased service provision with less resources.

One finding of such a consideration of trends is that there is a potential lowering of support, and cost, of service provision made available to children in care over the same timeframe. Children formerly in HSUs may now be placed in private children's residential centres, and many children formerly in children's residential centres may now be placed in fostering arrangements. This results in the reduction of the amount of higher-support services available within the system of care, in effect a reduction in strength of the care system.

	Children in Care	Foster Care	Residential Care	Private Fostering	High Support Care	Private Residential Care	Special Care	Out-of-State
2006	5,247	4,595	351		41		16	
2007	5,307	4,750	337		30		31	
2008	5,357	4,976	328		23		26	
2009	5,674	5,100	327	249	38		20	13
2010	5,965	5,354	382	304	26	100	32	22
2011	6,160	5,564	384	360	20	104	39	27
2012	6,332	5,821	334	251	19	142	26	25
2013	6,389	5,966	324	215	15	115	25	?
2014	6389	6014	327	256	3/0	152	17	21

Table 7: *The Data for the Period 2006-2014 used to Inform Figures 5 and 6 and Includes Data for Children in Special Care Placements and Out-of-State Placements. There is no data available for private residential care prior to 2010 or private foster care prior to 2009.*

Data on Children in Care

The lack of data on children in care has been the subject of repeated calls for improvement from numerous NGOs, academics, the UN-CRC and national inquiries such as the Ryan Report (2009). Whilst under Tusla management there has been an improvement in data availability with monthly National Activity Performance Reports and monthly Management Data Activity Reports, it is unacceptable that in 2015 we still do not have a figure for the number of young people leaving care each year. From a sociological perspective it can be informative to consider what is not being provided as opposed to what is being provided (Phoenix and Kelly, 2013). In this context, making a figure available of how many care leavers are in receipt of an aftercare service, but not how many are not in receipt of this service, assumes obfuscatory dimensions.

It must also be noted that the level of inaccuracy within data compiled by the HSE is revealed with even a cursory examination of the data, which renders accurate comparative analysis problematic. For example, one of many issues which arise when comparing Data Sets and Adequacy Reviews published by the HSE between 2006 and 2013 is evidenced by the inefficacy with regard to the calculation of simple mathematics within the Review of Adequacy for Children and Family Services 2008:27:

Type of Care	2006	2007	2008
Residential Care - General	351	337	328
Residential Care – Special Care	16	21	30
Residential Care – High Support	41	30	23
Foster Care – General	3,073	3,141	3,134
Foster Care – Relative	1,482	1,552	1,581
Foster Care - Special	40	31	27
Pre-Adoptive Placements	36	26	24
At Home under Care Order	44	41	38
Other	164	128	172
Total	**5,247**	**5,307**	**5,357**

Table 8: *Care Placements, 2006-2008.*

Situation in 2014

A Tusla Monthly Management Data Analysis Report (July, 2014) affords evidence of the current usage of residential care as of February 2014.

Total number of children in care	6,466
Number of children in Special Care	17
Number of children in High Support	3
Number of children in General Residential Care	339
Number in out-of-state secure residential care	7
Number in out-of-state non-secure care	15

Table 9: *The Total Number of Children in Care within July 2014 and the Breakdown of Placements within the Residential Care Sector.*

The July 2014, Tusla Monthly National Performance Activity Report, identifies the following on page 6:

Residential High Support
There were no children in care on the last day of July 2014 in a residential high support placement.

Residential General Care
5.0 per cent (339) of all children in care (6,466) at the end of July (2014) were in a residential general placement. 163 (48 per cent) are in a private placement. There has been an increase of 1 young person placed in a private residential centre in the last month, from 162 in June. This demonstrates an increase of 45 from 118 (36 of 327 per cent) since June 2013 in the use of this placement type. The percentage breakdown of children in a residential general placement who are in a private placement in each region is: Dublin Mid Leinster 50 per cent (61/121); Dublin North East 8 per cent (38/97); South 55 per cent (41/74); and the West 49 per cent (23/47).

2 per cent (7 of 339) of the children in residential care general placements at the end of July were in out of state placement.

Thus we can see that Tusla has succeeded in reducing the number of children in residential care to 5.9 per cent of the care population, with a total number in all residential centres, both in the Republic of Ireland and abroad, at 381. In terms of residential general placement, in February 2014, they have achieved the distinction of having hit their identified corporate target of 5 per cent which is all the more remarkable given that this has been achieved whilst numbers of children in care have increased by 20 per cent over the same timeframe (HSE, 2011, 2012; Tusla, 2014, 2014b). In fact, over a two-year period, 2011-2013, they reduced the usage of mainstream residential by 18 per cent going from 384 in 2011 to 315 in 2013 (Tusla, 2014d). The usage of residential care when High Support and Special Care are included over the same period reduced by 18 per cent, going from 443 to 364 placements. Notably, the Management Data Analysis Report also identifies that as of the end of February 2014 there were 505 children in care without an allocated social worker, and 811 children without a written care plan, with Dublin Mid Leinster reporting only 71 per cent of children in care with a written care plan.

With regard to the Detention Schools the 36 beds are appropriately only utilised for justice cases where young people are either on committal by court order, on remand, or on remand for the purpose of assessment. The classification of the new beds created at the Oberstown Campus as either justice beds or welfare beds will be critical to the development of a robust system of care for children given the closure of HSUs and the efficacy of current special care units (€19,230 plus per-child, per-week in Coovagh House). There were eight special care beds anticipated for June 2015 on the redeveloped Crannóg Nua site (Dáil Debate, Written Answer, 27325/14).

The HSE has systematically enacted what it terms the "rationalisation" of HSE/Tusla-operated residential children's centres which resulted in the closure of many such centres over the same time period (2005-2014). In 2005, there were 86 such centres (Smith, cited in Gibbons, 2007) nationally. By 2011, this had reduced to 60 centres and by 2013 to 45 centres (Joint Committee on Health and Children, 2013, Question 4). Nationally, in 2007 seven HSE children's residential centres closed (HSE, 2007) and in 2008 eleven HSE children's residential centres closed (HSE, 2008). There were 39 private for-profit centres in operation in 2008 (HSE, 2008) with 65 private children's residential centres in operation in 2013. Cumulatively, the elimination of the High Support Service and the "rationalisation" of statutory residential centres have combined to reduce the capacity to provide a robust system of residential placements for children whilst we continue to place children in residential children's services outside of the state (EPIC, 2013).

In September 2014, there were 324 children placed in residential care general placement with 159 (49 per cent) placed in private placement, thus rendering the private sector the largest provider of residential general placements (Tusla, 2014e). In January 2015, there were 90 private centres providing 318 placements; 49 statutory centres providing 209 placements and 32 voluntary centres providing 168 placements.

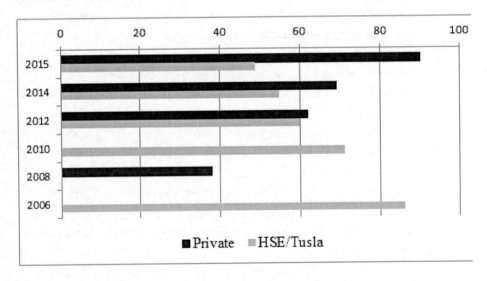

Figure 7: *The Number of Private Residential Care Centres and HSE/ Tusla (statutory) Centres over the Period 2006-2015.*

The issue of pensions with regard to staff is also relevant to trends within the private and statutory sectors. Here the systematic and phased withdrawal of the HSE and now Tusla from residential child care provision under the rubric of "rationalisation of services" can also be located within the developing public pension crisis in the Republic of Ireland. A recent report published in 2014 highlights the €440 billion "hidden" state liability for public servant pensions and the shortfall in the Social Insurance Fund, which it identifies as a far greater problem for the state than the €192 billion public debt (*Irish Times*, 2014c). Tusla social care staff are eligible for public pensions and within this context reducing the numbers of such staff can be located. Private providers' staff are not eligible for these public pensions.

Additionally, a recent Labour Court ruling in a case that has been ongoing for some time regarding the issue of overnight allowances and the Working Time Act is also significant. The court found in favour of the union representing Tusla residential social care staff and ruled that the hours where staff sleep over during 24-hour shifts must be counted as working time. Currently these are not counted as working hours and an allowance is paid for each such sleepover. This will have major ramifications for Tusla who argued that to implement these changes will entail a projected cost of €60,000,000 (RTÉ, 2014). The court recommended that both parties engage in talks over the forthcoming nine months to resolve this issue. These two factors, combined with our current neoliberally defined political paradigms, augur for continued, if not increased, levels of usage of private provision of children's residential child care in the Republic of Ireland.

As we have seen, the HSE Child and Family Services were subject to imperatives whereby "more for less" was the operational directive in force from 2009 onwards. In the UK similar demands of "more for less" were identified by Evans *et al.*, (2012), who pose the question, "how can social care achieve the seemingly impossible task of doing more for less" (2012:746). They propose that environmentally sustainable systems of social care offer a potential solution. As demonstrated, the HSE in fact achieved this seemingly impossible mandate over this timeframe with more children in care without a comparative increase in funding. The focus here, however, appears to have been exclusively on economic sustainability rather than environmental sustainability, or indeed the sustainability of a congruent system of care. Notably, over the same timeframe there has been a moratorium on most recruitment for HSE social services posts, which has resulted in a decrease in the numbers of employees within the HSE and an attendant increase in use of agency staff. This poses several dilemmas in terms of service delivery with consistency, safety and relationship continuity impaired by high usage of temporary agency staffing. This point was highlighted by HIQA with regard to a HSE run children's centre in Dublin as reported by the *Irish Examiner* (2014a):

> HIQA said that "staff sickness levels rose and culminated in the majority of the team being on leave" during the period of crisis. Agency staff were brought in and the "young people and external professionals informed the inspector that, given the unsettled atmosphere, the presence of unknown staff did not help the situation to improve".

The level of agency staff usage is recognised within the Policies and Procedures for Children's Residential Centres Dublin North East (2009) wherein policy 8.5: Policy on Agency Staff, states:

> This centre acknowledges that there are two levels of engagement of agency staff; engagement with those that work in the centre on an infrequent and intermittent basis and with those that are engaged by the centre on a frequent and regular basis. (HSE, 2009:49)

There is also the question of the cost of service provision with regard to agency staff where both recent EU Directive on Temporary Agency Work 2008/104/EC and pension costs are significant factors. The agencies in questions are private for-profit companies and charge rates accordingly. In 2011, the two largest contracted agencies supplying social care workers to the HSE were TTM, who charged an agency fee of 5.9 per cent to the HSE West, and CPL, which charged an agency fee of 8 per cent to HSE South, Dublin/ Dublin North East and Dublin Mid-Leinster (Dáil Debates, Written Answer, 36228/11).

Given the previously identified efficacy levels of data gathering and assimilation within the HSE and the identified anomalies with regard to the true cost of High-Support and Special Care when, for example, education costs are factored in, there is also the question as to the accuracy of the identified cost of service delivery within the statutory sector residential child care services. Here, akin to the public/private divide, where the public and private sectors were pitted against each other (an issue we shall cover in more detail in section 6), this data has been used as a frame of reference to determine value-for-money and acceptable costings within the private sector. The question as to whether the cost of agency staffing within statutory centres has been calculated within the identified costs of running these centres, as this cost certainly in 2011 and before was not categorised as a fixed cost, requires clarification. The omission of this cost has the potential to produce an erroneous lower cost of service provision, just as the omission of education costs produce a lower figure for High Support and Special Care Units. This, then, could potentially create myths regarding efficiency within the different sectors with serious implications when used to inform funding and costings within other sectors. Having worked within residential care services within the statutory, voluntary and private sectors it has been my experience that each sector has its strengths and limitations. A robust care system is only achievable with a robust system of care. This is best achieved utilising all three sectors and by focusing on developing services that maximise the strengths of each.

One such example is contained within the 2011 Analysis of Residential Child Care Centres and Places in Statutory, Voluntary and Private Sectors Used by the HSE. This was obtained under the Freedom of Information Act by the *Irish Times* and findings therein published on 22 April 2014. This analysis offers a cost-per-week for placement within HSE centres of €4,326 but, as referenced above, this figure may well be underestimated if agency costs are not included. The calculation of such costs would benefit from external oversight by an independent expert party given its potential ramifications.

We now have the private sector providing 80 placements at €4,500 per week, all but price-matching the statutory cost identified in the 2011 analysis. However, what is missing from the 2011 Analysis, and indeed from much of the official discussion regarding the services provided, is the level of need of the young people being cared for. Simply put, within currently configured children's residential centres, there is a direct correlation between the level of need and the numbers of children capable of being cared for within the one centre, with higher needs dictating lower occupancy. Thus a centre with children with low to mid-range levels of needs may be able to cater for five to six children, whereas a centre with young people with higher levels of need may only be able to cater for two to three such children.

There are also staffing implications in caring for children with higher needs with night staff often required and higher staff-to-child ratios thus inflating the cost of providing this service. An alternative analysis for the year 2011, where the operation cost-per-centre is compared rather than a per-placement cost, would yield a different picture. Here the 60 HSE centres, operating at a cost of €61.2 million, yields a cost per centre of €1,020,000 per annum, whereas the private sector with 56/62 centres operating at a cost of €47 million yields a cost per centre of €839,285/€758064. Within this methodology the private sector would present as more efficient than the statutory, and notably this was prior to the imposition of the pricing caps of €5,000 per week, followed by the €4,500 procurement price currently being implemented. Both of these factors would have the effect of exacerbating this private sector efficiency even further.

This example is not offered as an incontrovertible truth, but rather to illustrate some of the flaws inherent in simplistic and one dimensional financial comparisons, and thereby illustrate the fact that to compare sectors on price alone yields a biased picture of the market. This is a case in point of the previously cited issue of statistical integrity, referenced by Disraeli's famous line, "lies, damned lies and statistics", where figures can be manipulated to strengthen a particular case.

With regard to the aforementioned efficiency initiatives there is always the implicit danger that the law of diminishing returns will result in negative results, thereby rendering these efficiency initiatives mechanisms of false economy. In the case of social services, such negative economies hold potential for the gravest of consequences. After six years of rolled-over "more for less" initiatives, where each year more efficiency is demanded with fewer resources, there are inescapable consequences associated with risk as well as grave quality implications. It is the professional responsibility of social care/work professionals to query whether this point of negative return has been reached in 2015, if not earlier.

As a senior manager overseeing a company operating several children's residential centres, I came to recognise the necessity for built-in redundancy with regard to staffing levels. Built-in redundancy, more staff than the minimum requirement to accomplish the required tasks with elements of duplication and overlap, has been identified by Morgan and Murgatroyd (1994) in their influential book *Total Quality Management in the Public Sector* (TQM) as possessing strong similarity to the concept of "non-value-adding activity". Streeter (1992) identified that:

> In a perfect world, where everything is certain and predictable, there would be no need for redundancy... However, the real world is full of surprises. Human service organizations exist in an environment of uncertainty...Uncertainty is a normal part of organizational life. The greater the uncertainly the greater the potential for failure in organizational systems. Uncertainty is the reason that redundancies exist. (1992:109)

Streeter further identifies that the wholesale removal of these redundancies in the pursuit of efficiency is an inappropriate organising principle within social agencies. Additionally, Streeter identifies the propensity for the extra capacity, where available, to be harnessed for non-customer-related activity thus diluting its potential. A balance has to be struck between staffing costs and quality of service, and within a paradigm of "more for less" this balance can easily be tilted in favour of cost containment.

I have learnt that to incur extra staffing costs to proactively avoid potential crises is in fact cheaper in the long term than dealing with crises after the event. Additionally, and crucially, this also provides a better quality of care. In my experience in residential child care, it is far easier, and in reality often less expensive, to maintain an equilibrium than to have to regain one. Placement breakdown is financially expensive for both the organisation and to the system of care, and invariably occurs in a reactive, crisis-led manner. It is also deleterious to the developmental trajectory of both staff and the young person (Ward, 2009; Jones *et al.*, 2011).

Avoiding placement breakdown maximises financial efficiency whilst also optimising the benefit of services to young people's development and well-being, as well as promoting staff and service development (Dixon, et al., 2006; Hannon *et al.*, 2010). Administrators, financial departments, boards of management or business owners without practice experience may not readily perceive this, as sustaining the placement may require unplanned, and therefore unbudgeted, expenditure targeted at averting the crisis. In fact, it may appear counterintuitive if considered solely from a financial perspective. System reflexivity is critical in regard to accessing the resources that will be required at short notice, and systems that demand prolonged procedures with rigid financial control mechanisms to access such resources preclude such reflexivity. This is an area where a modest unplanned expenditure may result in a significant future cost saving, and is one example within our care system where negative returns have been invoked by an overly-dominant focus on cost containment.

. . . .

> *By focusing more on doing what services are intended to do, and doing this to the highest possible standard, the cost element of the service is optimised. The key, of course, is to do this well which includes taking account of financial parameters, but in the correct balance. Whereas by focusing more on cost containment both quality and cost efficiency may actually deteriorate.*

. . . .

With regard to the question posed in the previous chapter as to the move from institutions to community located settings, there are several questions arising here. The location of children's homes in rural settings, sometimes isolated, can be seen to be a significant factor in the context of community integration. These locations may be more conducive to managing the children's risk behaviours but often, and for the same reasons, they minimise potential for community interaction and integration. There may be few close neighbours or community resources within the locality. It may be that in meeting the needs of a specific cohort of children such locations are validated due to the reduced levels of negative peer influence or access to alcohol, or other negative stimuli in the immediate locality. However, in terms of medium to long-term placements their suitability requires ongoing review. The link between resilience development and community protective factors, including neighbourhood networks and appropriate role models, is well established (Daniel and Wassell, 2002; Zolkoski and Bullock, 2012). As far back as 1992, Gambrill and Paquin identified the benefits of positive relations with neighbours for children in care, whilst also identifying this as a neglected area of practice. It would appear to have remained underdeveloped subsequently.

> Community support through collective networks can act as a collective agency and socialisation (Fegan and Bowes, 2004).... In its absence, social isolation from community has been shown to be a critical feature in maltreatment and a host of negatively related youth conditions (Belsky, 1997). (Brennan, 2008:58)

Additionally, children's centres located in urban settings may strive for anonymity within the community as their goal rather than meaningful integration. This is understandable where staff and management err on the side of protecting the children from stigmatisation by not fully engaging with local resources. There is also the practical task of dealing with the resistance from residents in the community that can be a factor when establishing children's residential centres. Of the children's residential centres I have been involved in establishing (n=11), seven received community acceptance whilst four experienced strong resistance. Where there has been resistance this can be difficult to resolve as attitudes can be entrenched. Here the negative perception of youth in today's society may be a significant factor, but the question arises as to whether this alone would engender such resistance.

Vojak identified how the use of language stigmatises and excludes young people and how the community's perception of children in care can be shaped by the use of specific language when referring to children in care. She identifies commonly used terms such as client, risk assessment, accountability and foster, amongst others, as examples of such stigmatising language.

> The systematic use of stigmatizing language – language that implies power and status differences, language that assigns blame or moral deficiency, language of illness and abnormality and language of "otherness" – colours the community's perceptions and consequent sense of responsibility. (2009:943)

These points, then, prompt some further questions:

. . . .

1) Is there a lack of understanding within the general public as regards to the reasons why children are admitted to care?

2) Does this potential lack of understanding play a role in the public indifference to the plight of care leavers, who may be seen as undeserving, the subjects of criminal proceedings and delinquent, and therefore the authors of their own misfortune and/or perceived parental fecklessness tarring the child with the same brush?

3) Is there a case to be made for a public information and awareness campaign to educate the public to the plight of care leavers and the reasons why children come into care?

4) Has the striving for anonymity rather than real community integration been a factor in propagating this public lack of understanding?

5) What effect does this seeking of anonymity have on children in care? Do they, for example, interpret this imperative to not stand out as a reinforcement of their difference from others within the community?

6) Is this pursuit of anonymity a deficit-based model, and would a strengths-based model incorporating real community integration be more appropriate?

7) Have those who have left care been consulted on this issue to inform practice and could this be an example of a protectionist approach (where children are seen as weak and needing protection) as opposed to personhood (where they are perceived as capable in determining their own well-being, of rational and moral reasoning skills) with regard to children's rights?

8) Are children in residential care made more vulnerable by these practices than they are protected? Would improved community integration lead to positive relationships for children in care within their communities? Would these positive relationships afford enhanced protection via community networks and programmes such as Neighbourhood Watch, thereby enhancing the children's overall functioning as well as their safety?

9) Would a social pedagogical approach, which shall be examined in the forthcoming section, to residential care result in enhanced community relationships for children in residential care owing to the focus on community and society integral to social pedagogy?

10) Has the public associated the failings of institutional care with current residential care, and have the seemingly relentless litany of revelations of abuse and misery within some of these institutions reinforced this perception as to the ineffectiveness of residential care?

11) Should residential care be re-branded with the terminology of children's home or children's residential centre replaced by more positive terminology to break these connections in public and professional mindsets, and also to communicate to children that residential care is a positive placement rather than placement of last resort?

Clearly, there are balances to be struck in the transition from institutions to community-based centres and there is much work still to be done in this regard.

The problem is not residential care; the outcomes achieved in States such as Finland, Germany and Denmark which use residential care as the placement of choice in many cases confirms that residential care works. The problem is how, in the Republic of Ireland and the UK, it is utilised, under-resourced, assessed and misrepresented. A robust system of care providing a diverse range of placement options for children requiring out-of-home care is a fundamental prerequisite to achieving positive outcomes for all care leavers. This requires inclusion of a range of foster care options including relative care, mainstream residential care, enhanced-support residential centres, emergency, short-term and respite care and specialist residential centres, including secure care.

. . . .

> *Such has been the relentless drive to reduce/eliminate residential child care that the question as to whether we are now seeing residential care recreated within the foster care sector arises. In such cases the cost disparity is less pronounced as foster carers are highly supported with teams of outside professionals coming into the home together with structures, such as built-in time away, that, in essence, residential care has been re-created within the foster care sector. The lines of demarcation between group living and family living are becoming more and more blurred within some of these placements, which prompts the question as to what has driven this development? Also, if foster care becomes further professionalised will it still afford the same benefits and to the same degree that many identify it as providing over residential care?*

. . . .

Nevertheless, the boundaries between residential and foster care have become somewhat blurred, particularly in relation to the number of children in placement, which may be very small in some residential placements and relatively large in some foster placements. Concerns about cost have also played a part. In 2010 the weekly cost of care in a local authority children's home was estimated at £2,689 per resident per week, compared with an average cost of £676 for foster care, although the cost of specialist foster placements for adolescents with levels of need similar to those of young people placed in children's homes is likely to be considerably higher (Department for Education, 2011a; Berridge et al., 2008). (Berridge *et al.*, 2010:4)

James Anglin, one of residential child care's most articulate and respected advocates, has likened its place within the social services system as a whole to:

> ... the tip of an iceberg that protrudes out of the water; if you try to remove it, the iceberg moves upward to maintain its overall balance.... A service that is not valued, or that is considered to be always an unsatisfactory or second-rate option will inevitably deteriorate, and will ultimately reflect these self-fulfilling expectations. Our young people are asking for and deserve the best group care settings that we can provide. (Anglin cited in Eriksson and Tjelflaat, 2004:173,188)

A better way to consider what service best meets the needs of any individual child or sibling group is to focus on practice underpinned by theory rather than a basic focus on type of placement (foster/residential). Equally, a focus on developmental need rather than chronological age needs to be incorporated into placement selection. I also agree with Holland and Crowley who state:

> We follow Prout (2005) in wishing to abandon some of the cruder dichotomies such as sociological v psychological accounts of childhood, recognising that both disciplines (and, indeed, others too) help us to develop a holistic understanding. (2013:65)

This brings our attention to the subject of theory in social care and aftercare which we shall consider in the next section.

Summary

These two chapters illuminate the misunderstandings, myths and assumptions associated with residential care which it has been demonstrated have led to the residualisation of this service within the Republic of Ireland and the UK. The detailed examination of costs associated with all forms of out-of-home care have revealed additional reasons for this residualisation, and the negative implications for children needing specific levels of support which require residential placement have been identified. Trends within out-of-home care provision in the Republic of Ireland have also been outlined which informed an understanding of the service as it is delivered today.

The case has been made that a robust care system requires a robust system of care placements, which must include sufficient levels of well-resourced residential care placements to appropriately meet the needs of all children requiring out-of-home care.

SECTION THREE –
THEORY AND APPROACHES

Introduction

Birren and Brengtson (1998), Nolan and Downs (2001), Stein (2006b), Tweedle (2007) and Dima and Skehill (2011) highlight the lack of theory informing research and practice. Stein (2006a, 2006b) proposes that theories in addition to attachment should be considered when planning throughcare and aftercare. He explores developmental theories in relation to aftercare, reflecting on four in particular: attachment, resilience, focal and life course. Barton *et al.* (2012) proposes that a good relationship between therapeutic carer and child, accompanied by theoretical consideration, is essential in caring for children in care. Bloom (2005) suggests that by integrating theory into care systems, carers and other professionals work with greater synchronicity and shared understandings of both the problems and the solutions.

> He who loves practice without theory is like the sailor who
> boards a ship without a rudder and compass and never
> knows where he may cast. (Leonardo da Vinci)

In addressing some of the issues with regard to leaving care and aftercare identified by Keith, this section will consider three of the theories highlighted by Stein (2006b), namely attachment, resilience and focal theory. In considering attachment theory the focus will be on the area of relationships. Resilience theory is appropriate as Keith's is an excellent case study exemplifying the concept of resilience. Focal theory is also relevant as it affords insight into, amongst other things, transition processes. Next, some theory relevant to listening, the key element of communication, will be considered.

Then the focus will be on two approaches to care, social pedagogy and relationship-based practice, as these have much to offer in our pursuit of positive outcomes for children in care. Finally, the role of mentoring for children in care and aftercare will be addressed.

Chapter 5

Attachment Theory, Resilience, Focal Theory and Listening

Attachment Theory

Stein (2006b) and Howe (2005) identify attachment theory as a framework for making sense of the experiences of many young people leaving care, drawing on the work of Bowlby (1969, 1988), Ainsworth and Eichberg (1991), Downes (1992) and Rutter *et al.* (1998). Stein identifies stable placements in care as the most significant implication for attachment theory, and that from these strong emotional platforms, or secure bases (Maslow, 1962; Bowlby, 1988), young people can be best prepared for their journey into adulthood. These secure bases facilitate the young person experiencing what Winnicott (1986) termed "good enough" parenting, and thereafter moving forward in a psychologically healthy way. There is little doubt that attachment theory is highly relevant with regard to relationship formation, and all social work is relational at its core (Collins and Collins, 1981; Fahlberg, 1996; Cairns, 2002; Trevithick, 2010).

> ... attachment theory has come to singularly dominate children's services when thinking about child development and parenting skill. (Webb, 2006:120)

This dominance merits an examination of the role of attachment theory in practice so that we can understand its current place within the care system. Such a consideration follows Pierre Bourdieu's advice in relation to his concept of *field,* which offers an insightful methodology for considering the place of theory within practice and indeed the concept of the professions, which we shall explore further along in this book:

> ... there is a field effect were one can no longer understand a work and the *value*, that is to say the belief, which is accorded to it without knowing the history of the field of production of that work. (Bourdieu, 1984:117)

There are many definitions of attachment theory as it has been the subject of considerable debate. For this chapter I have selected two definitions.

> ... the strong affectionate ties we have with special people in our lives that lead us to feel pleasure when we interact with them and to be comforted by them in times of stress. (Berk, 2010:196)

and

> Attachment behaviour ensures the survival of the infants and young children by keeping their caregivers close and available to provide protection and comfort. The attachment relationship provides the context for the main developmental task of infancy and early childhood, particularly emotional regulation and development of the capacity to "mentalise". (Furnivall, 2011:1)

There was a strong recognition within the profession of social work from the 1940s to the 1980s of the importance of attachment theory within psychodynamic approaches, which were shaped by psychoanalytical influences (Ruch, 2005).

However, the dominant socio-political ideology in place at any given time has a profound impact on the service user and professional relationships (Foucault, 1977; Howe, 1997, 1998; Adams, 1998). Accordingly, the neoliberal policies in dominance in the Republic of Ireland and the UK since the 1980s have diminished the prominence of psychodynamic approaches.

> Neo-liberalism or "advanced liberalism" (Rose, 2000) refers to the policy, practices and values that privilege the market, individualism, global economic trade and deregulation

of businesses. One of the values underpinning neo-liberal policy changes is a disenchantment with "big government" and "the nanny state", both of which are seen as undermining economic and social prosperity. The social welfare state is thought to create dependencies and neo-liberal proponents suggest that less governmental controls in business will allow the market place to meet the social welfare needs of its citizens (Mullaly, 2007). The social welfare state has thus been reconfigured; social assistance benefits and eligibility criteria have been made more stringent; employment benefits have been reduced; there have been cuts to childcare, health care, social services and mental health services. (Pollack, 2010:1266)

The commercialised and audit/managerial model of social work provision (Harris, 1998; Clarke *et al.*, 2000; Ruch *et al.*, 2010), where transactional and fiducially-driven approaches replaced the therapeutic and interpersonal stance, has risen in prominence (Howe, 1997; Murphy *et al.*, 2013).

Performance indicators for professional excellence have been redefined as accountancy and managerial skills with a transfer of power from professionals to managers (Smith, 2009; Evetts, 2011).

As a result of these influences, workers' professional voices have been muted and their profession placed into a state of flux "without a robust identity capable of addressing public criticism or a strategy to fend off the ever-increasing demands of government" (Jordan and Parton, 2000:259). Practitioners are reduced to bureau-professionals (Pietroni, 1995).

It seems that the dominant attitude in many countries is that generous assistance will only encourage further expensive dependency on state support … and defines assistance to care leavers as "wasted money" because it "only" produces human wellbeing rather than creating financial benefits. (Munro *et al.*, 2011:2421)

In recent times the pendulum has begun to swing back with recognition of the many failings of the dominant managerial/audit models. There is an emerging recognition of the benefits of a relationship-based model of practice (Ruch, 2005; Leeson, 2010; Trevithick, 2010; Turney, 2012).

Relationship-based practice is informed by psychosocial approaches and psychodynamic practice. Psychodynamic practice has been described as:

> ... an approach informed by attachment theory, psychoanalysis and systems theory which offers ways of understanding the complexity and variability of the ways in which individuals develop and relate to one another in particular social contexts, via a focus on the past and present relationships. (McCluskey and Hooper, 2000:9)

Implicit in the relationship-based model is an understanding of the potential impact of anxiety in response to change and uncertainty (Trowell, 1995; Brearley, 2007). This is especially salient when considering care leavers who are experiencing "compressed and accelerated transitions to adulthood" (Stein, 2004:53), laden with uncertainty and therefore, oftentimes, anxiety as well (Bridges, 2002; Cashmore and Paxman, 2006; Goossens, 2006; Kilkelly, 2008).

> Making the transition from care to independence may prove to be one of the "betwixt and between moments" when young people find themselves between stages, which leaves them without a successful means of justifying their own continuity across time. (Ward, 2011:2516)

I have witnessed the stress care leavers are subjected to and recognise it as a major issue they face, and unfortunately Keith was a case in point. This can be exacerbated by a lack of preparation, loneliness, isolation, fear of the unknown, pre-existing trauma, separation and loss (Biehal *et al.*, 1995; Cashmore and Paxman, 2006). The behaviours which I have witnessed over the years, at times apparently self-sabotging and often accompanied with declining mental health, as care leavers approach their eighteenth birthday and step into the unknown are, I believe, often the symptoms of stress compounded by the underlying trauma resulting from previous exposure to toxic stress (Shonkoff *et al.*, 2012;

Centre for Youth Wellness, 2014). We must ensure that we address both the symptoms and the disease.

Research with young people in care highlights that leaving care is a major source of anxiety and stress. This appears to stem from the lack of planning and a general uncertainty about what is happening to them when they leave care. Many children turn 18 when preparing for their Leaving Certificate examinations, meaning that the stress about leaving care compounds existing worry and tension about their future. (Kilkelly, 2008:339-340)

Keith clearly identifies that he was still a child at age seventeen and this must not be overlooked. Despite being over six feet tall and broadly built, Keith, like others his age, was at times a child and at times a young adult. As we know, this is a typical part of adolescence. We know from Furnivall's (2011) above-cited definition that attachment theory is closely associated with child development.

> The variable which is most often studied in developmental psychology is *age*... It is very important to recognise that chronological age does not *cause* development, but simply reflects the fact that we have existed for a certain amount of time. In other words age is a *proxy variable* (Hartmann and George, 1999). By proxy variable, we mean that chronological age stands in for other developmental processes we have not measured... Age difference is only a small part of what developmental psychologists examine. The real interest lies in examining what mechanisms cause developmental change and, thus, performance difference between age groups. (Keenan and Evans, 2009:9)

David Pithers (2013) makes the point that, "We do not grow away from childhood, it grows with us." Thus from Pither's position and the field of developmental psychology we can see that human life-course development is not simply a chronological aging process, where we leave behind an existing life stage in order to move on to the next one, rather it is a dynamic process of acquiring the potential for new life stages which, ideally, complement the pre-existing stages. Piaget (1952) acknowledged this in his theory of human development where he posited that "new stage developments build on and incorporate what has come before" (Keenan and Evans, 2009:5). In this process of acquisition, human development involves both gains and losses (Baltes, 1987), and the actualisation of the new life stage may alter our internalised blueprints of the pre-existing ones. This conception of human development allows for our evolving capacities in physical (biological), emotional, social and cognitive domains, to act in tandem with chronological maturation with an understanding that each person may acquire the potential for new life stages at different ages. Furthermore, this construct also recognises that each may actualise this potential at different times, as we saw in Keith's case. Thus we can see that children making the fragmented transition to adulthood via emerging adulthood (Arnett, 2007), or deferred adulthood (Côte, 2000; Maguire *et al.*, 2001; Pais, 2003; Plug and DuBois-Raymond, 2006), are moving between the child and adult state as they "try out" the adult roles with "evolving capacities" (Lansdown, 2009) in what Stephens and Squire (2003) have described as "non-linear transition". These non-linear transitions have become increasingly fragmented with considerable movement back and forth between independence and dependence. We must remember this when we are setting our expectations of care leavers and judging them for their ability to meet these expectations.

. . . .

The importance of the anticipation of loss identified in this model of human development is of significance for care leavers given the prevalence of trauma and suboptimal attachment development in their biographies, coupled with their transitional positioning in a developmental context. Allen (2008) identified that there is an anticipation of betrayal in attachment relationships for those affected by attachment trauma, and that this has clear potential to be further compounded by experiencing an anticipation of loss in the transition from care. The antidote is to imbue care leavers with agency via rights-based entitlement to aftercare, coupled with continuity of relationships within a congruent system of care which appropriately meets their needs across the entire system.

. . . .

Keith clearly articulated the love he had for his mother, despite the serious harm he experienced as a child, and there is much to reflect on here for professionals when we consider attachment theory. Keith's experience in a family where there was both love and neglect affords insight into the concept of "good enough parenting" (Winicott, 1986; Bettleheim, 1987), and how the problems presenting may be the focus of professionals' attention at the expense of human dimensions. The temptation to be judgemental of others for their failings must be balanced with the realisation that all people have worth as human beings. This principle underpins good social care/work practice, as does the imperative, so seldom heard within practice, to operate from a basis of social justice. Social justice, and its converse, social injustice, is a theme we shall return to throughout this book.

Keith describes how he felt "safe" within the residential centre and how he was able to develop his identity from this "secure base". He describes the routines of the centre which nurtured this sense of belonging which, as Laursen (2005) states, "is fundamental to developing a sense of self-worth" (cited in Smith *et al.*, 2013:25). Keith's affinity for this residential centre is an example of an attachment to a place rather than a person, an issue which Giluiani (2003) and Scannell and Gifford (2010) have researched. Smith *et al.* (2013) also cite Jack (2010) who outlines attachment to a place which develops in ordinary daily-life events through "a large number of routine activities and everyday experiences" (2010:757).

> Drawing on psychoanalytical theory, Jack suggest that the way people think about places is "incorporated into the self" creating internalized objects that serve as sources of security at times of isolation ... the development of a sense of belonging, therefore, needs to incorporate attachment relationships with particular individuals but also to take into account the meaning attached to places. (Smith *et al.*, 2013:25)

Ward (2011) makes a pertinent point regarding the symbolic value of possessions:

> ... one relatively simple initiative that could be introduced to strengthen children's sense of a persistent and posi-

tive thread of identity that links their past to their present and future. Efforts should be made to promote greater understanding by carers and professionals of the symbolic value of possessions brought from home or presented as gifts that indicate that a child belongs to a particular family or culture: making arrangements to ensure that these are properly valued and carefully preserved could promote the development of a stronger, more resilient sense of self continuity. (Ward, 2011:2517)

Keith's experience validates these findings and has implications for how we conceptualise and support transitions, given that the potential loss is not restricted to relationships with people but also places and artefacts.

Keith's story also clearly challenges existing perceptions regarding residential care. He identifies how he felt safe and formed a meaningful relationship with me, and also with other staff who he identifies as possessing nurturing characteristics. Significantly, Keith talks of perceiving me as gentle in my interactions with the child in the coffee shop and that this was how he thought fathers should be with their children, but he had not experienced in his own life. This gentleness cannot be overestimated in social care although, along with kindness, it may often be given less acknowledgement in education, academia and practice. Misunderstandings around how to maintain consistency within a team, and around holding authority with children, can lead workers to overlook the simple value of being gentle in all their dealings with traumatised and vulnerable young people. It is entirely possible to be gentle and firm simultaneously. Keith recounts how this characteristic he perceived in me played a key role in his decision to trust me and the development of our relationship. Given that his time in the residential centre was brief, five months, and although our relationship continued for a time after he left, the experiences he had were clearly profound. Was it the sense of connectedness between us within a nurturing environment that has endured over the years? This challenges one of the previously identified assumptions associated with residential care as being un-conducive to attachment formation, and raises some interesting questions in the process:

· ·

1) What role does time play in attachment formation? How long does a relationship have to last to be meaningful in an attachment context? We know that some experiences, such as the age at which trauma occurred and the number of care givers involved, may play a role in determining how quickly a child will trust another primary care giver and time for such processes needs to be factored into lengths of placement in residential centres. However, we all know people who claim to have experienced love at first sight and this poses the question as to how long it takes to form a meaningful relationship?

2) Keith recalls how he felt safe in my presence prior to any significant verbal interaction but informed by observing me and, just as with emotional/chemical connections, this queries what stimuli and interactions are significant and to what extent in attachment formation?

3) What role does perception and observation of the other play in relationship formation, given that Keith references his perception of me as a gentle man and the relevance of this to his decision that I was trustworthy?

4) Where, if indeed they exist, are the lines of demarcation between attachment relationships and what can be termed meaningful relationships for adolescents, and what role does a sense of connectedness play within this?

5) Could we better identify or create turning points in adolescents' lives and then target these adolescents with specific attachment-informed interventions to engender resilience?

6) What role, if any, does the setting play in attachment formation?

7) What role does play hold with regard to attachment formation in adolescence?

· ·

In my experience children will form meaningful relationships with staff of their choosing and, just as each child is unique, so too is each staff. I have witnessed children form meaningful relationships with staff who I would have perceived as more structurally orientated than relational, and consequently I have come to recognise that there is a place for diversity in staff characteristics. Each child will match their need to a specific character. This is one of the benefits of residential care as children have a variety of adults offering different personal qualities and interests. I am especially conscious of this when facilitating mentoring relationships with the choice of male and female mentors within the match-making process, just as Holt and Kirwan (2012) have recommended for key worker selection. I have also facilitated successful mentoring schemes where mentees have access to more than one mentor for just these reasons. I implemented such practices in response to mentees' requests for this option over the course of several years.

Li and Julian (2012) propose a model of relationship which, in the context of working with children in care, is interchangeable with what I term meaningful relationships – development relationships. Developmental relationships, they posit, are the universally applicable active ingredients underlying effective interventions. Developmental relationships are characterised by attachment, reciprocity, progressive complexity and balance of power, and these consistently promote positive development of children across diverse developmental settings. Li and Julian (2012) outline how these relationships promote lasting positive outcomes drawing on the works of Brofenbrenner:

> Learning and development are facilitated by the participation of the developing person in progressively more complex patterns of reciprocal activity with whom that person has developed a strong and enduring emotional attachment and when the balance of power gradually shifts in favour of the developing person. (Bronfenbrenner, in Li and Julian, 2012:158)

The developmental model of relationship holds much promise when working with children in care, and especially with older children where power is such a salient, but often poorly understood, factor. Using the metaphor of magnets in social care, reciprocity can be seen to be a force that attracts the different poles together, whereas power is often associated with forces resisting each other, the clash of poles. This model is progressive by virtue of its pluralistically-based recognition of the roles of power and reciprocity within a continuum of complexity and located within a framework of attachment.

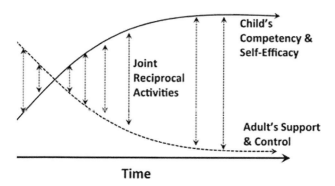

Figure 8: *The Idealised Model of Developmental Relationship (Li and Julian, 2012:159).*

Li and Julian define attachment as:

> ... not just the exclusive connection formed between primary caregiver and child, but an emotional connection that is natural, positive, and appropriate for the context. (2012:158)

Brofenbrenner's definition was termed the developmental dyad, which Li and Julian have broadened to becoming the developmental relationship. They reference the four components of development relationships as being "simple without being simplistic" and of "representing a particular style of relationship that can apply to both dyadic and group relationships".

These criteria "are interwoven and interdependent aspects of one coherent mechanism of developmental interaction, rather than simply four separate checklist figures" (2012:158).

The work of Li and Julian builds on existing theory and practice and holds much promise for further research and development. They conclude their paper with the following insight and recommendation:

> One common response we receive when discussing this article with professionals who serve children (funders, programme managers, researchers) is: "We do agree with the importance of relationship building. But funders pay for, and want, hard measurable outcomes, not soft, hard-to-measure relationships." We believe it is time to make development relationships the very outcome that is measurable and worth paying for. (2012:164)

This statement encompasses two issues we shall address in greater detail in later sections – outcomes and their measure and quantification – whilst also highlighting the paramountcy of the relationship in social care.

With regard to meaningful relationships, Keith identifies that he has kept in contact with some of the young people he lived with over those five months since he left care. This illuminates the potential for attachments/meaningful relationships between young people whilst living together in residential care where they are more often of a similar age than those placed in foster care.

These points certainly challenge conventional conceptions of residential care and foster care. There are clearly benefits from group living which afford children opportunities they may not experience in lower occupancy settings (Edmond, 2004).

There is also an issue of temporality and chronology with regard to attachment theory and children in care which warrants further consideration. As we see from Furnivall's definition, attachment formation is primarily concerned with infants and young children, and indeed this is where Ainsworth and Bowlby (1965) focused their research. Attachment theory undoubtedly affords insight into human behaviour across the full life-course (Howe, 2011) and, indeed, this can be especially relevant to young people in transition (Furnivall, 2011:12). However, given that attachment theory posits that these attachments are formed primarily in early childhood, and that children benefit from multiple attachments – with, for example, grandparents, siblings or pets – one has to question the validity of the preferred placement selection within foster care above residential care when one is considering older children. Clearly, it is the individual needs of the child that should determine the appropriate placement identification.

> The implication is that, despite very poor early care, infants were able to form secure attachment relationships to new carers if the foster parents provided sensitive care. However, that optimistic impression may be limited to infancy because older children in foster care, who are typically placed well after infancy, have been found to exhibit significant attachment and other relationship disturbances.

> Unfortunately, limited data exist on the likelihood that children who experience poor carly care would form a secure attachment relationship, particularly past early childhood. (Joseph *et al.*, 2014:68, 76)

It is also worth considering attachment from a behavioural perspective and the fulfilment of needs which we previously identified as the underpinning motivation for all human behaviour. In this case it can be seen that the infant has a need to bond with an adult figure to develop a sense of security and regulation leading to the formation of its own sense of self. This has been well researched and is now widely accepted in its significance to human development. However, as with human development theory, much of this research dates back to the mid- to late twentieth century and warrants reconsideration within the context of knowledge in the twenty-first century.

Questions arising from this perspective are:

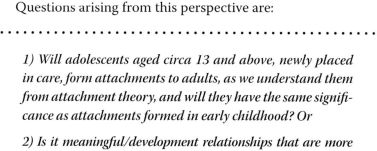

1) Will adolescents aged circa 13 and above, newly placed in care, form attachments to adults, as we understand them from attachment theory, and will they have the same significance as attachments formed in early childhood? Or

2) Is it meaningful/development relationships that are more appropriate to conceptualise when dealing with these children?

If it is meaningful/development relationships then perhaps, as previously noted, residential care affords multiple opportunities for such relationships. If this is indeed the case then the placement of these children at an older age into foster care rather than residential care on the basis of supposed conduciveness to attachment formation may require further research. Interestingly, John Bowlby (1953) advocated for such a model of practice where group care was employed for caring for adolescents, and only for short-term care of younger children and siblings prior to placement in fostering or adoption.

Certainly attachment theory is relevant to these adolescents as the internalised attachment blueprints which have been imprinted during the critical early years define many of the behaviours and needs of these adolescents. However, the question being posed has to do with whether these attachment experiences occur in adolescence as they do in early childhood?

Whilst internalised attachment blueprints may well be altered by positive attachment experiences during adolescence, this can also be facilitated both within small group settings as well as foster placements or familial setting.

Smith (2009) posits that group-work skills have been diminished within social care in recent years, and that there can be apprehension on the part of workers and policy-makers in dealing with groups of young people. It has been my experience, as both a residential manager and a supervisor of residential managers, that the one unwritten axiom for managers is, "You can never lose control of the group, or by extention, the centre". The consequences for a manager were this to happen would be grave. These factors, coupled with risk-averse paradigms of practice and oversight, have conspired to lead to lower occupancy numbers in residential care. With regard to the Republic of Ireland and the UK, the trend in recent years has been for ever decreasing occupancy levels within residential care centres with many centres now catering for between three to five residents.

· ·

Within adolescence we know that peer acceptance is of pro-
found significance and peer interaction of paramount im-
portance to adolescents' developing sense of identity (Cole-
man, 2000). If we then accept that attachments may not
necessarily be forming in care settings with older adolescents
and staff, but that meaningful/developmental relationships
can and do form, the questions arises as to how much of this
need for meaningful relationships can be met within the peer
group, and how much must be met by adults? Should devel-
opmental relationships rather than attachment be the focus
in moving the young person towards positive outcomes?

· ·

For adolescents, higher occupancy centres may present enhanced socialisation opportunities with positive role modelling
and the opportunity to experience a sense of belonging within this
peer group, as Keith identified in his story. There is also the potential for negative peer influence, but in my experience this can be
managed with informed admission processes and meaningful relationships with staff. The utilisation of self-contained apartment-
style accommodation for residents who are aged sixteen and over
further enhances their sense of self-efficacy and develops their
independent living skills within a supported setting. It has been
my experience that such settings dramatically reduce issues of aggression between young people and staff. In a fractious interaction
with staff or other residents, the young person can simply withdraw
to their own space thereby breaking the cycles of aggressive behavioural responses they may have exhibited in previous settings.
Furthermore, possessing a key to their own space is of major developmental significance to many young people. Such settings afford
experiential learning opportunities which can also include work
experience programmes, in supported environments, which may
better prepare young people for leaving care. Some things, such
as being alone at night, can only be mastered through experience.

The utilisation of mentors within such centres to support the
residents promotes the potential for relationship formation with

appropriate adults. Therefore, the combination of a larger mixed-gender peer-group combined with mentoring support affords enhanced opportunity for optimal development for adolescents. In our striving for improved outcomes for residential care and care leavers, it is innovative models such as this that we need to identify and resource. To this end the broadening out of our understanding of what family means is to be welcomed. Previous concepts of family along traditional parent/child lines have been limiting in terms of alternative options being developed.

A further point on attachments within residential care is from practice knowledge where children were known to form meaningful relationships with ancillary staff such as cooks, drivers and cleaners as well as, or rather than, care staff. Attachments cannot be demanded and young people are active agents in meeting their own needs (Bullock *et al.*, 2006).

With regard to the imperative for workers to be self-aware there are several factors to consider. Hiles Howard *et al.* have highlighted the significance of adult carer representations of attachment within the professional relationship with children. They make the point that, "Attachment support for child welfare professionals, regardless of attachment classification, is important" (2013:1590). They utilised the Adult Attachment Interview (AAI) in their research to evaluate the impact workers' attachment experiences have on their work with children, and suggest appropriate supports for workers based on their attachment profile and their history of trauma and loss. They cite Dozier *et al.* (1994) who found that adult case managers who were secure in their own attachments were better able to interact with clients, even in ways that were uncomfortable for them, such as discussing one's own maltreatment. This bears consideration by workers caring for children who may have experienced trauma and attachment disruption. The inclusion of AAI should also be considered for staff recruitment processes with weighting given to the prospective staff member's awareness of how their attachment experiences have impacted on, and continue to influence, them. This work builds on the research that:

... has documented the association between adult representations and client relationships and outcomes for professionals in relationship-based domains such as counselling
(e.g. Bernier and Dozier, 2002; Blakely et al., 2011; Dozier
et al., 1994; Romano et al., 2008; Tyrrell et al., 1999; White,
2004; Zeggers et al., 2006), clinical supervisors (e.g. Pistole
and Fitch, 2008; Riggs and Bretz, 2006), and early childhood workers (e.g. Constantino and Olesh, 1999). (Hiles
Howard *et al.*, 2013:1588)

Emotional co-regulation, as we saw previously in the case of
Sue, is an important area of practice in social care. This can, over
time, assist young people who are experiencing "emotional flood-
ing", where they are overwhelmed by their responses, to self-regu-
late these emotions. Alford *et al.* (2006) examined the relationship
between adult attachment representations and working models of
emotion. They found "that unique emotional schema were associated with distinct forms of adult attachment" (2006:55). Their
findings support the case that the worker's emotional competence,
a critical factor in practicing emotional co-regulation, is linked to
their attachment profile.

Furthermore, with regard to self-awareness, Digney and Smart
(2014) posit that our attachment to specific theories and epistemological positions renders us closed to considering alternatives as
illustrated by the "Backfire Effect". They cite Raney who posits that:

Once something is added to your collection of beliefs, you
protect it from harm. You do this instinctively and unconsciously when confronted with attitude-inconsistent information. Just as confirmation bias shields you when you
actively seek information, the backfire effect defends you
when the information seeks you, when it blindsides you.
Coming or going, you stick to your beliefs instead of questioning them. When someone tries to correct you, tries to
dilute your misconceptions, it backfires and strengthens
those misconceptions instead. Over time, the backfire effect
makes you less sceptical of those things that allow you to
continue seeing your beliefs and attitudes as true and proper.

> Popova makes the point that when considering our attachment to particular theories, it must be recognised that there is evidence to show that once we have established a particular way of thinking and later challenges to that theory or thinking, can actually make us more entrenched in this way or thinking – even if there is credible evidence to back up the challenge. (Digney and Smart, 2014:43)

Whilst Keith's story is powerful it is but one story. However, I am aware of numerous instances of such strong relationships between residential social care staff and young people they have cared for, many of which endure long after they have left the residential centres. Such relationships, what Wade (2008) terms "unsupported and unacknowledged interventions", emerge from a wide range of residential centres including foster care, secure care, mainstream and specialist care. Daly (2012) identified the importance of the social support afforded by professional relationships in aftercare. However, the fact remains that the low level of empirical data evidencing these relationships is a weakness in gaining recognition for their value. Notably, there is a lack of empirical data on foster care yet it is often considered more appropriate than residential care (Jones and Landsverk, 2006).

Workers seem to have become increasingly defensive in their practice in recent years and with good cause. This phenomenon has been highlighted by Smith (2009) and Kendrick (2013), focusing on the advent of consumer-focused practices under neoliberalism where service users are recast as customers whose complaints are seen as integral to their ability to exercise consumer choice (Malin, 2000; Newman and Vidler, 2006; Schinkel and Noordgraaf, 2011). Additionally, external regulatory bodies which judge and measure workers' practice, coupled with ill-defined calls for professional accountability, plus litigation and insurance industry requirements, have all construed to place workers on the defensive.

Examples include staff making entries in daily logs, ever mindful that what they write may be used in evidence at a later stage, and the maxim that "if it is not written down it didn't happen" (Smith, 2009). Consequently, they may write in a manner to limit their exposure to any potential unknown events. This preoccupation with documentation also holds significance when coupled with evidence-based practice wherein data is paramount, as outlined by Gilbert and Powell:

> Documentation fixes the objectification of individuals in writing codifying, calculating difference and drawing comparison and embedding this in discourse, that is "evidence-based practice" which in turn, disciplines and regulates professional activity. (2010:7)

Equally, practices around working alone with children, or physical contact, can create defensiveness for fear of allegations. As a profession we aspire to strengths-based approaches in our work, though we may not always use this to best effect. The fear of litigation and censure is a palpable undercurrent within the profession and needs to be challenged. Kelleher *et al.*, in their seminal publication *Left Out on Their Own*, highlighted this as far back as 2000:

> There is an increasing sense that the remedies being put in place to redress abuses of the past are leading to practices that lack spontaneity and are clinically devoid of feeling. The result is a lowering of morale among residential care workers. (Kelleher *et al.*, 2000:31)

This defensiveness associated with residential care particularly has knock-on effects for the children in care. If we accept the case argued by McCarter (2007:119) that "to instil hope in others one must have a sense of their own hope", as well as the relationship between hope and change previously cited, this raises the following question:

• •

Is the ability of social care workers to instil hope in young people in care diminished given that they themselves may be lacking in this regard?

• •

Attachment theory can be helpful in considering the plight of social care workers within the context of this defensiveness.

If we accept, as we obviously do, that children in care and social care workers have their humanness in common, then we can see that there are many commonalities that apply to both. If we also accept, and again our training tells us that this is true, that all behaviours communicate a need, and that we are skilled at interpreting the behaviour of children, then the same can be said of staff. Attachment theory can therefore be applied to staff and their relationship with both their employer and, on a wider level, their profession (Nelson and Quick, 1991; Mitchell and Lee, 2001; Lin, 2010; Strangleman, 2012). This affords an insight into how employment changes in recent years, where flexible working arrangements and contract changes, as well as the above mentioned factors, have altered the worker's relationship (attachment) to their employer. A job for life is now a scarce commodity and employment security has become increasingly precarious.

In this context, the worker is more likely to have disrupted or insecure attachments, or worse, to their employer. These employees are then potentially prone to the same maladaptive behavioural and emotional consequences as the child who has experienced insecure or broken attachments in early life, but for the employee these will be exhibited within a work environment. This can have clear implications for efficiency, effectiveness, retention and well-being. Put simply, we humans thrive on secure bases. Furthermore, the negative perception of social care, and especially residential care, is having a major impact on social care workers' professional well-being.

Ongoing research is informing our work constantly, such as that within neuroscience, where the findings of attachment are being confirmed by extensive research on the brain. We now have the vista of attachment science as well as theory on the horizon. However, attachment theory is not without its inherent issues (Bolen, 2002; Olafson, 2002; Yeo, 2003; Barth *et al.*, 2005; Chaffin *et al.*, 2006). We must be wary of the medicalisation of attachment (Kanieski, 2010), and the misinterpretation and misapplication of attachment theory with regard to children in care (Milner and O'Byrne, 2002; Anglin, 2013).

... a doctrinaire approach to attachment can serve children badly. It is good social and psychological parenting that is essential if children are to do well: but this is not the same as attachment. Neither is it the same as love. An attachment cannot be generated artificially, the best that can be hoped for is that carers are sensitive to attachment issues and capable of handling conflicting emotional roles that might affect them. If the context is right, attachment might develop or emerge from other things, but it will develop at a pace set by the child and cannot be demanded. (Bullock *et al.*, 2006:17)

• •

Has the "systemic bias" identified by Stuck et al. (2000) to place young people in the "least restrictive" placement option, together with misinterpretation and misapplication of attachment theory and residual bias created by John Bowlby's disregard for residential care, combined to relegate residential child care to its current lowly status?

• •

Attachment theory, which as previously noted has risen to dominance in social care, holds much potential for identifying and thereafter meeting the needs of children in care and care leavers. A thorough understanding, which requires a critical perspective, of attachment theory is therefore essential for effective social care work:

Attachment theory provides a framework for exploring young people's separation from their families and the circumstances surrounding it, including their patterns of attachment, care careers, placement disruption or stability, and the legacy of these experiences for their lives aftercare (Schofield, 2001; Howe, 2005, Schofield and Beek, 2006). (Stein, 2012:161)

What I have learnt in my time as a worker and manager in social care, my practice knowledge, is that there is a direct link between how staff are treated by their employer and how they then treat the children they care for. Staff need the appropriate support, at all levels, to successfully care for children with complex needs. This requires allocating sufficient time for them to spend "being with" rather than managing the children and record keeping. By applying our understanding of children's needs and behaviours, which attachment theory affords us, we can see the implications of the assertion that how we treat staff plays a major role in determining how they will treat the children.

Resilience Theory

Resilience has been reified in recent years as it apparently holds the potential to turn vulnerable young people into healthy active citizens (Gordon and Song, 1994). However, it remains a concept with inherent ambiguity (Kaplan, 1999; Masten, 2001) and with "no clear consensus of what resilience is, if it can be defined objectively at all" (Liebenberg and Ungar, 2009:6).

> Resilience is a broad conceptual umbrella, covering many concepts related to positive patterns of adaptation in the context of adversity. (Masten and Obradovic, 2006:14)

Mike Stein offers us the following definition:

> ... the quality that enables some young people to find fulfilment in their lives despite their disadvantaged backgrounds. (Stein, 2005b:1)

The elements most often identified in the constructs of resilience are themselves highly contested, such as health, well-being, disadvantage, fulfilment, and "heavily laden with subjective, often unarticulated assumptions and fraught with major logical, measurement and pragmatic problems" (Glantz and Sloboba, 1999:110). It is this "fuzziness" (Lerner, 2006) that can be problematic when coupled with, for example, evidence-based research and practice. Luther *et al.* (2000) and Schofield (2001) query whether resilience is just "a rose by another name, child development? Attachment?" (cited in Stein, 2005b:3).

The relationship between risk and resilience has been well documented (Haggerty *et al.*, 1997; Luther *et al.*, 2000; Keyes, 2004; Ungar, 2004). This highlights a dilemma when we consider the dominance of risk management and, by implication, risk elimination, within social work and child protection in recent decades (Smith, 2009; Ruch, 2010, 2012). The managerial/audit models currently dominant in the Republic of Ireland are founded on a belief that "the appliance of science" models (Alasuutari *et al.*, 2008) – taken from economics, natural sciences and business – will make "risk" manageable when applied to social care, giving the illusion that there is order in the world (Barrett, 1978; Ruch, 2012).

> In terms of emotions, attempts to control risk have the same purpose, i.e. a sense of security but, in contrast to the past, now we use scientific evidence to explain risks and also to invent ways how to manage the unpredictable. Rational thinking, systems of prevention and the identification of hazards are becoming the standard approach to the regulation of danger and threats (Lupton, 2004). We have developed a statistical and probabilistic science that is used to determine the norms and identify deviations from them. This deepens the rationalistic (but in fact partially irrational) belief that, by counting and classifying, we will establish control over "chaos" (Hacking, 1990). (Šabić, 2013:76-77)

The global economic crisis brought about by the business models of the money markets clearly illustrate these methodologies themselves to be flawed, as we now know to our detriment. They may have made the insurance industry into what it is today, but is that a good thing?

Deprived of exposure to risk by overzealous professionals, young people in care may also be deprived of opportunities to develop resilience (Newman, 2002; Luthar and Zelazo, 2003; Laser and Nicotera, 2011).

> There is no doubt that the identification of potential risk factors has led to substantial improvements in many areas of children's physical health. However, it has not always led to similar improvements in many aspects of children's emotional and psychological wellbeing. On the contrary, a substantial increase in psychosocial disorders of children has taken place in most developed countries over the past

half century, including suicide and para-suicide, self-injurious behaviour, conduct and eating disorders and depression. (Smith and Rutter, 1995; Slap, 2001)....The dilemma for child care services can be illustrated by the recent rise in the numbers of accidental drownings of children, a trend that has been associated with the overprotection of children by parents, and the corresponding failure of children to be offered sufficient opportunities to learn the management of risk. Over-protection may reduce morbidity, but a hidden price may be paid by children in industrialised countries "whose lives and childhoods are being newly circumscribed by unprecedented levels of parental concern" (UNICEF 2001:21). (Newman, 2002:2)

Research by Olsson *et al.* (2003) suggests that it may be healthy for young people who experience adversity and disadvantage to display distressed emotions, and that this is part of resilience. However, professionals supporting these young people may interpret these displays as evidence of unhealthy psychological development and try to suppress them:

> Ungar (2004) points out that for some marginalised young people, it is their problem behaviours that sustain their wellbeing "when resources that support healthy functioning are scarce". (Ungar cited in Canavan, 2008:3)

Practitioners need to be mindful that harm can be caused by classifying people into two groups, vulnerable or resilient. This is an example of the individualisation of problems to clients, in this case young people who already are perceived by large sections of society as "problems" rather than "victims", and thus diverting resources from the structural issues underpinning the "vulnerability" (Scraton, 2004, 2007; Devlin, 2005; Clarke, 2008; Mendes, 2008). Furthermore, a blame culture may develop for those young people who fail to overcome adversity, with individuals seen as lacking in some personality characteristic or not trying hard enough (Luthar and Zelazo, 2003). Families also can be subject to the same judgment in their endeavours to parent the resilient child, a key theme in parenting culture, a point made by Hoffman:

> Now even emotional competencies can be subject to measurement and those who don't measure up can be found lacking. In this sense, resilience (the antidote to risk) can be also a source of risk, as parents and children are increasingly tasked with managing it and producing it, and, inevitably for some, failing to produce enough. (Hoffman, 2010:391-392)

This potential for blame has particular relevance in our current social work and social care professions, which are defined within the prevailing neoliberal socio-political contexts. Here, discourses which may have originated for the benefit of marginalised groups, such as anti-oppressive and anti-racist practice, have been re-articulated to more conservative positions. Discourse is dynamic, and it is this dynamism which has facilitated this reframing beyond the original language and meaning which were historically specific (Gilbert and Powell, 2010).

> Indeed anti-oppressive practice has allowed the state to reposition itself as a benign arbiter between competing identity claims. Perversely, given its aim to make the personal political, it has allowed the problems of society to be recast as due to the moral failings of individuals who need censure and correction from anti-oppressive social workers. (McLaughlin, 2005:300)

The question posited by Luther *et al.* (2000) and Schofield (2001) as to whether resilience is "a rose by another name" is especially salient when considering care leavers. Often they have experienced major trauma which has resulted in their admission into care, and on leaving care many years may have elapsed since they experienced this trauma (Hannon *et al.*, 2010). Is resilience aimed at assisting them to overcome this trauma, or is it aimed at overcoming the ongoing negative issues associated with being in care (Cook, 1994; Mullan *et al.*, 2007; Dixon, 2008)? Or, is it targeted at steeling them for possible future hardships? If it is the first scenario, then perhaps it is a rose by another name – recovery; if it is the middle scenario, then this poses important questions about our care system and its potential to cause harm to children placed therein (Ombudsman for Children, 2013). If the latter scenario, then this poses the question of why it is anticipated that care leavers, amongst other marginalised groups, will potentially encounter hardships more than other groups and, if this is the case, should we be more focused on ameliorating these hardships rather than preparing the young people to recover after experiencing them?

A strengths-based perspective has much to offer researchers and practitioners (Saleeby, 1997), as does the resilience paradigm, but we must be ever vigilant for unintended consequences or, at times, intentional consequences by policymakers intent on promoting the policies of neoliberalism.

> The resilience paradigm takes challenges and adversity as a given, rather than as the exception (Antonovsky, 1979) and then asks how it is that many people continue to cope and sometimes even thrive (Ickovics and Park, 1998) despite these challenges. This is the heart of salutogenesis, a particular approach to research that focuses on health (or wellbeing) rather than illness (or vulnerability). The salutogenic question is, "Why, when people are exposed to the same stress which causes some to become ill, do some remain healthy?" (Antonovsky, 1979, 1984; Strümpfer, 1995). This approach, in common with the strengths perspective... (van Breda *et al.*, 2012:7)

Olsson *et al.* (2003) also make the point that resilience is not just an outcome, it is also a process, as Herrenkohl states:

> While resilience has been at times reduced to a single outcome, most researchers would agree in theory that resilience is far more complex. (2013:192)

This raises the question of what constitutes an outcome within a social care context and how is it measured? This is very important as outcomes are often cited as evidence when evaluating services, often for funding purposes, and especially within the domain of evidence-based practice. However, many have identified problems with quantifying and recording outcomes, an issue which shall be addressed in more detail in Chapter Nine.

For now, with regard to outcomes and resilience, it is notable that Keith returned to education at age 28 and completed his leaving certificate and thereafter received honours and master's degrees in social care and social work. As a statistic, Keith would have appeared as a poor outcome from ages 18 to 28, whereas from 28 to now he is a remarkably positive outcome, evidencing high levels of resilience. This validates that resilience is a process and Keith's description of the supports that were available to him aligns well with Ungar's (2010, 2012) social-ecology model of resilience:

> In the context of exposure to significant adversity, resilience is both the capacity of individuals to navigate their way to the psychological, social, cultural, and physical resources that sustain their well being, and their capacity individually and collectively to negotiate for these resources to be provided and experienced in culturally meaningful ways. (Ungar, 2008:225)

Ungar, building on previous works by Rutter (1987) and Lerner (2006), posits that resilience is a process to be nurtured by the quality of individuals' interaction with promotive and protective factors within their social environment. He places equal emphasis on the environment's ability to interact with the individual as on the individual's ability to interact with the environment, and thus places responsibility on policy-makers and service providers to meet this challenge:

> Rather than defining resilience as the individual's capacity to succeed under stress, I defined resilience as the capacity of both individuals and their environments to interact in ways that optimize developmental processes. (Ungar, 2013:256)

This construct of resilience offers much promise and, by virtue of its extrinsic dimensions, addresses many of the issues associated with individualisation. Ungar critiques constructs of resilience that focus on the individual with the following statement:

> An overemphasis on personal agency and other aspects of what has come to be known as 'resiliency' naively assumes that individuals survive only because of a positive attitude

or other fiction (Masten, 1994; Seccombe, 2002; Ungar, 2011c). (Ungar, 2013:256)

Research by Rutter (1990, 2006, 2007) into links between turning points, coping and resilience, including the social-ecology model, also holds much promise.

> Better understanding of the nature of resilience-promoting processes can inform the design of service ecologies. (Masten, cited in Ungar, 2011:13)

It is worthwhile considering the role mentoring can play in promoting resilience, as many have done (DuBois *et al.*, 2002; Colley, 2003; Clayden and Stein, 2005; Newburn and Shiner, 2005; Stein, 2005a, 2005b, 2008, 2012; Osterling and Hines, 2006; Canavan, 2008 and Avery, 2011). They showed the importance of one significant adult relationship in the life of a young person in the development of resilience, and identified mentors as ideally suited to this role. The power dynamic between mentor and mentee is significantly reduced compared to that between worker and client. This promotes engagement and communication whilst also generating an internal locus-of-control for the young person which promotes self-efficacy (Phares, 1979; Clutterbuck, 2002; Noe *et al.*, 2010).

> ... mentoring, including mentoring by ex-care young people (or peer mentoring), may assist young people during their journey to independence, and offer them a different type of relationship from professional support or troubled family relationships. (Stein, 2012:171)

Research carried out by the Princes Trust in the UK found that of those surveyed "95 per cent thought that, in principle, volunteer mentoring should be a service that is available to all care leavers" (the Princes Trust, 2004). (For more on mentoring, see Chapter 6.)

Masten's (2001) description of resilience as "ordinary magic" fits well within the mentoring approach to attachment, a normalised approach to an ordinary process. But until we can solve the how and the why of the process – for example, what if any role temperament or identity play in resilience (Fraser, 2004) – it retains elements of magic in as much as we cannot fully explain it. For me, it is akin to the electricity of social care. I know electricity exists and is powerful, and I know of people who understand how it works. It would appear that within the natural sciences, for example, electricity is quantifiable and predictable as is resilience. In fact, the origin of the word resilience, originating from the Latin verb *resilire* meaning to rebound or recoil, comes from the natural sciences where the ability of wood and metal to recoil was termed as these materials' resilience properties. Yet, neither resilience nor electricity is so well understood within the social or medical sciences. Humans are complex beings not readily given to quantification, standardisation and predictability, "shaped by early infant experiences, cognitive and affective capabilities and conscious and unconscious forces" (Ruch, 2009:351).

> It is not surprising then, that relying upon the tools and methodologies of the natural sciences for use in the social sciences has been rejected by many postmodern thinkers and scholars (Flyvbjerg, Landman, and Schram, 2012). (Fusco, 2013:200)

However, as Trinder and Reynolds (2000:129) argue:

> Human science, however, is concerned with the values and meanings of lived experiences, "the interrelation of life, expression, and understanding" (Dilthey, 1976, p. 175).

Scientific measures tend to generalise humans into bands based on statistical data analysis, but there are always those outside of these margins, albeit often in small percentages. This formula works well for insurance actuaries as the marginal figures represent acceptable financial losses. In the social professions, these small percentages represent people rather than commodities, and we cannot therefore accept that 3 per cent of these people will be written off as acceptable losses (Higgins *et al.*, 2005; Fitzgibbon, 2007; Littlechild, 2008). Indeed, it is these marginalised people who we predominately work with in social care.

In his 2005 publication *Resilience and Young People Leaving Care: Overcoming the Odds*, Stein concludes with the following paragraph which still holds true today:

> Promoting resilience will mean improving the quality of care: providing stability and a sense of identity, assisting with education and holistic preparation, enabling more gradual transitions from care, as well as providing more help for young people after they leave care. Finally, promoting resilience will also mean challenging the current separation in policy and practice of leaving care from caring for leaving – for too many young people experience them as divided and fragmented pathways instead of as a single journey. (Stein, 2005b:27)

Keith identified the significance of the hope that I gave him that Christmas night when he was struggling with deeply distressing family issues. Building on this evidence, and the previously cited work of Tomlinson, I see a strong correlation between nurturing of a sense of hope for children in care, who may have limited previous experience of their distress being contained by an adult, and the nurturing of resilience. Whilst there has been some research, such as by Horton and Wallander (2001), which focused on hope as a promotive resilience factor against psychological distress for mothers who care for children with chronic physical conditions, and by Margalit and Idan (2004) who focused their research in the intellectual disability sector, the area of hope and children in care warrants further research.

Keith also identified that it was the first time he was consciously aware of an adult male showing an appropriate interest in his welfare, which is significant in the context of mentoring and relationships. Keith also recalls how his relationship with me was so sacred to him that he took my advice on matters that he was struggling with, deeply personal matters where it is often difficult for workers to effectively intervene. This is one example of how behaviour can change through the power of the relationship. In my experience, mentors have the enhanced, though not exclusive, potential to develop such relationships with difficult to engage young people. Innovative behaviour change tools, such as Do Something Different (www.dsd.me), utilising mobile communications technology, offer complimentary programmes which, when coupled with mentoring, have much to offer. But the relationship is the key. It is this everyday human experience, a meaningful relationship, which enables traumatised young people to learn to cope and grow into healthy adults (Ruch, 2005; Smith, 2009; Cameron, 2013). As evidenced by Keith, for children in care, it may be the relationship that can turn the ordinary into the extraordinary and can render the seemingly impossible possible.

> We are broken
> within the context of relationships;
> and we are also healed
> within the scope of relationships.
> (Nadjiwan, 2010:1)

Focal Theory

> At different ages, certain relationship patterns emerge or come into focus, in the sense of being most prominent, but that no pattern is specific to one age only. (Coleman and Hendry, 1999:14)

Focal theory, which offers valuable perspectives on adolescent psychological development, argues "that transition between childhood and adulthood cannot be achieved without substantial adjustment of both a psychological and social nature" (Hendry *et al.*, 1993:9).

Erikson (1902-1994) and the psychoanalytical model propose adolescence as a time of "storm and stress", what Farrelly (1994) termed a "traumatic time" and the individuals undergoing it as "volatile". Erikson recognised the search for "self" and saw the crisis of adolescence proposed within the storm and stress model as a potential "turning point". Building on Erikson's model, developmental contextualism was theorised by Urie Bronfenbrenner (1917-2005) and Richard Lerner. Developmental contextualism is associated with the life-course perspective which takes account of the context of human development, timing, continuity of development and reciprocity and agency. Grabber and Brooks-Gunn (1996) proposed that by overlaying the concept of turning points with transitional periods one arrives at what they term "transition-linked turning points" (1996:769). They theorise that:

> ... turning points occurring in the context of transitional periods may be particularly salient to individuals or to subsets of individuals. These turning points may be more likely to result in behavioural changes, as described earlier, or in larger or more long-lasting changes than turning points that do not occur in the context of a transitional period. (1996:196)

Focal theory has close associations with developmental contextualism, and thus with the social-ecology model of resilience. It further explores the timing of specific issues that "come into focus" for adolescents at different ages, and that by focusing on one such issue at a time adolescents may cope with the change inherent in adolescence. The notion of stage development is present in both Erikson and Bronfenbrenner's and Coleman's models, but Coleman takes account also of the potential for multiple issues being addressed simultaneously for some young people.

Simmons *et al.* (1987:1221) offer the following overview of focal theory:

> According to this perspective it is easier if the child goes through the various adolescent changes at different times rather than simultaneously. The focal model argues that gradual adjustment to one change before confrontation with another will be beneficial. The ability to cope with the discontinuities created by major life transitions will be easier if they come into focus at different stages. Being able to tackle these issues one at a time will reduce the stresses inherent within the transitional process. (also see Rutter, 1980:181)

There is flexibility around the concept of age boundaries and the focal model is not centred on fixed sequence (Coleman, 2011). It is this flexibility that offers valuable perspectives on how young people, taking account of potential development issues, late bloomers or early developers, are able to manage the process of transition.

> An alternative and more balanced view of young people's social and psychological development is provided by Coleman and Hendry (1999) who argue that what is needed is a theory of adolescent *normality* rather than abnormality. Coleman and Hendry also stress the role of individual young people as *"active agents"* who play a significant part in shaping or determining their own development (rather than being helplessly swept along by unseen hormonal, biological or psychological forces). Furthermore, they support the argument of writers like Bronfenbenner (1979) that human development has an "ecology", meaning it is shaped by and interacts with its "environment". (Devlin, 2009:40)

The focus on adolescents' normality, as opposed to abnormality, within their development makes focal theory a strengths-based model, as opposed to deficit-based such as the psychoanalytical model.

Hendry *et al.* (1993) and Hendry (1996) highlight the significance of play and leisure to adolescent development, and how this is encompassed within focal theory:

> Our results for associations between relational issues and leisure preferences and behaviours in adolescence would further suggest that there is some linkage between psychosocial focuses and the "use" of leisure contexts by young people in order to meet developmental needs. (1996:319)

Focal theory holds particular relevance with regard to young people ageing out of care, as they have to undertake dual, highly-stressful processes simultaneously. They must make the transition from childhood to adulthood, and also from care to independence, in what Biehal and Wade (1996:443) term circumstances that are "both accelerated and compressed". The need for time and space to process these changes becomes evident when considered from the focal theory perspective as the impact of stress is taken into consideration. According to focal theory, young people focus on

151

one issue at a time and it is possible that this one issue may be the stress associated with the leaving care process itself. This can be the anxiety invoked by impending loss of relationships, familiarity and security (Dixon, 2008; Holt and Kirwan, 2012).

> ... those people who have to face a number of interpersonal issues at the same time are likely to experience problems of adjustment. (Coleman and Hendry, cited in Stein, 2012:162)

It is important to bear in mind that children often enter the care system having experienced trauma in their lives, both prior to entry into care and within the entry process itself, and these traumas may be re-experienced, as Keith did when the manager read him the riot act.

> Evidence suggests that many of the children and young people who eventually become looked after already have a high level of mental and physical health problems at their point of entry to care. (Hannon *et al.*, 2010:11)

This stress can manifest as re-experiencing the trauma associated with entering care and the associated experiences of loss, separation and anxiety (Roger, 2011; Ward, 2011), as well as the erroneously internalised sense of guilt at having been taken into care due to their own actions (Cashmore and Paxman, 2006).

Children enter care due to a range of issues, with family problems being the single largest reason (Eurochild, 2010:93). These family problems include parental separation, death, mental health issues, inability to cope and financial/housing problems. Other problems precipitating entry into care include neglect, physical, sexual and emotional abuse. For many children there can be a sense of abandonment attached with entry to care (Yates, 2001). The abrupt transition into "instant adulthood" can evoke a re-experiencing of these earlier traumas at the same time as they are attempting to deal with a range of other stressful factors associated with leaving care. Unfortunately, abandonment upon leaving care may not always be a re-experiencing of a prior trauma, but rather an all too real-time experience of abandonment, this time by their substitute parents. This was a finding with two prominent recent Irish inquiries, the Commission of Inquiry into Child Abuse (2009) and the Report of the Independent Child Death Review Group (ICDRG) (Shannon and Gibbons, 2012). Internationally, Philip Mendes (2008) identified this issue in Australia:

> Care leavers are literally abandoned by their substitute parents, and expected to transition directly from childhood dependence into adult self-sufficiency. (2008:255)

Failure to facilitate the time and space required to successfully process such experiences, and the stress which they induce, can result in the young person becoming overwhelmed or, within Maslow's hierarchy of needs, "blocked" and unable to progress beyond the present level of functioning. Furthermore, times of transition are identified as times of upheaval and vulnerability wherein an individual's psychological coping capacities can be consumed with managing the present stress, thus rendering them vulnerable to being overwhelmed by additional stressors. These additional stressors can come in the form of new issues to cope with or the emergence of dormant issues. As a result, the care leaver may regress to an earlier level of functioning and require additional rather than less support.

Whilst the transition can add to the burden of coping, it also represents an opportunity to focus on an issue which may be of profound significance for the care leaver, but has not been within their "focus" for some time. By addressing this issue healthy psychological development may be both restored and promoted.

This strategy is supported by the psychodynamic conception of adolescence, especially that espoused by Anna Freud (1958) and Peter Blos (1962). The theory suggests that adolescence is a second, and sometimes last, opportunity to address unresolved childhood issues, for example oedipal issues. These issues, if not resolved, thereafter become fixed as internalised, unhealthy blueprints for adult functioning and become entrenched psychologically. Therefore, by alleviating the stress in the life of the care leaver with targeted interventions and waiting to see what comes into focus, childhood traumas may be resolved. However, it may require addressing multiple issues to accomplish this task, as an underlying unresolved issue may be the cause of the stress.

Thus the crisis of transition from care may be turned into an opportunity for growth. With this potential in mind, professionals supporting care leavers need to identify the stresses and, with targeted support, enable the care leaver to work through the difficulties. This is of major significance for two reasons:

1. It allows the care leaver to resolve the current issue and move on to the next issue, thus promoting healthy psychological development.

2. This may be a "turning point" (Hannon *et al.*, 2010) for the care leaver as the issue which arises may be one which has been "blocking" their healthy psychological development for some time. By resolving this new developmental pathways may become open for the care leaver.

From a similar perspective of disruption to normal psychological development, the potential harm to children in care who are subjected to multiple movements between placements becomes clear when considered from a focal theory perspective.

Owen

An example of the application of this theory from my practice, and indeed the origin of its derivation, is the case of "Owen". Owen was a 17-year-old young man who was admitted to a centre I managed in order to assist him in the leaving care process. He had been in care for several years and had limited positive experiences of education, family or social aspects of his life. Contact with his parent was limited and not very positive, and it was not anticipated that he would return to the family home on leaving care. The private rental sector was his identified option. He was increasingly struggling with anxiety as he approached turning 18. This manifested in a range of high-risk behaviours which required medical, psychiatric and other interventions to attempt to keep him safe. His mental health declined to where what little sleep he managed was during the daytime as he was awake all night. He became increasingly agoraphobic and began to experience panic attacks whilst rapidly losing weight, despite staffs' best interventions to ensure a healthy diet.

Every support was unconditionally offered to him to meet the issues he appeared to be struggling with. Stating expectations of him appeared futile and unrealistic given his level of distress. One day he informed staff on duty that he wanted to talk to me when I was available. I chose to grant him his request in the full knowledge that I would most likely be on the receiving end of an apparently disjointed and irrational outpouring of unrelated issues with little possibility of meaningful resolution. The staff and I had sat through many such monologues previously. During our meeting I paid full attention to the content of his speech and sat in a silent but attentive position facing him. He spoke about a range of issues for approximately five to ten minutes, the content of which I have long forgotten, with me offering nods to confirm that I was listening. On this occasion I resisted the temptation to "tune out" which can sometimes arise in such situations. Then, within the seemingly unconnected monologue he interjected one apparently unrelated five word sentence, then reverted, seamlessly, back to the ostensibly irrational and illogical monologue.

Thankfully, on that occasion I heard what he was trying to tell me. What he said was along the lines of "and I need ... and ... is wrong and why can't I have ... and my father hates me ... and if only I was given ... and they are not doing what they should ... and if only I had ..."

Those five words were the window into his distress. I was stunned by this revelation and how he had communicated it in such an ostensibly hidden manner. I made no comment or even acknowledge that I had actually heard what he had said. Given the manner in which he had communicated this to me, I felt this was the most appropriate course of action, and we would discuss it when he was ready and able. I felt he was bringing it to my attention in an exploratory manner. He may have felt this afforded him the safety he required to broach this self-truth, possibly in the hope that I would act in some way to assist him. When he had finished his monologue I made reference to the fact that I had heard what he had said about his father, and asked if he wished to discuss it further. He did elaborate on it briefly, giving reasons why he believed his father felt that way about him, and then he ended the conversation. I accepted this as I felt he had gone as far as he was able to at this point.

The staff team had been directly tackling his anxiety with a range of interventions, and he had begun to focus on his familial relationships, which had not been in focus for quite some time. Because I had been attuned enough to hear what Owen was trying to communicate, the staff team and I were able to implement a range of interventions around his relationship with his father. The aim was to assist them to reconnect over a period of several months. This proved to be highly successful and Owen stayed in the residential centre until he turned 18. His anxiety began to diminish noticeably after this milestone. His panic attacks ceased, he gained weight, his sleep pattern returned to normal and he began to leave the centre to socialise. Shortly after this he left to live in the family home.

Owen taught us much about how to support young people in the leaving care process, and thereafter this strategy was implemented with all care leavers at the centre.

On this occasion I heard what Owen was trying to tell me, but I wonder on how many other occasions I failed to hear, when I was not attuned or attentive enough. He just wanted for me to hear what he was trying to tell me. Whether he intended to communicate this consciously or subconsciously I do not know, but I am grateful that on that day I was able to catch the finer detail embedded within his message.

It is noteworthy that focal theory has remained largely underutilised, despite validation for the theory in research in the 1980s (Simmons *et al.*, 1987; Call and Mortimer, 2001), and if not for the work of Mike Stein in identifying its significance in relation to care leavers it might have been consigned to the vaults of academia.

In recent times, research by Dima and Skehill (2011) and Ryzin *et al.* (2011) builds on focal theory by utilising the Bridges model (2004). This identifies that transition is composed of two distinct processes, the social and the psychological, and three distinct phases, ending, neutral and new beginnings. They also highlight the importance of temporal consideration to these processes, as highlighted within focal theory. Anghel (2011) also uses the Bridges model with reference to care leavers, which is an example of where further research has added to focal theory.

Focal theory has had its critics, notably Dohrenwend and Dohrenwend, who claim that "focal theory is nothing more than a theory of life events applied to adolescence" (1974:17), though perhaps they are missing the agency component where "the young person is an agent in his or her own development, managing the adolescence transition – where possible – by dealing with one issue at a time" (Coleman and Hendry, 1999:18). Also, Coffield *et al.* (1986) criticised focal theory for not placing sufficient emphasis on economic stress or social constraints that are increasingly impacting on young people in developed societies. This critique has been rebutted by Kloep (1999:50):

> In theory, this criticism is unjust, as focal theory was never meant as a model that can explain adolescent behaviour in all circumstances, but rather to describe "normal" or "mainstream" psychological development, very much as descriptions of physical maturation do not necessarily include non-normative factors like lack of nutrition or disease.

Hendry *et al.* (1993:11-12) respond to Coffield *et al.* as follows:

> ... whilst they are right to draw attention to the social circumstances of the individual, for these will obviously contribute in a substantial way to each adolescent's psychological adjustment.... This point has already been made by Hendry (1983) in his argument that ecological factors are as important as psychological ones in understanding the young person's development.

Hendry *et al.* (*ibid*) are referring to an adaption to the focal theory that Hendry published in (1983). Within this adaption Hendry proposed that the level of anxiety, fear or conflict that may be present can be determined by matching the self-image with the role ascribed to the individual by significant others. Thus, if a care leaver perceives themselves as mature and independent, whilst those supporting them perceive them as immature and dependent, there will be conflict or dissonance. This adaption suggest that "external social factors are just as important as personal internal ones in determining social, relational behaviour." (Hendry *et al.*, 1993:10)

Building on this adaption, Hendry *et al.* (1993:11) make the point that the external social factors "focal theory has to do with the psychological transitions of adolescence at a macro level, rather than the economic and social circumstances of the individual".

The links between focal theory and the social-ecology model of resilience are striking, especially when we consider that Coleman and Hendry were theorising focal theory more than 30 years ago. Further research, including work to integrate the focal model of adolescent development with its temporal dimensions of stage and process development and the social-ecology model of resilience, may prove rewarding in assisting young people through transition processes.

In summation, and in light of the factors identified in this chapter, focal theory clearly has more relevance than it is currently afforded due to its natural strengths base, its relevance to the social-ecology model of resilience, its recognition of young people as active agents in their own development, its relevance to transition theory, and its encompassing of the significance of leisure and play within adolescent developmental processes.

Listening

As listening has featured strongly as a core practice skill, I am including some theories I have found helpful in this critical area.

> Good communication skills lie at the heart of effective social work practice. (Richards *et al.*, 2005:409)

Listening is a core communication skill which can be said to be the one that contributes most to the communication process (Gast and Bailey, 2014).

If one word sums up most of what service users want form social care, it is "listening". (Beresford *et al.*, 2005:26)

Without effective listening there is the potential that communication appears to have happened whilst, in fact, it has only occurred superficially. It is all too easy to listen to respond rather than listening to understand.

The single biggest problem in communication is the illusion that it has taken place. (G.B. Shaw)

Children with a disability are over-represented within care compared to the general population in the Republic of Ireland (Clarke, 2015) and the UK (Baker, 2011). This group have a particular vulnerability which led to their entry into care (Gordon *et al.*, 2000) and also, as identified by Clarke (*ibid*) and Baker (*ibid*), on leaving care. However, there has been scant research into the experiences of disabled care leavers, although Baker (2011) highlighted that care staff may lack the skills to facilitate effective communication with them. We must also be mindful that these young people may have suffered developmental delay which can diminish their ability to function age appropriately compared to their non-developmentally delayed peers. Bryan *et al.* (2007), in a study of language and communication difficulties among young offenders aged 15-18, found that:

... 66-90 per cent of juvenile offenders in the sample had below average language skills, with 46-67 per cent of these being in the poor or very poor group. (2007:505)

This, they highlight, holds particular significance for practitioners in communicating with these groups of young people:

How effectively do these young people with lower than average language ability communicate, and does this level of language ability affect their ability to benefit from verbally mediated interventions? (2007:515)

Watzlawick's Five Axioms of Communication (1967)

One of the most helpful communication aids I have encountered is Watzlawick's Five Axioms of Communication. Understanding these axioms can significantly improve communication and listening. Though originally developed in 1967, and with inherent limitations to their applicability in all settings, these remain key concepts for those practicing within the social professions. Kleipoedszus (2011), in his insightful chapter on the role of conflict in social pedagogic relationships, outlines these along with the related Schultz von Thun's (2001, 2003) Four Sides Model of Communication, together with a social pedagogy perspective on listening.

1. One cannot not communicate

This means that all behaviour has to be seen as a kind of communication. Because behaviour does not have a counterpart (there is no anti-behaviour), it is not possible not to communicate.

2. Every communication has a content and relationship aspect such that the latter classifies the former and is therefore a meta-communication

This means that all communication includes, apart from the plain meaning of words, more information – information on how the talker wants to be understood and how he himself sees his relation to the receiver of information.

3. The nature of a relationship is dependent on the punctuation of the partners' communication procedures

Both the talker and the receiver of information structure the communication flow differently, and therefore interpret their own behaviour during communicating as merely a reaction to the other's behaviour (i.e. every partner thinks the other one is the cause of a specific behaviour). Human communication cannot be dissolved into plain causation and reaction strings; rather, communication appears to be cyclic.

4. *Human communication involves both digital and analog modalities*

Communication does not involve merely spoken words (digital communication), but non-verbal and analog-verbal communication as well (e.g. facial expression, gestures, body language).

5. *Inter-human communication procedures are either symmetric or complementary*

Symmetrical communication is based on equal power while complimentary communication is based on differences in power relations. A healthy relationship will have both types of power. Too much of one type can lead to conflicts.

Four Sides Model

Schultz von Thun developed the Four Sides Model of Communication, also known as the Communication Square or Four Ears Model, in 2001. The basic concept is that every message has four potential meanings and thus the recipient needs "four ears" to interpretive its true meaning. The four aspects are *factual, appeal, relationship* and *self-evaluation*.

An example of these aspects in communication would be where a child in care asks the social care worker for money for bus fare:

- **Factual**: the child requires the money as it is in fact necessary to buy a ticket to use the bus

- **Appeal**: the child hopes to go somewhere on the bus; thus the appeal is "please let me get there"

- **Relationship**: the child is asking in the belief that the care worker cares enough about them, due to their relationship, to support them in getting to where they want to be

- **Self-evaluation**: the child shares something about themselves in explaining why they need to be at the specific location and possibly why they need the social care worker's help with accessing the money.

This can become more complex when the response of the listener is factored in. The listener may choose to listen with "one ear", and respond with their own message which may also have four aspects or dimensions. Thus it becomes apparent that this communication model requires constant self-reflection on the part of the worker to identify which of the four "ears" they are employing, and to consider the four aspects of the child's communication. This tool requires practice but holds much potential for effective communication.

Kleipoedszus (2011) identifies the potential for the 3P's identified within the social pedagogy model of the private, professional and personal to influence the listening process. The professional pedagogue may hear with a "factual ear" employing various theories to explain the behaviour and meaning of the communication; the private pedagogue may hear with an "appellate ear" because the young person reminds them of their own child; and the personal pedagogue may hear with a "relational ear" as they may be seeking the relational aspect of the communication to facilitate the personal relationship. Thus Kleipoedszus reveals the many ears which the worker may use to interpret the communication from the child, and an awareness of these on the part of the worker can greatly aid the listening process.

SOLER

With regard to the setting for the above meeting with Owen, I consciously set this up to be conducive to effective communication by following the SOLER technique (Gast and Bailey, 2014:54):

Square on – angle of the body towards person at 90 degrees

Open body position – body conveys interest

Lean towards – conveys interest and equalises height differences

Eye contact – maintained (but avoid "stare" and become "culturally competent")

Relaxed manner/posture.

Perhaps the most important thing we bring to another person is the silence in us, not the sort of silence that is filled with unspoken criticism or hard withdrawal. The sort of silence that is the place of refuge, of rest, of acceptance of someone as they are. We are all hungry for this other silence. It is hard to find. In its presence we can remember something beyond the moment, a strength on which to build a life. Silence is a place of great power and healing. (Rachel Remen)

. . . .

S I L E N T is an anagram for L I S T E N

. . . .

Chapter 6

SOCIAL PEDAGOGY, RELATIONSHIP-BASED PRACTICE AND MENTORING

Social Pedagogy

Social pedagogy, as noted at the beginning of this book, has much to offer social care work, as together with relationship-based practice it offers an approach that integrates multiple theories and disciplines within a framework. Critical reflection is central to social pedagogy practice and, amongst other things, is utilised to determine what is private as opposed to what is personal in the 3P's. Many of the failings identified earlier, such as unilateral processes and singular approaches, as well as many of the strengths, such as pluralistic approaches and diversity, can be addressed within the holistic discipline that is social pedagogy. Social pedagogy is more about the how and the why than the what of affairs, and it places relationships, at all levels, at the core of practice.

> A central tenet of a pedagogic approach is to reject universal solutions and accept a multiplicity of possible perspectives, depending on personal circumstances, particular dynamics and events and sources of support. (Cameron, 2004:145)

Social pedagogy has a long history with its roots traceable back to the mid-nineteenth century. Although there are major cultural, socio-economic and political differences between the Republic of Ireland, the UK and the European countries that implement social pedagogy models of practice, it must be acknowledged that the outcomes for children in care are enviable in some of these countries by comparison to those in the Republic of Ireland and the UK.

Social pedagogy at its core is concerned with well-being, growth and learning, and it represents an approach to care or education which draws on disciplines such as sociology, education, psychology and philosophy. It has been strongly influenced by, amongst others, the works of Johann Heinrich Pestalozzi, Kurt Hahn, Paul Natorp, Maria Montessori and Janusz Korczak. It represents an approach drawn from the range of disciplines encompassed within social pedagogy which may be utilised depending on which best meets the needs of the individual. Currently in the UK and the Republic of Ireland there is much focus on models of care within residential care. Whilst having a model of care is clearly preferable to not having one, an approach to care offers broader scope for diversity of practice.

Social pedagogy can appear complex and difficult to accurately define as its practice and definition may vary from country to country. One definition is:

> Social pedagogy is a holistic way of working with children and young people in different settings. It:
>
> 1) Draws on related disciplines such as education, sociology, psychology and philosophy;
>
> 2) Encompasses all elements of living and learning, developing learning opportunities that are embedded in day-to-day activities;
>
> 3) Recognises the importance of relationships for positive wellbeing and growth. (Celcis, 2013)

The term "pedagogy" originates from the Greek words for child (*país*) and to bring up (*ágein*). Within social pedagogy the concept of *haltung*, which in English may be translated as stance, mindset or attitude, encapsulates being authentic and having actions shaped by beliefs. As with Carl Roger's concept of "unconditional positive regard", *haltung* requires a profound respect for an individual's human dignity. Such a concept may be considered in the Republic of Ireland and the UK as a "professional stance" or "professional attitude", which offers potential for unity within the profession. It also incorporates the necessity for workers to be activists to better empower those they support by endeavouring to change society to be more inclusive and equitable. In this sense, *haltung* speaks of how our actions are driven by our beliefs. As Banks (2006:133) has said, "the professional is political". This could be our common professional persona or beliefs, and clearly holds strong potential, if successfully developed as it is within social pedagogy, to be a force for ensuring ethical practice where social justice is repositioned to the fore of the profession.

To better understand social pedagogy and the concept of *haltung* it is worthwhile to briefly consider the life of Jansuz Korczak (1892-1942), one of its founding fathers. Korczak was a Polish-Jewish doctor who established orphanages in Poland in the early twentieth century. He was an early proponent of children's rights believing that:

> Children are not the people of tomorrow, but are people of today. They are entitled to be taken seriously. They have a right to be treated by adults with respect, as equals. They should be allowed to grow into whoever they were meant to be - the unknown person inside each of them is the hope for the future.

His ideas were as profound and challenging then as they are today. His beliefs can be distilled into three key points:

- a child's right to die;

- a child's right to live for the day;

- the right of the child to be what s/he is.

> "If you want to be a pedagogue you have to learn to talk with children instead of to them. You have to learn to trust their capacities and possibilities". Everything else follows on from this. (Korczak, cited in Eichsteller, 2010)

Korczak identified the paradox whereby by protecting the child from harm (death) we deprive them of the right to live fully and

166

with self-determination. This resonates still today with the right to die regularly featuring in high profile court cases for both adults and children, and also within research relating to risk-averse and over-protective practices – protecting the child may be depriving then of the opportunity to develop resilience and lead fulfilling lives.

In his orphanages Korczak established children's parliaments and children's courts to ensure all children were treated with respect. When the 200 Jewish children from his orphanages were transported to the concentration camp of Treblinka, he chose to accompany them. He was offered the chance to avoid death but he declined, choosing instead to walk with his children into the gas chamber to support and reassure them in their hour of greatest need.

Clearly his life was led based on his beliefs and in this sense his *haltung* meant that his work was inseparable from his life – he walked the talk in all aspects of his life. This is the embodiment of a "way of being".

Haltung is also associated with how we engage with others. A stance of equality and respect for the other underpins communication and a shared exploration of what meaning may result. Congruency is required so that each may see the personality of the other and how this impacts on the dialogue. This resonates with collaborative meaning-making and the previously identified significance attached to respect.

Social pedagogy brings with it a more holistic approach founded on humanistic principles and includes the 3H's of Hands (practical and doing with children), Hearts (emotions and connection to the work) and Heads (academic and theoretical base), all of which are brought to bear on the work with children. This facilitates the emotional aspects of care as children need emotional nurturing just as they do physical sustenance. Caring cannot become sterilised as it is inherently messy; it is a complex task and cannot be effective if devoid of emotion and/or feeling.

> Care that is neat and tidy and conforms to bureaucratic specification is not care at all. (Smith, 2009:166)

Another concept central to social pedagogy is the Common Third. This is essentially about using a shared activity to strengthen the relationship between worker and child whilst also developing new skills. If the worker is genuinely interested in this activity then the experience can be rewarding for both. There is also an implicit equality as both worker and child enjoy the activity. There is an expanding repository of knowledge addressing this area (Cameron and Moss, 2011; Cameron, 2013; Storø, 2013).

Together with the 3P's and the 3H's, the Diamond Model is central to social pedagogy.

WELL-BEING & HAPPINESS

EMPOWERMENT   **POSITIVE EXPERIENCES**   **RELATIONSHIPS**

HOLISTIC LEARNING

Figure 9: *The Diamond Model (Eichsteller and Holthoff, 2011).*

One of the most fundamental principles underpinning social pedagogy is the notion that every human being has intrinsic value. We are all precious and possess unique knowledge, skills and abilities. But as with a diamond, not all of this richness is necessarily visible. Not all diamonds are polished and sparkly, but all of them have the potential to be. Social pedagogy is about setting people's potential free.... Social pedagogy follows four core aims that are closely linked: wellbeing and happiness, holistic learning, relationship, and empowerment...The overarching aim of all social pedagogic practice is to provide wellbeing and happiness - not on a short-term needs-focused basis, but sustainably, through a rights-based approach. (Holthoff and Eichsteller, 2009:60)

Social pedagogy is essentially political in its practice as it focuses on inequality by promoting values of social justice. It is not aligned with any singular political ideology or political paradigm. The focus on relationship is not restricted to the context of practice but rather within society more widely. This entails what Paulo Freire calls conscientization of the people pedagogues are working with, supporting them in taking responsibility for their community and developing a strong support network – relationships in the broadest sense. Another anchor related to this is a rights-based approach that sees relationships as between human beings of equal value, conducted with dignity and respect. That leads to another essential anchor in social pedagogy: critical reflection, which aims to ensure consideration of the above principles and, more practically, as we have seen, helps draw the lines between the 3P's. There is a strong focus on life-world orientation, which focuses on the subjective experiences of people's everyday reality within the context of life-skills and self-responsibility.

> At a societal level, the concept of life-world also demonstrates social pedagogy's commitment towards social justice by aiming to improve living conditions and social circumstances, so that people have the skills and opportunities for social participation (Grunwald and Theirsch, 2009). Social pedagogy Haltung does not, therefore just refer to an attitude towards individuals but provides the context for social pedagogy's aims and purposes at the level of community and society. (Eichsteller and Holthoff, 2011:38)

Social pedagogy can be seen to encompass three distinct but interconnected fields: social policy, professional practice and theory. It is referred to as "social education" in some jurisdictions and its aims can be seen to be both educational and the promotion of social inclusion (Petrie, 2011).

Social pedagogy is implemented differently within the states where it is practiced. There are subtle but significant differences between models in Finland, Denmark and Germany, for example. It is this feature of social pedagogy which makes its replication uncertain in jurisdictions such as the UK and the Republic of Ireland.

It is not as simple as implementing a model developed in Germany and automatically achieving the same positive outcomes. Germany has different political and social structures and a significantly higher usage of residential care as opposed to foster care. However, social pedagogy does offer a proven model for uniting what are currently separate silos: social work, social care, youth and community work, restorative approaches, juvenile justice and educational models. Within such a model, the strengths of each would complement each other synergistically in a truly integrated model.

Relationship-based Practice

Relationship-based practice is a central theme within this book and warrants a more detailed examination. Gillian Ruch has given us this excellent example of one such definition:

> A fundamental tenet of the relationship-based approach is its focus on the individual in context and on the psychological and the social, as neither the individual nor the context make sense without the other. In essence, relationship-based practice emphasises the centrality of relationships and the principles informing it are relevant to the range of relationships encountered in professional contexts, e.g. with service users, colleagues, managers and other professionals. Relationship-based practice has several core characteristics:
>
> • it recognises that each inter-personal encounter is unique;
>
> • it understands that human behaviour is complex and multi-faceted, i.e. people are not simply rational beings but have affective-conscious and unconscious-dimensions that enrich, but simultaneously complicate, human relationships;
>
> • it focuses on the inseparable nature of the internal and external worlds of individuals and the importance of integrated-psycho-social-as opposed to polarized-individual or structural-responses to social problems; and

- it places particular emphasis on "the use of self" and the
  relationship as the means through which interventions
  are channelled (Wilson et al., 2008). (Ruch, 2009:350-
  351)

Relationship-based practice is not restricted to the relation-ship between worker and child, but also, as evidenced by Ruch's definition, to all relationships the worker has within a professional context. Relationship-based practice, in common with child and youth care (CYC) and social pedagogy, is an approach to our work, a "way of being" within our professional persona, and therefore must be practiced in all areas. This begins with our relationship with ourselves in terms of self-awareness and how we are impact-ing on others.

Perhaps the key relationship to be considered, is our own relationship with our self. (Ward, in Ruch *et al.*, 2010:65)

It is a cause of grave concern when the focus of the work in-creasingly shifts from relationships to bureaucratic tasks (Munro, 2011; Furnivall *et al.*, 2012). We cannot forget it is precisely in the area of relationships with adults that many young people experi-ence difficulties. Consequently, the relationship focus holds the potential for young people to address life-changing issues through a safe relationship with an appropriate adult, thus enabling lost trust to be restored (Howe, 1998; Trevithick, 2003).

A particular strength of this approach (relational) is to re-store trust in other human beings where it has been lost, or to provide a place to work though 'other relationship prob-lems, including problems arising from their environment (Wilson, 2000, p. 350). (Trevithick, 2003:168)

No social care worker wants to be a "bureau-carer" or a "care technician" implementing predefined programmes and adminis-trative functions. Keith's recollection of the time we played com-puter games in Cleary's twenty years earlier bears testimony to the value of relationship-based work, as well as the value of play in caring for children, even those in their middle teenage years. This vignette, and other examples from Keith's story, also challenges the perception that children in residential care are afforded living standards that they may not be able to sustain on returning home. Playing expensive computer games might be a case in point, albeit in this instance it was a free game in a department store. Nonetheless, the impact of this game play, and other recreational events Keith enjoyed during these five months, were some of the all too brief normalised childhood experiences that Keith ever experienced.

For Keith, it is clear that his time in residential care allowed him to experience some aspects of the childhood he had missed, which thankfully he got to experience second time around through the power of positive and meaningful relationships. Without endorsing short-term placements for traumatised children, one has as to ask what price could be placed on this experience of five months of normalised childhood which Keith experienced within today's fiduciary-led care system?

The logic behind denying him, or any child, such experiences because they might be "spoiled" harkens back to the workhouse days of the famine in the nineteenth century. Then, life was made extremely difficult for destitute souls needing to take refuge within these institutions to dissuade any undeserving souls attempting to benefit from the charity of the state – Dickensian stuff which has no place in twenty-first century society, and indeed poses questions as to the role of charity in caring for children. Ultimately, all children have a right to be cared for, at least up to age 18 in the Republic of Ireland, and it can be argued that having to depend on "charity" for receiving this care lessens the imperative on the state to meet its obligations, and therefore weakens children's rights and access to such care.

The lost opportunity implicit in not recognising the need to focus more on relationships and meaningful life-experiences, and less on managing risk and planning children's lives with scripted programmes, may be located within the quote often attributed to the late John Lennon: "Life is what happens whilst we are busy making other plans."

Mentoring

The place of mentoring in residential care, leaving care and after-care deserves special attention. Care leavers need psychosocial and emotional support, in combination with structural support, and face-to-face relationships are the optimum medium to satisfy these needs (Stein and Carey, 1986; Stein, 2012). Existing professional aftercare workers, coordinators, managers and social workers, many of whom are highly qualified, could be utilised to oversee the work of mentors. Mentoring is naturally aligned with the youth and community model of care, and there is much synergy yet to be developed which could bring benefit to both models. Mentors, working with existing staff and services, would then be able to meet the psychosocial and emotional needs of care leavers.

Mentoring has risen to prominence in both the UK and the USA in recent decades, and to a lesser extent in the Republic of Ireland. In the USA there are over 5,000 mentoring programmes serving an estimated three million young people (DuBois *et al.*, 2011). It is one of the most utilised forms of service provision, particularly with young people and those deemed "at risk", but also one of the least understood. In fact, it has developed to such an extent that it can be regarded as a social phenomenon (Freidson, 1999).

> The problem with any study of mentoring begins at the very beginning for, as Clutterbuck noted at the Third European Mentoring conference in 1996 "the biggest problem for researchers into mentoring is still defining what it is" (Clutterbuck, 1996). (Hall, 2003:3)

There are many different forms of youth mentoring including formal and informal programmes, employing paid and unpaid mentors within directive and/or engagement programmes. It has been said that "the very words 'mentor' has acquired a mythical status, suggesting almost superhuman power to transform the mentee in the face of all odds" (Colley, 2003:1).

A good definition for a formal youth mentoring programme is offered by Brooker (2011:22):

A formal youth mentoring program is one in which a young person (mentee) is paired with a non-parental older, more experienced person (mentor) with the expectation that a close relationship characterised by trust develops; within which the mentor can offer support and guidance to their mentee, and share companionship, with the intention of fostering the mentee's growth and development.

Mentoring has been linked to promoting resilience in young people (Clayden and Stein, 2005; Stein, 2005a, 2005b, 2008a; Gilligan, 2008a) with recognition of the importance of a single reliable adult role model. Thus it also has roots in attachment theory. Mike Stein (2006a) has written a seminal book on the subject called *Mentoring for Care Leavers*.

Engagement mentoring is a commonly used form and is often associated with specific goals and targets, such as improving employment prospects via educational achievement. I have implemented engagement mentoring with care leavers in both residential settings and within the community.

Its very malleability and lack of an evidence base makes mentoring a fraught enterprise. It can be adapted to promote a vast range of outcomes and can be delivered at very low cost, thus making it attractive to policy-makers. However, the integrity and values of those delivering it are key factors in determining its efficacy. Additionally, issues of cultural sensitivity are important. In my experience, local programmes are most effective for implementation within the Republic of Ireland. We must be mindful, as we saw in our consideration of evidence-based practice, that what works in one culture or for one specific group may not work elsewhere. Without this consideration, there is the potential for more harm than benefit to result from a poorly implemented programme (Philip and Hendry, 2000). While much of mentoring occurs in one-to-one sessions, which can promote relationship development, there is also a risk in terms of the absence of other people acting as observers. It is imperative that robust policies, procedures and protocols are put in place and enacted.

An appreciation of the role of power and a willingness to "negotiate" is highly salient in working with young people in care. For many, they have the experience of little agency in their lives and as they progress into adolescence naturally strive to achieve a sense of self-efficacy. This is a normal and healthy part of adolescent development. It is also important to recognise that a power differential is a significant factor in communication, as we saw in the section on listening. This is a critical factor within disciplines such as counselling, psychotherapy and supervision (Taylor, 1994; Guilfoyle, 2006). The listener has to consider the range of possible responses, bearing in mind the potential implications that the exercise of this power might have. Therapeutically, the lesser the power differential present the more effective the communication as there are fewer "barriers" and "filters" in place.

Peer mentoring can have particular advantages in this regard with the enhanced identification and reduced power differentials between mentor and mentee.

> Because of the inherent equality among (peer) group members, relationships are more mutual, and ideally, each participant has something of value to contribute and gain. These relationships are likely to offer more personal feedback and friendship than traditional mentoring relationships. (Bussey-Jones, 2006:675)

Li and Julian (2012) identified the relevance of power to meaningful relationship development and how mentors can capitalise in this area. Ideally, mentors should hold the least amount of power possible within their relationship with mentees. Clutterbuck (2002:115) recommends that mentors "park" their power at the onset of the mentoring relationship, though he also points out that little is known of just how to do this. Mentee and mentor need to agree on an ongoing basis the goals and targets of the mentoring. The goal of this form of mentoring for care leavers is the promotion of their continued engagement with wider support services, whilst promoting the development of social skills and nurturing interdependent living skills. It is not specifically to target singular goals such as involvement in education, work or training, though these areas most often do benefit from the mentoring relationship. As we saw in the section on focal theory, different issues may arise for care leavers in transition. The mentor is available to address these issues as they arise by not being bound to pre-defined goals set by management. By agreeing together what both parties expect from the programme there is an internal locus of control (Noe *et al.*, 2010; Lefcourt, 2014) which has a known benefit in promoting self-efficacy. Ideally, mentoring should be a beneficial experience for both mentee and mentor. However, the impact of an external locus of control is not limited to the mentee alone:

> The imposition of external goals tends to drive the mentors practice towards the more directive end of the spectrum. (Colley, 2003:37)

Within the residential settings where I employed paid mentors alongside residential social care workers the mentors did not have the authority to make decisions on structural issues such as curfew times, access to money, visitors, etc. These decisions were made by care staff or management. This was deliberately constructed to promote the reduced power dynamics known to be beneficial to the mentoring relationship. Mentees enjoy their time with the mentor, just as Keith recounts he did with regard to the time we spent together, and this is sufficient to promote prosocial behaviour. The novelty of having an adult in their life who is only there "for them", rather than to tell them what to do, is priceless to many of these young people.

As highlighted, both resilience and attachment theory identify the importance of one significant appropriate adult relationship to the developing person. It is this holistic development that this form of mentoring targets.

Gerry

An example of mentoring's potential within a residential setting is the case of Gerry, who was placed in a dedicated preparation for leaving care centre and had a male mentor with whom he had a particularly meaningful relationship. Approximately midway through Gerry's placement things became tense between Gerry and staff at the centre. Gerry was involving himself in issues which brought known risk to the centre and staff were attempting to intervene to curtail this behaviour. As things escalated Gerry began to detach, spending more time away from the centre and communicating less with staff and not at all with me, the manager. A dynamic of "us" and "them" began to enter the relationship. In my previous experience such scenarios can precipitate a breakdown of placement in residential settings. However, in Gerry's case this did not happen. Gerry continued to engage with his mentor during the time he was away from the centre, as clearly he did not perceive the mentor as being one of "them". This was interesting to me, as Gerry knew that I supervised the mentor and that there was no confidentiality attached to the information he received. Gerry appeared to attach more value to the relationship with the mentor than concern for any role I may have had in this relationship.

Over a period of time, and with input from the staff team, which was communicated back to Gerry via the mentor, we were able to successfully resolve the issue that had caused the problem originally. Gerry returned to live in the centre and saw out his placement successfully. He transitioned to independent living with the support of his mentor and has kept contact with him over the intervening years. It must be acknowledged that Registration, Monitoring and Inspection Services were supportive of including mentors within the staff team, which is a good example of the promotion of needs-led best practice on their part.

Mentoring clearly has much to offer as a complimentary support service to care leavers. It encompasses principles from attachment, resilience and focal theory as well as being aligning with the principles of relationship-based practice, social pedagogy and the youth and community approach.

In Northern Ireland, the role of personal advisers, with strong links to mentoring, achieves this objective. This is a good example of how the redeployment of existing resources allocated to aftercare services can make a major difference to the well-being of care leavers.

Finally, it must be acknowledged that professionalisation has brought many benefits to social care but some losses as well. Mentors have the potential to address some of these losses. For example, I am conscious that my use of language has changed as I have progressed academically and that this could have a negative impact on my relationships with young people. I am more prone to speak in a professionalised fashion, using specific words and phrases whilst avoiding other ones. Perhaps I have also become overly correct in my attempts not to offend or to be perceived as politically incorrect or insensitive. This can be seen by young people as less authentic. Mentors may be less likely to speak in this way and therefore be perceived as more authentic. Many years ago I learnt from a former 17-year-old key child that he was more likely to retain the information he heard from someone he identified with than from a professional. In this instance, it was a recovering heroin addict who had come to make a presentation to a group of young people in care. My key child was able to recite word-for-word some of what this presenter had said some weeks previously, whereas he couldn't remember any details of what I and other professionals had said the day previously. He taught me the power of identification in communicating with young people, and the relevance of this to relationship formation, and this single incident was the genesis of my interest in mentoring.

Summary

Clearly a deeper understanding of theory affords workers a better understanding of the needs of the young people they seek to care for and aids the development of practice to best address those needs. Such practice can create opportunities to enable young people to achieve a sense of mastery in their lives and to meet their needs over longer timelines with structured programmes. A singular theoretical approach affords limited possibilities, whereas combinations of approaches has much greater potential for success. As the aphorism often attributed to Abraham Maslow (1908-1970) states: "When the only tool you have is a hammer you tend to see every problem as a nail."

There is potential for compatibility between theories and approaches, as we saw in terms of the significance of meaningful relationships within both attachment and resilience theory, but there is also the possibility for tension, as shown between exposure to risk and resilience development, or between behavioural and psychodynamic approaches. This point is particulary salient when considering the potential dominance of one theory or approach over others.

As identified, my relationship with Keith developed without the benefit of significant theoretical knowledge. Clearly, this relationship was beneficial to him which highlights that theory is not everything in social care and workers cannot become slaves to theoretical approaches or dominant paradigms. It is imperative that workers practice responsively, reflexively and reflectively and uses their professional judgement (D'Cruz *et al.*, 2007; Banks, 2013). Cooper (2011) posits that professional judgement requires embracing uncertainty, which by default means that our knowledge is always forming and reforming:

> ... the only certainty entails being sure of your best judgment in particular situations at particular moments in time and with the fully considered evidence of incomplete knowledge so that you can defend and justify your assessments, plans and interventions. (Cooper, 2011:23)

No singular theory, approach or paradigm should dominate our profession, just as the proponents of the various approaches should lead by their actions and embrace diversity and multiplicity (Anderson-Nathe, 2010). The whole of such integrated practice would certainly be greater than the sum of the parts.

Erik Erikson's famous line with regard to his own theoretical model, redolent with humility for such an eminent theorist, still holds true today and bears contemplation when considering the role of theory and professional judgement in practice:

> ... a tool to think with rather than a "prescription to abide by". (Erikson, 1950:243)

Section Four –
Children's Rights and Policy

Introduction

This section commences with a chapter affording an overview of children's rights and underpinning principles. It then addresses the National Policy and Procedure for Aftercare Service Provision (2011) through a discussion of its relevance with regard to the United Nations Convention on the Rights of the Child (UNCRC). Relevant articles are then examined as are Committee commentaries and recommendations and ECHR hearings. Thereafter there is an overview of policy relevant to children and young people in the Republic of Ireland.

The reader is encouraged to reflect on Keith's experiences in Chapter 1 while reading this section. In particular, bear in mind his experiences of stigmatisation and labelling in his childhood, and then of moving into aftercare and the impact poverty and loneliness had on him. Rights and policy are key factors in shaping both practice and welfare provision, and thus any impetus to promote change in service structures, availability and entitlement requires inclusion of these areas.

Chapter 7

Children's Rights

The twentieth century may arguably be called the century of rights with diverse groups demanding the same freedoms enjoyed by others. Historically, childhood only came to be seen as a separate life stage in the eighteenth to nineteenth centuries with children previously being seen as mini-adults (Lee, 1998; Pole *et al.*, 1999; Rogers, 2001). Childhood finally emerged in its own right, partly through the work of philanthropic societies in Victorian times highlighting the hardships being endured by children (Aries, 1965; Pollock, 1984; Dekker, 2002; Prout, 2005). In the twentieth century childhood came into focus as a separate life stage and was researched by psychologists and sociologists alike with the age of 18 becoming recognised as the ending of childhood and the onset of adulthood. Psychological data of that time indicated that at this age humans were cognitively fully developed (Piaget, 1936; O'Kane, 2000). Sociologists in turn recognised that pathways to adulthood commenced with the employment opportunities available to young people in industries such as manufacturing and mining. In the last decades of the twentieth century enormous change took place with youth pathways to adulthood becoming fractured, and youth unemployment and dissatisfaction rising (Lister, 1998; Coleman, 2000; MacDonald, 1997, 1998, 2007).

> All young people today making the transition to adulthood have to 'negotiate a set of risks which were largely unknown to their parents' and contend with a pace of change that creates 'increased uncertainty (that) can be seen as a source of stress and vulnerability. (Furlong and Cartmel, 1997:1)

It is only in recent times, since the 1970s, that the rights of children have been considered on their own merit (Mayall, 2000; Freeman, 2000, 2007). The United Nations Convention on the Rights of the Child (UNCRC) has been ratified by most world nations since 1989 and contains 54 articles referring to children's rights and their implementation. The impact of the charter is evident in how nations incorporate its concepts into child care legislation. One example is the Republic of Ireland where "the best interest of the child" (Art. 3) underpins legislation. The Committee on the Rights of the Child (CRC) have regular discussions on the articles, passing comment and recommendations to nation states.

There are numerous ways to conceptualise children's rights. Amongst the key principles underpinning the UNCRC are another 3P's, namely, provision, participation and protection (Kilkelly, 2008: Alderson, 2008). All three principles are found in UNCRC Articles Two (non-discrimination), Three (best interests of the child a primary consideration), Six (right to life, survival and development) and Twelve (the right to he heard in matters concerning them), what might be called the charters "guiding principles" (Fortin, 2005). The traditional dominant principle of children's rights and laws has been protection. "Paternalistic" has been a word often used to described this approach (Lansdown 1995, 2009; Franklin, 2002). Provision or implementation of protective rights, can be found in a number of UNCRC Articles outlining the responsibility of state governments. Provision has raised questions regarding the role of the state and the parent in determining, firstly what standards of care are appropriate and who should provide those standards (Freeman 2010, 2011). The final principle, participation, feeds into discussions on protection and provision in light of a growing recognition of the capacities, agency and autonomy of young people (Freeman, 2000). This has also arguably been the most challenging aspect of the principles of children's rights (Alderson, 2008) as well as fundamental human rights (Thomas, 2007).

These principles are found internationally in contemporary children's rights legislation. For example, in Australia with the New South Wales Children and Young Persons (Care and Protection) Act 1998, in the UK with the Children Act 1989, and in the

Republic of Ireland with the Child Care Act 1991. The Child Care Act 1991 recognises children's vulnerability, engendering the protection and provision principles with measures for the removal of a child from an environment not serving their best interests and placing them in more appropriate surroundings. The Act also recognises the child's right to be heard, facilitating their place at meetings and involvement in the planning of their care. The development of the National Children's Strategy (2000) is arguably as significant as the 1991 Child Care Act (Kilkelly, 2008). The strategy also focuses on protection, provision and participation, highlighting that children will have a voice, greater assessment and research on their needs, and that children will receive quality supports to promote their development.

The Children's Referendum in the Republic of Ireland in 2012 was another significant development with regard to promoting children's rights and advancing the implementation of the UNCRC. The fact that a referendum was required to address children's rights makes explicit the political dimensions. The positive outcome of this referendum led to changes to the Irish Constitution, with the repeal of a former Article, 42.5, and the insertion of a new Article, 42A, sitting between Articles 42 and 43, titled "Children". This Article enshrines the place of children's rights in the Irish Constitution. It recognises children in their own right and promotes the voice of the child whilst also enshrining the "best interest of the child" principle within the Constitution. Formerly, the Irish Constitution recognised children as parts of a family whereas now they will be recognised as individuals with their own rights, and where decisions are made regarding children it is these rights that must matter the most. Formerly, children may have been subject to different treatment depending on the marital status of their parents in situations such as eligibility for adoption. The amendment allows for the adoption of children who have been in care for substantial periods of time where this is in the child's best interests. This is significant as currently there are circa 2,000 children in foster care who formerly could not be adopted, despite the fact that they will not be returning to their birth families (Children's Rights Alliance, 2012). Adoption, and therefore potentially permanence, will now become an option for some of these children, thereby affording them a "second chance" at having a secure and stable family life.

The UNCRC is an example of internationally combined efforts to, on the one hand, protect children from the traditionally understood risks they face, but also to imbue them with certain rights, such as the right to participate responsibly. However, the existence of the UNCRC could be couched very differently. The individualisation of childhood as a generational unit can have unintended negative consequences. Individualisation is a strong feature of neoliberalism where individuals and families can be identified as "problems" in states such as the USA and UK (Freeman, 2000; Hill *et al.*, 2004; Besson, 2005; Wyness, 2009).

> When problems are framed as individual rather than collective, the solution is similarly framed as a matter of individual rather than collective responsibility. (Hawkins *et al.*, 2001:8)

Therefore, by individualising childhood as a generational unit this may exacerbate the vulnerability of children who have already been rendered vulnerable by neoliberalism. As previously noted, the dominant socio-political ideology in place at any given time has a profound impact on people using services.

It is notable that as children's rights have gained prominence so too have the number of young people being incarcerated, as rights become increasingly synonymous with responsibilities. In the United States the number of children being incarcerated annually jumped by 48 per cent between 1993 and 1999 (National Policy Paper, 2000). A 2004 report by the Ann E. Casey Foundation (AECF) identified that there were 600,000 children incarcerated annually (Goldson in Scraton and McCulloch, 2009:89). In 2015 one out of every 28 children has a parent in prison, meaning that "the cycle of poverty and unequal opportunity continues a tragic waste of human potential for generations" (Roder *et al.*, 2015:1).

In the UK throughout the 1990s, the statistics were in many ways worse with an increase of 90 per cent in the numbers of 15 to 17 year old prisoners, a 400 per cent increase in the number of girl prisoners and a 800 per cent increase in the number of child prisoners aged 14 or less (Goldson, 2006; Narco, 2005). At the end of December 2014, there were 981 children incarcerated in the UK. This represents a decline of 203 from the previous year, which evidences a similar decline in youth incarceration since 2009 as in the USA (Ministry of Justice, 2014; Howard League, 2015). These declines in youth incarceration rates are welcomed as positive developments which extend the de-institutionalisation trends in social care. However, rates of youth incarceration in the USA and the UK still remain very high. We must be mindful that care leavers are first and foremost young people and as such their destiny is in part shaped by the opportunities, policies and attitudes that are common to all young people (Stein, 2005b, 2012). We must also be mindful that young people are human beings and not human becomings (James, 2009; Freeman, 2010) who are in need of protection in order that they may develop into productive adults. Whilst overtly benign, as it places value on young people, this actually diminishes them as human beings in their own right. They are not a lesser group of human beings in the making; they share the same human rights as adults which, for those aged under 18, children's rights add to rather than obviate.

Beck (2000) argues that it is a growth of intergenerational conflict linked to employment competition and the greying population, amongst other intergenerational factors, that facilitates the acceptance of such high levels of youth incarceration. Beck also highlights the contradiction that the older generations who demonise young people are in fact dependent on them for pension support through their labour. Intergenerational division has further been exacerbated by the rise in managerial approaches in social services directed to "at risk" children (Ruch, 2005: Ruch *et al.*, 2010; Trevithick, 2010). As previously noted, there has been a move away from the relationship-based, person-centred approaches employed prior to the 1980s. Garside (2009) highlights the UK's contemporary authoritarian approach to the risk of child criminality and various Labour government responses such as the "Youth Crime Action Plan" (2008). The association between risk and labelling is made clear. The rise of child protection services and the risk-averse approaches adopted by social services has further individualised young people and, as Beck highlights, "It is part of the logic of risk to polarize, to exclude and to stigmatize" (Beck, 2010:140).

Beck's theories of risk society may be challenged as all socio-logical theories can be. O'Malley (2008) outlines how the negative perception of risk associated with Beck's risk society is misplaced. Nonetheless, Beck offers a new way to understand intergenera-tional relationships as does the work of others such as Alanen (2009) and Mayall (2009). Indeed, so great has the divide become that young people today can be seen to be at risk of being genera-tionally marginalised, thus adding to the social exclusion burden to which they are already susceptible (Berridge, 2006; Stein, 2012). Through understanding the concept of risk society as one perme-ated by fear and division (Furedi, 2006), as seen in the media ap-proach to youth crime, we can start to look to solutions involving the healing of divisions (Scraton, 2004, 2007).

The potential for what ought to be a force for good for children paradoxically resulting in harm illustrates the complexity which the children's rights agenda presents. This complexity is further exacerbated when we consider the issue of the age of criminal responsibility, which is a major factor in the high rates of youth incarceration highlighted above. Advocates of children's rights lobby for raising the age of criminal responsibility from their cur-rent ages which they consider to be set too low. Goldson (2009), in arguing for the age of criminal responsibility to be raised across the board, points out that other articles and commentaries in the convention, such as Article 4 (1), encourages nations to align the criminal age of responsibility with other age-appropriate respon-sibilities such as marriage, although this would not make much change in many countries. Such arguments have not as yet had ef-fect, and the UNCRC remains permissive by nature, although UN-CRC instruments such as the Riyadh Guidelines (1990) and the Beijing Rules (1985) compel signatory nations to aspire to setting their age of criminal responsibility at "not too low a level" whilst also recognising the role of culture.

In the CRIN (Child Rights Information Network) Review 2009, Lansdown discusses the UNCRC in terms of evolving capacities (UNCRC, Article Five). She identifies its permissive nature in how it provides signatory states with the leg room to apply each article in its own cultural context. Lansdown conceptualises the idea of evolving capacities in emancipatory, developmental and protective terms. The introductory article finishes off with the following appeal:

> There is an urgent need for better understanding of how to promote the cultural change necessary to ensure that children are protected in accordance with their evolving capacities, and that they are respected, whatever the levels of those capacities. (CRIN, 2009:9)

In the rush over recent decades to recognise cultural and individual difference, initially a practice emerging from the works of Carl Rogers, individualised approaches to the care of children have become prevalent. Policies that promote person-centred care are commonplace, and yet in focusing on such practices attention is diverted, inadvertently, away from the social and cultural influences that result in the high levels of youth incarceration in so-called "developed" (minority) nations. This has been addressed somewhat by Davis and Vander Stoep (1997) and Woodhead and Faulkner (2000) in their recognition of social function and personal development as central themes within maturation, and that children's competence is "different" from adults' and not "lesser". They called this "transition to adulthood" and highlighted the complex interplay between, on the one hand, social environments, and on the other hand, the developmental nature of childhood itself. Davis and Vander Stoep make clear that age is not necessarily a delineator of maturity as numerous factors come into play, as do Solberg (1996), Bentley (2005) and Thorne (2008).

Scraton (2004, 2007) has explored the cultural and societal influences on youth crime and justice. He argues, amongst other theories, that person-centred culture, manifest through policies of individualisation with a strong neoliberal economic identity, has contributed, alongside a frenzied media, to the growth of intergenerational and class distinctions and the criminalisation of youth. Scraton (2007) follows the progression of youth criminalisation and demonisation through the development of the Clinton and New Labour Third Way. He describes how the labelling of nonconformist family units and socio-economically deprived youth has resulted in heightened rates of incarceration, as seen in the UK by the Anti-Social Behaviour Order (ASBO), whereby young people are punished for non-criminal behaviours. It is clear that Scraton is influenced by the criminologists Howard Becker and Scandinavian criminologist Nils Christie, who also argue against the understanding of crime as personal or developmental. Becker and Christie suggest that crime does not exist at all, but rather is a socially constructed concept based on moral judgements regarding human actions.

The age of criminal responsibility in the Republic of Ireland is currently set at twelve, although in certain case of serious crimes such as murder, rape, manslaughter or aggravated rape this is reduced to ten. This was raised from age seven by the Criminal Justice Act, 2001. This was a welcome and progressive development but regrettably the Criminal Justice Act, 2006 abolished the long-standing rebuttable presumption of *doli incapax*. *Doli incapax*, translated as "incapable of deceit" with deceit becoming "guilt" for legal reasons, was a presumption in law that a child under a certain age, in the Republic of Ireland 7 to 14, cannot be held legally responsible for their actions and thus could not be criminally charged. This could not be rebutted by evidence, regardless of the nature of the evidence. The abolition of *doli incapax* means that any child aged over 10 can be charged with a criminal offence as they are deemed to comprehend the consequences of their action. The Director of Public Prosecutions must now be notified if a child under 14 is to be charged, but the legal defence of *doli incapx* no longer exists to protect children from criminal charge. The Republic of Ireland, as with England, now has one of the lowest ages of criminal responsibility in Europe (Arthur, 2011).

> The presumption of doli incapax should be re-established, and children who commit offences should be dealt with through a welfare-based approach. The adoption of a welfare approach to child offending, does not imply that the harms caused by youth offending should be tolerated, but means ensuring that all children who are alleged to have offended have access to the range of health and social care

services they require whether they are formally prosecuted or not. (Arthur, 2011:18-19)

Central to the argument for raising the age of criminal responsibility is that young people are not fully responsible for their actions. Yet there is a conflict here with the argument propagated by advocates of children's rights that children are in fact social actors capable to be consulted in deciding on matters which affect their lives (Prout and James, 1997; Mayall, 2000, 2002). This paradox whereby children are portrayed as incompetent, when this is in their best interests, yet competent when also in their best interests, can be best deciphered within the context of evolving capacities as outlined by Lansdown above.

Gordon Jeyes, CEO of the Child and Family Agency (Tusla), makes the point that the age of criminal responsibility should be raised to 18, other than for serious crimes, from a rights and responsibilities perspective:

> If they don't have a full set of rights they shouldn't have the full set of responsibilities. (Jeyes, cited in *Irish Examiner*, 17.2.2014)

Clearly, children's rights present many complexities that require the attention of those supporting children to ensure that policies aimed at enhancing children's well-being achieve their intended goals. Social policy is itself a highly complex field (Kemshall, 2002) and we need to be ever vigilant to prevent policies being subverted by policy-makers with politically motivated agendas.

Set within the complexity of children's rights, the UNCRC may be perceived as a flawed convention without teeth to enforce its articles (Hill *et al.*, 2004; Wyness, 2009). However, frequently, the European Charter of Human Rights (ECHR) and its Courts refer to the UNCRC (Kilkelly, 2001; Lyon, 2007). The ECHR convention refers little to children but does entitle them to the same rights as adults.

Nevertheless, the UNCRC has been the mechanism for much progress in promoting the cause of young people since its inception in 1989 (Mendes *et al.*, 2014). It holds much potential, as outlined by Munro *et al.* (2011:2418):

> The UNCRC may not always have the strength of national or even some regional cross national jurisdictions but it has shown itself to be very effective in promoting the convergence of perceptions and expectations about children as active citizens with rights which should be protected and promoted.

The UNCRC has published *Guidelines for Alternative Care of Children* (2009) and Munro *et al.* (2011) have identified the potential benefits for care leavers contained within these guidelines. Notably, the guidelines identify three important phases of leaving care:

1. Preparation and planning;

2. The transition process from care to aftercare which should include recognition of the child's age, gender, maturity and particular circumstances;

3. Aftercare support which should include ongoing educational and vocational training opportunities and access to social, legal, and professional services and financial support.

In April 2011, the Republic of Ireland published policy on aftercare for the first time. This occured despite the fact that numerous reports had highlighted the inadequate supports available to care leavers over a forty-year period. These commenced with the Kennedy Report in 1970, the Task Force Report on Child Care Services in 1980, the Madonna House Report in 1996, Youth Homeless Strategy in 2001 and the Ryan Commission's Report in 2009. Notably, the UNCRC's recommendation to the Republic of Ireland in 2006 was to "strengthen its efforts to ensure and provide for follow up and aftercare to young people leaving care centres" (UNCRC, 2006).

Section 1.3 of the new policy acknowledges that due to the discretionary nature of the legislation service provision has been fragmentary. The legislation in question is Section 45 of the Child Care Act 1991:45(1):

Where a child leaves the care of a health board, the board *may*, in accordance with subsection (2), assist him for so long as the board is satisfied as to his need for assistance and, subject to paragraph (b), he has not attained the age of 21 years.

The word "may" gives rise to the discretion referred to by the policy, as this affords Tusla the authority to provide a service should it choose to do so.

Gilligan (2008) speaks briefly of the Republic of Ireland's leaving care services, describing them as neglected and noting a dearth of general data on aftercare in the Republic of Ireland, a point also highlighted by Stein *et al.* (2000), Stein (2008) and Carr (2014).

The new policy document (p. 4) describes aftercare as:

A process of preparation for leaving care, follow up and support in moving towards independence for all those young people who are eligible. It is a through care process, in consultation with the young person, beginning from reception into care and including comprehensive assessments, care plans and reviews.

This definition sets an outline to the purpose and stages of aftercare, but infers that not all care leavers are entitled. Notwithstanding the pioneering nature of the document, it appears to share an exclusionary characteristic facilitated by the Child Care Act 1991 itself. The new policy document cites Section 45 of the Act as its legislative base, thereby perpetuating the flaw which caused service provision to be fragmented.

The word "may" could in theory include or exclude anyone. Children in the juvenile justice system, children in care less than one year (here all new admission into care aged over 17 would be ineligible) or who are not officially in care but are out of home and children who do not have an appointed social worker are excluded from the policy (IASCW, 2013).

A number of inspections carried out in 2013 identified that not all young people in foster care had an allocated social worker (HIQA, 2013a, 2013b, 2013c). For example, in (2013) one area (Dublin South/Dun Laoghaire), just 62 per cent of children in foster care had an allocated social worker. (HIQA cited in Carr, 2014:93)

Paradoxically, this potentially excluding policy grants the rights of Tusla to offer care but denies rights and agency to young people, akin to the UNCRC which has been critiqued as granting rights to autonomous parents more so than children (Freeman, 2010:6).

With regard to comprehensive assessments and care plans identified in the policy description it is highly relevant that in October 2014 only 91.8 per cent of children in care had an allocated social worker, and only 87.4 per cent had a written care plan (Tusla, 2014f). Furthermore, in some regions the figure was as low as 74 per cent for children in foster care, thus illustrating both the improbability that the cited comprehensive assessments and care plans will be in place for all care leavers, and the continuance of regional variation with regard to the quality of service provision. This acknowledged regional variation was one of the driving factors behind the proposed Aftercare Bill (2014) and these statistics highlight an inherent flaw in the propose Bill:

· ·

Given that written care plans have been compulsorily mandated under Article 23 of the Child Care Regulations 1995 for children in care for many years, yet 100 per cent compliance never achieved, just as 100 per cent compliance with statutory requirement for each child in care to have an allocated social worker has never being achieved, the likelihood of all care leavers having an aftercare plan prior to leaving care is, at best low, but most likely nil. Therefore, gaps will remain and it is through these gaps that often the most needy young people fall.

· ·

Carr (2014) locates the significance of the new policy within the context of aftercare provision and makes the point that "beyond the development of a national policy, which aims to standardise service provision nationally, leaving and aftercare provision in the Republic remains discretionary, ad hoc, and inadequate" (2014:88).

The policy appears to poorly mimic the progressive UK Children (Leaving Care) Act (Northern Ireland) 2002. The UK policy sets out a detailed framework that is structured, clear and definitive, making aftercare a statutory entitlement, establishing five-year pathway plans with regular review, ring-fenced funding and proactive measures to reach out to non-engagers. This detail is not to be found in the new Irish policy.

The policy's opening statement (1.3) claims that there has been much research in the Republic of Ireland on aftercare which has informed the document. As already noted by Stein and Gilligan, however, there is in fact very little research available. Nor does the policy refer to consulting with young people during drafting, a cause of grave concern to those working on behalf of care leavers:

> Barnardos is disappointed at the lack of consultation in drafting the proposed policy and framework.... Similarly, the absence of engaging with young people leaving the care system in the drafting of this policy is also significant. (Barnardos, 2010b)

A further point regarding the listed legislations and publications that have informed the new policy must be made. The UNCRC is not mentioned, nor is the UN *Guidelines on Alternative Care* or the ECHR. This, despite the fact that the policy recognises that work on preparation for leaving care ideally commences on entry into care, and that preparation must commence prior to leaving care, with needs assessment completed ideally at age 16. Thus in both instances the policy addresses those aged under 18 which then requires referencing this policy to the UNCRC. The Roscommon and Ryan reports, which both call for adherence to the UNCRC, are cited. In claiming to accord with both reports the authors of the policy may unknowingly be misstating the truth. The fact that neither the UNCRC nor the ECHR is mentioned amongst other legislative considerations is significant from a children's rights perspective.

As noted previously, all policies can be located within the prevailing socio-political ideology in place at the time (Foucault, 1977; Adams, 1998; Howe, 1997, 1998; Gregory and Holloway,

2005). Considered from this perspective, the National Leaving and Aftercare Policy perpetuates the social injustice so evident today where the gap between the haves and the have-nots is ever widening. Currently, at a minimum, 40 per cent of care leavers do not participate in work, education or training, and thus are not the focus of the current National Leaving and Aftercare Policy, the focus of which the proposed Aftercare Bill (2014) will not change. This Bill will be examined in further detail in Section Six. What this means is that, in reality, the Republic of Ireland has a two-tiered aftercare service with winners and losers analogous to the disaggregating and shadow-making social policy in evidence.

National Leaving and Aftercare Policy (2011) and the UNCRC

We shall next consider the National Policy for Leaving and Aftercare Services (2011) from a children's rights perspective employing the UNCRC as an evaluation framework. Such a methodology has recently been used in the National Policy Framework for Children and Young People 2014-2020 in the Republic of Ireland.

The definition of childhood within specified age parameters is a critical factor when considering the transition to adulthood. Article one of the UNCRC defines what is meant by a child, but there are arguments that this definition is insufficient. Evidence emerging from a new sociology of childhood calls for the traditional age defined boundaries to be re-addressed (Foley, 1998; Sinclair, 2004; Faulkner 2009). A theme in this revisionist front has been how adults perceive and engage with children, and particularly how capacity must be included in discussion and planning.

Mayall (2000) highlights a universal concept infused within the UNCRC, one in which childhood is on a particular developmental "trajectory". Traditional views of childhood like Piaget's stages of development are being challenged. Arnett's concept of emerging adulthood calls for a new approach to the end of childhood with a realisation that children are "emerging" adults rather than actual adults at eighteen (Tanner and Arnett, 2009). Similarly, Bentley (2005) in questioning the UNCRC's concepts of childhood, reveals the relativity of the concept, stating that the UNCRC assumes children to be passive objects without responsibility. Veerman (2010) highlights brain scan evidence that the end of childhood is only complete at the age of 24 when the frontal lobe is fully formed. Veerman also cites Dutch psychiatrists, psychologists and biologists who question the wisdom of using age to understand childhood. In particular, Veerman cites the argument of Doreleijers (2009) that young people accused of crimes should be brought before a juvenile court as they are still emerging from childhood, their irresponsible behaviour itself proof they are not fully developed adults. Blakemore and Choundhury (2006) and Steinberg (2007) further expand on the greater tendency for risk-taking and "over-emotionality" evidenced in adolescents. Although neuroscience has its critiques within childhood studies, with some crying "biological determinism or reductionism" (Ames, 2010), when coupled with evolving capacity approaches to children's rights (Landsdown, 2003) it does highlight the case for reviewing the age definitions of childhood. Additionally, legal precedents, such as *Roper v. Simmons* (2005) in the USA where it was decided that it is unconstitutional for a juvenile to receive the death penalty for reasons of "comparative immaturity", unite the bio-medical, psychosocial, legal and children's rights fields in making this case. This concept has been recognised by the UN through the Beijing Rules (1985) section 2.2 which states:

> This makes for a wide variety of ages coming under the definition of "juvenile", ranging from 7 years to 18 years or above.

The UNCRC has been ratified by most States, with the notable exception of the USA and South Sudan, Somalia having ratified the Convention on 20 January 2015 and South Sudan currently working towards ratification. However, it is certainly not universal in how those rights are to be understood. The rights it affords children are tempered by the concept of "evolving capacities" (Lansdown, 2009) which, as we have seen, in itself is invariably linked to the concept of maturity. As previously noted, developmental psychology focuses more on mechanisms that cause human development than on chronological age (Keenan and Evans, 2009). In the end, of course, the UNCRC fails to make any definite directives and allows for national cultural differences to be the final arbitrator in deciding when a child is responsible, criminally and otherwise:

> For the purpose of the present convention, a child means every human being below the age of 18 years unless, under the law applicable to the child, majority is attained earlier. (UNCRC, Article 1, 1989)

The UNCRC does recognise the definition of childhood as set out in Article 1 as a matter of great significance and consequently this is one of eight areas where states are obliged to submit reports on progress under the Convention's reporting mechanism (UNCRC/C/5/2001).

Further doubt is thrown on the current definitions by Schaffner (2002) who illustrates the many paradoxes that exist when considering age and adulthood, and Corsaro who makes the point that:

> Defining the boundaries of childhood ... is a difficult task. Childhood is a social construction that is clearly related to, but not determined by, physical maturation, cultural beliefs about age, and institutional age grading. (2005:191)

The fact remains, however, that the UNCRC sets the boundary at 18. It must be noted that the National Policy Framework for Children and Young People 2014-2020 identifies children as those aged up to 18 and young people as those aged between 18 and 24. The fact that this policy addresses both cohorts within the one framework is commendable and reflects well on those who developed it. Unfortunately, the National Leaving and Aftercare Policy (2011) does not do likewise.

Archard recommends that:

> In fact we should drop the word "age". For what matters is not so much age as associated maturity. (Archard, 1993:65)

The issue of age is also addressed in Article 12 where point 12.1 addresses children's views having a weight proportionate to their age and maturity.

The new aftercare policy reflects the sudden move into adulthood, what Stein (2004:53) refers to as the "compressed and ac-

196

celerated" transitions, through a change in primary role, with the social worker being replaced by the aftercare worker. The charter is also reflected in the aftercare policy by its general recognition of the needs of children leaving care.

In 2006 the UN Committee adopted recommendations following a day of discussion themed "The right of the child to be heard" recognising the fundamental changes Article 12 will bring, stating it "implies in the long term, changes in political, social, institutional and cultural structures"(UNCRC, 2006).

The Committee has been clear too that the right to be heard must extend to children as a collective. In Committee Recommendations to Chile (CRC/C/15/Add.173, para. 29), Morocco (CRC/C/15/Add.211, para.30) and India 9 (CRC/15/Add.228, para. 36) they referred to the seriousness with which the respective governments considered the opinions emerging from children's parliaments, councils and other such bodies (UNICEF, 2007:150).

How and to what extent children's voices are heard, both individually and collectively, has been an area of substantial exploration over the last 20 years (Sinclair, 2004; Faulkner, 2009). Debates centre around the capacity of children to understand situations in which their voice should be heard (Opie and Opie, 1969; Prout and James, 1997; Woodhead and Faulkner, 2000). Other areas of debate include what mechanisms are best suited, on a collective level, to deliver children's voices (Kilkelly, 2008). Pinkerton (2004) highlights Article 12 as "perhaps the most challenging aspect of the global agenda for children and young people set by the Convention" (Pinkerton, 2004:119).

It is far from clear that such discussions have occurred when drafting the aftercare policy or are reflected in prescribed procedures. Section 1.2 of the policy states, "This policy seeks to be informed by the young people and their carers" (HSE, 2011:4). There is no information relating to methodology or data collection available. Barnardos (2010) have been particularly critical of this.

A final comment on how the voice of the child is heard within the aftercare process. The language used refers to procedures such as including the child in an "assessment in order to inform the care plan". The purpose of the assessment is vague. Equally, the role of the aftercare worker according to the policy is to advocate on behalf of the child. It is important to note that all of the children concerned will be 16 years or over, considered able by many, but their voice is not heard directly.

As we have seen child development and the concept of evolving capacity are central to the UNCRC and also highly relevant to the National Leaving and Aftercare Policy (2011). Article 6 addresses survival, development and the inherent right to life. However, by failing to underpin what the measure of "maximum extent possible" is or define "development", this article permits nations to interpret the text unilaterally. The Committee has again added substance to the text but can only do so in an advisory capacity. They recognised a purpose of childhood as development towards adulthood and suggest "development" to have holistic connotations grounded in the child's right to health (Art. 24), an adequate standard of living (Art. 27), education (Art. 28), and leisure and play (Arts. 29 and 31) (UNICEF, 2007).

The new aftercare policy refers to developmental areas of the young person's life such as social skills and resilience. However, there is no detail on how exactly this is to be manifested into reality.

Children being excluded by the new aftercare policy infringes the requirements of Article 6. In commenting on the case of an Ombudsman investigation into the death of a child in care, Kilkelly (2011) links the investigation findings of HSE failings to Article 6 in that the child was denied the right to "life, survival and development". As the new policy recognises the increased adversities faced by children leaving care, the requirement on states to ensure to the "maximum extent possible" their survival and development is not being met (Barnardos, 2010; Children's Rights Alliance, 2010). It reflects poorly on the HSE that they stated that 23 children had died in care and aftercare over a 10-year period, when we now know that 196 died in that period and 27 in the past year alone (Barnardos, 2010).

This lack of clarity in data collection breaches Article 6 and as of March 2015 we still have no accurate national figure for children leaving care annually. The UNCRC raised this matter with the Republic of Ireland (CRC/C/SR.1182). The European Court of

Human Rights ruled in the case of *Edwards v State (UK)* (2002) that a State must investigate deaths not only where its agents are directly responsible for deaths but also where the State is indirectly responsible by failing to discharge its duties.

The guiding principle for decision making is that they be in the young person's "best interest", ideally with the input of the young person as per Article 12. This is laid out in Article 3 which many consider to be one of the most important of the Convention, with many other articles relating to it (Articles, 9, 18, 20, 21, and 37). This article has raised much discussion, except by the Committee themselves (Freeman, 2007). A serious problem arises as a result of the failure by the UNCRC to discuss the "best interest" of the child. This is reflected in common usage of the term by many nations who themselves have failed to define "best interest".

Although the UNCRC fails in defining "best interests" they may be inferred through other articles including the right to life, protection from violence, education, etc. Oddly, the Committee has commonly referred to the "best interest principle" when commenting on areas of children's welfare and care (UNICEF, 2007:39).

Article 3 recommends that the interest of the child be "a primary consideration". Freeman (2007) comments on the dilution of the Declaration of the Rights of the Child (1959), which provided that the best interests be of paramount consideration This dilution in effect allows some to escape their responsibilities to children, permitting the prioritisation of agendas other than the children's rights agenda. Freeman (2007) provides plenty of examples where Article 3 fails, ranging from female genital mutilation to early marriage to corporal punishment, not to mention the right to be heard. All of these have conflicted with cultural interests. The wording of Article 3 fails to address this when it declares the best interests of the child to be only "a primary consideration".

The new Irish aftercare policy, like the UNCRC article, fails to offer clarity. In excluding certain groups of children, the new leaving care policy arguably fails to take their best interests into consideration. In a complaint made against the HSE for failing to provide for a mother and baby in the care of the state, Kilkelly (2011) commented that the HSE failed to act in the best interests of the mother and child, infringing Article 3 in that they did not make primary the best interests of the child, did not establish a cohesive policy and had not established standards.

As Article 2 of the UNCRC establishes that the rights held within a state's jurisdiction are for all children without discrimination, those excluded by the aftercare policy must also have their best interests taken into account as a primary consideration. In failing to establish procedures for particular groups of children whose best interests are clearly not being met, the new Irish aftercare policy infringes on all of the paragraphs of Article 3.

Article 2 does address non-discrimination however it does not define discrimination, nor has the committee issued commentary on the article specifically. It has said, however:

> This non-discrimination obligation requires states actively to identify individual children and groups of children the recognition and realisation of whose rights may demand special measures.... (UNICEF, 2007:18)

Such a recommendation means that Article 2 goes beyond just protecting the named victim groups of discrimination. For example, currently children leaving care who are not in care over twelve months, who are not officially in care but out of home, and many children within the juvenile justice system are excluded. Whether each of these groups of children fit appropriately into the "other status" grouping as defined within the UNCRC remains to be seen.

Kilkelly (2011) cites a case presented to the Children's Ombudsman regarding the provision of school transport to a group of school children, referring to Article 2 highlighting the right to protection from discrimination on any grounds. In this case it was the children's geographical location that was the discriminating factor. This finding reflects the imaginative ways in which the "other status" phrase can be interpreted. For named groups of children excluded in the new policy, the factors of their discrimination differ but do not detract from their rights to leaving care services.

Preparation for leaving care has been identified in this book as paramount to the task of promoting better outcomes for care leavers. Article 40 is related to the new aftercare policy in the context of Articles 1 and 4. Preparation for leaving care and aftercare is precluded from young people incarcerated within the juvenile justice system. Kilkelly (2001) refers to an ECHR case in which a child was allegedly denied his right to a fair trial. The judge noted the charter's preamble promising assistance in assuming their responsibilities within the community, and Article 40 requiring states to "establish procedures and institutions applicable to children alleged as, accused of or recognised as having infringed the law" (Kilkelly, 2001:320). Children leaving care have needs that set them apart from ones who have grown up in their own families, as has been well established (Wade, 2003). All those within the juvenile justice system are entitled to have those needs met. Article 40 takes into account "the child's age and the desirability of promoting the child's reintegration and the child assuming a constructive role in society".

Considering paragraph 4, that children should be treated within the juvenile justice system "in a manner appropriate to their wellbeing", a failure to include many children within the juvenile justice system infringes their rights under Article 40.

Critical for children in care and aftercare is their right to protection from harm and maltreatment, and appropriate alternative placement in the event that out of home care is required. These rights are stipulated in Articles 19 and 20 of the Convention. The implementation handbook for the CRC makes a direct link between Articles 6 and Article 19 (UNICEF, 2007:249). The Article's emphasis on preventative measures necessary on the parts of governments was re-iterated in a 2006 United Nations report titled *Report of the Independent Expert for the United Nations Study on Violence Against Children* (UNICEF, 2006). In its recommendations the report rests responsibility firmly with the state and requests that:

> States develop a multi faceted and systematic framework
> to respond to violence against children which is integrated
> into national planning processes. (UNICEF, 2007:251)

The same report recognised that children in care, particularly children in residential care settings, are more prone to violence of varying natures. To not adequately prepare young people for leaving care, followed with provision of aftercare services, arguably infringes the rights of certain groups of children under Article 19.

Kilkelly (2001) cites the employment of Article 19 by the ECHR in the case of *Z and Others v. UK* (1999), in which it was claimed that the state failed to adequately protect children from abuse and neglect by their parents. It was found that the state did indeed breach its obligations under Article 3 of the ECHR, to protect the children from abuse and neglect, even though they were aware of it. Similarly, it could be argued that the state is well aware of the increased dangers to children leaving care, yet protection is not guaranteed to every child within the new aftercare policy.

There is a clear emphasis in Committee commentary on Article 20 on the removal of a child only as a last resort, prioritisation of family reunion and a tier system of care services. The "individualisation" of care has also been a strong theme (Kemshall, 2002). The new policy refers to individualised care plans to "entitled" children but doesn't reflect "creative solutions". A system whereby children in alternative care are left unprepared when they enter official adulthood is one that is failing its obligations. In its recommendations to Lithuania, the Committee made clear nations must provide "targeted services" to children who will soon become adults.

The new aftercare policy fails to provide detail of the "targeted" services available, and does not guarantee the "special protection and assistance" to all children leaving care. Nor does the policy require "due regard for continuity of care" as stipulated in paragraph 4 of Article 20. However, enforcing this Article would be difficult. There is no corresponding ECHR legislation and, as noted by the UNCRC in 2002, the Republic of Ireland, despite UNCRC recommendation in 1999, has failed to incorporate or reflect the Covenant in domestic legislation (UNCRC, 2002).

Chapter 8

Social Policy

Capitalism, as noted previously, played a central role in defining childhood after the industrial revolution. Poorly regulated, however, globalised capitalism, with its all-powerful markets, the very "market forces (that) were proposed to substitute for state regulation" (Evetts, 2011:16), has redefined childhood, but not in a benign way. Where once there were secure pathways to adulthood and independence, now there is risk and insecurity as the markets no longer value young workers. Post-modern capitalism, as posited by Beck, has heralded a sweeping process of change with the individualisation of experience and the changing logic of risk distribution (Mythen, 2004). In this process neoliberal policies of the dominant political regimes appear to have been designed to adopt Roman philosophies of divide and conquer, thus enabling neoliberalism to become the dominant force within developed states in recent decades.

Keith identified the importance of leisure and play in his time within the residential centre. This was considered within the chapter on attachment and referenced again with regard to social pedagogy, whilst within the chapter on focal theory the significance of leisure and play to human development was addressed. Gilligan (2008a) has highlighted the resilience development potential of recreational activities for children in care. Additionally, it must be noted that Article 6 of the UNCRC, which addresses the right to survival and development, has been expanded on by the CRC, as we saw earlier:

They recognised a purpose of childhood as development towards adulthood and suggest "development" to have holistic connotations grounded in the child's right to health (Art. 24), an adequate standard of living (Art. 27), education (Art. 28), and leisure and play (Arts. 29 and 31). (UNICEF 2007:286)

The National Policy Framework for Children and Young People 2014-2012, which recognises young people as being aged 18 to 24, states that the Government recognises:

• Play is important for all ages.

• Play, sports and recreation are an immensely important part of the lives of children and young people, and are highly valued by them." (DCYA, 2014b:56)

These factors pose two questions:

. . . .

1) Does the current perception of youth influence the lack of value attached to play for adolescents in care, as it may be perceived as a luxury and not conducive to promoting responsibility, or worse, in some cases rewarding the undeserving?

2) We now know of the critical importance of play for human development from the works of, amongst others, Russell (2012) and Sutton-Smith (1997), and specifically with regard to care leavers (Hollingworth, 2012). Given the importance attached to play and leisure within the UNCRC, and the recognition afforded to its critical role for children and those aged up to 25 years of age by the National Policy Framework for Children and Young People 2014-2020, why is there no reference to play or leisure within the National Policy for Leaving and Aftercare 2011?

. . . .

As a species humans tend towards the social and are not the unconnected, self-managing individuals, or independent consumers, rampant neoliberalism would have us be (Turner, 1997). We are interdependent and function best when connected with others. We must reclaim our sense of community within our profession where individuals are valued for their inalienable humanness and market individualism is challenged for its "cancerous effects on community life" (Tam, 1998:3).

Mathew Taylor, writing within a Joseph Rowntree Foundation report on Contemporary Social Evils, states:

> The greatest (social) evil is society's retreat in the face of rampant individualism. (2006:215)

In order to value children in care we must also value those working with children in care. This point was made by the Centre for Excellence in Child and Family Welfare (2006). They cite Anglin who advocates for an upgrade in the status of residential care:

> ... we owe it to children – they need to know they are cared for by someone who is respected... Good care is not produced by tools – it's provided by people and investing in carers is investing in the heart and soul of children. (Anglin, cited in Hillan, 2005:51)

Accepting these findings regarding society's retreat in the face of rampant individualisation, could it be that the one of the major flaws of the former HSE Child and Family Services was that its workers were also reduced to individuality within a mammoth hierarchical organisation, the largest employer in the state? Workers, as a protective strategy, may have adopted the view that they were only one person and could not singlehandedly change such a large organisation, one itself in a constant state of change. Few would deny that, as a system, Children and Family Services within the HSE, was a classic example of "the whole being less than the sum of the parts".

Gillian Ruch has addressed from a psychodynamic perspective the anxiety inherent in social work, together with the emotional impact on workers, teams and managers when these professionals are not appropriately supported:

> ... the potential for unacknowledged emotional and interpersonal dynamics to encourage basic assumption group

behaviours that impede a team's capacity to effectively address its primary task. In so doing, the primary task – safeguarding and promoting the welfare of adolescents – is distorted into the phenomenal task that serves the survival needs of the team rather than the interests of the service users with whom they work. (Ruch, 2012:1324)

Carr locates the "inadequacy" of aftercare provision in the Republic of Ireland, partly within a wider historical and political context where care leavers are perceived as a "'threat' to social order" (2014:99). Similarly, Holohan (2011:309) found that:

While today victims of child abuse are viewed with sympathy and concern, anxiety about the threat to the social order which troubled and troublesome young people represent continues to permeate the responses of agents of the State and wider society to children in care. In their examination of child sexual abuse in residential institutions in the United Kingdom, Colton, Vanstone and Walby argue that this "ambivalence is further fuelled by the social class background of these young people and ... by factors such as racism and negative attitudes towards disability".

In a similar vein, Scraton (2004, 2007) and Devlin (2005) illuminate how young people, and we must remember care leavers are first and foremost young people, have been reframed as "problems" rather than "victims" of society. Carr (*ibid*) identifies that care leavers are "invisible from view" in the Republic of Ireland.

Minister Fitzgerald voiced a similar opinion in 2013 whilst also acknowledging the absence of data relating to children in care and aftercare:

Children in care were hidden. They were out of public sight and there was not enough information on them. (Dáil Debates, 2013, Topical Debate, Children in Care)

The reframing of the perception of young people has been well researched and documented:

> Young people who are seriously troubled and may have come to be regarded as troublesome. (Bullock *et al.*, 2006:14)

Shannon and Gibbons (2012:xvii) support Carr's position of inadequacy of aftercare provision in the Republic of Ireland:

> In some cases no aftercare at all was provided to young persons who left the care of the HSE. This is a very serious cause for concern. In other cases aftercare was offered but solely at the option of the young person. Such an abdication of duty on the part of the HSE is unacceptable, and fails to properly meet the welfare need of these vulnerable young people.

Shannon and Gibbons (*ibid*) highlight an area of very real cause for concern with regard to provision of aftercare support whereby the "offer" of assistance can be seen as sufficient evidence of intent to provide the service, and the "voluntary" nature of the service used to support such practice. There are many reasons why a care leaver might refuse a service on leaving care. For example, they may have had fractious relations with the social work department or poor experience of being in care, or an unrealistic expectation of what living independently actually entails. There are many ways to make an offer and the aftercare service, which is still located within social work departments in many counties, needs to employ creative and less conditional methodologies to engage with such vulnerable care leavers.

Carr (*ibid*) also identifies the impact of cultural attitudes (perception) in shaping social policy. We have seen that neoliberalism reframed the "undeserving", as defined by the Poor Laws, to the "irresponsible". Consequently, the perception of care leavers as problems and irresponsible can be seen to be a powerful factor in perpetuating the exclusionary practices currently associated with leaving care and aftercare. This exclusionary aspect of the national policy can then be located within the wider socio-political landscape. Within this context the social justice dimensions are rendered manifest and therefore the imperative to implement a rights-based aftercare service as advocated within this book is equally made manifest. In recent times, the issue of social justice for care leavers has been made by researchers within a global context with a special issue of *Australian Social Work: Young People Transitioning from Out-of-home Care: An Issue of Social Justice* (2014, 67, 1) being devoted to this topic. In the Guest Editorial of this special edition Mendes, Pinkerton and Munro state:

> Services and supports need to be based on strong legislative mandate and sufficiently detailed policy and procedures. (2004:1)

There is, however, some cause for optimism in 2015. There has been significant progress made in aftercare provision in recent years, albeit slowly and with notable regional variation in availability and quality. The following table, comprised of information provided in response to Dáil questions (Written Answers 32587/13) by Minister Fitzgerald, illustrates the improvement in provision of aftercare support services for 18 to 21-year-olds in the period 2006 to 2014, although the fluxuations between 2007 to 2010, and again in 2012, are curious.

2013	1,427
2012	1,053 (June)
2011	1,213
2010	1,046
2009	847
2008	979
2007	1,051
2006	810

Table 10: *The Number of Care Leavers in Receipt of an Aftercare Service over the Period 2006-2014.*

However, this progress is constrained in its effectiveness by the inherent inequity of service provision. Only a fully developed policy coupled with rights-based legislation will effectively address this.

As previously noted, a further point in relation to the efficacy of aftercare services and the new policy is the association between preparation before leaving care and the ability to "cope" when in aftercare (Dixon and Stein, 2005). From this it can be seen that preparation is key to success, as it is in many situations, and therefore preparation for leaving care will certainly have a major bearing on achieving the elusive "positive outcomes". Ursula Kilkelly highlights a serious deficiency in this regard:

> The Child Care Act 1991 makes provision for a leaving care plan to be prepared for children in care (beginning at age 16), but there is no statutory requirement on the HSE to prepare children for leaving care. (Kilkelly, 2008:340)

. . . .

It has long been my observation, based on my practice experience, that in the absence of a National Standard for Leaving Care assumption plays a harmful role in preparation of young people for leaving care. Each individual service provider may, or may not, undertake this task as they best see fit. For those who do, workers may assume that a young person possesses knowledge that in fact they do not. Just as with developmental delays caused by trauma (van der Kolk, 2005), there may be gaps in their knowledge base. Also, young people may feel too embarrassed to ask adults or their peers questions about what they assume is common knowledge. To reveal this ignorance might show vulnerability. This assumption and ignorance can then be the cause of serious harm to ill-prepared care leavers when they leave care and no longer have the facility to make mistakes or be afforded second chances.

. . . .

For social policies to be empowering, equitable and effective they need to be based on firm foundations of social justice and be adequately funded. Services not so underpinned will always posses inherent flaw and never truly achieve their intended purpose. Consequently, there are major weaknesses and gaps in this policy, as we have seen, with perhaps its greatest flaw being one it shares with much policy for children, namely, incomplete implementation resulting in the chasm between policy and practice. Doyle *et al.* (2012) reviewed relevant guidelines relating to leaving care and aftercare since the Kennedy Report (1970) and made the following finding:

> Thus, many of the existing published guidelines on aftercare provision in Ireland bear the hallmarks of international best practice in the field. Significantly, however, policy and practice differ both within and between HSE regions. In any case, the nature and scope of aftercare provision is contingent on the allocation of resources within individual Health Service Executive regions. (2012:213)

The Republic of Ireland has had several statutory inquiries into child abuse cases since the 1990s, and although their findings may not have been fully implemented they have had an impact on practice, a point made by Burns and MacCarthy.

> Depending on when one studied to become a professional in child care and protection, one's training and practice was influenced by which post-inquiry era you studied in: for example, post-Kilkenny (McGuiness, 1993), post-Kelly-Fitzgerald (Western Health Board, 1996), post-Ferns (Murphy, Buckley and Joyce, 2005) or post-Ryan (Ryan 2009). (2012:26)

The National Policy for Leaving and Aftercare (2011), despite its significant flaws, can be seen as a positive development for care leavers in the absence of any previous policy. However, in the interests of balance, a consideration of wider social policies is necessary for an understanding of social policy as it impacts young people.

Two examples which warrant consideration are the aforementioned Ryan Report (2009) and the National Policy Framework for Children and Young People 2014-2020: Better Outcomes Brighter Futures.

The Report of the Commission to Inquire into Child Abuse (2009), better known as the Ryan Report, is a seminal publication. This inquiry was the largest ever investigation into child abuse in the Republic of Ireland. The findings deeply shocked and galvanised public opinion as to the plight of vulnerable children and the deficiencies of the state in caring for these children. The magnitude of its impact can be measured in terms of its unifying effect, the changes it initiated and the fact that, although not all its recommendations have been implemented, it is still influential in shaping children's services in 2015. Its legacy is having far-reaching beneficial impact for vulnerable children.

In response to the Ryan Report the government issued a 99 point Implementation Plan in 2009. Some of the actions that can be directly attributed to this report have been:

- The establishment in 2011 of the dedicated Department and Minister for Children and Youth Affairs (DCYA);

- The establishment and launch in 2014 of Tusla;

- The inspection of social work, fostering and residential children's services by the independent agency HIQA;

- The Children's Referendum, 2012;

- The employment of extra social workers and aftercare workers;

- The Implementation of Children First on a statutory basis which will be facilitated by the Children First Bill 2014;

- Closure of hostel accommodation service for Unaccompanied Minors seeking asylum.

There are still recommendations to be fully implemented, not the least being the recommendation regarding aftercare services (Implementation Plan, Recommendation 16):

> ... aftercare services should be provided to give young adults a support structure they can rely on. In a similar way to families, childcare services should continue contact with young people after they have left care as minors...the provision of aftercare by the HSE should form an integral

part of care delivery for children who have been in the care
of the state....In particular, and in common with all young
people, care leavers need the type of flexible support provided by families to young people exploring independence.
(DoHC, 2009:47-48)

However, it must be acknowledged that the Ryan Report
undoubtedly focussed attention on and brought much improvement to services. Let us hope that it does not take the 37 years it
took for the Kennedy Report to be fully implemented:

> ... it was not until 2007 that the policy recommendations
> articulated in a series of reports and other documents, par-
> ticularly the Kennedy Report and the Task Force on Child
> Care Services, were by and large fully implemented (Com-
> mission's Report, Volume IV, p. 423). (DoHC, 2009:3)

The National Policy Framework for Children and Young People 2014-2020 is the first overarching national policy framework
for young people (aged up to 24 years). It is a visionary policy
framework laying out a comprehensive and joined up strategy for
promoting the well-being of all children in the Republic of Ireland.
It recognises that almost all policy areas have a direct or indirect
effect on young people's lives and has a stated purpose of coordi-
nating policy across Government to promote better outcomes.

The policy incorporates robust implementation and evaluation
mechanisms within an integrated approach and undertakes to:

1. Align Government commitments to children and young peo-
    ple against the five national outcomes;

2. Identify six areas that have the potential to improve outcomes
    and transform the effectiveness of existing policies, services
    and resources in achieving these national outcomes;

3. Commit to measuring progress across the outcomes, with
    some key indicators selected to benchmark progress on key
    policy areas;

4. Establish new cross-Government structures to support imple-
    mentation and monitoring of the Framework and, as a result,

realise improved coordination of policies and services for young people. These structures provide a fora for external advice and oversight from experts in the field and from children and young people themselves.

It measures better outcomes within five domains and identifies six transformational goals for achieving these outcomes. The outcomes are:

1. Activity and Health
2. Achievement in All Areas of Learning and Development
3. Safe and Protected from Harm
4. Economic Security and Opportunity
5. Connected, Respected and Contributing.

The transformational goals are:

1. Support Parents
2. Earlier Intervention and Prevention
3. Listen to and Involve Children and Young People
4. Ensure Quality Services
5. Strengthen Transition
6. Cross-Government and Interagency Collaboration and Cooperation.

This policy framework addresses many critical issues affecting young people. For example, it sets out to tackle childhood obesity, food poverty and to lift over 70,000 children out of poverty by 2020. Additionally, it commits to services for child victims and aims to reduce the harm often caused by court proceedings. For children in care and those "at risk" this policy represents a significant development in addressing their needs and can be seen to build on the work of the Ryan Report (2009) in this regard. It also promotes the integration of the UNCRC throughout the policy framework. All six of its Transformational Goals are highly relevant to children in care and those deemed "at risk", and its full implementation would mean that the needs of these young people will be met with far more efficacy and equality than ever before.

The high incidence of targeting the needs of children in care, those "at risk" and those transitioning within care and leaving care is notable with this policy. As previously highlighted, the fact that this policy addresses young people aged up to 25 is also commendable. The Government commits to 69 actions to achieve transformational goals. Amongst those of particular significance are:

> **G7.** Provide and commission both universal and targeted evidence-informed parenting supports and ensure early identification of "at risk" children and families to strengthen families and reduce the incidences of children coming into, and remaining in, care.

> **G19.** Facilitate children and young people in care to have meaningful participation in their care planning and decision-making, including through training and support of the professionals.

> **G37.** Ensure all young people leaving care, detention or residential disability settings are adequately prepared and supported to negotiate the system and transition to stable independent living, further education, training or employment through the development and implementation of a quality aftercare plan and the development of protocols in relation to accessing housing, education and training (DCYA, Tusla, DH, HSE, DECLG). (DCYA, 2014)

However, it must be noted that despite a comprehensive listing of policy relevant to supporting each stated goal, there is no reference to the National Policy for Leaving and Aftercare (2011). Whether this is a poor reflection on those responsible for the National Policy Framework for Children and Young People 2014-2020 or the National Policy for Leaving and Aftercare (2011) is an interesting question.

By addressing many of the flaws indentified with previous policies, namely implementation, evaluation and accountability, the potential for full implementation of this policy is enhanced over previous policies targeted at this area. In this regard, this policy can be seen to be learning the lesson of the past, as advocated within the Ryan Report (2009).

Summary

The leaving care and aftercare policy under scrutiny is pioneering in the absence of any prior policy. In assessing how it fits with the UNCRC a number of themes have emerged.

1. The drafting of the aftercare policy reflects many of the criticisms laid against the UNCRC, notably its permissive and vague nature and a lack of consultation with young people during drafting.

2. It has been shown that the traditional trajectory of ageing employed by the UNCRC is insufficient. In precluding young adults over the age of 18 from the rights inherent within the UNCRC, it is possible that many young people with child-related needs may be excluded. Again, Irish child care and aftercare policy reflects the UNCRC definition of the child, although the National Policy Framework for Children and Young People 2014-2020 is progressive in binding children and young people together up to age 25.

3. The new policy, in continuing to use the word "may" to define eligibility contravenes Article 2 of the UNCRC. It is further contravened by the exclusion of named groups. This is a point that has serious implications when assessing whether or not the new aftercare policy adheres to the other Articles in the UNCRC. In its lack of a rights base for children it arguably empowers the state to be permissive.

4. The lack of consultation and voice of young people in the construction of this policy is a significant failing and represents a major missed opportunity by its authors.

5. It is reasonable to conclude that the new aftercare policy is not in the spirit of the UNCRC in its lack of detail. A number of articles contain paragraphs specifically requiring the development of systems of data collection, targeted services and

detailed operating procedures. This is not evident in the new policy.

The singular most effective mechanism to counter-balance the political pendulum effect and embrace ideals encompassing over-arching human values is to enact statutory entitlement to aftercare supports and services for all care leavers. Political views may change but values such as social justice, respect and dignity will not.

There is much good policy emerging which is focusing attention on the needs of children in care and young people in aftercare. The UNCRC has been influential in promoting children's rights but flawed implementation of policy and short-term political vision, an issue which will be examined in more detail in Section Six, remain challenges that must be surmounted.

Section Five – Research

Introduction

Having considered practice, theory and approaches, children's rights and policy, the next sections assesses the contribution research has made to the social sciences. Keith's story clearly illustrates the potential of qualitative data to offer real insight into the human dimensions of research. This validates consideration of the role of such research in social care as discussed in this chapter. Within this consideration, a particular focus will be afforded to the role of evidence used to inform the pedagogy, policy and practice of professionals working with young people leaving care.

Chapter 9

Research in Care and Aftercare

The issue of children leaving care has been recognised as a global problem, and one that needs further exploration through comparative research (Mendes and Moslehuddin, 2006; Pinkerton, 2006).

A notable theme emerging from the research literature on aftercare relates to how services are delivered at national levels. It is clear from a comparative analysis of aftercare services and outcomes in ten countries, including the UK, Germany, Canada and Ireland, that the quality of aftercare can vary greatly within one country (Stein, 2008).

For care leavers, entering adulthood is a more complex experience than it is for children living within a family. They must undergo normative changes experienced by their peers living permanently at home, but also an accelerated leap from childhood in State care to adulthood with little supports (Goossens, 2006). For many, trauma related to early formative experiences are revived as a result of impending adulthood (Downes, 1992). Despite this, it is only in the last decade that this subject area has emerged as a focus for research (Munro, *et al.*, 2011; Pinkerton, 2011).

A broad search of literature on throughcare for young people reveals two distinct concerns. The first involves the origins and outcomes for young care leavers (Courtney, *et al.*, 2005; Broad, 2006; EPIC, 2012; Pinkerton, 2012). There is a particular, if not almost exclusive, focus on accommodation, educational and occupational attainment and criminal activity, with lesser recognition given to the less tangible issues of emotional well-being and resilience. Much research highlights the high rates of homelessness, broken accommodation arrangements, low educational achievement and high unemployment amongst care leavers. These findings are pan-national and are reflective not only of aftercare service outcomes but the entire field of child welfare social work. For example, in 2007, care leavers in Northern Ireland were 18 times more likely to have no qualifications than general school leavers (DHSSPSNI, 2007).

Even among researchers there is disagreement on the number of care leavers in the Republic. Gilligan (2008:98) states that "there is almost a complete dearth of official data or evidence on outcomes for care leavers" and the same article estimates the number of care leavers at 250 to 300 per annum nationally. However, EUROCHILD (2010) give a figure of 435 care leavers in Ireland for 2005. This figure was extrapolated from HSE datasets, though notably the HSE omits those aged 18 thus obscuring the statistics on care leavers.

Key publications of outcomes-based research in Northern Ireland by Pinkerton and McCrea (1999) and in the Republic of Ireland by Kelleher *et al.* (2000) have focussed attention on the plight of care leavers. However, effective outcomes-based research has its limitations and recent critiques by Stein and Frost (2009) question their accuracy as much of the research compares care leavers to their peers from all sectors of society. They posit that this is flawed as care leavers, by and large, come from specific strata of society with associated educational achievement levels not representative of all strata. This potentially paints a more negative picture than is really the case for social services' effectiveness and has implications for evidence-based research. This is a key area for the informed professional and will be explored in greater detail following consideration of research methodologies. A UK-wide study by Goddard and Barrett (2008) examined the health of care leavers. The study highlights the well known deficiencies in aftercare but also some less researched aspects too. These new aspects were the results of interviews and reflect a growing qualitative approach to aftercare research, an approach encouraged by Stein (2008). The study found that many young people, on leaving care, lack a "significant other" to offer support. Aftercare workers often found themselves being that significant other, offering counselling and other services that went far beyond their defined occupational remit.

The second area of concern for researchers regards descriptions of services that young people use whilst transitioning from being "in-care" to adulthood, and associated national legislation and policies (Stein, 2006; Pinkerton, 2012). There is, nevertheless, a new perspective emerging in which theoretical models of child development, adolescence and transition are considered (Cashmore and Paxman, 2006; Goossens, 2006; Stein, 2006; Tweddle, 2007; Dima and Skehill, 2011; Barton *et al.*, 2012).

During this period of increased research into care and aftercare, outcomes for young people leaving care have not changed significantly, remaining less than positive (Martin and Jackson, 2002; Stein, 2006b; Dixon, 2008; McCrystal and McAloney, 2010; Hiles *et al.*, 2013).

Key Contemporary Findings

In the UK a recent report issued by the Centre for Social Justice (CSJ) in 2014 titled "Survival of the Fittest: Improving life chances for care leavers" published the following findings. Although concerns have been expressed regarding the political affiliation of the CSJ to the Conservative Party, the research is nonetheless valid. These findings are broadly in line with past research findings and also highlight the less well researched link between care, aftercare and the sex trade:

- 20 per cent of young homeless people were previously in care;

- 24 per cent of adult prison population have been in care;

- 70 per cent of sex workers have been in care;

- Care leavers are roughly twice as likely not to be in education, training or employment at 19 than the rest of the population;

- Only 6 per cent of care leavers are in higher education at age 19 compared to roughly 30 per cent of young people nationally;

- A care leaver who has a "negative journey" can cost the state £337,204, over the course of his or her lifetime.

In the Republic of Ireland, "outcomes for care leavers are poorly researched with Kelleher *et al's* (2000) research providing the only comprehensive published study on this topic (Gilligan, 2008)" (Doyle *et al.*, 2011:207). It was one of the recommendations of the Ryan Report (2009), Implementation Plan Action 65, that a ten-year longitudinal study of care leavers be undertaken to map their transition into adulthood in response to this deficiency in research. This recommendation has yet to be actioned. Kelleher *et al.* (*ibid*) found that the vast majority of care leavers came from backgrounds of poverty and social disadvantage, and had experienced various traumas owing to a range of factors in the home and associated with family separation. Subsequently, there have been several smaller scale studies evidencing poor outcomes with care leavers directly linked to homelessness, alcohol and drug problems, mental health problems, incarceration, poor educational attainment and social exclusion (Mayock and O'Sullivan, 2007; Mayock and Carr, 2008; Mayock *et al.*, 2008; Doyle *et al.*, 2012; Daly, 2012; Darmody *et al.*, 2013).

The final point identified by the CSJ study of cost to the state of negative care journeys will be explored within the Economic Case presented in the appendix to this book.

One area where there is a serious deficiency in research in the Republic of Ireland is the link between care, aftercare, sexual exploitation and the sex trade. Whilst there is a growing body of research in the UK (Munro, 2004; Montgomery-Devlin, 2007; Barnardos, 2011b; Beckett, 2011; Brodie *et al.*, 2011; Melrose, 2013; Smeaton, 2013), though a notable dearth specific to aftercare, there is no comparable research in the Republic of Ireland. The limited research that exists (Eastern Health Board, 1997; Shannon, 2010; Barnardos, 2012a) identifies the link between sex working and living in care in broad and imprecise terms. Barnardos (2012a) has identified the categories of children involved in prostitution as:

- Those who have left the care system;

- Those who have experienced homelessness;

- Those who suffer from alcohol and/or drug addictions;

- Separated or trafficked children.

The Eastern Health Board Report (1997) found that of 57 women interviewed who were or had been involved in prostitution, 47 were aged under 18 years, 10 were aged 18 or over and 80 per cent had, or were, experiencing homelessness.

Shannon (2010) identifies that those who have left the care system are of particular concern with regard to working in the sex trade. Furthermore, he identifies the need for adequate aftercare provision for all children leaving care by contrasting the legal duty of parents for their children beyond age 18, as opposed to the State's duty ending at age 18.

> ... children involved in child prostitution...These are children brought into care by the State because the State was obliged to care for them in circumstances where the biological parent(s) would not, or could not. A biological parent(s) moral duty to care for his or her child does not end on the child reaching the age of majority; indeed nor does the legal duty*. Why then should the duty on the State to care for such children end upon the child reaching the age of majority? (*See by way of example Succession Act 1965, Section 117). (Shannon, 2010:112)

The issues identified above associated with child prostitution feature prominently in research as areas of vulnerability for children leaving care. Furthermore:

> ... the factors which lead a young person to being placed in care may of course, contribute to their vulnerability to prostitution. However, the experience of being in care itself is said to put young people at particular risk of entry into prostitution because of social stigma, marginalization and "otherness" related with being in care (Kirby, 1995). (Cusick, 2002:237)

With specific regard to residential care, Beckett (2011) found in her study of child sexual exploitation (CSE) in Northern Ireland that children in residential care were more vulnerable to exploitation than those in other care settings. Her study found that of the sample of 1,102 cases, "sexual exploitation was identified as a cause of concern for almost two-thirds (63.6 per cent) of young females in residential care" (2011:22).

The dearth of research in the UK and the Republic of Ireland identifying the link between care, leaving care and aftercare with sex working is curious given that this is a known vulnerability for this cohort of young people. In the Republic of Ireland, in addition to the above cited, Kelleher *et al.'s* publication *Left Out on Their Own* (2000) identified prostitution as a "difficulty" two years after moving on for 14 per cent of the Health Board population and 3 per cent of the Special School population. Gilligan (2008:90) identified that young people with poor relationships with carers were at "a high risk and unstable lifestyle possibly involving illicit drug use and exposure to the sex trade."

It would appear that researchers, at least within the UK and the Republic of Ireland, have, en masse, been influenced by some factor which has resulted in a phenomenon analogous to that which Fintan O'Toole (2009) posits the citizens experienced with regard to the Celtic Tiger, political corruption and institutional child abuse. He labelled this phenomenon the "unknown known", an insightful extension of Donald Rumsfeld's famous phrase, "there are known knowns ... there are known unknowns ... there are also unknown unknowns" (*New York Times*, 2011). According to O'Toole, this phenomenon leads to people "choosing" to unknow the easily known, the obvious or as Holohan (2011) termed it, that which is (unrecognised) "in plain sight" – or in fact, actual known truths.

> At its most extreme this worked as a kind of collective psychosis, analogous to the idea of dissociation in psychiatry, where, in response to trauma, the mind distances itself from experiences that it does not wish to process. (O'Toole, 2009:181)

This is not denial on the part of researchers, as the facts are known and not disputed; rather, they have been neglected and inadequately referenced. This deficit highlights the importance of research, not just in developing understanding of specific issues, and theory associated with them, but also in creating the webs of knowledge amongst practitioners and policy makers with regard to these issues. These webs may then capture issues which otherwise might appear as isolated or unconnected events and afford a joined-up perspective. As previously noted, we are more likely to find what we are looking for than stumble across the unexpected. Consequently, by contextually locating these matters research has the potential to identify trends and systemic issues which otherwise might evade detection.

* *

My practice experience in residential child care confirms the vulnerability of young people in care to sexual exploitation and prostitution. This can both be misinterpreted as, and conflated with, what is euphemistically referred to as promiscuity and/or inappropriate sexual behaviour. This deflects attention from the underlying causes and wider factors involved (Cusick, 2002; Lalor and McElvaney, 2010; Melrose, 2013) by casting the issue as a immoral failing on the part of the young person. In order to effectively safeguard young people, research is essential to better understand these issues and to inform practice on how to effectively address them. This deficit in research and support, including educational programmes for both workers and young people, is a matter of grave concern requiring immediate attention.

* *

The fact that outcomes have ostensibly not improved to the extent desired requires further examination in an effort to establish:

1. The availability and usage of qualitative research data when creating aftercare pedagogy, policy and practice;

2. The origins and underpinning theories, influences and processes of qualitative research into aftercare;

3. The potential for qualitative research to better contribute to future evidence-informed practice initiatives and aftercare policy creation.

Conducting such an examination requires an understanding of the distinctions between quantitative and qualitative research, necessitating an overview of ontological, epistemological and positivist attitudes. Epistemology is primarily concerned with typologies of knowledge – what we know and how we know it – as opposed to ontological concerns regarding the essence of being and/ or self (Hesse-Biber, 2010). Epistemological debate as a process of methodological categorisation primarily delineates between quantitative and qualitative approaches to knowing.

> Qualitative methods focus on understanding constructed meaning. Whereas positivistic research assumes that phenomena are best understood from an objective standpoint, qualitative research assumes that meaning and knowledge are constructed in a social context. Qualitative researchers seek to understand research participants' subjective perspectives. (Merriam, cited in Adena *et al.*, 2006:1)

It is not my purpose to argue in favour of one epistemological branch, such as quantitative, over another, such as qualitative. Rather, it is necessary to understand these approaches in the context of their relationship during aftercare policy formulation. A reasonable model of the functional dynamic between quantitative and qualitative data and policy-making suggests qualitative methods are useful in the development of theoretical understandings. Quantitative methods can then be used to test the validity of the qualitative results (Strauss and Corbin, 1998; Crabtree and Miller, 1999). Accepting this sequential equation on face value, the task of examining the contribution of qualitative research takes on not only an assessment of contribution, but an explanation as to why qualitative research is not contributing more and what can be done to rectify the matter.

There has been a significant increase in research into aftercare internationally in the past decade as noted above. Equally, in the Republic of Ireland there has been an increase in aftercare research, some of which claims to be of a qualitative design, but quantitative methods continue to dominate pedagogy, policy formation and practice culture (Stein 2004, 2006b; Gilligan, 2008). It will be demonstrated that quantitative influences in social science research in general, and aftercare by implication, are sourced in the traditional bio-medical culture, left-right political/ideological oscillation, and contemporary administrative interests linked to efficiencies and risk management concerns (Lather, 2004; Hesse-Biber, 2010; Ceglowski *et al.*, 2011; Staller, 2013). In this context, the factors that influence the current research construct of aftercare are laid bare, and steps to establishing a rational model of policy formulation can be considered.

There has been an increase in the number of qualitative studies undertaken within the social care sector, but to a lesser degree regarding the experiences of children leaving the care of the State to independent living (Stein, 2004, 2005a). However, the current (under-represented) research interest in the relational, psychodynamic and psychosocial aspects of leaving care have not trickled down into aftercare policy formulation (Trevithick, 2003; Ruch, 2005; Stein, 2006; Bellefeuille and Ricks 2010). Instead, quantitative measurements appear of primary concern to policy-makers, not only in the Republic of Ireland but throughout the English-speaking world. Legislation and policies emphasise the need to address quantifiable problematic outcomes in housing, education, crime and substance abuse (Stein *et al.*, 2000). Matters of social justice and psychosocial well-being, factors that impact the lived experience, are rarely touched upon in legislation and policy. There have been many calls for social justice to be revitalised within the social professions (Allen *et al.*, 2009; Ferguson and Woodward, 2009) and both social work and social care cite social justice as a core principle of their mission statements. Social justice is a contested term which, as O'Brien (2011:145) states, "there is no clear definition of what social workers or social work associations mean when they refer to 'social justice.'"

Craig (2002:671-672) offers the following definition which O'Brien endorses:

> ... a framework of political objectives, pursued through social, economic, environmental and political policies, based on an acceptance of difference and diversity, and informed

by values concerned with: achieving fairness, and equality of outcomes and treatment; recognising the dignity and equal worth and encouraging the self-esteem of all; the meeting of basic needs; maximizing the reduction of inequalities in wealth, income and life chances; and the participation of all, including the most disadvantaged.

O'Brien (2010, 2011) concludes that at a micro-level social justice considerations are addressed at times by on-the-ground practitioners, but at a macro level such issues are ignored.

There is a concern that without change social work values atrophy: social movement ties are severed, opportunities to transmit social justice skills to new generations are removed and social justice skills gradually fade from consciousness and practice. (Baines, 2010:941)

There is of course a need to know and address quantities regarding the meeting of basic human needs, but statistics can be easily misunderstood or manipulated (Best, 2002; Ward, 2004). Additionally, there are always those who are not included, particularly in terms of aftercare research where the young people most in need of assistance often can no longer be traced (Cashmore and Paxman, 2006; Holt and Kirwan, 2012). Statistics fail to explain the "why" of a particular issue, instead only the "what", the cause and effect of interventions. Aftercare policies are still underpinned by quantities of prevalence, quantities of change, quantities of loss, and quantities of strategy, despite a slowly growing body of qualitative research into leaving care (Stein, 2004). This lack of "trickle-down" of qualitative data is not surprising as it would appear a "trickle-*up*" effect is required to influence the ultimate policymakers, the legislature and civil service.

There are a number of explanations for the hegemony of quantitative research that are transferable to an Irish aftercare context. Firstly, the historical emphasis on quantitative, deductive reasoning that has underpinned humanities research is only recently (in real-time terms) being challenged. Oakley observes that prior to 1960 there was little evidence of the argument between so-called

"quantitative" and "qualitative" methods in the professional literature (Oakley, 1999).

> The arrival of feminism as a political and social movement
> underscored the importance for political reasons for doing
> "qualitative" research methods, and gave an altogether new
> gloss to anti-science critiques of quantification. (Oakley,
> 1999:248)

The legacy of the natural sciences, the quest for perfect definition, formulae and reliable change-stimulus models, has not been
exorcised from humanities research by qualitative approaches.
Indeed, the often compulsive-like demands for scientific rigour in
qualitative research reveals that there appears to be a strong residue of quantitative aspirations (Kelliher, 2005; Alasuutari, 2010;
Brown, 2010; Hesse-Biber, 2010).

Furthermore, Ceglowski *et al.* (2011) consider what they term
the "censorship" of qualitative research through legislation, the establishment of a "gold standard" of research and the quantitative
demands of international social science publications. They cite
Denzin *et al.* (2006) when highlighting the impact of a resurgence
of quantitative emphasis in education research:

> The scientifically based research movement (SBR), first in-
> troduced by the federal government in the Reading Excel-
> lence Act of 1999 and later incorporated by the National
> Research Council (NRC) has created a new and hostile po-
> litical environment for qualitative research. Connected to
> the No Child Left Behind Act of 2002, SBR embodies a re-
> emergent scientism, a positivist, so-called evidence based,
> epistemology. (Ceglowski *et al.*, 2011:1)

Secondly, policy-makers, namely the legislature, do not come
to the drafting table as participants engaging in ontological/episte-
mological debates regarding the rationale for more complex, psychosocial interpretations of service user experiences. They bring
to the table *a priori* their own considerations, beliefs, expectations
and intentions. Howe (1997), O'Brien (2010, 2011) and Redmond
(2010) discuss the influences of left-right political dialect on wel-

fare policy formulation, highlighting the rise of the neoliberal right and an accompanying focus on the individual, freedom and rights. Trinder and Reynolds (2000:237) describe research as an "inherently political process ... that creates a false sense of security". Howe (1998) portrays the disembodiment of psychosocial and emotional concerns about relationships in social work as they are replaced with notions of individualism and free will, concepts that place the responsibility for personality development and behaviours on the shoulders of the individual.

Neoliberal policy-making betrays a number of discernible traits, namely the omission of community and society and the impetus on individualising the problem (Miller, 1993; Howe, 1997; Ruch *et al.*, 2010). In terms of aftercare, policies are devoid of community, focus on quantifiable outcomes and are underpinned by basic developmental theories (Stein 2004, 2006). By focussing the pedagogy of aftercare on statistical data and singular, basic psychological theories, it is the young person and their immediate environment that comes under the spotlight, and many social variables are ignored. Why is this so? The answer may lie in the projected implications of genuinely considering qualitative data during policy-making.

Contemporary understandings of liberalism centre on the contribution of the State within the wider context of the economy. Liberals generally, and particularly neoliberals, argue that State care provision should be significantly curtailed as it interrupts what they see as the natural dynamics of the "free market" (Evetts, 2011). Neoliberals cite political philosophers such as Adams and Bentham (reformers against feudalism) as proponents of free market ideologies (Harris, 1983). An implication of State intervention in the free market is that the "caring" free markets may be manually distorted by those wishing to apply concepts of social justice to policy formation. "Those" are the people wishing to re-balance economic distribution and address embedded poverty. The emergence of qualitative methods appears to have threatened the status quo, resulting in their playing second fiddle to quantitative modes of inquiry (Howe, 1998).

A third phenomenon maintaining the current influence of quantitative research relates to the growth of managerialism which has developed under neoliberalism, the authority of administrative functionaries in the care sectors (Clarke and Newman, 1997; Parrot and Maddoc-Jones, 2008; Redmond, 2010; Noordgraaf and Schinkel, 2011). The growth of administrative departments and influence can be linked to systemic political changes whereby the public are increasingly expectant of information, intervention and "progress" (Howe, 1997; Hanlon, 1998; Ceglowski *et al.*, 2011). Statistics and other quantitative accounts of practice are systemically gorged upon. Qualitative data cannot be readily quantified, however, and administrative personnel do not have the social science training necessary to understand it. Ward (2004) concludes that managerialism and administrative statistical tools have somewhat emasculated social care researchers. Senior administrators have access to increasingly complex quantitative datasets indicating trends and effects, omitting the qualitative essences of such data and simultaneously failing to increase measured variables alongside the advancement of technology.

Giddens explains the promise of modernity is the assessment and control of "risk" by expert knowledge (Giddens, 1991). Administrative concerns are often tinged with an aversion to the "risks" associated with policy implementation, risks that can be associated with political aggrandisement, fiscal imbalance and litigation (Beck, 1992; Brown, 2010). As such, it is explicable that administration departments prioritise the maintenance of physical (bio-medical) well-being over relational, psychosocial and psychodynamic concerns.

All of these factors impact on frontline professional practice in aftercare, dominating current standards and setting protocols, with benchmarks increasingly manifest as perceptions of evidence-based practice (EBP). EBP promises more efficient services (Gibbs and Gambrill, 1999) involving the use of research data to heuristically inform pedagogy, policy, practice culture and change (Magill, 2006). However, there has been some concern that a focus on efficiency and costs, rather than outcomes, has become the main driving force of EBP. It is described by the Centre for Evidence Based Social Services (CEBSS, 1998) as:

> The starting point for evidence-based social care is the principle that all decisions in our field should be based on the best available research evidence. Research evidence should inform both our understanding of the origins and development of social problems and our knowledge of the likely outcomes of different types of service provision.

This definition of EBP suggests that there is a "best" type of research which happens to be quantitative designs that can (allegedly) prove generalisability, pass rigorous stress tests and are most suitable to random control testing (RCT). This has resulted in the materialisation of the above-mentioned Gold Standard of research that is exclusive to quantitative designs (Stein, 2004; Lincoln and Cannella, 2004; Ceglowski *et al.*, 2011). The word evidence is laden with power by virtue of its role in deciding life and death in a courtroom context, and this perception of a proven truth transfers favourably to EBP. Equally, the reference to gold has implicit connotations. It is an unsettling picture in a field consistently under scrutiny by internal "auditors", the Health Information and Quality Authority (HIQA), political parties and the media. The compulsion on researchers and practitioners is to standardise practice based on quantitative "evidence" of cause and effect, and to ignore their own clinical experiential knowledge. Quantitative methodologies are primarily utilised in EBP (Trinder and Reynolds, 2000) and clearly this plays a significant role in diminishing the contribution of qualitative methods in social care research.

The intrusion of EBP-based policy on the independence of practitioners is a matter discussed by Staller (2013). She questions the merits of a strict policy based on so-called "evidence", arguing that there is no value in applying population-based scientific results (statistics, probabilities, averages, amongst other factors) to highly individualised circumstances, citing Rolfe (1999) in this regard. Furthermore, Staller contends (citing Cordingley, 2004) that the fundamental principles of evidence-based medicine (EBM) do not migrate readily to the social sciences. Staller notes also the surprising disparity between EBM, which seeks to integrate clinical practice with external evidence, and EBP in social care, which tends to focus only on the external evidence.

Nevo and Slonim-Nevo cite Rubin in identifying potential flaws within EBP:

> EBP has had its share of critics. Rubin (2007) summarises four disadvantages of EBP that have been pointed out in the literature, and defends the model against them:
>
> 1) it is too mechanistic and ignores the unique characteristics of both clients and practitioners;
>
> 2) it is not clear enough, ignores research flaws and makes exaggerated claims about the evidence at hand;
>
> 3) it is hard to implement due to resource limitations such as time, training and supervision;
>
> 4) due to the nature of the scientific process, the empirical findings are outdated by the time they appear in print (for further arguments and counter-arguments. (Nevo and Slonim-Nevo, 2011:1177)

Gilbert and Powell cites Scheyett (2006) with reference to evidence-based practice and the silencing of service users from a Foucauldian perspective:

> ... discourses of evidence-based practice effectively silence both the service user and the practitioner. This occurs as the dialogue between service users and practitioners over experiences and knowledge of the "real world" becomes subjugated to disciplinary knowledge external to this dialogue which, through its status as truth, discredits alternative conceptions of events and their meanings (Foucault, 1978). As tactics of government, information technologies objectify and render visible but in the same movement silence the targets of policy. (Gilbert and Powell, 2010:13)

Trinder and Reynolds locate the emergence of EBP within the context of the risk society (Beck, 2010) and changing understandings of professional expertise:

232

The timing of evidence-based practice is not accidental. It has developed within a specific context, particularly the current preoccupations with risk, ambivalence about science and professional expertise, and the concern with effectiveness, proceduralisation and the consumer...The response to the critique of science is to place renewed emphasis on science with a constantly revisable and transparent process that excludes uncertainty, and in the age of anxiety, promises security for practitioners, researchers, managers and consumers. Trust is transferred from the fallible individual and placed in the revised system. (Trinder and Reynolds, 2000:12-13)

There is also the cost implications involved in satisfying EBP criteria to be considered. The cost of large-scale RCT trails with independent verifiers prohibits many of those financially less well resourced from participating in EBP-approved studies, utilising the aforementioned Gold Standard. This requirement for major financial resources renders EBP susceptible to being used by vested corporate or state interests to promote their products or agendas.

Just what is considered as "evidence" is a cause of great concern, as is who decides and how is it recorded and quantified.

Not everything that counts can be counted, and not everything that can be counted counts. (Albert Einstein)

One of the most pervasive items of evidence, particularly when considering policy formation (Aldgate *et al.*, 2007; D'Cruz *et al.*, 2009) and residential child care research and provision (Butler *et al.*, 2009), is the concept of outcomes. However, many flaws have been highlighted with measuring and quantifying outcomes both generally and with specific regard to care leavers.

Mercer and Pignotti (2007) highlight the complexity of assessing the quality of outcomes research due to the evolution of the term and the variety of protocols for such assessments. Daining and DePanfils (2007) and Stein and Frost (2009) have highlighted the fallacy of comparing care leavers to young people from the general population, as care leavers, by and large, originate from less affluent socio-economic groups not representative of the general population.

> When the groups to be compared are different right from the outset, comparisons can be quite dangerous. If the cases of difficult adolescents are not advisable for foster care, and usually end up in residential care, comparing results tends to serve only to conclude time and time again that the latter cases have worse outcomes. Furthermore, while the importance of working with more specific developmental variables is beyond doubt, studies using psychological variables such as intelligence or personality traits often appear to forget that social intervention pursues social goals, such as social inclusion and the opportunity for young people to make a positive contribution to society. (del Valle, 2008:21)

Stein (2006) highlights the fact that normal life-course development encompasses ups and downs and thus measuring at any specific point in time is flawed. Bhabra and Ghate (2002) identify the need for professionals to take account of factors including age at entry to care, reasons for admission and duration of the care episode. Davis and Ward (2011) and Rees *et al.* (2011) identify the impact of poor parenting, including maltreatment, and social disadvantage that require inclusion when considering expectations about what constitutes a good outcome for an individual child. Winter (2006) and Howard *et al.* (1999) point out the adult-centric nature of currently defined outcomes which are devoid of the voice of the young person. Holland *et al.* (2008:20) highlight that young people should be recognised as "active members of society ... rather than just the outcomes they will become". They also identify a propensity when focusing on outcomes to divert attention from the here and now, which presents a risk that the current quality of life may be ignored in pursuit of future outcomes.

Fulcher and Garfat (2012) highlight that it is often outputs (everything that carers, teachers, social workers, youth workers or others do to provide targeted out-of-home care services under court jurisdiction) rather than outcomes (developmental achievements) that are recorded. Taylor and Bullock (2005) make the point that decisions as to what should be measured and how are inherently political, yet these dimensions have to date been under-researched. Pinkerton and McCrae (1999) make the key point that considerations of outcomes can reduce what is a process to a product. Devaney (2008) illuminates the debate as to "whether the focus on outcomes is actually about improving the life chances of children or is primarily designed to give greater influence to policy-makers in directing funding and priorities" (Devaney and Coman, 2011:39).

Holmes and McDermid (2012) put forward an argument in support of the case for revising how we conceive of outcomes relative to the each individual's pre-intervention biography:

> Progress may be small and slow compared to non-disabled children. However, given the level of needs, vulnerability and disadvantage experienced by families with disabled children, the impact of small improvements may well be magnified. A great deal of support (and cost) may be required to use a spoon to eat. Achieving this outcome may have a significant impact on the child, their parents and siblings. In such cases, the amount of improvement made since the provision of a service or "distance travelled" may be a more accurate form of measurement (Holmes, McDermid and Soper, 2010). (Holmes and McDermid, 2012:143-144)

A 2010 DEMOS report, *In Loco Parentis,* identifies this potential for harmful mistruths with regard to care through the misinterpretation of outcomes:

> This negative view of care in England and Wales is closely related to how it is evaluated and the way that data on young people's outcomes is misinterpreted — both of which tell a misleading story about its impact. (Hannon *et al.*, 2010:9)

Mike Stein has also made the highly relevant point that:

> ... the excessive focus on poor outcomes had helped to create a climate where social workers saw care as the worst possible option, and had contributed to vulnerable children being left too long with failing parents. (*Guardian*, 2009)

With regard to mistruths generated by the ambiguity associated with outcomes, the phenomenon of emotive mistruths and sensationalist hype to suit specific agendas (Best, 2002; Murphy, 2010), such as the continued reduction in the usage of residential child care services, becomes a reality.

One measure of an outcome for a child placed in residential care affording a more contextualised perspective is: Where would this young person be today if they had not been brought into residential care? This question encompasses the realities of the child's pre-care circumstances, the harm caused to them and the likelihood of what would have happened to them if they were left exposed to this harm. It also encompasses recognition that all other placement options have been exhausted and were it not for residential care there would be no service available to them.

It is also noteworthy that outcomes are currently recorded via positivistic quantitative methodologies, and it may require an epistemological shift for a more meaningful understanding of just what constitutes an outcome when we consider care leavers.

. . . .

> *Evidence and outcomes are important factors in promoting best practice for children in care. However, the professional needs to be able to synthesise the findings in the context of the individual they are working with, and be wary of letting the evidence do their thinking for them. They must analyse the data using informed professional judgement, in particular their knowledge of the individual young person.*

. . . .

In a similar tone as Staller (2013), Ruch (2005) calls for what she terms greater levels of "relationship-based practice" with more elbow room for the practitioner to reflect upon the client, the professional self, the organisational context and the knowledge informing practice.

Relationship-based practice explores not only the "how and what" but also the "why" of practice and is compatible with understandings of social work practice, which

236

recognise the interpretative nature of social work activity, the importance of reflexive responses to unique and unpredictable situations and the holistic nature of human behaviour. (Ruch, 2005:113)

However, such calls from the wilderness are not being heard as the dogmatic application of quantitative EBP dilutes the authenticity of qualitative research itself. This is all the more remarkable when we consider the point made by Rosenberg and Donald (1995):

> Ironically, despite the centrality of measuring the effectiveness of interventions in evidence-based practice, it has not escaped the notice of either critics or champions that there is not, nor ever likely to be, any empirical evaluation of the effectiveness of evidence-based practice itself. The lack of empirical justification for the approach has meant that advocates have relied on intuitive claims, whilst critics have countered on similar terms. (Rosenberg and Donald, cited in Trinder and Reynolds, 2000:213)

The issue of knowledge being used to inform practice is critical within our current neoliberal hegemonies. This knowledge frames the practice of professionals and determines their eligibility to be included as professionals if they implement policies and practice models prescribed by (neoliberal) policy-makers thus directly impacting on both workers and those they support (Fournier, 1999).

Qualitative researchers themselves often try meeting quantitative demands for scientific rigour through mixed-method design (Kelliher, 2005; Adena *et al.*, 2006; Brod *et al.*, 2009; Hesse-Biber, 2010). Processes of cross-tabulation and triangulation have developed involving qualitative and quantitative methods (Paterson *et al.*, 2001; Alasuutari, 2010). There may be a realisation amongst qualitative researchers that quantitative elements are essential, but more likely it's the appeasement of funding masters at play (Brown, 2010). As such, the same variables are examined again and again in grander surveys of greater longitudinal expanse, but to what end must yet be discerned.

From a deconstructionist viewpoint, the scientific drive towards certainty through measuring generalisability, sometimes referred to as "the appliance of science", is the folly of contemporary social science research (Alasuutari *et al.*, 2008). Derrida argued that we will never know anything for sure and as such social science research is a never-ending process of deconstruction and reconstruction (McCarthy, 1989).

> ... in the last 20 or so years, even those professions that rely most on the natural sciences, such as nursing, medicine, and psychoanalysis, have rejected episteme (knowledge derived from science) as the basis of clinical judgments (Bishop and Scudder, 1990; Groopman, 2007; Hafferty and Castellani, 2010; Orange, 2011; Rafferty, 1996). As Hafferty and Castellani (2010) point out, "the uncertainties of knowledge and its application to patient care, and the tremendous variabilities that exist with the patient population continue to demand some measure of individual expertise and discretionary decision making" (p. 299). (Fusco, 2013:201)

In a less critical vein, the notion of seeking broader clarification of qualitative findings within the population is not in itself unsound, but there is an insinuation that the mixed method researcher is substituting qualitative research potentials (time, focus and funding) with quantitative methods, and thus sacrificing latent qualitative possibilities. Hesse-Biber (2010) points out that the qualitative elements of mixed-methods research are "hand-maidens" or "second best" to the quantitative elements. Brown (2010) describes how researchers must compromise their qualitative epistemological principles in an effort to acquire funding.

Oakley puts forward a balanced argument with regard to mixed-methods, including the employment of RCTs, whilst also making the key point that it is the research question, or problem, which ought to dictate the method to be used:

> The challenge as we saw it - is to integrate the collection and analysis of "qualitative' and "quantitative" data so as to arrive at an interpretation which makes productive use of both.

and

> Of course it is the case that research methods must fit the question being asked and this means that "qualitative" methods are undoubtedly sometimes the most appropriate choice. But all methods must be open, consistently applied and replicable by others. (Oakley, 1999:251,252)

The authenticity of qualitative research is addressed by Bellefeuille and Ricks (2010) who, as previously noted, outline an alternative approach to youth care research, what they call relational inquiry. This is a qualitative approach to research that defies the desire to establish a definitive research question and linear methodology. Instead, relational inquiry facilitates an explorative, "messy" process of inquiry that is collaborative and centres on "inciting dialogue" (2010:1238). Relational inquiry suggests a hermeneutic methodological approach based on the works of Heidegger and Gadamer. As such, Bellefeuille and Ricks appear to be calling for authenticity of purpose in qualitative research into youth care, a return to the epistemological essences of the qualitative approach.

In an aftercare context, particularly in the Republic of Ireland, there is a paucity of authentic (in an epistemological sense) qualitative data within the overall construct of aftercare research. Stein's (2004) overview of available qualitative research highlights this lack, and he notes the dearth in theory when it comes to aftercare research, pedagogy and practice (Stein, 2006b). Most if not all the factors contributing to this scarcity of authentic qualitative research are associated with the perspectives of people involved in the social construction of aftercare pedagogy and practice. While the forces contributing to maintaining the current construct of research are powerful, change will come. The positivist attitude by its very nature demands change, and in this can be found hope that a new, post-positivist (Ryan, 2006) construct of research into aftercare, a more equitable distribution of resources and impetus, may materialise.

Chapter 10

An Alternative Research Construct

Pessimistic as the picture for qualitative research into aftercare may appear, it is not suggested, however, that the dominance of quantitative data in policy formation is in some way irreversible. An interactive model of social science research and policy formation exists that maximises the potential of both qualitative and quantitative methods. This might be termed a post-positivist model in that there is a recognition that the questions posed do not rely upon a dualistic answer, an either-or solution, either qualitative or quantitative methods (Ryan, 2006). In this ideal construct, qualitative research begins by establishing theories and hypotheses. Quantitative methods can then be engaged to determine the generalisability of the theory, the results used to inform policy (Strauss and Corbin, 1998; Crabtree and Miller, 1999; Magill, 2006; Alasuutari, 2010). Sinuff *et al.* (2007) describe this relationship when they state that: "Whereas the quantitative researcher's emphasis is testing theory, the qualitative researcher's emphasis is the construction of theory." (2007:105)

This model is not necessarily supportive of the mixed-methods approach adopted by certain studies and critiqued by Hesse-Biber (2010) as adding "vignettes" of qualitative data to largely quantitative studies. Rather, it recognises quantitative and qualitative approaches as distinct and uniquely functional to social research, but beneficial when combined for the purpose of policy-making. Sinuff *et al.* (*ibid*) cite numerous contributions made by qualitative research to the Intensive Care Unit (ICU), such as exploring complex phenomenon not immediately accessible with quantitative methods, behaviours and interpretations and the consequences

240

of practice changes. They conclude that when brought together qualitative and quantitative methods can "provide greater insights to guide clinical policy" (2007:108).

Vostanis *et al.* (2008) highlight the rarity of aftercare theory (other than attachment) indicating the construct of research in aftercare (particularly in the Republic of Ireland) is upside down. The traditional modes of research are continuously being recycled and nothing new emerges, whilst authentic, epistemologically diverse qualitative approaches are sidelined. A reconstruction of the model of aftercare policy formation in which qualitative research develops new ways of understanding social phenomenon may address the poor outcomes associated with young people leaving care.

Establishing such a construct of research will pose some significant challenges, such as getting qualitative and quantitative researchers to adopt a post-positivist attitude in which they revise their epistemological assumptions; to view their roles as that of learner rather than merely a tester (Ryan, 2006; Morowaski, 2011); to recognise the important contributions of both perspectives; and to engage them to work together without compromising their principles. This will require deep systemic change that broaches not only issues of epistemology, but matters of political, administrative and funding influences.

Before achieving symbiotic inter-working between research teams, a certain unity of purpose may be required amongst qualitative researchers. With varying methods available, and varying study objectives, comparing small-scale findings from different studies to establish a solid theory for further quantitative analysis can be difficult. Pinkerton has stated that, "There is an almost total absence of a comparative literature which could lay the groundwork for a global theory and practice of young people leaving State care." (2006:192)

Pinkerton (*ibid.*) suggests that cross-cultural differences in research emphasis makes comparison difficult, and infers that differences in language and culture render English language research ethnocentric. Even in the same country the variations in methods means comparison of qualitative data can be difficult. The solution would seem to be some form of methodological consensus between different qualitative research teams exploring the same subject area, such as aftercare. The suggestion of standardising qualitative research smacks somewhat of another form of emasculation of qualitative approaches. It seems as though by seeking consensus a certain level of freedom to interpret may be removed from the researcher. This may indeed be the price paid for developing a coherent inter-dynamic between quantitative and qualitative methods.

A re-assessment of how we prioritise current EBP tools over clinical experience may also be required. Directives from the top of the organisational hierarchy to specifically act in a certain way when presented with clinical situations must not be allowed to curb the application of experiential clinical learning, as is the current situation (Reynolds, 2000; Ruch *et al.*, 2010; Staller, 2013). Indeed, a broadening of qualitative interests to include more the clinical experiences of practitioners, what Staller (2013) described as practice-based evidence (PBE), could contribute to our understanding of the nuances of social phenomenon and also offer quantitative researchers a rich treasure trove of theories to test.

The data that might emerge from this inter-working must be accessible to those who formulate policy if research and practice are to be authentically integrated. Accessible databanks and cross-comparative tools have been developed for other child care fields such as foster care (Pinkerton, 2006), but this is not the case with aftercare. It would appear that of all the care fields disadvantaged by lack of qualitative research, the aftercare field is most deprived.

Authentic qualitative research offers opportunities to understand the complexities of social phenomenon relevant to particular sectors. By examining the subjective experiences of service users and providers, the meanings they apply to phenomenon, and the psychosocial and psychodynamic aspects of "care", new ways of understanding can influence how we work.

The influences that have resulted in the emergence of this construct of research in the social sciences, particularly in aftercare over the last three decades, are arguably but not exclusively: the historical context of research and the dominance of the bio-medical approach to knowledge; the political and economic ideologies of research funders (private and public); the growth of managerialism, and administrative inexperience with qualitative data and comfort with quantitative data.

Not only will the historical, political, economic and administrative shapers of aftercare research need to be relieved of their current influence, but a re-appraisal of the relationship between qualitative and quantitative research is needed if the balance is to shift. Furthermore, the dominance of evidence-based practice, which removes autonomy from the researcher and practitioner, must also be addressed. Rather than omitting clinical practice experiences, future research should focus on such knowledge, systematically bringing it together for comparative analysis and contribution to theory formulation.

Knowledge

Much has been written regarding knowledge, from Plato and Aristotle in ancient Greece throughout the whole history of philosophy and allied disciplines. The links between knowledge, theory and practice have equally been well researched (Trevithick, 2011). Of the three domains of knowledge – theoretical, factual and practical – it is the latter that requires elevation. The absence of the workers' voice in the academic domain has been a limiting factor in the promotion of practice knowledge. This, as previously highlighted, has significant implications, in particular with the evidence-based paradigms, and the leaving and aftercare domain.

> There is little research on the contribution of residential workers in assisting young people with their accommodation on leaving care. (Bostock *et al.*, 2009 cited in Stein, 2012:67)

Knowledge creation and dissemination is pivotal to the profession's recognition, in the battle for space in a congested arena (Beddoe, 2011). Paucity of practitioner research leaves the "numbers game" to the accountants and evaluation to the recipients of compliance reports. The voice of recipients may be muted and government reliance on so-called independent research effectively silences both users' and practitioners' experience of the world (Scheyett, 2006; Beddoe and Harington, 2013).

Unless workers get their voice heard in this arena the existing hegemony shaping practice will prevail longer than may be in worker's or children's best interests. Knowledge, as previously stated, must be utilised to influence practice in order to be meaningful and here the process of praxis – in its simplest construct meaning theory plus action or "theory-into-practice" (Garfat *et al.*, 2013:23) – is salient.

> It could be argued that when certain structures, social relations or practices exist for any significant period of time they can convey a sense of normality. Subsequently, attempts to challenge these practices can be interpreted as disruptive or unreasonable. There are emerging concerns that while social work publications contribute to knowledge they make little or no contribution to practice. (MacGregor, cited in Heron and Murray, 2004:204)

There may be impediments to workers undertaking such writing, as identified by Heron and Murray (2004), but these are not insurmountable. Social care workers report that they have participated in many research studies undertaken by undergraduate and postgraduate students into aftercare provision. However, the majority of this research has not been published. This, then, can be seen to satisfy the needs of the researcher in fulfilling their degree award requirements, but by not publishing this research they are not best meeting the needs of the researched.

. . . .

Social care workers and managers need to reclaim their rightful place within the profession and to write for academic publication, as peer-reviewed, high-impact journal articles are generators of evidence. The continued absence of such research has far-reaching consequences both for workers and those they support.

. . . .

We cannot accept a situation as identified by Heron and Murray (*ibid*) where of 700,000 articles published over a 25 year-period in two academic databases, Sociological Abstracts and Social

Services, only 63 referenced residential child care in the title. For tacit knowledge, use of self-knowledge and intuition (Polanyi, 1967; Collins and Evans, 2007), and practice knowledge to become change agents workers and managers need to publish their learning for this knowledge to fulfil its potential.

> The lack of a practice-based body of knowledge for residential child care reflects the fact that the discipline is under-researched and much of what does exist, in the UK at least, is predicated upon social work's current fixation with inquiry reports and outcomes studies. It does not conceptualise what might be different. (Smith, 2003:240)

Summary

All in all, it can be concluded that qualitative research approaches are not contributing significantly to aftercare pedagogy, practice culture and policy-making in the Republic of Ireland. Indeed, there is ample reason to suggest that qualitative research has not in fact reached its full potential in any of the care fields. Perhaps a time will come soon when the research economy of scales will re-adjust as it is realised by policy-makers that quantitative data alone are not adequate when considering relationships between human beings. For their part, workers need to write for publication, both to meet the needs of those they represent and to develop a body of knowledge to challenge dominant paradigms.

SECTION SIX –
RETHINKING RESIDENTIAL CARE,
LEAVING CARE AND AFTERCARE

Introduction

The preceding chapters have offered a perspective on social care, residential care, leaving care and aftercare with a specific focus on the Republic of Ireland. Several themes have emerged, such as the impact of neoliberal policies and their attendant focus on individualisation, the importance of relationships to social care work, and professionalisation and the role of the worker within social care. In further examining these, I acknowledge that my evolving epistemological position is anti-positivistic, wherein I conceive of human beings as inherently complex beings, socially constructed within unique circumstances and imbued with free will, all of which makes scientific quantification and predictive analysis problematic. I offer this personal position to illustrate my awareness of this bias and to enable the reader to factor it into their own interpretation of the contents of this book. Despite our goal of seeking a balanced and nuanced position, we all have inherent biases.

Chapter 11

The Profession, the Professional and Professionalisation

The Profession and the Professional

At the time of writing, there is a new Graduate Placement Scheme for social workers being proposed in the Republic of Ireland. This scheme will have newly qualified social workers working for lower salaries than those currently in employment, and will potentially have a major impact on the profession of social work (SWAN, 2014). Concomitantly, and interestingly from a profession perspective, there is also a scheme announced in early 2014 whereby social workers will receive specialised legal training to enable them to undertake court work currently being done by legal professionals (IASW, 2014). Government schemes to address unemployment, such as the Job Bridge Scheme (http://www.jobbridge.ie/), whilst potentially of benefit for many, are also impacting negatively on professional status, pay and conditions of employment. The interface between social care workers, social care attendants and Job Bridge interns in tandem with the aforementioned social work schemes means that the professions of social care and social work are being redefined within unprecedentedly rapid timeframes.

These changes are happening at a time when social care workers and their representative bodies such as Social Care Ireland (http://socialcareireland.ie/) are pursuing professional registration with CORU (http://www.coru.ie/), the body tasked with regulating health and social care professionals. However, the requirements of the state and the markets may not be best served by having established professional social care workers.

Workers, for their part, need to reclaim their rightful place within the care system and advocate with, and on behalf of, those requiring their support.

> ... there is a need for practitioners to reclaim their professional expertise in reflective practice in order to address the excesses of a "zombification" process on the dogma of crude risk assessment based on actuarial factorisation. (Hester, 2012:37)

There was an absence of activism within the social professions in response to paradigms such as social partnership, which ostensibly brought accord to labour relations but also promoted the policies of the State (Allen, 1999, 2000; Moran, 2010), while suppressing the voice of community activists. Funding and salaries became the weapons of neoliberal policy-makers, which was exacerbated by relentless globalisation and market-driven policies.

A prime example is the inclusion of a non-advocacy clause in the Service Level Agreements (SLA) issued by the HSE to voluntary and charity bodies it funds, though it has to be acknowledged not within the former Child and Family Services (Harvey, 2014). In the 1980s and early 1990s champions of the excluded regularly challenged the state for its failings in supporting marginalised individuals and groups. While the Catholic Church has much to atone for with regard to children in the Republic of Ireland, the work of Fr. Peter McVerry and Sr. Stanislaus Kennedy in securing resources for those most in need must be acknowledged. Though both remain influential figures, who else currently challenges the state as vociferously?

For the worker to be fully empowered, the role of personal relationships needs to be valued again within the social professions.

> Whilst the ability to forge good interpersonal relationships is desirable, but often not essential for highly developed professions such as medicine and law, it is an absolute precondition of effective social work practice (Chu and Tsui, 2008; Chu et al., 2009; Proctor, 1982; Ward et al., 2010). Be-

fore all others, the core skill required by social work is the capacity to relate to others and their problems. (O'Leary *et al.*, 2013:137)

Better outcomes can only come from better practice with better supports that are appropriately resourced. Meaningful relationships are central to best practice and predictors of positive outcomes (Green *et al.*, 2001; Brendtro *et al.*, 2002; Lemon *et al.*, 2005; Osterling and Hines, 2006; Harder *et al.*, 2008).

The relevance of relationships is captured well by the following quote taken from a study of outcomes over a forty-year period of psychotherapy outcomes for youth:

> ... relationship factors (the strength of the alliance that develops between the youth and the worker, built upon perceived empathy, acceptance, warmth, trust and self-expression and defined by the youth as a helpful connection) and the ability of the worker to work positively with the client's ways of understanding themselves and others, account for 70 per cent of behaviour change. Two other factors, hope and expectancy that change will occur, account for 15 per cent of behaviour change (and also depend on a positive relationship between worker and youth) while intervention models and techniques account for only 15 per cent. Fundamental to any prevention or intervention that has a chance of success, is a strong positive relationship. (Clarke, cited in Smith, 2009:120-121)

Furthermore, the current situation where bureaucratic models invest power in external managers who may have limited, outdated or indeed no experience in caring for children with complex needs must be challenged. Agency needs to be reverted to the workers to enable them to act responsibly and thereby place the child back at the centre of practice, rather than the fiduciary agendas of state agencies with which these external managers are aligned. Otherwise we run the risk of repeated failures to safeguard children where workers have failed to speak out, as evidenced in the findings of repeated abuse inquiries (Madonna House, 1996; Ryan Report, 2009). Amongst the lessons we need to take from these shocking cases is not that residential child care is the location of systemic abuse, but that workers, properly empowered, are an effective child protection mechanism.

A significant study in 2010 by Stevens *et al.* identified altruistic motivation, what I refer to as the desire to make a difference, as the most important motive for students to undertake social work courses. It may be the motivation for staff to challenge practices which they believe are not in the young person's best interest, such as by whistle-blowing, which increasingly is being recognised as a critical mechanism in protecting those in care. Furthermore, my practice knowledge would highlight a connection between this desire and strengths-based practice, as most such practitioners are looking for the positives in young people.

> I strongly believe that it is the actions of people that ultimately protect children, or the failure to act that places children at risk. (Elliott, 2012:69)

As previously stated, we are more likely to find what we are looking for than stumble across that which we are not seeking. In fact, the very act of seeking something may cause it to become manifest, for example, in the case of self-fulfilling prophecies. This, then, holds very different potentials for strengths-based and deficit-based approaches.

Professionalisation, Commercialisation and Managerialism

Professionalisation of social care, at times erroneously conflated with professionalism, is a topical issue. In the Republic of Ireland professional registration of social care workers is anticipated to commence in 2017 (Jeyes, 2014). This places a greater imperative on workers to engage with their profession. If not, we may find that the professionalisation agenda will be determined by bureaucrats, politicians and administrators, and implemented by managers aligned with their agendas. For example, managers implementing these models use the tools of audit management where key performance indicators (KPIs), which have become part of the nomenclature within social care management in recent years, are aligned more with the requirements of management than the well-being of children. Abbott (1988) posited that a better way to consider professional work is to see it as something that is defined within the continuous struggle between different occupational groups. Abbott's thesis can be informative to consider the addition of the "new managerialism" agenda (Clarke, 2000; Kirkpatrick *et al.*, 2005; Ruch, 2005; Meade, 2012) as representative of a new occupational group. This group includes managers who, paradoxically, whilst attempting to reduce the professional autonomy of occupational groups in order to control them, in this case social care/work professionals, seek to claim the very professional status formerly associated with these groups for themselves (Noordegraff and Schinkel, 2011).

Examples of this "new managerialism" can be found in many official publications in social care. For example, in the aforementioned 2011 HSE Review of Adequacy Report, under Point 9.3, Service Developments within Foster Care, the development of standardised business processes is clearly linked to care plans:

> The development of Standardised Business Processes to provide consistency in assessment tools and care plans. (HSE, 2011:47)

This conflation of business with care has become pervasive over the past two decades. The pernicious tentacles of free market-defined corporatism, which poorly regulated led to what the economist Susan Strange famously labelled "casino capitalism", have spread from the private sector to the statutory sector. Significant drivers of this corporatisation were the shift to neoliberal paradigms coupled with the imperative to achieve international competitiveness (Hanlon, 1998). In the UK, New Labour championed the "Third Way" (Ietto-Gillies, 2006). Halpern and Misosz (1998:43) point out "there is no clear definition of the third way", but certainly a cultural shift towards attitudes of welfare provision which focused on paid work rather than welfare assistance, and the role of the state in "enabling" its citizens to become economically independent by modifying welfare provision was, and remains, a central tenet. Basically, the mantra was that the state has no role in supporting families. This was facilitated with a shift in social policy outlined by Miliband (1994:88-89):

> Welfare has to be preventive rather than ameliorative, economic as well as social: the most potent social policy is a successful economic policy.

Rees (2010:332), commenting on Powell's (2000) observations of the Third Way, stated:

> The Third Way is as Powell (2000) pointed out, hard to define but in practice it has led to the marriage of the public and independent sector. In entering into this marriage, the public sector has acquired all the relatives of the independent sector as "in-laws"; market processes, financial primacy, competition and organizational streamlining.

These processes in the UK influenced developments in the Republic of Ireland in promoting the neoliberal agenda and the influence of the private sector within the public sector.

As we have seen, neoliberalism promotes entrepreneurial behaviour with government intervention perceived as an impediment to enterprise culture. Additionally, enterprise defines the conduct of organisational and individual activity which is focused on producing autonomous, self-regulating and self-limiting organisations and individuals (Beck, 1992; du Gay *et al.*, 1996).

> Basically, one is no longer concerned with attaining something "good", but rather with *preventing* the worst; *self-limitation* is the goal that emerges. (Beck, 1992:49)

> One might want to say that the generalization of an "enterprise form" to *all* forms of conduct – to the conduct of organizations hitherto seen as non-economic to the conduct of government, and to the conduct of individuals themselves – constitutes the essential characteristic of this style of government: the promotion of an enterprise culture. (Burchell, 1993:275)

Within this enterprise culture and the belief in the superiority of private-sector management (Doolin, 2002) the inclusion of

Public Private Partnerships (PPP) can be seen to have facilitated a further corporatisation of the public sector. PPP commenced in the Republic of Ireland with eight pilot projects in 1999 with, in more recent times, PPP becoming a major pillar of the Irish government plans to stimulate the stalled economy with €2.5 billion in investment announced in July 2012 (Reeves, 2013). Coupled with PPP, we had the emergence of highly-paid consultants along with government advisers, predominately from within the private sector, taking up powerful shadow-roles within government. The privatisation of the welfare states in major economies has been identified as a prime avenue of future business opportunity for corporations (Cogman and Oppenheim, 2002; Hanlon and Fleming, 2009).

These neoliberally-spawned enterprise actions have reshaped Irish social, economic and state structures with the cumulative effect being the corporatisation of the public sector. In this process the state has reduced its liability to supporting the needy and marginalised, and thereby facilitated its retraction from the welfare state (Hanlon and Fleming, 2009). In the same process the state also seeks to shifts risk to the private sector. The Department of Public Expenditure and Reform website states:

> The PPP approach has the potential to offer value for money and timely delivery of infrastructure when applied to projects of the right scale, risk and operational profile. One key aspect of the PPP approach is that risk is transferred to the party that can manage it best.

However, there is scant evidence that these PPPs, totalling €6 billion since 1999, have in fact met these objectives (Reeves, 2013). With Irish Water we have witnessed the enormous expenditure on consultancy, often to internationally-based firms, with contracts awarded to IBM for €44.8 million and Accenture for €17.2 million (*Irish Times*, 2014). Additionally, the scale of expenditure on government special advisers has been unveiled at €3.4 million, with many instances of salaries above agreed pay caps (*Irish Independent*, 2012), coupled with numerous exposés of questionable actions associated with these advisers, often relating to their appointment.

Through such dynamics the public sector became subject to corporatisation and the assimilation of business practices within government departments, including social services. This then passed to the voluntary and community sector, as the state expected these sectors to provide services which were formerly the preserve of the state (Harvey, 2014). This process was in part facilitated via a type of osmosis-like legitimising mechanisms of organisational isomorphism.

> Research in institutional theory has examined the causes of isomorphism, that is, the factors that lead organizations to adopt similar structures, strategies and processes (Davies, 1991; DiMaggio and Powell, 1983; Mezias, 1990; Jennings and Zhou, 1993). (Deephouse, 1996:1024)

This version of rampant corporatism masquerades under the guise of efficiency. It espouses the mantra of value-for-money with the underpinning assumption that business models will yield more-effective services at the lowest possible cost. This "corporatisation of care" assumes that any enterprise will benefit from applied business practices and systems of risk, quality and performance management, thereby emulating, on a reduced scale, the trajectory of private corporations (Jessop, 1994).

> The assumption that public healthcare providers can be organized as commercial entities and run as successful businesses is based on the belief in the efficiency of a competitive market mechanism and the superiority of private-sector management practices. (Doolin, 2002:385)

There is an unquestioning belief that corporate success was as a result of skilled leadership, further propagating the "cult of the individual/entrepreneur" so reified by neoliberal paradigms. This assumption is at best one-dimensional and at worst dangerous. It assumes that only by the ruthless implementation of audit-based management and managerial-based models of practice can value-for-money be achieved. In the drive for efficiency the focus is all on the administrator implementing corporate practices with little or no focus, other than cost cutting and "flexible" efficiency strategies, on the workers actually delivering the services.

Clearly any service needs to operate efficiently and waste should not be tolerated. Indeed, most businesses would not remain operational if run at a loss for prolonged periods of time, which in the case of social care means that those needing support would no longer get a service (Forster, 2001). Also, it is true that areas of the public services, social care included, needed reform after the excesses of the Celtic Tiger era and the recession which followed. However, the state's response, with the compliance of certain sections of the media, is a further example of the procrustean practice of individualisation and fragmentation inherent in neoliberalism. Here, the public sector was castigated for waste and pitted against the private sector which was extolled for efficiency (Murphy, 2010; Monaghan *et al.*, 2013).

However, the singular focus on value-for-money with reliance on the likes of SWOT analysis and KPIs as indicators of professional excellence is flawed. This disavows the key place of ethics, values and the intrinsic motivation and commitment present in the majority of social care professionals – the desire to make a difference. This unilateral approach is not working in promoting better outcomes for children in care and needs to be correctly integrated into the profession, but in balance with other factors such as the empowerment of staff and the value of practice-based wisdom. It cannot, for the sake of children in care, remain the dominant paradigm.

These managerial and audit models of practice are redefining the social professions within the neoliberally-defined parameters set by state, a point succinctly made by Gerald Hanlon:

> ... in short the state is engaged in trying to redefine professionalism so that it becomes more commercially aware, budget focused, managerial, entrepreneurial and so forth. (1999:121)

The evidence of this phenomenon is present within all sectors of social care. Most notably, there has been a "blurring of the lines" between the voluntary and private sectors. As we saw earlier, Rees

(2010) identified some voluntary companies do in fact generate profits but label these profits as "surpluses". This financial mandate is evident with the revelations in 2014 of the salaries paid to some senior executives. We have senior managers in a considerable number of voluntary bodies being paid six-figure salaries with the often citied rationale being that if we want the best people for the job we must pay salaries equivalent to those in the private sector. This places little emphasis on the value bases of such managers and seriously calls into question their appropriateness for employment in leading roles in social care. Within these agencies the service ethic, originally defined in 1939 by Marshall as the professional service ethos with service provision determined by need rather than ability to pay, is being eroded by the focus on personal monetary reward. If people want to make six-figure salaries they could more appropriately achieve this goal within private-sector employment. However, to serve others within the caring professions is, and should be, itself part of the reward, the job satisfaction. It is with some irony, given that he was formerly a bank official and currently operates predominately in international financial circles, but also with respect, that I quote one of Ireland's more successful entrepreneurs, Gerry Murphy, with regard to personal monetary reward:

> It is, however, incidental rather than an end in itself. What excites me is creating something from nothing, solving problems and improving other people's lives. (Murphy, 2014:xii)

Earning six-figure salaries in agencies providing care to the marginalised, and being supported partly or wholly by public money is, at a minimum, incompatible with the service ethic. It is also inappropriate within the context of the shrinking resources available which are vital for the sustenance of those in need.

This rationale of employing the "best people for the job" is flawed on several levels, not the least of which is by virtue of what our definition of "the best" actually means. Hanlon (1998) outlined a form of commercialised professionalism which we are seeing within these voluntary bodies. These leaders are often identified as "the best" within the three parameters of commercialised professionalism:

1) Technical ability – this will allow one to practice in the profession but will not guarantee advancement nor success

2) Managerial skill – this is the ability to manage other employees, the ability to balance budgets and the capacity to manage and satisfy clients

3) The ability to bring in business and/or act in an entrepreneurial way. (Hanlon, 1998:13)

Such selection parametres result in a range of consequences which impact on support services for children in care and after-care, as well as other marginalised groups. Firstly, the ability to act entrepreneurially and generate profit or "bring to the table" networks which have the ability to attract funding weakens the focus on providing a service based on need. "In short, personal professional success is related to profitability not to servicing clients in need" (Hanlon, 1998:50). Secondly, as previously highlighted, the people in care are often those on the margins of society and helping these "clients/customers" means that their voices must be heard above others. This has clear repercussions for many marginalised young people, as it is the more successful ones who often receive the most support, while the less successful, those more prone to social exclusion and without a voice, will receive the least. Thirdly, the technical function has been downgraded as a focus on managerial and entrepreneurial skills is preferred (Hanlon, 1998).

Furthermore, organisational culture comes from the top down (Schein, 2004) and clearly leaders play a pivotal role in this process. However, little heed appears to be paid to the fact that some leaders in the voluntary sectors are getting paid six figure salaries, whilst the lower grade employees are experiencing salary reductions and increased workplace demands in the guise of flexible working arrangements. This engenders a conflict between what these leaders espouse in terms of what they demand from their workers and what they receive themselves. We have a clear case of double standards where "do as I say not as I do" is the practice in evidence, which results in a disavowal of the service ethic that is integral to the caring professions. Solidarity and transformation are preached but the price is paid by the workers and those they support, not the leaders. This clearly has the potential to demotivate the workforces of such organisations and alienate public support.

An appropriate model for remuneration within the voluntary sector would be the model of "maximum wage" as outlined by Sam Pizzigati (1992, 2012). Pizzigati develops the pre-existing concept of maximum wage that had previously been endorsed by businessmen such as J.P. Morgan (1837–1913). Central to the concept is the linking of maximum salaries in any company to the minimum salary within the same company within a defined ratio. So, for example, a company operating a ratio of 5:1 would mean that the highest paid person could only earn five times what the lowest paid employee earns. Thus, if leaders want to pay themselves higher salaries they must also raise the salary of the lower paid employees to keep within the 5:1 ratio. This model ensures equity within any company and, in the case of voluntary agencies, would be in keeping with the service ethos.

The appointment of senior managers based on management skill-sets at excessive salaries is a self-perpetuating model. Anyone seeking to be considered for such roles must undertake training to satisfy the personal specifications requirements. These specifications are often stipulated by existing managers or private recruitment firms, and thus new managers become exposed to the paradigms associated with such models. This ability to ensure continuity via mechanisms of leadership and reward, seductive rather than coercive, is a feature of neoliberalism and the beneficiaries are the managers, administrators and state. The workers and those in receipt of services are relegated in importance, in the case of the worker, with lower pay and employment rights, and for those in need of services, with reduction in supports and entitlements.

With growing levels of poverty the rationale of employing increasing numbers of managers to micro-manage budgets and effect cost savings is flawed on at least two levels.

Firstly, this obviously consumes more of the resources available in salaries to these administrators which has the effect of reducing what is available for those in need. Secondly, the raison d'être for these administrators is to effect efficiencies to achieve cost savings and these targets validate their role, and salaries. The needs of those requiring services thus become secondary. One of the dangers is that it is possible for these administrators to make savings far in excess of their salaries, thus appearing to validate their role, but at the cost of reduced service quality. Motivation is a key factor in the social professions, and we must always question whether the end justifies the means. Alfie Kohn's seminal publication, *Punished by Rewards* (1993), offers valuable insight into the pitfalls of motivation by reward where performance is shown to suffer where motivation is promoted solely by financial incentives and rewards.

We need to set our expectations higher than merely achieving targets, such as the elimination of waiting lists. Having no waiting list but a service that does not meet the needs of care leavers is not an acceptable achievement. It is difficult to conceive of just how an aftercare worker can have a meaningful relationship with an individual client when they have caseloads of 25 and as high as 40 (Tusla, 2014a), an issue addressed in some detail in the Irish context by Burns and McCarthy, (2012) and internationally by Ridley *et al.* (2013).

> There is a clear link between caseload levels and quality of service as important both for outcomes for children and social workers' job satisfaction (Landsman, 2001; Strolin, McCarthy and Caringi, 2007; United States General Accounting Office, 2003). (Burns and McCarthy, 2012:26)

Whilst there has been progress made, for example within Dublin North East where there is emerging clarity around what aftercare support is and who is in receipt of it, there is still unfortunately strong evidence of this "target focus" with regard to aftercare nationally. This is evidenced in Dublin North East (DNE) within the "Aftercare Service DNE Review Report", 2014. This report is welcomed as an example of both willingness to make available what formerly may have been restricted in terms of internal reports, and also as a detailed account of aftercare services in DNE. It is important to acknowledge the poor history of the former Child and Family Agency within the HSE, which Carl O'Brien (2012), at the *Irish Times* correctly castigated for its excessive unwillingness, originating at senior management level, to make available data to external stakeholders.

In an informative book chapter, that commences poignantly with the tragic story of David Foley's death, O'Brien identifies some of these practices and their consequences:

> Furthermore, this information vacuum feeds a largely negative stereo-type about the image of social workers as a kind of over-zealous social police. This does a huge disservice to social workers...Far too often, even the most basic information seems to be shrouded in a veil of secrecy...It ultimately allows inadequate and under-funded social services to limp along, and it increases the pressure on committed social workers on the ground. (O'Brien, 2012:115-121)

Additionally, he identifies how when reports into serious failings in keeping children safe are eventually published, having been heavily censored, they invariably focus on "statistics and examples of good practice – criticism of the HSE's own employees is almost entirely absent" (2012:116). This is one practice that senior management within Tusla must guard against, not to deflect from the failings identified through highlighting any positive elements within these reports. Senior management must lead by example in accepting responsibility for failings and be mindful that in balancing the needs of maintaining essential public trust that same public will recognise when they are defending the indefensible. As Brien (2009:404;405) has stated with regard to trustworthiness and public confidence in a profession:

> Quite literally, for a professional all else flows form it...in order to be trustworthy and trusted, the professional must be ethical and be seen to be ethical.

Richard Stivers, in his book *Technology as Magic: The Triumph of the Irrational* published in 2001, identifies a management strategy which resonates with Irish statutory Child and Family Services. Stivers identifies how simply making a change in a management technique, such as the introduction of a new audit method, is viewed as success. Consequently, constant change is viewed as success when in fact there is no assessment of outcome or any evidence that the new technique either improves service quality or is accurate. Gambrill (2013:590) identifies such a strategy as "goal displacement", citing authors who have similarly written about this strategy as Power (1997) and Munro (2011). Implicit in this strategy is the deferral of accountability as each change, it is claimed, must be given time to effect its stated goals, and it is only after sufficient time has elapsed that assessment of its outcomes can be determined. Stivers further identifies how:

> Formal information is requested no matter how much managers already have and even while ignoring what they do have. Information is sometimes requested after a decision has already been made. In short, managers request more formal information, whether useful or not, at any time and ignore much of it. (Stivers, 1999:198)

This brings us back to the previously identified issue of the "appliance of science" within social professions, with Stivers putting forward an excellent case to unveil the illusionary aspects associated with such applications. The reality is that no management system can remedy issues of insufficient staffing and resources to accomplish tasks which only skilled human beings can accomplish. The more we try to achieve such technologically-based practice the further we distance our services from the core task, which demands that practitioners have time to support people through meaningful relationships and thereby effect change.

As noted, the aforementioned DNE Aftercare Service Review Report (2014) has much to recommend it. The publication of detailed statistical data on the Tusla website is another good example of transparent practices by Irish Child and Family Services. In making this report available critical analysis can inform the development and ultimately improvement of aftercare services. One such analysis of this report is the interpretation of Mike Stein's research. In Section 1.7:18, which addresses aftercare provision, the following statement is made:

> The most important requirements for young people leav-
> ing care are secure, suitable accommodation, access to
> further education, employment or training and supportive
> relationships. (Stein, 2009)

The reference citation is for Stein 2009, an internet web link
to a presentation he gave at a conference in Dublin in 2009, which
does not work and is in unavailable as it was given six years ago.

Another example of questionable interpretation of Professor
Stein's research is contained within another Tusla publication, *Alternative Care: Practice Handbook* (2014), which states:

> Stein (2012) identifies four major tasks of professionals
> supporting young people into adulthood:
>
> 1) finding settled, safe accommodation;
>
> 2) starting and maintaining employment;
>
> 3) further education or training;
>
> 4) being responsible for their own health and well-being.
> (Tusla, 2014g:138)

These are curious interpretations of Professor Stein's research
given that since 1986 all his research into leaving care and resilience has consistently highlighted the emotional and psychosocial
needs alongside the above. Whilst his 2012 book does identify the
above-cited issues in Part 2, other sections of Part 2 have headings
like Homelessness, Housing Outcomes and Leaving Care Services;
and Young People Needing More Support.

The best source of interpretation of the work of Professor Stein
is, unquestionably, the author himself. From the following two
statements it can be seen that he has in fact consistently identified a wider range of needs other than those cited in the two Tusla
publications, both with regard to preparation for leaving care and
aftercare:

> Preparation (for leaving care) should be holistic in ap-
> proach, attaching equal importance to practical, emotional
> and interpersonal skills… (Stein, 2006b:430)

> Reflecting upon the main "lessons learned" from research studies carried out over four decades suggests that the foundation stones of supportive pathways to adulthood are providing young people with: stability; continuity of attachment; emotional security; a positive sense of identity; compensation for educational deficits and opportunities to maximise progress; leisure activities, new opportunities and turning points; and holistic preparation – or put simply, good-quality care. (Stein 2015:199)

The interpretation of Stein's research is an important issue as these findings are used to influence policy development and service configuration.

Additionally, within the above-cited DNE report the issue of achieving targets as opposed to achieving what is in fact the required outcome, standardisation, which would challenge regional variation and therefore iniquity, is made manifest in the passage cited below. Here, achieving the target of providing a dedicated aftercare service is evidently seen as sufficient, and standardisation is identified as not worth changing what is apparently working, that is to say, what is achieving the target:

> However, at the time of writing this report, confirmation received from the Child and Family Agency national office with regard to the organizational structure for aftercare services informs that "Further to the aftercare audit (national audit) completed in 2011, it is clear that some areas have already in place a structure that meets the criteria of providing a dedicated aftercare service to young people leaving care … where the current structure although not standardised nationally works well and does not need to change." (Tusla, Aftercare Services DNE Review Report, 2014:53)

Meeting identified targets such as eliminating waiting lists may produce excellent results in management reports, however, although important, this is only one dimension of the complex combination of factors that constitute an effective aftercare service. What we cannot determine with this methodology is just what support the care leavers are actually getting, or how many are not in receipt of a service. Thus we have no insight into the quality of the service being provided or, indeed, as previously highlighted, whether or not we are getting value-for-money for the €17 million spent on aftercare in 2012 (Dáil Debates, 2013, Written Answers, 19073/13). Furthermore, this same report refers to developing the best aftercare service possible, which is to be lauded as an aspiration, although settling for achieving identified targets is tantamount to accepting mediocrity. Worse than accepting mediocrity, it is also a case of the needs of an organisation being put ahead of the needs of those people it is there to serve, in this case care leavers. There may be times where not fixing what isn't broken is indeed good practice, but only after considering that what worked previously may no longer be appropriate if things have changed. Equally, when the desired outcome is an equitable service without regional variation, this cannot be achieved without standardisation and thus change is essential. However, standardisation can be problematic, and the DNE Review Report provides an example where the case loads of the voluntary sector were raised to match those in place within the statutory sector. In this standardisation process the replication of the statutory sector is made manifest by what can be described as an "isomorphic hammer". Here, without compliance by the voluntary sector there would be serious ramifications from their main source of funding, the HSE/Tusla.

. . . .

This is an example of the potential for quantity to be prioritised over quality through focusing on readily quantifiable targets. This highlights a risk within the social care profession where focusing primarily on targets can lead to unethical actions.

. . . .

What I have learnt through my management and practice experience is that complex problems, no matter how challenging, are to be welcomed. Whilst often difficult to resolve, they largely involve management of people and resources and therefore are what we are trained to do. It is the problems that lie beyond our control that are most difficult to deal with and therefore the least welcome – societal, political and macro-economic, to name but three. When our work is impacted by these problems this makes social care management and practice much more difficult.

> What decision is made and whether it is implemented will also depend on the strength of commitment, integrity and determination of the professionals involved. (Banks, 2006:177)

As we saw earlier, the terms professionalisation and profession are both highly contested (Neal and Morgan, 2000; Devlin, 2005) and this ambiguity renders them susceptible to being appropriated by politicians and policy-makers to further their agendas. This ambiguity is added to by the fact that the meanings attributed to these terms in Anglo-American societies are not directly translatable or applicable in other languages (Jarausch, 1990; Neal and Morgan, 2000).

Much that is wrong with the market-defined, neoliberal conception of professionalism and the resultant welfare provision, as well as the need to provide care as opposed to making money, is encapsulated by Henry Tam, who outlines the potential harm to our sense of community:

> One of the most pernicious aspects of market individualism is its suggestion that individuals have within them the power to lift themselves out of all hardships, and that those who do not exercise this power deserve to be the victims, only surviving at the mercy of those who use their power to the full. Capricious fortune may endow some of us with better initial conditions than others to live a fulfilling life, but it can just as easily throw us into tragic circumstances. It is the deep seated feeling that we need to care for others, just as we need others to care for us, that lies at the heart of human solidarity. When this feeling is dismissed as unworthy of competitive market heroes, it threatens to undermine the possibility of communal existence. (1998:129-130)

Evetts describes the changes which result from such forms of professionalism:

... the appeal to the discourse (of professionalism) by managers in work organisations is a myth or an ideology of professionalism (Evetts, 2003). The myth includes aspects such as exclusive ownership of an area of expertise, increased status and salary, autonomy and discretion in work practices and the occupational control of the work. The reality of professionalism is actually very different. The appeal to professionalism by managers most often includes the substitution of organisational for professional values; bureaucratic, hierarchical and managerial controls rather than collegial relations; managerial and organisational objectives rather than client trust and autonomy based on competencies and expertise; budgetary restrictions and financial rationalisations; the standardisation of work practice rather than discretion; and performance targets, accountability and sometimes increased political control.

The use of the discourse of professionalism as operationalised by managers in work organisations is also a discourse of self-control which enables self-motivation and sometimes even self-exploitation. (2011:12-13)

Evetts is not alone in identifying this potential for self-exploitation as many others have also referenced it as a strong feature of neoliberally-shaped practices. The inherent potential for achieving the desired control by the state or corporate interests – veiled behind smoke screens and spin employing emotive and powerful terminology such as empowerment, choice, rights, inclusion, professionalism – bears constant vigilance on part of today's professionals. Foucault's concept of neoliberal government where control is exercised through the production of subject positions and moral conduct "has inspired a whole tradition of work on the various institutions, mechanisms, techniques and groups through which conduct is regulated" (Fournier, 1999:283). In this way the state seemingly conducts itself in a rational manner through the co-operation of free-willed subjects (Burchell, 1993). Foucault (1997) outlined a concept of "subjectification" which involved a range of "technologies of the self" where individuals engage with processes Foucault likens to the confessional. He posits that individuals engage in reflective processes which lead to them acting in a self-regulating manner, thus producing the self-managing individuals central to neoliberal rule (Dreyfus and Rainbow, 1982; Miller, 1993; Turner, 1997; Gilbert and Powell, 2010).

> Techniques of self-assessment, counselling, refection and professional supervision all provide examples of confessional practice (Gilbert, 2001; Rose, 1999). (Gilbert and Powell, 2010:7)

This is not to say that the techniques outlined above are themselves flawed; correctly used they can be beneficial by improving self-awareness, practice and well-being. Rather, it is the potential for manipulation and misuse by agents of the state and corporate capital that we must guard against.

> "Governmentality" has come to depend in crucial respects upon the intellectual technologies, practical activities and social authority associated with expertise.... (Miller and Rose, 1990, 1)... It is through their "professionalization", through their inscriptions into systems of expert knowledge, that individuals become the targets of liberal governments (Foucault, 1978)... The professions are central to liberalism, to the microphysics of power (Foucault, 1973) through which the governed are constituted as autonomous subjects regulating their own conduct (Miller and Rose, 1990). (Fournier, 1999:284)

As we have seen, there are several prerequisites for achieving professional status, summed up succinctly by Schinkel and Noordegraff:

> Professionalism, it is argued (e.g. Wilensky, 1964; Freidson, 1994, 2001), exists when workers are part of an occupational association that institutionalises a technical base (knowledge and skills) as well as a service ethic (some sort of calling or higher purpose). (2011:69)

From this perspective it can be seen that social care in the Republic of Ireland has achieved, to varying degrees, a reasonably defined base with regard to the first two issues. With regard to knowledge and skills, both of which can be acquired, the Applied Social Studies in Social Care degree course at third level has addressed this area, albeit with some issues relating to, inter alia, oversupply and thus the dilution of professional status. With regard to occupational associations, the formation of Social Care Ireland (SCI) should address this area. However, it is the third issue, the service ethic, what I refer to as the desire to make a difference, which is the one essential prerequisite to good social care practice. This cannot be taught or technically developed. Of course, a focus on training and accreditation are very positive elements within the profession.

· ·

> *We must be mindful that what is at stake within the professionalism agenda is "the ability to make a difference". (Schinkel and Noordegraff, 2011:88)*

· ·

A further factor in the establishment of a robust professional status is a defined code of ethics, which establishes expectations for practitioners and can be seen as a "reflection of the profession's collective values and principles" and the "hallmark of professionalism" (Francis and Dugger, 2014:131). From this perspective it can be seen that social care has much to do to match the developed code of ethics of social work in the Republic of Ireland. However, with regard to the enforcement of codes of ethics to regulate professional practice, and highlighting the importance of the vocational aspect of the desire to make a difference, Brien (2009:393) cautions that "using legislation to regulate ethical behaviour – as opposed to using legislation to constitute a vocation as a profession – would tend to de-professionalise the profession".

Seen from the cautionary perspective presented by Schinkel and Noordegraff (*ibid*) and Brien (*ibid*) we must be vigilant that the "cure" sought via professionalisation – the claim to professional status for social care – does not turn out to be worse than the disease.

Chapter 12

The Socio-Political and Socio-Economic Context

We must recognise, as previously stated, that social care work and policy is, in the widest sense, largely framed by the dominant political values in place.

> These politically defined purposes of social work also influences the psychological and sociological theories chosen by practitioners to help them "make sense" and practice. (Howe, cited in Davies, 2000:86)

Clearly paradigms come in and out of favour (Hannon *et al.*, 2010) which requires practitioners to be well informed to differentiate the factors driving these shifts, as "uncritical acceptance of change, however, can be dangerous for an individual, an organisation or a society" (Partington and Brown, 1997:210). Esping-Anderson's (1990) study of welfare capitalism affords good insight into how the dominant political philosophies have shaped welfare provision in European countries. There are a multitude of theories to explain psychological and sociological functioning. No one theory should dominate practice, just as no one epistemological paradigm should dominate the other.

We must be wary of becoming overly politically correct in what we say or advocate for fear of censure, loss of standing or access to funding streams, or worse perhaps, perceived incompetence. It is within this context that I accept that my views will not be embraced by all and that my methods may well be subject to criticism. The words of Aristotle hold true still today:

There is only one way to avoid criticism: do nothing, say nothing and be nothing.

Milligan (1943) employed the analogy of baking a cake to illustrate the flaws inherent in democracy. Using this analogy for the social professions, and for offering critical perspectives, it can be seen that there is much truth in the maxim that "you cannot bake a cake without breaking some eggs". If, in the process of creating a cake (writing a book), wherein conflict (difference of opinion) is inescapable as eggs must be broken (convention challenged), we occasionally get the recipe wrong and end up with egg on our faces then, well, this is the price of progress. More importantly, in the ensuing process truth-seeking (investigation) collaborative meaning-making (Bellefeuille and Ricks, 2010) is facilitated, even if driven by ulterior motivations on the part of some of those instigating these processes. Furthermore, as demonstrated within Keith's story, getting egg on one's face by virtue of being fooled due to one's belief in people's positive potential can also sometimes be a good thing. However, when we get the recipe right in our practice, whether intentionally or not, great transformations can be facilitated with traumatised children developing into healthy young people and thereafter adults.

Social Justice

Social care/work professionals are tasked with practicing from a principal base of social justice and to operate with anti-discriminatory practices (Ruch, 2005). Perhaps it is this supporting of the underdog, the marginalised and excluded, the oppressed and those in need, that constitutes the previously referenced desire to make a difference. However, as all behaviour meets a need, many of us enter social care to fill our own need to care. This need may make holders of such character traits well suited to caring work, but that is not to say that they will be better functioning human beings than those with different characteristics. The pitfalls to what could be also construed as a character flaw are many, and self-awareness is vital to mitigate these potential pitfalls.

These principles are made explicit within the Irish Association of Social Workers Code of Ethics and the International Federation of Social Workers (2014) Global Definition of Social Work. The Irish Association of Social Workers Code of Ethics states:

> The members of the Irish Association of Social Workers (IASW) acknowledge:
>
> • That every person is unique and has an intrinsic worth;
>
> • That society has an obligation to pursue justice, in all its forms, on behalf of every person including the assertion and protection of their human rights.

The International Federation of Social Workers (2014) Global Definition of Social Work states:

> Social work is a practice-based profession and an academic discipline that promotes social change and development, social cohesion, and the empowerment and liberation of people. Principles of social justice, human rights, collective responsibility and respect for diversities are central to social work...

If we accept that principles of social justice and anti-discriminatory are central to our work, then we should also apply these to our profession. By re-framing theories to focus on workers and organisations, rather than young people and their carers, as we did earlier with attachment theory, light can be cast of less well illuminated issues.

For example, we might see the dominance of evidenced-based and managerial models of practice as oppressing relational work and psychosocial approaches. Once recognised, we then would hold a professional responsibility to seek a redress of such an imbalance. But, could it be that the dominant market forces and neoliberal policies have diminished the professional autonomy, and therefore the ability to seek redress, of social care/work professionals? Have the demands for flexibility, standardisation, accountability and inter-professional collaboration weakened the claim to professional status of many professions including the social professions?

> ... the neoliberal dogmas of managerialism and market relevance actively undermine professional authority and independence. (Meade, 2012:906)

Standardisation of practice may improve consistency but it also weakens claim to esoteric knowledge mastery, as does the ability to access information rapidly and from most any location in the increasingly digitalised world (Evetts, 2011).

> Positive developments include increased accountability and standardisation of social work practice however this may be at the cost of producing a punitive environment and reducing social work to a simplistic description of practice that operates within a culture of blame and protocolisation (time spent on activities such as paperwork or electronic form filling). (Gilbert and Powell, 2010:12)

Accountability and Competence

Those professionals who carry statutory responsibility can come under sustained attack with increasing calls for individual accountability for the failings in protecting children (Smith, 2009; Ruch, 2011). The expectation that by the implementation of better management models and risk assessments, the appliance of science approach, complex situations will be made manageable can result in false expectations being placed upon under-resourced professionals. Dekker (2007) argues that accidents are no longer perceived as uncontrollable events, but rather as failures of risk management, and behind these failures, Dekker argues, there is a person or group who are to be held accountable. It is the task of experts to give meaning to these "accidents" and to explain which risk factors were not controlled, when, where and by whom. Through such patently flawed processes the illusion that the uncontrollable is rendered controllable is propogated. The media, political and abuse inquiries, which inevitably result in a raft of new policies and procedural directives aimed at eliminating risk factors, add to this clamour for accountability, which Gillingham (2006) argues is fuelled by the risk discourse which proposes that accurate risk prediction is possible.

> Despite the acknowledgment that complexity, risk, uncertainty and ambiguity are intrinsic dimensions of child-care social work, government directives frequently contradict this belief. The exhortations to "learn the lessons" from public inquiries and serious case reviews, for example, alongside the expectation that, if the "right" systems are in place, risk can be eliminated, create false illusions that the eradication of risk is possible. (Ruch, 2012:1317)

Accountability can also be a mechanism for controlling the professional by employers and regulatory bodies. This form of accountability "entails not just undertaking work that can be justified in terms of recognised standards of practice (process) but also in terms of benefits (outcomes or products)" (Banks, 2013:594).

It is not accountability alone that should be the focus of this "moral panic" (Cohen, 2002; Clapton, 2013; Krinsky, 2013), but rather competence combined with accountability. Within the domain of competence accountability is a sub-domain. Accountability is critical as it can delineate responsibilities which are essential for effectively safeguarding children, but it can also be associated with a blame culture, a point made by Holohan (2011:9):

> But our focus seems not to be on the broad application and value of the principle of accountability as an essential tool to guide good decision-making and governance, but rather on accountability as a means to apportion blame for past failings and to impose sanctions upon those who have failed or wronged us.

The expectation of accountability and competence rests not just with the individual worker but also structurally, in that workers must have the correct resources to competently undertake the task. Correctly resourced workers can then be accountable to those they support. The relentless calls for accountability do little to engender confidence in a sometimes beleaguered profession and indeed can be seen as promoting risk-averse practice. In 2015, the British Prime Minister, David Cameron, in reaction to the Rotherham and Rochdale Abuse Investigations, proposed to change legislation regarding the offence of wilful neglect within the Criminal Justice and Courts Acts 2015. This would allow for social workers to be imprisoned for up to five years for failing to keep children safe. Mr Cameron stated that this would send an "unequivocal message that professionals who fail to protect children will be held accountable" (Community Care, 3.3.2015).

This proposal prompted the following response from Brigid Featherstone, Chair of the College of Social Work's Children and Families faculty who stated:

> ... the move will reinforce a climate of persecution. The proposals also fail to address the incredibly important safeguarding issues that recent serious case reviews have raised. We must address the severe lack of investment in child protection services, which has put organisations and systems under incredible strain and reduced their capacity for in depth work with children and their families. (Community Care, 3.3.2015)

The retraction of the state from welfare provision leaves many vulnerable and a social justice perspective would require us to consider the status of the worker as well as the young person. By recognising that the residualisation of residential child care is a form of social injustice, as also is the virtual complete absence of positive discrimination for care leavers, we then recognise that this clamour for accountability may best be focused at policy-makers and government rather than individual workers.

> ... an emerging social structure of accumulation in which the state has cast aside a number of its "social welfare" functions, creating the requirements for an autonomist civil social order if capital is to reproduce itself. (Hanlon and Fleming, 2009:9)

Expecting individual accountability when the resources are not there is making a difficult task into a near impossible one

(Burns and MacCarthy, 2012). This is akin to the empowerment conundrum (Peters and Savoie, 1996), whereby theoretically giving individuals the power to make choices empowers them (to be self-regulating consumers), but in reality they do not have the wherewithal to actually make these choices.

> Consequently, empowerment takes on a purely individualistic meaning, rendering structural/systemic factors irrelevant. As Rose (2000) states, empowerment "codes the subjective substrate of exclusion as lack of self-esteem, self-worth, and the skills of self-management necessary to steer oneself as an active individual in the empire of choice" (Rose, 2000, p. 334). Social exclusion is reconfigured to be "a state of mind" amendable to cognitive restructuring and empowerment. (Pollack, 2010:1268)

Concomitantly, professionals are required to complete a job despite it being commonly accepted that they do not have the right resources to do so. This requires those who want to progress within this system to "work with what they have"; otherwise they can be seen as difficult, inflexible or, paradoxically, incompetent and unprofessional. Within such paradigms authority compliance (Bushman, 1984) becomes embedded.

Yalloway *et al.* (2012:96-97), with reference to Irish Child Protection Services, identify how:

> ... the inherent danger in the implementation of rapid reforms to a system, which demands increasing standards of performance management and accountability, is that the focus of the service becomes increasingly managerial rather than practice based (Tilbury, 2004; Buckley, 2008, 2009).

Mark Smith, as cited in the introduction to this book, has stated, "Actually being professional is about getting the job done, competently and ethically" (Smith, 2009:136). I would add that a key component of competence in social care is found within the minutiae. Attention to detail within all aspects of the work, including knowledge of the child and their social ecology, implementation of programmes, assessment and the completion of documentation as well as practice skills such as listening, as we saw in Owen's case, is critical to competent practice. This precludes making assumptions and raises standards and therefore expectations. My practice learning merely confirms what Winnicott already identified, originally in 1947:

> In no work is attention to detail more important than in work with children (Winnicott, cited in Winnicott *et al.*, 2013:63)

Attention to the minutiae demands reflective (Perry, 2000) and reflexive (Cunliffe, 2009) practice on the part of the worker. D'Cruz *et al.* (2007) undertook an interrogation of the meaning of reflexivity and its relevance to social work. They identify how the term is often used interchangeably with critical reflection, but is in fact a different construct. They identify three different forms of reflexivity that are relevant to social work:

1. A worker's response to their immediate context and making choices for further direction;

2. A worker's self-critical approach that questions how knowledge is generated and what role power relations play in this process;

3. A worker's awareness of the relationship between thought and feeling in how knowledge is constructed and how this informs their emotional responses to a situation.

D'Cruz *et al.* cite Schön (1983) and Sheppard *et al.* (2000) in identifying a crucial difference between critical reflection and reflexivity. They identify the distinction between reflection-on-action (past tense) as opposed to reflection-in-action "in the moment" (Sheppard *et al.*, cited in D'Cruz *et al.*, 2007:83). Within this construct, workers operating competently identify those whose needs are paramount, the young people and their families, as opposed to other vested and, at times, competing interests.

There is much to reflect on in the commonly cited adage that with power comes responsibility, and the power that comes with statutory authority comes with a responsibility to seek the right resources to meet the needs of those requiring support. This is a vital form of competence and those professionals who may be labelled as troublesome, incompetent or unprofessional for seeking the right resources to undertake the work are in fact being highly competent and therefore professional.

This is a point made explicit in Section 4.2.4 of the International Federation of Social Workers Statement of Ethical Principles:

> 4. Challenging unjust policies and practices – Social workers have a duty to bring to the attention of their employers, policy-makers, politicians and the general public situations where resources are inadequate or where distribution of resources, policies and practices are oppressive, unfair or harmful.

Social care work is becoming increasingly complex, which, when considered from a psychodynamic perspective, can be seen to be anxiety-inducing for those working within the profession.

> In recent years, wider societal awareness of the impact of risk and uncertainty on social structures and behaviours has penetrated into the domain of social work practice (Broadhurst et al., 2010; Parton, 2008; Power, 2004; Warner and Sharland, 2010). This recognition of the complexity of practice in social work, and more broadly across the human service professions, has been accompanied by the widespread growth of managerialism (Munro, 2010; Skinner, 2010). (Ruch, 2012:1316)

Ruch (*ibid*) has identified the tension between relationship-based child care work and managerial practice as being the tension that lies at the heart of current social work management. She identifies managerial practice as being based on principles that focus more on predictability, cognition and rationality, and less on the emotional, irrational and unpredictable aspects of human behaviour. Relationship-based practice, she posits, is founded on a holistic understanding of human beings that encompasses all of these dimensions of behaviours (Ruch, 2005, 2011, 2012). She identifies how the anxiety and pain inherent in social work is potentially avoided though the employment of managerial approaches, the aforementioned "appliance of science" approaches. These offer the illusion that risk can be made manageable, thus making their employment an enticing proposition. This can occur either consciously or unconsciously for anxiety-burdened professionals, both workers and managers alike (Trinder and Reynolds, 2000).

> By adopting more managerialist approaches, the potentially anxiety-provoking aspects of practice are avoided. (Ruch, 2012:1318)

. . . .

At a minimum what is missing from this appliance of science approach is an acknowledgement that it is the human being delivering such programmes – the worker, and their skill and relationship with the young person that will determine whether or not these programmes will be effective or not. These programmes, including attendant policies, procedures and assessments, are not ends in themselves, rather they are a means to an end.

. . . .

Currently, Tusla is accountable for large elements of the protection and well-being of all children under 18 and, in reality, as we have seen, fulfil this growing mandate with limited resources. This is very challenging, at times warranting the title of "the impossible task", and seldom are the successes acknowledged to the same extent the failings are. Nonetheless, this is the duty employees undertake on taking up employment within Tusla.

However, systems which facilitate practices such as the expectation of individual accountability without sufficient resources can be seen to be dysfunctional. It is entirely plausible to perceive of such systems as posing a real threat of harm to workers. Here, the risk of what can be termed "system trauma", where the lack of support and resources afforded by the system of care is equally, if not more of a reality for workers than vicarious trauma. Young people are equally exposed to such "system trauma" within a system which, for example, in 2014, had 405 children waiting for an appointment within our Child and Adolescent Mental Health Service (CAMHS) for longer than 12 months (Children's Mental Health Coalition, 2015).

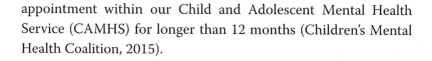

> *By placing aftercare on a robust legislative basis, Tusla would become accountable to care leavers which would ensure that aftercare develops in the optimum format. This form of accountability would offer the most benefit to those who depend on the service.*

Interdependence and Statistics

With the launch of Tusla there was a real opportunity to redress the past failings of children's service, some of which have been identified within this book. The potential for better outcomes for children leaving care will be promoted by focusing on the in-care development of children services. This includes the effective and statutorily prescribed preparation for leaving care targeting psychosocial and emotional well-being (Action for Children, 2014). Additionally, the focus on fostering interdependence (Stein, 2008a), the nurturing of autonomy within webs of dependence, rather than independence, will lead to better outcomes. It is these webs of dependence that constitute the supports identified within the social-ecology model of resilience. As posited by Rutter and Ungar, access to these resources is the critical factor in nurturing resilience. Resilience, within this construct, may be seen as the enactment of interdependency. Thus, to develop resilience in care leavers it is interdependence we need to be facilitating, rather than independence.

> This social ecological understanding of resilience implicates those who control the resources that facilitate psychological wellbeing in the proximal processes (e.g., making education accessible; promoting a sense of belonging in one's community; facilitating attachment to a caregiver; affirmation of self-worth) associated with positive development in contexts of adversity. (Ungar, 2013:255)

279

Supporting care leavers in education, as we currently do, is beneficial and education is undoubtedly a cornerstone of independence. However, not all care leaves, as was the case for Keith, will take up this option on leaving care:

> Given that young people in care often get stereotyped about their care experiences, it is interesting to note that after the age of 18, some 61.1 per cent of those young people were in some form of education or training and some 55.8 per cent of them were in full-time education. I accept that obviously means almost 40 per cent of them were not in education. (Dáil Debates, 2013, Topical Issue Debate: Foster Care Supports)

The fact that it is claimed that 38.9 per cent of care leavers do not participate in either education or training upon leaving care means that a large number are excluded from meaningful aftercare support. This potential is made explicit in Section 2.1 of the National Leaving and Aftercare Policy clearly states:

> It is emphasized that the most important requirements for young people leaving care are for secure, suitable accommodation as well as further education, employment or training. These core requirements will be prioritized in the provision of aftercare services.

. . . .

> *This section of the National Policy makes explicit the two-tiered aftercare service currently available. Those participating in work, education or training receive one form of service, whilst those who do not, or indeed in many case may not, receive a different, and lesser, service.*

. . . .

However, there is a simple fact which renders these statistics as questionable. As cited previously, Tusla cannot give a figure for the total number of young people leaving care in any one year, so how can they calculate the number who are not involved in work, education or training. Without a total sample figure it is impossible to derive any statistic which is representative of the total cohort of care leavers. As we have seen, the only figure Tusla is capable, or willing, to offer is a figure for those in receipt of an aftercare service. The National Activity Performance Report Quarter 4, 2014 Point 1.4 (i) crucially states that the statistic of 58 per cent in full-time education relates only to those care leavers who are in receipt of an aftercare service, and therefore is not representative of all care leavers:

> The number and percentage of young people aged 18-23 (inclusive) *in receipt of an aftercare service* who are in full-time education: Of the total number of 1,685 young adults aged 18-23 inclusive *in receipt of an aftercare service* on 31st December 2014: 975 (58 per cent) were in full-time education. (Tusla, 2014g:14)

Minister Reilly in response to a Dáil questions made the same statement in 2015:

> At the end of December 2014, 58 per cent of the 1,685 young people aged 18 to 23 years *in receipt of an aftercare service* were in full-time education. (Dáil Debates, 2015, Written Answer, 19541/15)

This casts doubt over the statistic given by Minister Fitzgerald to the Dáil in 2013. This same statistic is also frequently cited by senior Tusla management to support claims of effectiveness via comparative analysis with aftercare services in "other" jurisdictions (McBride, 2014).

> Some 60% of care leavers, as of January of this year (2014), were in some form of education or training. This compares favourably with other jurisdictions, where my experience is the figure can be as low as 30%. (McBride, 2014a)

However, it would appear that the number involved in education at circa 58 per cent is a percentage of those in receipt of a service which is being cited erroneously as a percentage of all care leavers. The percentage cannot be 58 per cent for both groups and in any event an accurate percentage cannot be calculated for the total number of care leavers as this total sample is an unknown figure. Therefore, the real figure for all care leavers who are in full-time education is lower than the cited 58 per cent and the numbers who are not in education would be higher than the cited figure of circa 40 per cent. In 2012-2013 in Northern Ireland 66 per cent of 19 year old care leavers were participating in work, education or training whilst in England the percentage was 63 per cent and in Wales 58 per cent (DHSSPSNI, 2014:13).

· ·

Based on an estimated 450 care leavers per annum, there would be 2,250 young people aged 18-23 over the course of the five years who have left care. The percentage of the 1,685 who are in receipt of an aftercare service and who are involved in education is given at 58 per cent, which equates to a figure of 928 young people. Based on the total sample figure, this would yield a real percentage involved in full-time education of 41 per cent, and not the 58 per cent as claimed. Of course, this figure is not truly accurate as we do not know precisely how many leave care each year, nor the educational profile of those who have left care but are not in receipt of support. It does, however, demonstrate that the real statistic will be much lower than the cited 58 per cent, and therefore much lower than that achieved in neighbouring jurisdictions.

· ·

One example of where the critical omission, whether intentionally or not, of the qualification "in receipt of a service" can lead to distortion of the facts is the following statement given by Fred McBride, Chief Operating Officer of Tusla, to the Joint Committee on Health and Children in the Houses of the Oireachteas (Vol. 2, No. 139) in 2014. It is important to note that there are circa 450 care leavers per year in the Republic, as we still have no exact figure for this group, whilst there are circa 1,600 aged 18 to 23 in receipt of a service per year.

With reference to the question about aftercare, we have approximately 1,600 care leavers per year. At the end of July, I was made aware of only four who had ended up in hostel accommodation directly after their care placement. There were explanations for all four of them. The four had ended up there as a result of a crisis. Their placement had temporarily broken down and they had ended up there through our out-of-hours service or crisis intervention service. They were very quickly removed from that hostel accommodation either back into their placement or into an appropriate aftercare placement.

I am aware of some information being bandied around by Focus Ireland and others as to there being large numbers in that category. I have yet to see that substantiated. When I looked into some of that information, it transpired that some of those young people were well into their 20s, so they were not leaving care. They might have been termed "care leavers" but they had been away from care for a number of years and thereafter ended up in homeless accommodation. It is regrettable, but these people were not directly leaving care at 18 years of age. That point should be made. (McBride, 2014a)

Mr. McBride accuses Focus Ireland of misleadingly categorising those who have been away from care for a number of years as "care leavers", yet he employs the very same technique by claiming that there are 1,600 care leavers per year. Also, four out of 1,600 is clearly very different from four out of 450.

Empowerment

Current discourses within the social professions acknowledge empowerment as a pillar of effective practice with the fostering of enhanced levels of self-efficacy. Bandura (1997) identified an individual's self-efficacy beliefs as the most powerful determinant of human agency and action (behaviour) (Ellett, 2008). Yet, paradoxically, we are currently empowering the wrong party – the state and its agents.

Watts conducted a comparative study of homeless service provision in Scotland and the Republic of Ireland in 2014. She identified that Scotland affords a legal right to accommodation for people experiencing homelessness, whereas the Republic of

Ireland does not. The Republic of Ireland retains discretion as to what supports it makes available to individual people experiencing homelessness, analogous to how it provides aftercare support. She concludes:

> Nonetheless, the experience in Scotland demonstrates the potential for clear and simple legal rights to minimise provider discretion, "crowding-out" non-needs related considerations in responding to homelessness, as well as to enhance the assertiveness of service users, and reinforce the perceived legitimacy of this assertiveness amongst service providers. Moreover, it seems to achieve this without fatally undermining self-reliance, and indeed may be argued to support self-reliance rather better than the highly-discretionary Irish model. (2014:13)

Watt's findings support the case for empowering care leavers with rights-based entitlements to specified aftercare supports, thereby enhancing their self-efficacy and promoting their participation in society as active citizens.

Aftercare Support

It is notable and curious that the reference to social support as one of the most important criteria for young people leaving care that Minister Fitzgerald repeatedly acknowledged within her Written Answers to Dáil Debates (33365/12; 24027/12; 5502/12; 5503/12) has been omitted from the National Policy statement of most important requirements, and thereby demoted in significance. Care leavers are not a homogenous group (Stein and Wade, 2000; Skuse and Ward, 2003; Barnardos, 2012; Doyle *et al.*, 2012) and to limit conceptualisation of their most important requirements within the domains of just accommodation, education, training and employment is, at a minimum, reductionist.

> The most important requirements for young people leaving care are for secure, suitable accommodation as well as further education, employment or training and social support. The most vulnerable group of young people leaving care are those that have dropped out of education and

training and those that have left residential care. (Dáil Debates, Written Answers, 33365/12)

It is to be welcomed that Minister Flanagan, the successor to Minister Fitzgerald, in his earliest written answers to Dáil Debates (23989/14 on 5/6/2014) included continuity of relationships within his definition of most important requirements for young people leaving care.

The most important requirements for young people leaving care are for continuity of relationships; secure, stable accommodation as well as further education, employment and training.

The above statement causes the National Policy for Leaving and Aftercare, as well as the proposed Aftercare Bill 2014, to be considered as deficient in this area. The implication implicit within the aftercare plan proposed by the Aftercare Bill 2014 is that some care leavers may not need aftercare support. How this can be reconciled with their need for continuity of relationships is difficult to see. In fact, the latter would appear to disavow the former. It is entirely correct that continuity of relationships is vital for care leavers and there is no question that they absolutely need these relationships to be maintained (Ridley *et al.*, 2013; Action for Children, 2014). The challenge is to make this support available in such a manner that is accessible and acceptable to the care leaver. My practice experience has confirmed that many of the most difficult to reach young people, who may have fractious relationships with authority and social work departments, are capable of forming meaningful relationships with some staff. The important point is that these staff are chosen by the young people rather than be allocated to them. The rupturing of these existing relationships when young people leave care staff or foster families represents the severing of any possibility to meet their essential need for continuity of relationships.

Meeting this challenge is possible as this is one of those areas where we can exert influence and bring our training, experience and resources to bear. One such solution would be to introduce mentors to care leavers whilst they are still in care, and thereby allow time for the relationship to form before the young person leaves care. The mentor would then continue to support the care leaver in aftercare thereby ensuring continuity of relationships. Aftercare workers generally work Monday to Friday during office hours whereas mentors have the advantage of being accessible to care leavers when they may need them the most, including weekends and out-of-hours times. This can be a key factor in promoting engagement. We know how vulnerable care leavers are during this transitional phase of leaving care, before, during and after, and having the support of a "transition mentor" during this process would make a major difference for many care leavers.

Those care leavers who do not participate in work, education or training are, often, the ones in need of most support, yet paradoxically, within this model of aftercare provision they may get the least. At a minimum, these young people representing more than 38.9 per cent of care leavers are "invisible from view" (Carr, 2014) as current data only addresses those in receipt of aftercare support and excludes any data on those not in receipt of a service.

Values

The significance of values has been referenced repeatedly and therefore warrants more detailed examination. The range of values across human experience is diverse and therefore discussion of common values is open to argument. However, Tam has offered us what he has determined to be four deeply valued human experiences of core values:

> First, there are experiences of loving and being loved, caring for others, passion, tenderness, friendship, sympathy, kindness, compassion and devotion. These can be grouped together as the *value of love*. Second, there are the experiences of understanding, clarity of thought, being able to think for oneself, to weight evidence and make good judgements. These constitute the *value of wisdom*. Third, are the experiences of being fairly treated by others, of being able to relate to other without the sense of discrimination or subjugation, and of knowing that reciprocal relationships are

respected. These values are encapsulated in the golden rule "do as you would be done by", to be found in the core moral code of every advanced culture. It is the *value of justice*. Finally, there are the experiences of developing and realizing one's potential, being able to enjoy oneself, to feel satisfied, and to take pride in one's actions and achievements. These can be viewed together as the *value of achievement*. (Tam, 1998:15)

There is a growing recognition of the overarching importance of values and the place of the worker within social care and, more specifically, residential care. This is encapsulated by the following quotation from HIQA in 2013:

The quality of children's residential services is almost entirely dependent on the commitment and quality of the staff team and its leadership. (HIQA, cited in Cúram, 2014, 48:19)

Banks (2006) advances an interconnected positioning of practice within the social professions. Within this she acknowledges the influence of values in the decision making processes of professionals.

Most decisions in social work involve a complex interaction of ethical, political, technical and legal issues all of which are interconnected. Our values will influence how we interpret the law. (Banks, 2006:12)

The Role of Language

[B]eing aware of the terminology we choose, and the way in which we use it can be critical in determining whose view of "reality" we are accepting, what power relations we wish to reinforce, the sort of world we wish to adopt, and in identifying the type of social work we wish to create. (Hawkins *et al.*, 2001:3)

It is not my intent to promote one model or approach above another (Ford and Harding, 2007). Rather, it is to seek balance and use whichever model best aids the individual young person. Positivistic approaches can play a key role with, for example, neuroscience adding greatly to our work in recent years. Of course, we should seek value-for-money in our work. Truly integrated practice, with theoretical and practice equality, offers the optimum way to achieve this. But we must be vigilant not to be seduced by powerful rhetoric, mindful of the role of language (Ruch, 2009; Vojak, 2009) and that "words become actions" (Hartman, 1991). The language we use to describe things plays a major role in how we think about them, as we saw previously with regard to the words institution and residential care. Relationships alone are, like knowledge, islands in the sea of human need. It is actions that count and the relationship must be meaningful, which requires that the power dynamics are addressed. Ideally, relationships are reciprocally promotive of growth and change, just as knowledge needs to be catalysed into practice to become meaningful. In a similar vein, Freire (1972) argued that "reflection without action results in 'mentalism' and action without reflection in 'activism'; and both are empty" (cited in Banks, 2006:160).

Of course the relationship itself is a therapeutic intervention, as is highlighted by the interdependence (Antle *et al.*, 2009) and relationship-based (Ruch, 2005) models. The ability to sustain a healthy relationship with an appropriate adult is a significant life skill which once acquired can be replicated. Whilst also acknowledging the psychological benefits accruing from "connection" with another person, the worker must be regularly assessing the relationship for developmental opportunities to promote the holistic growth and well-being of the young person. We must learn from the mistakes of the past, such as in the 1980s, where the relationship was often seen as the end in itself. This was one of the reasons for the subsequent decline in the psychodynamic practices in place from that time (Ruch, 2005; Olson, 2007).

With regard to the use of business language in our profession – service user, client, performance indicators, value-for-money to name but a few – we must be mindful that:

... as the discourse of enterprise culture becomes increasingly influential as a vocabulary of social calculation, more and more areas of human activity become conceptualised and treated in terms of commodity, production, distribution and consumption. (du Gay and Salaman cited in Doolin, 2002:372)

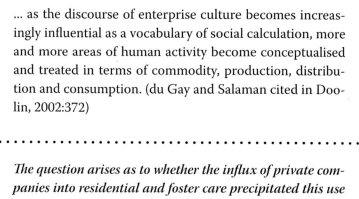

The question arises as to whether the influx of private companies into residential and foster care precipitated this use of language, or was this in place prior to the emergence of the private sector?

This then poses two further questions:

1) When did our profession become a business, and how has this impacted on the care provided to children?

2) Are we conscious that every time we use the language of business management in our work we reinforce the commodification of our profession (Gregory and Holloway, 2005)?

Clients are no longer perceived as "individuals with difficulties", but as "service users", or "consumers" who may – or may not – be eligible for services, depending on their circumstances and the relevant assessment criteria (Adams, 1998; Munro, 2000; Parton, 1998). (Richards *et al.*, 2005:413)

Language is also important when we consider the terminology associated with leaving care and aftercare. The term "aftercare" is potentially self-negating as it implies that care has finished and something else comes *after* this, and not necessarily to the same standard. A more dynamic title needs to be coined, ideally by young people, using active rather than passive terminology, and reflective of the high-quality service needed by care leavers. For aftercare to cease to be an afterthought, especially in the Republic of Ireland, the word "after" needs to be removed.

Examples might include Care2Adulthood Service, which can be written as C2A, or Pathways2Adulthood Service which again could be written as P2A. Both these afford opportunities for catchy URLs such as www.P2A.ie.

Language is also important with regard to social policy. For example, we no longer have unemployment assistance support as this has been reconfigured as job seekers allowance, making the conditionality of this support explicit. This is administered by a re-configured Department of Social Protection where previously we had a Department of Social Welfare. Formerly we had social security and social welfare, now we have a multitude of schemes and programmes, all geared towards achieving employment, termed by some "workfare", with sanctions for those who do not or cannot participate as required. The *welfare state*, where citizens' welfare was prioritised with the state playing a key role in the economic and social well-being of its citizens, is being replaced by the *welfare of the state*, where the state's welfare is prioritised. This is achieved by the state withdrawing from supporting its citizens who are notionally either self sufficient, or capable to become self-sufficient, through achieving employment and ultimately becoming responsible for themselves in all but the most severe circumstances of incapacity.

· ·

> *The question arises, as it does with any statutory protection service, of who is being protected? Is it the individual citizen or the state?*

· ·

The employment of the term "system of care" throughout this book has been deliberately chosen on the recommendation of Stuck *et al.* (2000) and Professor James Anglin (2004). They identified how the usage of the terms "continuum of care" or "spectrum of care services" have a tendency to influence thinking that relegates "residential care to an 'end of the line' or 'last resort' status" (Anglin, 2004:181).

With regard to the term "care leavers", the reality for many of these young people is that care leaves them regardless of their ability to function without it, and often within what should be a managed process but in reality becomes an event over which they have little or no control. Thus the term care leavers is misleading and in reality "care losers" more accurate, albeit with negative overtones. Care leavers are conceived of as moving on in a managed process within which they have power to exercise choice, though in reality they do not. They must seek the essential resources formerly available to them to meet their most basic needs for survival and development. This renders them more accurately and less disparagingly conceived of as "care seekers" or "support seekers". Aftercare for these young people really means after care has gone, posing the question – what and who is left after care is gone?

The Impossible Task – Poverty, Risk and Resilience

As noted earlier, social care can be seen as the "impossible task" with reference to Bruno Bettleheim's concept. Some may question this choice of metaphor, but it is often used with regard to social work (Balbernie, 1971; Taylor, 2007; Littlechild, 2008; Burns and MacCarthy, 2012) or other professions such as law enforcement:

> Manning (1978, p. 8) observes that "Based on their legal monopoly of violence, (police) have staked out a mandate that claims to be efficient, apolitical and professional enforcement of the law". Manning calls this the "impossible mandate" which is driven by public expectation rather than the reality of police work. The heroic public image of the police is as "crook-catchers" and "crime-stoppers" is reinforced by the police themselves. (Chan, 1997:76)

In social care, the task of "curing" or ameliorating the ills of years of exposure to poverty, violence, neglect, abuse, prejudice and social exclusion can be extremely difficult for the individual workers with stress at extremely high levels (Söderfeldt et al.. 1995; Lloyd et al., 2002; BASW, 2012; Wilberforce et al., 2014). However, when we factor in the implications of years of neoliberal policies we can see that the task has become exponentially more challenging than it was in the past. To deal with the ever increasing gaps between those who hold wealth and those living in poverty, with diminished resources yet growing demand for service provision, is becoming increasingly more difficult. Central Statistics Office data for 2012, the Survey on Income and Living Conditions, published in 2014, reveals that 755,591 people were living in poverty in the Republic of Ireland, including 220,000 children. The gap between the richest and poorest is increasing, as has the numbers living in "consistent poverty" which has risen from 4.2 per cent in 2007 to 7.7 per cent in 2012 (CSO, 2014). It is not that children are more difficult to care for than previously, as some would argue, rather the absence of resources and supports from the state. This coupled with a less than heroic public image of the profession propagated by numerous high-profile failings and subsequent inquiries, and the negative perception of young people in general (Devlin, 2006) causes the work to be more difficult than in former years.

. . . .

> *Could it be these realities that inculcate the reification of re-silience with researchers and policy formulators? We know that the concept of resilience in the social professions rose to prominence at the same time, from the 1970s onwards, as neoliberalism in the UK and Ireland (McAslan, 2010). We have also seen that research and the psychological and so-ciological theories chosen by practitioners are heavily influ-enced by the dominant political hegemony. Could it be that the construct of resilience has been exploited to represent a form of magic elixir which offers a remedy for disaggregat-ing social policies spawned by the neoliberal hegemony and compounded by austerity? Those who refuse to imbibe this elixir, or those who imbibe but fail to succeed, are then held solely responsible for their own fate – having "chosen" their situation and being personally responsible for it. (Howe, 1997:166)*

. . . .

This raises the question of where the worker is located with regard to risk and resilience. Resilient workers are essential to support children through difficult periods when behaviours can be unpredictable and the risks heightened. Workers who will "stick with" children through these times and not seek to move on the risk, thereby pre-empting placement breakdown and the attendant harm that results (Jones *et al.*, 2011; Ombudsman for Children, 2013), are essential to best practice in residential care. Clearly the work is highly stressful (Coffey *et al.*, 2004; Tham and Meagher, 2009), often with many setbacks, and workers therefore need to be resilient, just as do their clients.

• •

Deprived of ability to operate with risk and uncertainty, can workers become resilient workers?

• •

It is further interesting that, as previously noted, seeking security for care leavers has become a preoccupying pursuit in recent times. Considering that workers are also striving for security means that there is much scope for transference between the two groups. There is potential for cycles to be created and stress to be magnified through such processes. There is much truth in the maxim that, "As we treat our staff so they will treat the children", and in this context we need to engender resilience in our staff for them to nurture the same in the children they care for.

From an attachment perspective, and reinforcing this maxim, Walker (2008:12) states:

> Attachment theory maintains that one of the key functions of a healthy organisation should be to function as a "secure base" (Bowlby, 1988) for its staff. Attachment theory is clear that the more secure, safe and "held" that a social worker feels, the more likely he or she will be able to continue to hold on to some reflective function when under stress.

With regard to staff, a few workers seem more concerned for their own professional and physical welfare than the children's well-being. They may stick rigidly to guidelines taught in academia and training courses. This is a dangerous recipe when working in social care. Whilst the Duty to Rescue may not be legislatively pre-

293

scribed here as it is in many countries, social care professionals have moral responsibilities which supersede the professional ones. The potential for unpredictable scenarios makes it impossible to cover every eventuality within risk assessments, procedure manuals or models of care documents (Castel, 1991).

> The world is therefore manageable through the myth of calculability or statistical probability (Reddy, 1996), where the concept of "risk" is built on the technocratic rationality of control over the hazards or prevention of irruption of the unpredictable (Castel, 1991). Therefore, Castel (ibid., p. 289) speaks of the "... myth of absolute eradication of risk, they construct a mass of new risks which constitute so many new targets of preventive intervention". (Šabić, 2013:77)

Risk is a part of normal everyday life and as human beings imbued with free will we all make risk management choices daily, often without even being conscious of doing so. As parents we manage the risks present in our children's daily lives and make choices for them, as risk management is strongly associated with the ability to exercise choice. As their capacity evolves we, ideally, allow for them to exercise more choice in their lives and make risk-based decisions for themselves. So risk and risk management are not only inescapable, they are, in fact, essential to a healthy and fulfilling life.

Whilst the relationship between risk and resilience has been well researched, and indeed referenced earlier in this book, there is another less well researched relationship as well. This is the commonality between the two constructs with regard to how they are interpreted within other areas and then applied within the social sciences. The connection between risk and quality is that by eliminating unfavourable occurrences from manufacturing or service systems, for example, the quality of the product or service will be improved. However, in social sciences these concepts do not transfer so well. They do not take account of the positive and essential place of risk in child and adolescent development (Newman, 2002). Yet, even within human sciences, a sub-domain of which is the social sciences, the same dilemma arises. The medical model perceives risk as solely a harmful construct. This can be seen in the development of services for children and families which, prior to the establishment of Tusla in 2014, were located within the behemoth Health Service Executive operating an overarching medical model of care.

> In 2007 the HSE adopted the Australian New Zeeland Risk Management Standard (AS\NZS 4360:2004) which was subsequently updated to the ISO 31000:2009 Risk Management: Principles and Guidelines. (HSE, 2011b:3)

The HSE Risk Assessment Tool and Guidance (2011a) makes explicit the negative perception of risk when outlining the ICC (Impact, Cause, Context) Approach to Risk Assessment with the following statement: "Risk is inherently negative, implying the possibility of adverse impacts" (2012:3). Furthermore, the HSE (2011a) Risk Assessment and Risk Register Process makes the following expectation clear on the HSE website:

> Managers must seek to eliminate or minimise all foreseeable risks in their service. All risks identified must be assessed in terms of the their impact and likelihood of occurrence.

It is the negative perception of risk that poses a major problem in preventing the crucial positive potential of risk in the social professions. Whilst ISO 31000 includes recognition of the positive potential of risk within its definition as "the effect of uncertainty on objectives – positive and/or negative", this is always overshadowed by the negative construct. Stating that risk can be a positive construct, but then framing it within wider systems which identify risk as solely negative, is ineffective.

Systems which seek to manage and control risk have the potential to pathologise what is, in fact, a normal process. Clearly risk management is critical in safeguarding young people, but this must be achieved within a holistic framework which also recognises the value of risk with regard to human development (France *et al.*, 2010). Whilst risk management systems may allow for different levels of risk, and therefore different levels of intervention, this must be made explicit for practitioners to correctly interpret the place of risk management within an overall framework.

. . . .

> *This raises fundamental questions as to why we place such emphasis on risk assessments in our work when, at best, whether clinical, actuarial or holistic, they are an uncertain tool (Littlechild, 2008)?*

. . . .

We must be mindful that whilst the reduction or indeed elimination of risk may improve quality in manufacturing and professional service industries, within the social sciences this relationship between risk and quality requires more nuanced consideration.

Additionally, it raises the question as to whether we are justified in changing the everyday life, and in this process potentially causing some degree of harm by depriving the young person of a normal life, on the basis of mitigating some future harm that may never happen?

The question of our position within a protectionist stance with regard to the rights of young people is critical to this issue (Holland *et al.*, 2008).

. . . .

> *The area of risk needs further development with the engagement of practitioners, policy-makers and administrators. This is an area where Continuous Professional Development modules may prove effective in challenging the dominant negative perception of risk.*

. . . .

Dealing with risk is itself a risky business. (Kemshall, cited in Davies, 2000:130)

Incorporating a risk and strengths-based approach to our work requires us to recognise that resilience development is dependent on exposure to risk, and that without such exposure resilience cannot develop (Laser and Nicotera, 2011). We need to consider the opportunity present within a crisis, as well as the danger. Working from this base would require more consideration of managers' and practitioners' recognition that ideally all risk-assessment tools would include the identification of such promotive factors before an action plan is devised.

> Sense must be made of cases by well qualified professionals; care needs to be taken that risk assessment technologies do not short-circuit "workers" ability and willingness to be intellectually active and critical. (Benbenishty *et al.*, 2003:152)

Regulatory bodies need to look at their own approaches and consider whether they are strengths-based or deficit-based in their actions and not just their verbal communications.

Security and Mortality

The world is changing at an unprecedented pace and this is impacting on young people more than any other age group. Globalisation, unemployment and ruptured pathways to adulthood have all added risk and uncertainty into the lives of today's young people (Bryner *et al.*, 2002).

As noted, the search for security has become preoccupying yet elusive in an incessantly changing world (Pinkerton, 2012). So great has this pursuit of security become that it has been said that, arguably, "We desire security more than freedom" (Tocqueville in Stivers, 2001:211). The impact on a search for identity, an issue at the core of all young people's development (Meade, 1934; Erikson, 1980; Grotevant and Cooper, 1985), but more complex for young people in care, is profound within such undefined futures (Stein, 2008a). For example, in the Republic of Ireland 40 per cent of young people aged 18-25 are at risk of poverty or social exclusion (OECD, 2013), with youth unemployment at 26.5 per cent in 2013 (DCYA, 2014b). Care leavers, however, have the added disadvantage of having been exposed to trauma in their childhoods, having been in care, and on leaving care being at risk of a range of poor outcomes. For care leavers, these forces are both magnified and multiplied whilst they are also experiencing transitions that are "compressed and accelerated" (Stein, 2004:53).

Paradoxically, at the very time of major vulnerability when they most need the stability of significant attachment figures, care leavers experience broken relationships with care staff they are leaving behind (Holt and Kirwan, 2012). For some, predominately though not exclusively those leaving residential care, they also experience a re-traumatisation induced by past experiences of loss, separation and abandonment. The cumulative effect of these factors and forces renders leaving care a time of heightened risk across multiple domains including, tragically, the risk of death (Shannon and Gibbons, 2012).

> Suicide levels among young people in contact with the State's child protection services are almost 10 times the rate of those who are not. Dr Ella Arensman, director of research at the National Suicide Research Foundation, described the findings as "extremely worrying"... An analysis of the report by the foundation showed that between 2005 and 2009, the average rate of suicide per 100,000 for adolescents aged between 15 and 19 in care, aftercare or known to the HSE for the period from 2005 to 2009 was 117, compared with 12 for the general population. (*Irish Examiner*, 2012)

In fact, a care leaver who has just exited care at 18 years of age is more vulnerable to death from non-natural causes that at any other time from infancy to the age of 23. Shannon and Gibbons recorded eleven such deaths at age 18, as opposed to three up to age 13, two for ages 14 and 15, four for age 16 and six for age 17. From age 19 to 23 Shannon and Gibbons recorded sixteen deaths. Clearly as children approach the age of leaving care their risk to non-natural death increases exponentially and peaks at the age of actually leaving care, 18. Of further concern is the fact that in the first two years after this report, which covered 2000 to 2010, the numbers of deaths of children in care from non-natural causes more than doubled, from six in 2011 to 16 in 2012 (*Irish Examiner*,

2013a). The figures for children known to the HSE for 2012 are even more disturbing:

> Barnardos is deeply saddened by the findings of the National Review Panel that 23 children and young people who were either in care or known to the care services died in 2012. It is particularly alarming that nine of these children died by suicide, the youngest only being 13 years old. (Barnardos, 2013)

These tragic statistics bear testimony to the risks care leavers are exposed to and the vulnerability they experience during the transition from care. This vulnerability to suicide is a known risk for care leavers with a study by Saunders and Broad (1997) finding that nearly two-thirds of their sample had considered suicide and 40 per cent had actually attempted it on leaving care. These statistics also highlight the paradox that at the time of highest vulnerability, and often after many years of intensive and expensive intervention by the state, when young people most need the support it may not be available to them. This is especially pertinent to those most in need, the non-engagers and those care leavers who may not participate in further education or training, and who get the least support in our current inequitable two-tiered system. For them the unacceptably high mortality rate for care leavers as evidenced by these statistics confirms that aftercare support may be the difference between life and death.

Whilst making precise comparisons between these statistics and the general population is difficult, an issue addressed by the ICDRG and Minister Fitzgerald (Dáil Debates, 2013, Written Answers, 21773/13) partly due to the small amount of data available over limited timeframes, nonetheless some comparisons can and should be made.

· ·

It is shocking that 25 per cent of all deaths from non-natural causes for young people in care and aftercare, over a 23-year age span, occur within one year, age 18. Additionally shocking is the fact that for young people in aftercare non-natural deaths outnumber natural deaths by a multiple of more than 5:1 (27:5) whilst for children in the general population suicide accounts for 21.9 per cent or 1:5 of all deaths of children aged 10-17 (DCYA, 2012). This statistic is truly shocking and profoundly worrying for the health and well-being of all our young people. Within the 15-24 age range in 2012 there were 95 suicides, again a 1:5 ratio (IMO, 2013). These statistics highlight the shocking disparity in suicide rates amongst children in care and aftercare and children in the general population. A care leaver is five times more likely to die from unnatural causes, including suicide, than any other cause of death, whilst within the general population a young person of the same age is five times less likely to die by suicide than any other cause of death.

. . . .

Norah Gibbons, then Director of Advocacy with Barnardos, made the following statement in 2010:

> It is simply astounding that the Government is writing off the very notion of a mandatory provision for aftercare. In the past year we have seen numerous reports on cases of children whose young lives were cut short because of failings in the aftercare system; Government is refusing to learn the lessons of the past and continues to put vulnerable children's lives at risk with an aftercare system that is inconsistent and under-resourced. (Barnardos, 2010)

Corporate Parenting

The Department of Health, Social Service and Public Safety in Northern Ireland published guidelines in 2007 on corporate parenting that are notable for their reference to the state acting as a "good parent" as opposed to just any parent:

> ... must ensure that we are everything a good parent should be, offering a quality home and experience of childhood, ambition, hope for the future and demand the best schools and services for these children. (DHSSPSNI, 2007)

In the Republic a HSE report published in 2010 identified corporate parenting as:

The In Loco Parentis Role of the HSE

The HSE, acting in loco parentis has the responsibility of seeking the best possible outcomes for children in its care. Such a role encompasses three key elements:

• The statutory duty of the HSE to promote the welfare of children and young people who are in its care;

• Co-ordinating the activities of many different professionals, carers and partner agencies who are involved in a child or young person's life and taking a strategic, child-centered approach to service delivery;

• Shifting the emphasis from "institutional" to "parenting", defined as the performance of all actions necessary to promote and support the physical, emotional, social and cognitive development of a child or young person.

Stein (2012) makes several points in regard to corporate parenting:

> For looked-after children and young people, it is the foster carer or residential worker who gives meaning to "corporate parenting"… the essence of corporate parenting responsibility is to provide high-quality placements. (2012:93)

He outlines a corporate parenting case model "with legal responsibility held by personal advisers embedded within formalised intra- and inter-agency processes." (2012:9)

The formalised intra and inter-agency processes have in the past been problematic for the HSE Child and Family Services. This has been exacerbated by the focus on accountability of staff and independence for, and the individualisation of, children in care and care leavers. Considered from a psychodynamic perspective it is possible to see how:

> Acute and chronic feelings of anxiety about difficult cases or work situations impede the capacity for practitioners to think clearly and exacerbates the tendency to resort to defensive behaviours as responses to the emotionally charged situations they face (Taylor *et al.*, 2008). (Ruch, 2009:351)

The focus on independence may have caused the HSE Child and Family Services, via mechanisms of isomorphism and defensiveness, to itself become isolated and subject to individualised status within state structures and agencies. The HSE was left holding responsibility for care leavers where passing of problems between departments and agencies was the norm. As seen in a similar situation in England:

> ... this places an unreasonable burden of responsibility on social workers and risks reinforcing the prevailing tendency towards individualising blame for mistakes and scapegoating a professional group, which usually targets social workers (Munro, 2010). (Ruch, 2011:440)

The climate of distrust and blame became pervasive and partnership working and inter-agency cooperation were poorly developed.

The focus within such corporate parenting models is on risk aspects of the corporate body rather than the norms, values and better parenting aspects implicit in the use of the word parenting. Evans (2014) makes the following notable points in relation to corporate parenting, referencing the oxymoronic aspect of the term:

> Part of the difficulty lies in the paradoxical basis of the concept itself – parenting denotes intimacy which is at odds with the idea of a corporation. The term "corporate parent" is, thus, something of an oxymoron – how can a corporation be a parent? The irony is that the more accountable the "corporation" becomes, the less parental it is, as Smith, in his review of residential care, has highlighted: "...demands for accountability in public care have gone too far and now detract from the act and the art of caring." (2009:118)

In her examination of the state's role as "corporate parent", Mooney poses the following question:

> Ordinarily a good parent will fight for the rights of its child but when the parent also provides the services, who wins? (2012:141)

The solution, she suggests, is to adopt the idea of "parallel parenting" in line with the "social pedagogy" model of care which characterises the Danish approach to social care. (Evans, 2014:66)

Paradoxically, the one action which the HSE refused to take may well have led to the resolution of some of these problems. Placing aftercare on a legislative basis would require that formalised inter-agency processes were agreed with all stakeholding agencies. This process would have benefited the HSE by bringing all stakeholders together in a coherent forum with resources input mandated from all stakeholders, thus ultimately reducing the resource demands on the HSE. Corporate parenting, as outlined by Stein (2012), implicitly involves developed interdependency between all relevant stakeholders where responsibility would be shared just as good parents share responsibility with each other. Legislation would afford aftercare a foundation of equitability and simultaneously facilitate enhanced corporate parenting.

There is much learning for the new Child and Family Agency to take from such experiences, and it is not the derogation of the former HSE Child and Family Services that motivates this consideration. Rather, in the sociological tradition, it is the unveiling of the forces at play so that we learn from them. We need to be able to consider practice and policy developments, locally, nationally and globally within a wider socio-political context so that we can better represent those we are tasked with supporting. In this regard the actions of the HSE/Tusla can be located within the wider context via examination of the reductionist policies from alternative perspectives:

> In the current climate, when the principles of the welfare state are under threat, and we face ever increasing demands to measure our work in simplified ways, it is more crucial than ever to ensure that we can defend and sustain complexity. An important way to do so is through bringing a number of different perspectives to bear on our work. (Burck and Cooper, 2007:193)

Examples of effective corporate parenting can be found in the UK where positive discrimination (affirmative action) prioritises care leavers for supports as well as employment opportunities. In the Republic of Ireland, examples of positive discrimination are few and far between, other than social welfare payments where young people who have left residential care receive the full allowance at age 18, Students Universal Support Ireland (SUSI) maintenance grants and Youthreach allowances for care leavers. We have multiple opportunities to effect positive discrimination and here Tusla/HSE could lead by example. As previously noted, the HSE is the single largest employer whilst also being a corporate body owned by the state. Were the state to act as an authentic corporate parent it might follow the example of parents who are fortunate enough to own businesses that can offer employment. These parents, understandably, prioritise their own family for such employment. Apprenticeships, trainee and starter employment opportunities could be targeted towards care leavers within the workforce of the HSE, which numbers circa 100,000; 55,000 direct employees and 35,000 in funded healthcare organisations. Creating such opportunities for care leavers, just as caring parents do for their children, would be an example of positive discrimination. This would have a major impact on the well-being of care leavers whilst also being cost-neutral. Similar positive discrimination occurs across multiple domains in the UK with universities, housing agencies and local and county councils all positively discriminating in favour of care leavers.

Clearly, there is major financial benefit to the state in implementing such practices, a benefit not yet being realised in the Republic of Ireland. The focus on the positive has most to offer in caring for young people. Consequently, the opportunity to turn negative discrimination (social exclusion, marginalisation) into a positive force via positive discrimination (affirmative action, empowerment), just as the manager in Keith's story turned a negative into a positive and achieved the impossible task, is a missed opportunity for children in care and aftercare.

The inherent tension between the organisational, administrative and financial needs of the corporate body and the need to act as a caring parent means that the proposed Aftercare Bill (2014) is inherently flawed. Tusla has to operate within its budgets, as do its employees. There is a clear potential conflict of interest in such a scenario where the best interest of the child, the recognition of the need for ongoing aftercare support, may place the organisation under further financial pressure. After six years of remorseless austerity measures many boundaries have become blurred. Naomi Klein (2007) illuminates such processes whereby under the influence of "shock and awe" tactics, where bewilderment and confusion are created to stun the general population, seditious changes can be implemented by state and corporate powers without resistance from the population. This is informative in the Republic of Ireland's case given events subsequent to September 2008. Faced with catastrophic bank failure where public services may have ceased to operate, sweeping changes were implemented on a population stunned but stoic, who to this day do not know exactly what happened.

This potential for unchecked changes to become entrenched as norms holds particular importance in the case of the Republic of Ireland. As the country begins to exit recession we must be mindful that what may have, arguably, been unavoidable during a time of emergency may be unacceptable now that the emergency has passed. Social justice needs to be brought to the fore and we must guard against these draconian crisis measures becoming entrenched as new norms.

As we have seen, social care has adopted many of the mechanisms from the commercial professions, with accountancy and business management to the fore, but in a non-reciprocal relationship.

An analogy, appropriately also defined by the markets, is the price of oil. We have seen that when there is a crisis that threatens oil supply, such as the OPEC-induced crisis of 1973 when oil went from $3.00 a barrel to $12.00 a barrel or the Oil Crisis of 1979 when oil again rose from $12.00 a barrel to $32.00 a barrel (Leddin and Walsh, 2003), that the price of petrol at the filling station inflates dramatically. However, when the oil supply crisis abates and production returns to normal, the price of petrol does not return to its pre-crisis cost. In fact, it remains at the crisis-induced cost thereafter as the new "normal" price. Subsequent to these crises in the 1970s it now only takes the "threat" of a potential crisis to induce the same phenomenon of inflating prices (Beck, 2000, 2010).

> As the risk society develops, so does the antagonism between those afflicted by risks and those who profit from them. The social and economic importance of knowledge grows similarly, and with it the power over the media to structure knowledge (science and research) and disseminate it (mass media). The risk society in this sense is also the science, media and information society. Thus new antagonisms grow up between those who produce risk definitions and those who consume them. (Beck, 1992:46)

In such strategies can be seen the principles of cognitive dissonance (Festinger, 1962; Cooper, 2007; Gawronski and Strack, 2012), which are so effectively used by the advertising industry.

> Festinger (1962) developed cognitive dissonance theory in the 1960s as a "consistency theory" so designated because it emphasizes the premise that humans desire congruence in their thinking and will act to reduce inconsistency among thoughts, and between thoughts and behaviours. He defined cognitive dissonance as "the existence of non-fitting relations among cognitions" (p.3). In other words, a person who has two cognitions that are inconsistent, experiences dissonance – a negative drive state similar to hunger or thirst (Aronson, 1997). (Taylor, 2007:95)

An allied phenomenon, professional dissonance, has been identified and defined by Taylor (2008:90) as "a feeling of discomfort arising from the conflict between professional values and job tasks". She identifies how social workers often have to formulate practice decisions which protect society as well as maximising the rights of the individual. She identifies this as perhaps an impossible task "when these two objectives are incompatible social workers find themselves in the position of making a practice decision that may be unwanted and/or directly opposed by the consumer" (2008:90).

Therefore, decisions where tensions of cognitive and/or professional dissonance are present, as when assessing the need for aftercare support, requires that they be made by an independent body. It is generally accepted, and for the same reasons, that no organisation should act as its own oversight body or watchdog.

In Scotland the Children and Young People Act, 2014 became active in 2015. Part 9 of this Act outlines, in detail, the corporate parent role and responsibilities with regard to young people in care and aftercare. This progressive legislation, which has received widespread international acclaim, prescribes a mandate for after-care up to age 26 in certain cases and for young people in all settings to have the right to opt to remain in these care placements until 21. However, as we noted previously with reference to Professor Stein's research, Tusla is prone to questionable interpretation of data when it comes to aftercare. This is again evidenced with regard to this progressive rights-based Scottish legislation for care leavers. Minister for Children, James Reilly, is of the belief that services afforded young people in Scotland via this legislation are "akin to aftercare services for children leaving care in this State" (Dáil Debates, 2015, Written Answers, 17451/15). This is a curious interpretation of the Scottish legislation as it dismisses any recognition of the rights aspect of young people to, amongst other rights, opt to remain in their care placement until age 21 and for all care leavers to aftercare support up to age 26. Rather, Minister Reilly references "continuing care" as prescribed within this progressive Scottish Act not as a right for care leavers but as a "new legal term to describe care leavers who remain in their "looked after" (care) placements up to the age of 21." He perpetuates the entrenched propensity of former ministers and senior HSE/Tusla management, which shall be considered in more detail in the next section on the Aftercare Bill 2014, of focusing on the duty of the state to provide support, rather than the right of all care leavers to access support.

Furthermore, Minister Reilly identifies care leavers as children and yet contrasts them with young people aged 18-26 in Scotland. Elsewhere, Gordon Jeyes, CEO of Tusla, has identified young people who have turned 18 and who may seek to remain in their foster care placements as both youngsters and adults:

... and ensure we not only support those youngsters who remain in education but those who choose to remain in foster care. We will fund this irrespective of their education arrangements. Those involved will at that stage be adults and as such there will be no free rides. (Jeyes, 2014a)

Consequently, it is unclear whether care leavers in the Republic of Ireland are seen as children or adults. Furthermore, there would appear to be concern which Mr. Jeyes seeks to assuage that some care leavers, specifically those not involved in education, may seek "free rides". However, just what is meant by "free rides" is left ambiguous and therefore may reasonably be seen, in the absence of any supporting evidence, to be based on assumption. This is reminiscent of the rhetoric of the "undeserving child".

. . . .

Could it be that the definition of care leavers as children or adults is offered to fit the particular agendas of the corporate parent in different contexts?

Where does this assumption that some care leavers may seek "free rides" come from? Is there any evidence underpinning it and what role might this assumption have with regard to the corporate parent's steadfast refusal to make aftercare a rights-based entitlement for all care leavers?

Whilst such an attitude towards welfare provision may align well with the neoliberal master narrative, can it co-exist with an understanding of the consequences of the often horrendous price involuntarily extracted from children admitted into state care?

. . . .

One issue where there is no lack of clarity, however, is that some of the principal officers of the Irish corporate parent, the Minister for Children and the CEO of Tusla, both attest that aftercare services are good: "By international standards, our current aftercare arrangements are good" (Jeyes,2014a). Just what international standards Mr. Jeyes is referring to is curious given the failings that have been identified throughout this book. These include representations from the NGO sector, the judiciary, independent inquiry boards, politicians, the media, academia, care leavers themselves, international children's rights organisations and the questionable statistics proffered to support claims regarding the number of care leavers involved in education. What is certain, however, is that if we compare our aftercare services with those available in our closest neighbouring states of England, Scotland, Wales and Northern Ireland, all of which have placed aftercare on a statutory legislative base, the Republic of Ireland is deficient by this standard. Furthermore, as a direct consequence of these deficiencies our aftercare arrangements for those young people who do not engage in work, education or training are equally deficient.

It is appropriate considering the outcomes for care leavers achieved within the rights-based and equitable aftercare service in Northern Ireland. In 2012-2013, the Trusts in Northern Ireland remained in contact with 98 per cent of care leavers aged 19; 66 per cent of 19-year-old care leavers were participating in work, education or training and of the care leavers the Trusts were in regular contact with 69 per cent were involved in work, education or training.

To conclude this section on corporate parenting it is worthwhile considering one of the most influential research papers on corporate parenting, "Can the corporate state parent"? (Bullock *et al.*, 2006). This research found that there are three factors necessary for the state to effective corporate parent:

> 1) The framework must be right to be conducive for optimal outcomes for children and families – this requires legislation and provision that meets the needs of a wide variety of young people and that professionals have equal opportunities to use the legislation to access a range of services and placement options as they deem to be most appropriate in each case. The state must also accept long-term responsibility for these young people into early adulthood with all agencies serving children and young adults contributing to young people's welfare and not just social services. The state must also recognise the need to support those chil-

dren who have left care in order to identify and apply clear principles and values that underpin services for children

2) The second requirement is to ensure that care offered is of a high quality. The minimisation of placement breakdown is essential. To achieve this "planning for children, support for carers, contingency plans, and the handling of difficult behavior and complex contact arrangements with birth relatives have to be well coordinated and effective (Sinclair, Wilson and Gibbs, 2004)."

3) The third requirement is the tackling of the weakness that ensues upon the ending of children's care in the late teens. They recommend that a more informed approach to matching, permanence and attachment be implemented and clarity be brought to bear on just what is meant by permanence.

The findings of Bullock *et al.* (*ibid*) reflect some of the very issues highlighted throughout this book: the necessity for legislation to mandate quality services; a robust care system which requires inclusion of residential care (Hillan, 2005); inter-agency and partnership working; the necessity for values in the work with children; and the need for support after young people leave care.

Aftercare Bill 2014

We have seen the launch of the Child and Family Agency (Tusla), in January 2014, initially under Minister Frances Fitzgerald. It is significant on many levels that Tusla has had three different ministers, from three different professional backgrounds, overseeing its first seven months of operations. Minister Frances Fitzgerald, a former social worker, was replaced by Minister Charles Flanagan, a former solicitor, on the 8 May 2014. She was moved to the Department of Justice after what many have identified was a highly effective term as Minister for Children. Minister Flanagan was moved on 11 July 2014 to the Department of Foreign Affairs and replaced on the same date by Minister James Reilly, a former doctor.

The proposed amendment to legislation underpinning aftercare (DCYA, 2014a), strengthening the entitlement to the preparation of an aftercare plan where the need for aftercare support is identified prior to leaving care, is welcomed as a step in the right direction. However, granting a right to an assessment of need for support via the development of an aftercare plan can also be seen to represent, whether intentional or not, yet another manoeuvre aimed at avoiding taking the one essential step of granting statutory entitlement.

> It is proposed to strengthen the legislative provisions for aftercare, by amending the Child Care Act, 1991 to provide for a statutory basis for the preparation of an aftercare plan. The purpose of the proposed amendment is to provide clarity around eligibility and the arrangements for preparing, reviewing and updating the aftercare plan. (DCYA, 2014)

Granting a right to the state to provide support to those it determines require it via assessments, and describing how this may be done, is a very different, and lesser, thing than granting a right to a care leaver to a service.

Incorporating within this Bill the legislative imperative to prepare an aftercare plan merely addresses one aspect of the complex task of caring for and supporting care leavers, and mimics the focus on the preparation of care plans within residential and foster care. The definition around eligibility appears to be somewhat analogous in terminology to that from Northern Ireland, but nonetheless is welcome in bringing enhanced clarity to this critical issue.

It can be said that "just because we give something a name does not mean we understand it", and also, that "just because we know the right thing to do does not necessarily mean we will actually do the right thing". Making more explicit the statement of the duty on the Child and Family Agency is reminiscent of former Minister Andrews' 2010 statement that the existing legislation, Section 45(4) of the Child Care Act 1991, was sufficiently robust and that, having being advised by the Attorney General, he was assured that it placed a statutory duty on the HSE to provide aftercare and that henceforth the HSE would do so. This, as we have seen, had limited efficacy historically (Dáil Debates, 2010, Written Answers, 27230/10).

It is somewhat of a rhetorical question to consider whether any 18-year-old *may* need some form of ongoing support. I know of none who does not, and for care leavers this is even more assuredly the case given their ongoing vulnerabilities.

> All children need support during their transition from adolescence to adulthood. Young people leaving care are a particularly vulnerable group who often have no family supports available to them. If they don't receive adequate aftercare they are cut adrift and left to cope with situations most adults would find impossible to navigate. (Barnardos, 2010)

Support can come in many forms, including assistance with holidays, knowing that someone cares about your well-being and is there to listen if needed, emotional support and a "felt-sense of security", financial, social, somewhere to fall back on in emergencies and general advice and encouragement, to name but a few. It is also important to recognise that the transition process is not necessarily linear and needs may vary accordingly (Stein, 2008). The question to be asked is whether we are providing the supports they actually need, and how, and on what basis, are the supports being made available to care leavers.

In some cases care leavers may return to the family home from which they were removed and the family may not want any further dealings with the social work departments. Equally, some young people may stay on in a foster home beyond 18 and the foster family may not desire any further dealings with social work departments. However, we have no way of accurately knowing how many children are actually in foster placements without aftercare support due to the unacceptably inchoate data recorded and made available by the HSE/Tusla. In some instances it may not be the support that is being rejected but the interaction with social work departments. This represents a failure to engage with these families on a meaningful level across various services ranging from social work to family support.

Disenfranchised young people, or their families or foster families, refusing any contact from aftercare services upon turning 18 does not mean they do not need support. In reality, these young people need support all the more due to negative experiences, but this support needs to be made available in a format that is acceptable to them. We know that children in care may not be able to accept feelings of trust, affection or intimacy, and we work to build their capacity to sustain these feelings, yet we do not always extend such understanding to these older children and their families. Making this support available on terms they can accept is, as previously identified in Chapter 2, one of the core challenges of caring for these vulnerable care leavers. As ever caring parent knows, "no" does not necessarily mean "no" in every incidence when it comes to adolescents refusing to take direction or accept input from their parents. There are times where they are testing their boundaries and may just want to see how much the adult actually cares, which they may determine by assessing the adult's perseverance. Sometimes it takes encouragement, patience, cajoling, humour, change of approach or rewards, coupled with a thick skin, to persevere beyond the refusal and get children and adolescents to say yes, even though they may really like doing what they are being asked to do. This is a vital form of emotional co-regulation (Butler, 2013).

Keith recounts how I had the tough conversations with him on sensitive matters, such as family relationships, and how he took my advice. He finishes his chapter with some excellent advice for those working with children in care:

> Take the time to get to know the person in your care. Always show an interest in what is going on in their social circle. Have the tough conversations with them, if required, as you won't say anything to them that they are already not aware of or about which they have some understanding.

It has been my experience, based on observing colleagues interacting with children in care, that those who were direct and spoke their mind tended to have close, meaningful and trusting relationships with the children, despite the fact that, at times, these workers would be addressing behavioural or interpersonal matters. Children tended to value this authenticity very highly, perhaps as Keith has posited because they may have already known of these matters at some level themselves. Such workers had the ability to challenge children when needed, yet maintain a strong and meaningful relationship with them. They were comfortable dealing with conflict and therefore capable of providing care and control in the correct balance. The young people knew where they stood with such workers, which afforded them some certainty in their often very uncertain lives.

The consequences of workers "playing it safe" and being less direct with the young people, perhaps from a professionally defensive position or a focus on "first causing no harm", would include the loss of such trusting relationships. This loss would in fact represent "harm" to these children with the opportunity for growth being wasted. Equally, deliberately avoiding conflict when conflict is required can be harmful (Kleipoedszus, 2011). The key to such relationships, as Keith has identified, is the worker having a meaningful relationship with the child and having the courage to speak their mind. As previously noted, children in care, through harsh necessity, learn to discern authenticity in adults. This was evidenced in Keith's story where he identified how, as a growing child, he developed this ability to quickly discern adults' intent where he talks of being able to determine his "parents' mood or mental state by observing how they dressed, stood, or even to how my mother had her hair brushed. This is a state of mind where one is hypersensitive to the environment and the individuals in it" (p. 11).

. . . .

This issue, where the lines between being an educator, fire fighter or abuser are very fine, encapsulates the absolute necessity to both know and have meaningful relationships with the young people we work with so that we can make the correct interpretations.

. . . .

As a corporate parent this is a core challenge for aftercare services. It is too easy to just accept the no and say they refused the service and there is little more that can be done. Whilst being respectful of their right to decline, there is usually more that can be done, although there is no guarantee of success. As every caring parent knows it can be a thankless task but, nonetheless, this is what it means to be a "good enough" parent – we put the child's needs above our own needs and comfort.

We prioritise our children's needs above their wants as we recognise that as they mature they are acquiring the ability to regulate these matters, and therefore need our support during this developmental process. As a good corporate parent Tusla should do the same and recognise that there is a world of difference between wanting something and needing something. Therefore, Tusla should, as a good corporate parent, extend the paramountcy of the child principle, where the child's needs rank the highest. Making aftercare a "core business" for Tusla by implementing statutory entitlement represents the singular most effective mechanism to achieve such an extension of the paramountcy principle. This would make the core challenge of creating the circumstances for young people to access resources become core business for Tusla, thereby enhancing its desired transformation from the former Child and Family Agency located within the HSE into a congruent agency supporting all young people in care and aftercare.

To accept the rejection of the offer of support, tantamount to an "abdication of duty" as Shannon and Gibbons (2012:xvii) termed it, represents yet another missed opportunity on the part of Tusla to support these vulnerable young people. Furthermore, if we accept the assertions of eminent theorists such as Anna Freud and Erik Erikson, who posit that adolescence is the second, and sometimes last, chance to address the crises of earlier childhood, then aftercare can be the second, and last, chance to address the crises of negative in-care and pre-care experiences. Endings and beginnings are intertwined, so eloquently put by T.S. Eliot (p. 54), and for these young people having a positive ending to their care experiences can facilitate positive beginnings in their adult lives, but unfortunately the converse it also true.

With regard to the support and assistance that may be made available to care leavers, the wording of the National Leaving and Aftercare Policy bears consideration:

Section 45 of the Child Care Act 1991 places a statutory duty on the HSE to form a view in relation to each young person leaving care as to whether there is a "need for assistance" and if it forms such a view to provide services in accordance with the section and *subject to resources*.

Having reviewed the past failings of the state in supporting care leavers, and with specific regard to the final three words "subject to resources", the above statement inspires limited confidence in the policy, and also the Aftercare Bill, achieving its aims. What is needed is sufficient ring-fenced funding.

Minister James Reilly, the current Minister for Children and Youth Affairs, in one of his first written answers to Dáil questions, made the following statement which appears to develop the theme of available resources further:

> The prioritisation of services for young people receiving aftercare is considered in the context of the statutory and administrative criteria and rules relating to State provision of services and the requirement of all State bodies to provide services in accordance with resources available to them. The Agency and officials of the DCYA have been and continue to explore these matters further with the relevant Departments and agencies, on a bi-lateral basis, to continue to support the improvement of aftercare for this vulnerable cohort. (Dáil Debates, 2014, Written Answer, 35541/14)

By making aftercare support a statutory entitlement for care leavers Tusla can make its proffered commitment to children in care and aftercare real and meaningful. Then, as active agents in determining their own futures, care leavers will be empowered to ensure that they receive the support they absolutely need.

> When accorded rights, individuals are legally recognised as members of a social order and this enables self-respect to develop, as well as respect for other. Social esteem is expressed through acknowledgement of individual's achievements and abilities and enables self-esteem. (Ridely *et al.*, 2013:3)

A further observation with regard to the proposed Aftercare Bill (2014) is the usage of the word "may" as outlined by Minister Reilly in 2015. As we have previously noted, the usage of the word "may" has long been identified as the problem with the existing legislation with campaigners seeking to replacement it in the Child Care Act 1991 Section 45 with the word "shall". It would appear that the proposed Bill merely perpetuates the employment of this permissive word, may.

> Section 45 of the Child Care Act 1991 provides that the Child and Family Agency *may* assist a child leaving its care if it is satisfied that the person has a "need for assistance". The provisions have been interpreted and applied on the basis that young people who have had a care history with the Agency are entitled to an assessment of need, from which an aftercare plan *may* be prepared and an aftercare service *may* be offered (based on the assessed needs). (Dáil Debates, 2015, Written Answers, 9659/15)

A final observation on the Aftercare Bill (2014) in its proposed format is the import of a forthright statement by Gordon Jeyes to the Joint Oireachtas Committee on Health and Children regarding aftercare provision in 2015:

> We have the minimum guarantee, but out legislative basis is for us to support the young people who are in full-education or training.

No clearer statement of the absolute imperative to place aftercare on a statutory rights-based footing for all care leavers can be made than this acknowledgement that Tusla interpret Section 45 of the Child Care Act 1991 as not affording a legislative mandate to support care leavers who are not participating in education or training. Mr Jeyes is to be commended for placing this statement into the public domain.

However, with specific regard to the many care leavers who do not engage in full-time education or training, but who often have the most need for support, how does this statement accord with the previously cited statements from Mr Jeyes that:

> By international standards, our current aftercare arrange-
> ments are good and ... ensure we not only support those
> youngsters who remain in education but those who choose
> to remain in foster care. We will fund this irrespective of
> their education arrangements. (Jeyes, 2014a)

Indeed, the same is true for any of the numerous statements over recent years by former ministers, senior HSE management and even the Irish Attorney General regarding the interpretation of this Act as placing a statutory duty on the HSE/Tusla to support care leavers. It does, however, reveal Tusla's future intent.

This, then, poses the question as to whether it was the omission, deliberate or otherwise, of the one word – "all" – from previous interpretations of this Act that has led to our current inequitable two-tiered aftercare system? It also begs the questions as to just what, currently, is the claimed minimum guarantee for the many vulnerable young people excluded from aftercare support, and what impact will this interpretation have on those care leavers currently receiving support who are not involved in education or training, including those supported to remain in their foster placements beyond 18? We know the number of care leavers not in education or training identified as receiving some form of service to be circa 757 (McBride, 2014a).

Clearly, merely replacing the word "may" with "shall" or "must" in the Section 45 of the 1991 Child Care Act would not be sufficient to achieve an equitable aftercare service. The legislation must be sufficiently robust to compel, with sufficient ring-fenced resources, the State and its agents to meet its corporate parent responsibility to all care leavers. Unfortunately, the Aftercare Bill (2014) in its proposed format does not achieve this.

The Political Dimension

Political short-term planning, together with changes in political direction, are major factors in Irish child care provision. We have seen with the launch of Tusla that there have been three different ministers responsible for overseeing its beginning. The significance of this can be located both in terms of continuity of relationships and also when we consider that each minister came from a different professional background. This one example, then, reveals a major flaw in the development of integrated child care services, namely, short-term political vision. Politicians must constantly seek voter's preference and consequently are prone to making promises whilst seeking election that fail to materialise once elected. Children cannot vote, and the marginalised of society are typically not the highest level of voters. Thus the needs of these two groups do not rate as highly for politicians seeking a mandate as those who are known to vote.

> Children have been set low on the list of political priorities in Ireland for far too long. Too often they have been sidelined and voiceless. Those living in communities who are disenfranchised and marginalised are even further away from the political table. (Barnardos, 2011a:3)

We know that in 2014 there were 9,450 reported cases of abuse, neglect or welfare concerns awaiting social worker allocation with 3,450 of these being categorised as high priority cases (Dáil Debates, 2014, Written Answers, 36155/14). Burns and MacCarthy (2012:34) suggest that:

> ... entry thresholds to the (child protection and welfare social work teams) are increasing to respond to issues of capacity, which means that children and families who normally would receive a service are being placed on a waiting list or are not worked with at all, and opportunities for preventive work are being lost.

Yalloway et al., (2012) identify that the 2005 HSE Dublin North Interim Data Set Returns confirms that:

> Large numbers of children are being "screened out" for services because of the need to prioritise available resources to respond to children who are most in need ... this reflects the wide variation in practice across the country concerning referral and assessment of child abuse and service capacity issues in each HSE area. (2012:93).

There is a growing body of evidence demonstrating the fallacy of delaying entry into care, which entrenches harm and makes re-unification with family less successful whilst also costing the state substantially more in the long term (Ward *et al.*, 2008; Holmes, 2012). However, to tackle this issue would require government to prioritise children's services for funding when they are increasingly under pressure for poor health services and other public services deficiencies. It may be that tackling the public health system will prove more beneficial to the current, or indeed any, government in terms of retaining its mandate. Thus the problem accrued by not providing investment in children's services is deferred, potentially for a different government, for political reasons.

Political responsibility for child protection failings, linked to negative public perception of children in care and their families, was a major finding of Holohan's (2011) research report "In Plain Sight: Responding to the Ferns, Ryan, Murphy and Cloyne Reports."

> This research makes clear that political and societal attitudes to those living in poverty contributed significantly to the situation whereby children at risk and living in poverty were victims of human rights abuses. Families at risk of or living in poverty were somehow blamed for their socio-economic status. They were viewed as morally suspect, degenerate and unworthy. (Deasy in Holohan, 2011:325)

The need for political leadership and vision in order to develop children services effectively is not down to any one particular political party or politician – it is a challenge to all and therefore to the political system itself. Children and their services need to be prioritised by Government, a challenge which has been acknowledged, but a robust solution has yet to emerge. This acknowledgement is evidenced within another policy document published by the DCYA whilst under Minister Fitzgerald's leadership in September 2013. This policy, "Right from the Start: Report of the Expert Advisory Group on the Early Years Strategy", contains the following observation within its preface:

> A set of recommendations, of course, is not enough. If the people of Ireland really do want to change the future – to

ensure that right from the start all our children have the best possible chance – that requires a major statement of political purpose and a radical re-orientation of structures, organisations, resources and policy priorities. (DCYA, 2013:1)

We have seen the political influence on social care through-out this book, its role in social policy, research, children's rights, theory and the professions, all of which shape services and practice. There is also a political dimension with the media coverage of social care issues, a point made by Carl O'Brien:

The problem with social issues is that most politicians and political parties – but not all – see them as being of relevance only to the most marginalised, who are less likely to vote or to be active members of "civil society". Because the issues are marginalised politically they, they are also marginalised in the media....Ultimately social work needs to be higher on the political agenda if it is to receive wider coverage. (O'Brien, 2012:118-119)

Given the extent of this influence we can see the magnitude of the impact of the short-term focus on children's services outlined above.

. . . .

The politically induced short-term focus on children's services development can be seen to underpin much that is wrong with Irish children's services (Kennedy, 2014).

. . . .

Aftercare and Positive Outcomes

At the risk of stating the obvious, it is necessary to make the case for aftercare in terms of promoting positive outcomes for children leaving care. As far back as the Kennedy Report (1970) and as recently as the Ryan Report (2009), aftercare provision has been highlighted as an essential service for children leaving care:

> Aftercare, which is now practically non-existent, should form an integral part of the Child Care system. (Kennedy Report, 1970:14)

> ... comprehensive aftercare services that assist young people in the transition to independent living are vital. (Ryan Report, 2009:396)

Recent research by Harder, Kalverboer, and Knorth (2011) and James *et al.* (2013) highlights the link between aftercare and positive outcomes, and this research builds on the existing body of works previously cited by Mike Stein, Robbie Gilligan and John Pinkerton within the UK and Irish contexts. There is a growing body of research validating the place of relationships in aftercare.

This is not to say that repositioning the relationship back at the centre of practice will alone resolve all that is wrong with social care. However, by acknowledging the centrality of the relationship, which requires that we also acknowledge the importance of the worker and elevate both within current models of practice, then the elusive "better outcomes" may begin to come into clearer focus.

Quality Assurance

There is also the issue of quality assurance of service delivery which requires consideration. There is little doubt that registration, inspection and monitoring regimes have brought significant benefits to social care for children since the introduction of the SSI in 1999, and more recently with HIQA. The current situation where Tusla Registration and Inspection Service monitors and inspects private and voluntary children's residential centres, whilst HIQA inspects statutory children's residential centres, is not ideal. Although identified by the DCYA as a priority issue to resolve, there is as yet no set date for the assimilation of these private and voluntary centres within the scope of HIQA inspection services (Dáil Debates, 2013, Written Answer, 53791/13). Some of the benefits attributable to Inspection and Monitoring Services for children in care have been previously identified, such as their role in the elimination of abuses that formerly occurred within residential care settings. What is needed is quality assurance achieved through the evaluation of services against a framework of National Standards for Aftercare Services. In order to empower HIQA and Registration and Inspection Services to have a similar mandate extending to aftercare, legislation is required. Therefore, any legislative change to place aftercare on a statutory basis requires the inclusion of the necessary wording to create the mandate for HIQA and Registration and Inspection Services to hold authority of compliance enforcement within identified standards for aftercare services.

. . . .

The fact that 93 per cent of children in care are in foster care (Tusla, 2014), and that of the four HIQA Inspection Reports on Foster Care Services carried out from January - July 2014 (ID 687; 683; 674; 669) all services were found to be non-compliant with the standard for preparation for leaving care and adult life is a shocking indictment. This represents the clearest evidence of why preparation for leaving care, aftercare and the inspection of aftercare services must be placed on a statutory basis and inspected by HIQA.

. . . .

Summary

These two chapters have covered many issues germane to children in care and aftercare, whilst also acknowledging the professional as a critical component of care, the "face of the corporate parent". Some of the implications of the professionalisation agenda have been revealed. The relevance of issues of social justice, values, empowerment and the impact of language, as well as the need for external inspection and monitoring, have been considered. There are many factors impacting social care and social work, which require better understanding on the part of the professional to inform their practice and on policy makers to inform service development and configuration. These include political, economic, social and professional processes. The professional must be able to evaluate these to inform their decision making so as to best represent and support those they are tasked with assisting. This section has been wide-ranging and intended to promote thinking on the part of the professional across a variety of areas to better inform their professional judgement. There are many perspectives to be considered to inform our decision making. As such this section, as is the entire book, is intended to be thought-provoking rather than provocative.

My intent has been to make a contribution to the knowledge base with the goal of improving outcomes for young people in care and aftercare. In so doing my purpose is also to align with the advice of the Munro Report (2011:84), previously cited in the introduction to this book. Munro identified the importance of workers' professional judgement and the paramountcy of the relationship in social care, and said that it:

> ... requires social workers to be in possession of the right knowledge and be capable of clear reasoning. Children need and deserve a high level of expertise from their social workers who make such crucial decisions about what is in their best interests. This expertise should include being skilled in relationships where care and control often need to be combined, able to make critical use of best evidence from research to inform the complex judgements and decisions needed and to help children and families to solve problems and to change." (Munro, 2011:84)

Conclusion

Some of the best professional advice ever given to me was from Professor James Anglin. He said, "Always stay curious and question everything." This book is intended to promote the reader to be curious and question everything, seeking their own answers through their endeavours, professional development and practice as well as their knowledge of the young people, their families and their social ecologies. This is the surest way to promote better practice and keep young people safe which will result in better outcomes for children in care. Informed workers will be professionally-active and seek to increase the resources and opportunities of those they support. On the face of it, to advocate questioning everything may appear to promote paralysis and indecision, whereas in reality it does not. We may question something today and, indeed, find an answer, however tomorrow the same question may be in a different context and thus require a different response.

Keith's experiences of poverty and loneliness within his aftercare placement makes clear the need to always maintain an inquiring stance. I now know that I assumed that he would be well cared for in this placement as it was with a long-standing and well-known service provider. Additionally, it was the only such service available in Dublin at that time and securing a placement there was in itself an achievement. However, I didn't verify this for myself, even though I visited him there several times and witnessed his circumstances. His poverty was "in plain sight" but I did not see it for what it was. I now see that my assumption may have obscured my objectivity, just as, historically, assumption prevented so many adults from hearing and acting on children reporting abuse. Assumption underpins the discrimination and stigmatisation Keith experienced within the community as a child growing up in a dysfunctional family. Had I inquired beyond my assumption Keith may not have suffered the harm and hardship to the extent he endured. No young person should endure such experiences in 2015.

We must be prepared to question convention, a point made explicit by the eminent Professor Eileen Gambrill:

> Helping clients requires asking hard questions of professors and alleged "experts". It will take courage to ask questions others chose to ignore; it will take caring about clients. (2013:x)

A working hypothesis is very important to inform our work, but we must always be mindful that it requires verification employing critical thinking, incorporating practice and research informed evidence and knowledge. We must remember that theory is a "tool to think with" and not let it become an assumed truth for all, "a prescription to abide by" (Erikson, 1950:243).

We must be ever vigilant to guard against our assumptions, and the influence of the assumptions of others, becoming our beliefs. As Hartman (1991) has identified, "words become actions" and as we have seen, theories used by practitioners to understand human behaviour are heavily influenced by the dominant political hegemony. Add to this the contested nature of outcomes and evidence and we can see why we must resist the temptation to allow these constructs to do our thinking for us by employing doctrinaire approaches to singular theories or methodologies. We have also seen the overarching importance of values in social care and social work. Consequently, there is much to reflect on in the famous quote of unknown origin:

> Your beliefs become your thoughts,
> Your thoughts become your words,
> Your words become your actions,
> Your actions become your habits,
> Your habits become your values.

In questioning some of the assumptions surrounding residential care and aftercare, as well as practice, theory and research, this book has attempted to dispel some mistruths whilst promoting an inquiring stance on key issues shaping social care. However, within this process some facts have also been revealed.

Residential care, as currently configured, is a residualised service, a placement of last resort. Children are mixed with others with disparate levels of needs, and thereby the ability of the service to function in the best interest of each child is compromised. Residential care needs to become a placement of first choice for those young people identified as needing a residential placement and at the time this need is first identified. The care system cannot function optimally without all elements operating in an integrated manner. The current usage of residential care in the Republic of Ireland is set too low by international standards.

Preparation for leaving care needs to be placed on a statutory footing and given the recognition it warrants. There is a pressing need for an implemented National Standard of Preparation for Leaving Care in the Republic of Ireland.

There needs to be a paradigm shift with regard to how we care for children requiring out-of-home care. We need to place values of social justice at the core of all that we do. We need to cease configuring services within existing budgetary allocations. This enables superficially convincing planning whereby, on paper, a care system can operate without the required range of placements. The tragedy of the current system is that only after it has been proven to be ineffective, after young people have come to harm, will it be changed. We need to rethink what services are necessary to meet the needs of young people, and then put in place a strategy to implement them accordingly.

Statutory entitlement to aftercare support is a means to, and guarantee of, change, rather than the conversation about change which has been ongoing since the Kennedy Report in 1970. Mendes *et al.* (2014) make the point that far more is known today about leaving care and aftercare, which places policy-makers and practitioners in a much better position to address what is required. Over the past two decades we have had numerous inquiries and investigations into the failing of the former Health Boards and the HSE Child and Family Services in attempting to care for children and care leavers. We have had the Madonna House Inquiry (1996), the Commission of Inquiry in Child Abuse (2009) and the Investigation in Deaths in Care (2012), to name some of the most prominent, and all highlight the inadequacies of aftercare provision. Concomitantly, we have had numerous publications by a variety of NGOs – Barnardos, Focus Ireland, EPIC, the Children's Rights Alliance, Office of the Ombudsman for Children to name but a few. Additionally, there have been media investigations as well as academic publications all highlighting these failures in supporting care leavers. All the while, the plight of care leavers has been revealed with the *Left Out on Their Own* publication in 2000 unveiling what previous reports had highlighted but had remained largely unresolved. Burns and MacCarthy (2012:36) describe change following these reports as "glacially slow", echoing Gilligan's (1993:366) observation regarding the implementation of the 1991 Child Care Act in the Republic of Ireland as "the genteel pace of reform".

Given that four neighbouring states – Northern Ireland, Wales, England, and Scotland – have all placed aftercare on a firm legislative basis it is difficult to understand why the Republic of Ireland has not done so. Based on the experiences within these states it is true that legislation alone is not the solution, however, it is also true that improvement is not possible without rights-based legislation. Aftercare needs to become "core business" for Tusla as opposed to its current status as "non-core business". The fact that many care leavers achieve positive outcomes is commendable and must be acknowledged. Nor should such a focus fail to acknowledge the dedication and commitment of many aftercare workers, social care workers, foster carers and social workers who go above and beyond the call of duty in very difficult circumstances. Rather, it is intended to achieve equity and the opportunity for positive outcomes for all care leavers.

Whilst there has been a notable focus on aftercare services in recent years, for aftercare to cease being the "poor second cousin of social work" legislation is needed. Legislation would empower care leavers to access the resources they need to become resilient. It would also empower workers by providing role clarity and ring-fenced funding. Legislation, together with policy, regulation and education, shapes practice. Currently, practice is deficient legislatively and educationally, under-resourced, weak in policy and with notable regional variability in terms of availability and quality of support.

Support services for young people who have left state care that were made available solely on the basis of chronological age and training or education status were never equitable or sufficient to meet the needs of all care leavers. It was not a service fit for purpose then nor is it now.

By enacting statutory provision to aftercare support for care leavers the Republic of Ireland may become the authentic corporate parent she aspires to be, rather than the obdurate one she has been. Responsibility would be shared across all stakeholding agencies and government departments. Coupled with this, single case-holder legal responsibility would ensure both the mandate to access resources with statutory authority and the continuity of relationships for the young people leaving care. Such an aftercare service would be equitable, values-based and developmentally-appropriate, with an expectation that all care leavers would thrive as opposed to many merely surviving.

We cannot rewrite history and erase the harm caused to many young people who left state care in the past but we can right the wrong now.

Appendix

The Economic Case for Statutory Aftercare in the Republic of Ireland

It is not my intention to make a precise economic case for legislative change in this book, nor to prescribe what such a service should entail. Rather, I will carry out a review of some of the available data to give context to this proposition and challenge any false assumptions that seem to exist. To achieve this I propose a tripartite piece of analysis, based on the available data in the Republic of Ireland and Northern Ireland to frame a cost/benefit analysis. This research will constitute the evidencing of:

1. How much is currently being spent on aftercare in the Republic of Ireland.

2. How much it would cost to provide a statutory aftercare service in the Republic of Ireland.

3. The benefits of providing a statutory aftercare service compared to the costs of provision.

As previously noted, there is a lack of available data with regard to care leavers in the Republic of Ireland which renders accurate analysis problematic. There has been an improvement in the availability of data in recent years, albeit with major deficits remaining in many areas. However, it must be acknowledged that the willingness to make available known data by the Department of Children and Youth Affairs (DCYA) and Tusla in recent times is a welcome development and augurs well for more complete data becoming available in the future.

Due to the inconsistencies in available data for the Republic of Ireland, contrasted with the complete and accurate data from Northern Ireland, it will be necessary to extrapolate figures from 2007 and 2013. This is largely due to the fact that the only published figure for care leavers in the Republic of Ireland was published by Eurochild (2010), which identified the number of care leavers in 2007. There is no available published figure for the number of young people who left care in the Republic in 2013. Additionally, there is no known expenditure on aftercare in the Republic prior to 2011. We do, however, have a figure for 2012 which was made available by DCYA which is €17 million (Dáil Debates, 2013, Written Answers, 19073/13). This figure, which represents 3 per cent of TUSLA's 2014 budget (Jeyes, 2014) affords us the starting point for this research.

Costs for the implementation of statutory aftercare provision in Northern Ireland over the years 2002 to 2005, and annually thereafter from 2005 to 2010, have very kindly been made available by our colleagues in Northern Ireland. Indeed, it has been my experience over the years that I was secretary of the Irish Network of Aftercare Workers that our colleagues in Northern Ireland have been very supportive of endeavours to develop aftercare in the Republic by giving generously of their time and knowledge.

There is a growing body of research available regarding the benefits afforded to the state by the provision of effective social services, including leaving care services. For comparative value to the Republic of Ireland (welfare regimes, socially and culturally) and the scope and range of the available research four publications from the UK and two from Australia shall be examined. From the UK: Dixon *et al.*, (2006). *Young People Leaving Care: A Study of Costs and Outcomes;* Hannon *et al.*, (2010), *In Loco Parentis;* HM Treasury, (2007), *Policy Review for Children and Young People;* Audit Commission, (2010), *Against the Odds.* From Australia: Raman *et al.*, (2005), *Investing for success: The economics of supporting young people leaving care;* Forbes and Inder (2006), *Measuring the cost of leaving care in Victoria.*

Research Point One

Current Expenditure in Republic of Ireland

The amount currently being spent by the State in the Republic of Ireland is a known figure and thus we have a figure for the first part of our research: €17 million for 2012. (Dáil Debates, Written Answers, 7314/13)

Research Point Two

Cost of service provision in Republic based on Northern model

We are fortunate to have detailed information which affords comprehensive information on the real costs and also the format of the services being delivered within these budgets. This is a detailed document and is available in full at www.empowerireland.ie/resources. What is extrapolated below is the financial costs of implementing this service for the years 2006-2010.

Estimated regional annual costings:

- 2005/06 – £3,880,395

- 2006/07 – £4,823,763

- 2007/08 – £5,051,826

- 2008/09 – £5,127,359

- 2009/10 – £5,456,504

This document clearly sets out the costs of implementing the statutory aftercare service in Northern Ireland, and the composition of the service on offer within this budget. It can be seen that the cost in 2007 was £5,051,826, which equates to €6,112,000. In Northern Ireland in 2007 there were 241 young people who left care, which equates to a cost per care leaver of €25,347 per annum. In the Republic in 2007 there were 411 care leavers which would yield a cost of €10,422,220. However, there are many differences between the jurisdictions which impact on costings for like-for-like services. For example, salaries for social care staff are higher in the Republic. If we allow an additional weighting for salary differences, the figure for the Republic for 2007 would be €11,985,553 or €29,161 per care leaver. This is a conservative weighting given that salaries in the Republic have dropped significantly since 2009.

Whilst we have no published figure for the number of young people who left care in the Republic for 2012, we do know that the numbers of children in care have increased year-on-year from 2006 to 2011 by 17.4 per cent, rising from 5,247 in 2006 to 6,260 in 2011 (HSE, 2012). We also have an approximate figure of 450 per year given by Minister Flanagan on 5 June 2014 in Dáil Debates, Written Answers, 23989/14. This would equate to a cost of €13,122,450 for an aftercare service based on that in Northern Ireland. This is less than the declared figure of €17,000,000 currently expended on aftercare disseminated by the DCYA (*ibid*).

Thus, even including a conservative weighting for salary differences between the Republic and the North, it is clearly evident that delivering a statutorily-based aftercare service would, at a minimum, be cost neutral. That is to say, the cost would be no more than what we are already spending.

Year	Care Leavers Pop.	Total Service Cost	Cost Per Care Leaaver	Adj. Total Service Cost	Adj. Cost Per Care Leaaver
NI 2007	241	€6,112,000	€25,347		
ROI 2007	411	€10,417,617	€25,347	€11,985,553	€29,161
ROI 2011	450	€11,406,150	€25,347	€13,122,450	€29,161

Table 11: Cost Comparison Northern Ireland and the Republic of Ireland.

It must also be said that without accurate data it is impossible to operate a service within an accountable or indeed value-for-money or performance-led framework. The inability to determine how many people require the service renders all calculations determining such parameters as inherently flawed. Thus we cannot know if we are getting value for the €17 million currently being spent, as we don't know how many people are eligible for the service. We do know how many are in receipt of the service, but without knowing the true number eligible, and those not currently in receipt of a service but who would benefit from a service, this figure is incomplete causing its meaning and significance to be biased and inaccurate in yielding a true representation.

Research Point Three

Benefit-cost analysis to the state for implementing statutory aftercare services

The 2010 Demos report by Hannon *et al.*, *In Loco Parentis* and *Young People Leaving Care: A Study of Costs and Outcomes* by Dixon *et al.* (2006) are both solid pieces of research into the costs associated with children in care and positive outcomes for care leavers. Rather than examining either report in any depth, it is proposed to select the figure identified by Hannon *et al.*, as the cost difference to the state in the UK between two children leaving care up to their thirtieth birthday, where one leaves care successfully and the other less successfully. This figure, which Hannon *et al.* (2010:167) declare is most likely to be underestimated, is €161,400 per person. Whilst this figure incorporates elements of within care costs, thus reducing the potential amount of benefit figure as the costs of within care services are included, this does not weaken the case for this piece of research. Preparation for leaving care has been clearly identified within this book as key to positive outcomes, thus validating investing in high-quality care services which will then lead to improved outcomes for care leavers.

Another notable piece of research from the UK is a HM Treasury Report from 2007, *Policy Review for Children and Young People: A Discussion Paper*. Within this report the following points are made regarding the costs associated with care leavers who are not involved in education employment or training:

- Children in care experience many poor outcomes, including poor educational attainment. It is estimated that if attainment of all children in care could be raised to that of all children, there might be a gain to society of around £6 billion in terms of increased productivity over these children's lifetimes.

- The additional lifetime costs of being NEET (not in education, employment or training) at age 16-18 have been estimated at around £8.1 billion in terms of public finance costs. It should be noted that these figures are based on a number of assumptions and do not include potential health and crime effects.

A 2010 Audit Commission Report, *Against the Odds*, found that:

> Research by York University estimates an average lifetime public finance cost of £56,301 for a young person who is NEET aged 16 to 18. (Audit Commission, 2010:14)

In 2011, the economic cost to the Republic of Ireland of NEET young people was estimated to be €4.3 billion, or 2.8 per cent of GDP (Oireachtas Library and Research Service, 2013). These include many young people who may have been placed in residential care as a placement of last resort. They will often have experienced multiple placements and, on leaving care, may not engage on the terms stipulated by aftercare services.

There are a minimum of 38.9 per cent of care leavers in the Republic of Ireland not participating in education or training (Dáil Debates, 2013, Topical Issue Debate), which means that of the 450 care leavers in 2012 (Dáil Debates, Written Answers, 23989/14) 175 were not in education or training. We know this figure to be based on flawed methodological practice which misrepresents the cohort of care leavers in receipt of an aftercare service as the total figure for all care leavers, meaning that the real number of care leavers who are NEET will be significantly higher. In December 2014, the Republic of Ireland had a youth unemployment rate of 21.6 per cent (Eurostat, 2015).

> The scale of the problem is also masked by a very significant increase in the number of young people re-entering or remaining in education and a very considerable increase in the number of young people emigrating. (National Youth Council of Ireland, 2010:8)

Consequently, it is unlikely many of these 175 care leavers will be in employment.

The Australian research is appropriate to this exercise as it affords a cost analysis up to age 59. Also, the care population in

Victoria is very similar to Ireland with circa 6,000 young people in care in both jurisdictions and with similar usage of residential services and foster placements.

> The general approach to estimating the cost of the exist-ing Victorian policy is to determine the additional support from State funded services required of young people who have previously been in care beyond what is typically re-quired of young people from the wider community. To do so, the total cost of services over the adult lifetime (taken here as 18-59 years of age) of a representative young person from the general population in Victoria is estimated and compared against a similar estimate of the total lifetime cost of services of a representative young person from the leaving care population. The difference between these two estimates provides an estimate of the average total cost to the State of leaving care in Victoria for each person who is released from care. (Forbes and Inder, 2006:10)

> To cover the main areas of State government support, out-comes are segregated into the eight categories [as shown in Table 12].

> The figure of $738,741 (€496,225) is associated with a single, representative adult lifetime after leaving care... It should also be stressed that this is a conservative estimate – where assumptions have been needed in the cost calcu-lations, these have generally been made to understate the cost differences rather than overestimate them. The true savings are likely to be significantly higher. (Forbes and In-der, 2006:22-23)

Appendix

Table 12: *Lifetime Costs per Person Leaving Care in Australia.*

Category	Care Leavers	General Population	Gap
Child Protection	$98,812	$540	$98,272
Gov./State Tax Revenue	-$67,317	- $119,434	$52,117
General Health	$39,887	$16,074	$23,813
Mental Health	$45,012	$6,302	$38,710
Drug and Alcohol Treatment	$18,853	$1,244	$17,609
Police	$240,134	$4,543	$235,591
Justice and Correctional	$175,598	$2,918	$172,680
Housing	$108,883	$8,934	$99,949
Total	**$659,862**	**-$78,879**	**$738,741***

* *$738,741 = €496,225

Significantly, the figures from the UK and Australia are similar thus adding credibility to the research findings as well as international comparative authenticity. This validates their employment in the Irish context. The UK research by Hannon *et al.*, (2010) identified a cost to the state per unsuccessful care leaver which equates to €13,450 per annum, whilst for Australia Forbes and Inder (2006) identified a cost to the state which equates to €12,301 per annum. Additionally, the 2014 CSJ research identified in Section Five identified a cost to the state of €458,551 per person over the life course in the UK whilst Forbes and Inder (*ibid*) identified a cost of €496,225 in Australia up to age 59. All these calculations are acknowledged as conservative by the researchers.

Forbes and Inder (*Ibid*) also considered the cost to the state of establishing a "wrap around" model of support services to help care leavers. This model included support in areas such as health, education, housing, employment and mentoring. Costs were estimated against existing programs that provide some level of support to young people, such as the mentoring and housing programs. They estimated the cost, based on a 50 per cent take up

337

of the service, at €57,800 per person for a seven-year period. This cost equates to circa 11 per cent of the estimated average state cost for each young person were they not to receive such a support. Whilst they cannot, owing to insufficient data in their study, accurately calculate benefits accrued to the state in terms of savings, they do estimate that:

> Based on international and interstate evidence (for more details see Raman et al, 2005) which suggests that the leaving care phase is vital in influencing outcomes, we estimate that if the integrated and on-going program described in our model can produce an improvement of 10 per cent in life outcomes for young people leaving State care, then it will have virtually paid for itself in cost savings. (2006:23)

With 6,400 children in care in 2015, the magnitude of financial benefits accruing to the Irish state as identified with this research from the UK and Australia takes on real and profound dimensions. This benefit is in the order of hundreds of millions of euro in the medium term, and in the billions of euro over the life-course of the current cohort of children in care. It may be helpful to consider investment in our care system as an early intervention strategy where many multiplies of the investment are recouped in the following years. What must also be acknowledged is the human benefit in terms of quality of life for so many young people and their families. This, coupled with the breaking of generational cycles of entry into care and the advancing of Ireland's goal of achieving an equitable and inclusive society, represents a benefit that is beyond quantification.

In conclusion, we are currently spending a minimum of €17 million per annum on aftercare with no way of knowing if we are getting value for money. It would cost us no more than this to implement a rights-based service with the benefits to the state and our young people being of profound and life-changing proportions.

Bibliography

Abbott, A. (1988). *The System of Professions: An Essay on the Division of Expert Labour*, Chicago, University of Chicago Press.

Abramovitz, R. and Bloom, S. (2003). Creating Sanctuary in Residential Treatment for Youth: From the "Well-Ordered Asylum" to a "Living-Learning Environment", *Psychiatric Quarterly*, 74, 2, 119-135.

Acott, K. (2015). *The Three Phase Conversational Model of Communication: An Introduction.* https://www.academia.edu/12123216/The_Three-Phase_Conversational_Model_Of_Communication?auto=downloadandcampaign=weekly_digest

Action for Children (2014). *Too much, too young: Helping the most vulnerable young people to build stable homes after leaving care*, Watford, Action for Children. http://www.actionforchildren.org.uk/media/9663662/14_15-0276-too-much-too-young-english_final_a-web-lr.pdf

Adams, R. (1998). *Social work processes*. In Adams, R. Dominelli, L. and Payne, M. (Eds.), *Social Work Themes, Issues and Critical Debates*, Basingstoke, Macmillan.

Adena, B. Meyers, B. and Sylvester, A. (2006). The role of qualitative research methods in Evidence-Based Practice, *NASP Communiqué*, 34, 1-5.

Ainsworth, M. and Bowlby, J. (1965). *Child Care and the Growth of Love*, London, Penguin Books.

Ainsworth, M. and Eichberg, C. (1991). *Effects on infant–mother attachment of mother's unresolved loss of an attachment figure or other traumatic experience.* In Marris, P. Stevenson-Hinde. J. and Parkes, C. *Attachment across the life cycle*, London, Routledge.

Ainsworth, F. and Hanson, P. (2009). *Residential programmes for children and young people: The current status and use in Australia.* In Courtney, M. and Iwaniec, D. (Eds.), *Residential care of children: Comparative perspectives*, Oxford, OUP.

Ainsworth, F. and Thoburn, J. (2014). An exploration of the differential usage of residential childcare across national boundaries, *International Journal of Social Welfare*, 23, 1, 16-24.

Alanen, L. (2009). *Generational Order.* In Qvortrup, J. Corsaro, W. and Honig,

M. (Eds.), *The Palgrave Handbook of Childhood Studies*, Basingstoke, Palgrave Macmillan.

Alasuutari, P., Bickman, L. and Brannan, J. (2008). Introduction: Social Research in Changing Social Conditions. In Alasuutari, P. Bickman, L. and Brannan, J. (Eds.), *The Sage Handbook of Social Research methods*, 1-8, London, Sage.

Alasuutari, P. (2010). The rise and relevance of qualitative research, *International Journal of Social Research Methodology*, 13, 2, 139-155.

Alderson, P. (2008). Children as researchers: Participation rights and research methods. In Christensen, P. and James, A. (Eds.), *Research with children: perspectives and practices*, London, Routledge, 276-290.

Aldgate, J. Healy, L. Malcolm, B. Pine, B. Rose, W. and Seden, J. (Eds.) (2007). *Enhancing Social Work Management: Theory and Best Practice from the UK and USA*, London, Jessica Kingsley.

Alford, D. Lyddon, W. and Schreiber, R. (2006). Adult attachment and working models of emotion, *Counselling Psychology Quarterly*, 19, 1, 45-56.

Allen, J. (2008). *Coping with Trauma: Hope through Understanding*, Arlington, American Psychiatric Publishing.

Allen, K. (1999). The Celtic Tiger, Inequality and Social Partnership, *Administration*, 47, 2.

Allen, K. (2000). *The Celtic Tiger: The Myth of Social Partnership*, Manchester University Press, Manchester.

Ames, D. and Fiske, S. (2010). Cultural neuroscience, *Asian Journal of Social Psychology*, 13, 71-81.

Anderson-Nathe, B. (2010). *Youth workers, stuckness, and the myth of supercompetence*, New York, Routledge.

Andrew, E., Williams, J. and Waters, C. (2013). Dialectical Behaviour Therapy and attachment: Vehicles for the development of resilience in young people leaving the care system, *Clinical Child Psychology and Psychiatry*, 0, 0, 1-13.

Anghel, R. (2011). Transition within transition: How young people learn to leave behind institutional care whilst their carers are stuck in neutral, *Children and Youth Services Review*, 33, 2526-2531.

Anglin, J. and Knorth, E. (Eds.) (2004). *International perspectives on rethinking residential care* [Special Issue], New York, Kluwer Academic/Human Sciences Press.

Anglin, J. and Knorth, E. (2004a). Competing declarations on residential care for children and youth: Stockholm versus Malmö, *Child and Youth Care Forum*, 33, 3, 141-149.

Anglin, J. (2002). *Pain, Normality, and the struggle for Congruence: Reinterpreting residential care for children and youth*, Binghamton, Haworth Press.

Anglin, J. (2004). Creating "Well-Functioning" Residential Care and defining Its Place in a System of Care, *Child and Youth Care Forum*, 33, 3, 75-192.

Bibliography

Anglin, J. (2013). *New Directions in Policy and Planning for Residential Care*, Paper Presented 17.5.2013 at Melbourne, Australia.

Anne E. Casey Foundation (AECF) (2013). Reducing Youth Incarceration in the United States. http://www.aecf.org/m/resourcedoc/AECF-DataSnapshotYouthIncarceration-2013.pdf

Antle, B., Johnson, L., Barbee, A. and Sullivan, D. (2009). Fostering interdependent versus independent living in youth aging out of care through healthy relationships, *Families in Society: The Journal of Contemporary Social Services, 90*, 3, 309-315.

Archard, D. (1993). *Children: Rights and Childhood*, London, Routledge.

Aries, P. (1965). *Centuries of Childhood: A Social History of Family Life*, New York, Vintage.

Arnett, J. (2007). Suffering, selfish, slackers? Myths and reality about emerging adults, *Journal of Youth and Adolescence*, 36, 23–9.

Arnold, S. (2012). *State sanctioned child poverty and exclusion: The case of children in state accommodation for asylum seekers*, Dublin, The Irish Refugee Council. http://www.irishrefugeecouncil.ie/wp-content/uploads/2012/09/State-sanctioned-child-poverty-and-exclusion.pdf

Arthur, R. (2011). *Rethinking the criminal responsibility of young people in England', Opportunities and Challenges: Implementing the UN Convention on the Rights of the Child*, Queen's University Belfast, June 1-2, 2011, in Book of abstracts. p.26. http://tees.openrepository.com/tees/bitstream/10149/134598/2/134598.pdf

Audit Commission (2010). Against the Odds: Targeted Briefing: Young Carers, http://lincolnshire.moderngov.co.uk/Data/Children%20and%20Young%20People%20Scrutiny%20Committee/20100910/Agenda/Document%2018.pdf

Avery, R. (2011). The potential contribution of mentor programs to relational permanency for youth aging out of foster care, *Child Welfare, 90*, 3, 9-26.

Baines, D. (2010). If we don't get back to where we were before: Working in the restructured non-profit social services, *Australian Social Work*, 59, 1, 20-34.

Baker, C. (2011). *Permanence and Stability for Disabled Looked After Children*, Insight 11, Glasgow, IRISS.

Balbernie, R. (1971). The Impossible Task? In Fees, C. (Ed.) (1990), *Residential Experience*, Birmingham, Association of Workers for Maladjusted Children.

Baltes, P. (1987). Theoretical Propositions of Life-Span Developmental Psychology: On the Dynamics Between Growth and Decline, *Developmental Psychology*, 23, 5, 611-626.

Bandura, A. (1997). *Self-Efficacy: The Exercise of Control*, New York, Freeman and Co.

Banks, S. (2006). *Ethics and Values in Social Work*, 3rd Ed., Basingstoke, Palgrave Macmillan.

Banks, S. (2007). The social professions and social policy: Proactive or reactive,

European Journal of Social Work, 2, 3, 327-339.

Banks, S. (2013). Negotiating personal engagement and professional accountability: professional wisdom and ethics work, *European Journal of Social Work*, 16, 5, 587-604.

Barnardos (2010). *Child Deaths: No More Excuses, No More Delay: Press Release*, http://www.barnardos.ie/media-centre/news/latest-news/child-deaths-no-more-excuses-no-more-delay.html

Barnardos (2010b). *Feedback on the HSE National Policy and Procedure Document on Leaving and Aftercare Services*, http://www.barnardos.ie/assets/files/campaigns/children-in-care/submission%20on%20draft%20aftercare%20policy%20July%202010.doc

Barnardos (2010a). Children Cast Adrift by Failure in Aftercare System. http://www.barnardos.ie/assets/files/Advocacy/2012-08%20Barnardos%20Submission%20on%20the%20Review%20of%20Legislation%20on%20Prostitution.pdf

Barnardos (2011). No room for complacency in child welfare and protection: Saving Childhood group marks 2nd anniversary of Ryan Report, *http://www.barnardos.ie/media-centre/news/latest-news/no-room-for-complacency-in-child-welfare-and-protection.htm*

Barnardos (2011a). *Stand Up for Children: The Children's Manifesto*, Dublin, Barnardos. http://www.barnardos.ie/assets/files/Advocacy/MANIFESTO-SINGLE.pdf

Barnardos (2011b). Puppet on a String: *The urgent need to cut children free from sexual exploitation*, Barkingside, Barnardos.

Bardardos (2012). Moving On; Aftercare Provision in Ireland. http://www.barnardos.ie/assets/files/campaigns/children-in-care/submission%20on%20draft%20aftercare%20policy%20July%202010.doc

Barnardos, (2012a). *Submission into the Joint Oireachtas Committee on Justice, Equality and Defence on the Review of Legislation on Prostitution*. http://www.barnardos.ie/assets/files/Advocacy/2012-08%20Barnardos%20Submission%20on%20the%20Review%20of%20Legislation%20on%20Prostitution.pdf

Barnardos (2013). Deaths of Children in Care 2013. http://www.barnardos.ie/media-centre/news/latest-news/deaths-of-children-in-care-in-2012.html

Barrett, W. (1978). The illusion of technique: A search for meaning in a technological civilization, Garden City, NY, Anchor Press/Doubleday.

Barry, M. (2001). *A Sense of Purpose: Care leavers' views and experiences of growing up*, Edinburgh, Save the Children. http://strathprints.strath.ac.uk/10343/1/sense_of_purpose1.pdf

Barry, M. (2010). Youth Transitions: From Offending to Desistance, *Journal of Youth Studies*, 13, 1, 121–36. http://strathprints.strath.ac.uk/10343/1/sense_of_purpose1.pdf

Bibliography

Barth, R. Cree, T. John, K. Thoburn, J. and Quinton, D. (2005). Beyond attachment theory and therapy: Towards sensitive and evidence-based interventions with foster and adoptive families in distress, *Child and Family Social Work*, 10, 4, 257-268.

Barton, S., Gonzalez, R. and Tomlinson, P. (2012). *Therapeutic Residential care for children and young people*, London, Jessica Kingsley Publishers.

Bates, B., English, D. and Kouidou, G. (1997). Residential treatment and its alternatives: A review of the literature, *Child and Youth Care Forum*, 26 (1), 7–51.

Baxer, C., Archibong, U., Giga, S. and Kular, R. (2008). Critical Success Factors in the Implementation of Positive Action in the NHS UK, *The International Journal of Diversity in Organisations, Communities and Nations*, 8, 2. http://www.Diversity-Journal.com

Beck, U. (1992). *Risk Society: Towards a New Modernity*, London, Sage.

Beck, U. (2000). *The Brave New World of Work*, Cambridge, Polity Press.

Beck, U. (2010). *World at Risk*, Cambridge, Polity Press.

Beckett, H. (2011). *Not a World Away: The Sexual Exploitation of Children and Young People in Northern Ireland*, Belfast, Barnardos. http://www.barnardos.org.uk/13932_not_a_world_away_full_report.pdf

Beddoe, L. and Harington, R. (2013). Civic Practice: A New Professional Paradigm for Social Work, *Journal of Social Work*, 14, 2, 147-164.

Beijing Rules, United Nations Standard Minimum Rules for the Administration of Juvenile Justice (1985), http://www2.ohchr.org/english/law/pdf/beijingrules.pdf

Bellefeuille, G. and Ricks, F. (2010). Relational Inquiry: A child and youth care approach to research, *Children and Youth Services Review*, 32, 1235-1241.

Benbenishty, R., Osmo, R. and Gold, N. (2003). Rationales provided for risk assessments and for recommended interventions in child protection: A comparison between Canadian and Israeli professionals, *British Journal of Social Work*, 33, 137–55.

Bentley, K. (2005). Can there be any universal children's rights? *International Journal of Human Rights*, 9, 1, 107-123.

Beresford, P., Shamash, M., Forrest, V., Turner, M. and Branfield, F. (2005). *Developing Social Care: Service Users' Vision for Adult Support*, London, SCIE.

Berne, E. (1964). *Games People Play – The Basic Hand Book of Transactional Analysis*, New York, Ballantine Books

Berridge, D. and Brodie, I. (1996). In Hill, M. and Aldgate, J. (Eds.), *Child Welfare Services: Developments in Law, Policy, Practice and Research*, London, Jessica Kingsley.

Berridge, D., Beecham, J., Brodie, I., Cole, T., Daniels, H., Knapp, M. and MacNeill, V. (2003). Services for troubled adolescents: Exploring user variation, *Child and Family Social Work*, 8, 269–279.

Berridge, D., Biehel, N. and Henry, L. (2010). *Living in Children's Residential Homes*, Research Report, Department of Education. https://www.gov.uk/government/uploads/system/uploads/attachment_data/file/184079/DFE-RR201.pdf

Berridge, D. (2006). Theory and Explanation in Child Welfare: Education and Looked-after Children, *Child and Family Social Work*, 12, 1, 1–10.

Berk, L. (2010). *Development Through the Lifespan*, Boston, Pearson.

Besson, S. (2005). The Principle of Non-Discrimination in the Convention on the Rights of the Child, *International Journal of Children's Rights*, 13, 4, 433-461.

Best, J. (2002). Monster-hype: How a few isolated tragedies-and their supposed causes-were turned into a national "epidemic", *Education Next* (Summer), 51-55.

Bettleheim, B. (1976). *The Uses of Enchantment: The Meaning and Importance of Fairy Tales*, New York, Vintage Books.

Bettleheim, B. (1987). *A Good Enough Parent: A Book on Child-Rearing*, New York, Random House.

Bettmann, J. and Jasperson, R. (2009). Adolescents in residential and inpatient treatment: A review of the outcome literature, *Child and Youth Care Forum*, 38, 161–183.

Bhabra, S. and Ghate, D. (2002). *Consultation analysis: Raising the educational attainment of children in care*, London, Policy Research Bureau.

Biehal, N., Clayden, J., Stein, M. and Wade, J. (1995). *Moving On: Young People and Leaving Care Schemes*, London, HMSO.

Biehal, N. and Wade, J. (1996). Looking back, looking forward: Care leavers, families and change, *Children and Youth Services Review*, 18, 4-5, 425-445.

Biehal, N., Cusworth, L., Wade, J. and Clarke, S. (2014). Keeping Children safe: Allegations concerning the abuse or neglect of children in care: Final report, University of York, NSPCC. http://www.york.ac.uk/inst/spru/research/pdf/Abuseincare.pdf

Birren, J. and Brengtson, V. (1998). *Emergent Theories of Aging*, New York, Springer.

Blakemore, S. and Choundhury, S. (2006). Development of the adolescent brain: implications for executive function and social cognition, *Journal of Child Psychology and Psychiatry*, 47, 296-312.

Bloom, S. (2003). Caring for the Caregiver: Avoiding and Treating Vicarious Traumatization. In *Sexual Assault, Victimization Across the Life Span: A Clinnical Guide and Color Atlas*, Giardinio, A, Spencer, M. Faungo, D. Girardin, B . and Asher, J. (Eds.), St. Louis, STM Learning Inc, (459-470). http://www.koms.rs/wp-content/uploads/2014/05/Bloom-Caring-for-Caregiver.pdf

Bloom, S. (2005). Creating sanctuary for kids: helping children to heal from violence, Therapeutic Community, *The International Journal for Therapeutic and*

Supportive Organizations, 26, 1, 57–63.

Blos, P. (1962). *On Adolescence: A Psychoanalytical interpretation*, New York, McMillan Company.

Boeckel, J. (2013). *Individual and Family Factors Related to the Reduction of Risk Behavior in Asian Youth*, Unpublished Dissertation, Faculty of the Graduate School of Social Work, In Partial Fulfilment of the Requirements for the Degree Doctor of Philosophy, University of Denver.

Bolen, G. (2002). Child Sexual Abuse and Attachment Theory: Are We Rushing Headlong into Another Controversy? *Journal of Child Sexual Abuse*, 11, 1, 95-124.

Bonanno, G. (2004). Loss, trauma, and human resilience: Have we underestimated the human capacity to thrive after extremely aversive events,? *American Psychologist*, 59, 1, 20-28.

Bourdieu, P. (1984). *Questions de sociologie*, Paris, Minuit.

Bourdieu, P. (1986). The forms of capital. In (Ed.), Richardson, J. *Handbook of Theory and Research for Sociology of Education (241-58)*, New York, Greenwood Press.

Bourdieu, P. (1990). *The Logic of Practice*, Cambridge, Polity Press.

Bourdieu, P. (2000). *Les structures sociales de l'économie*, Paris, Seuil.

Bowlby, J. (1953). *Child Care and the Growth of Love*, London, Penguin Books.

Bowlby, J. (1969). *Attachment and Loss, Vol. 1*, New York, Basic Books.

Bowlby, J. (1988). *A Secure Base: Parent-Child Attachment and Healthy Human Development*, New York, Basic Books.

Brearley, J. (2007). *A Psychodynamic Approach to Social Work*. In Lishman, J. (Ed.), *Handbook for Practice Learning in Social Work and Social Care: Knowledge and Theory*, London, Jessica Kingsley Publishers.

Brendtro, L., Brokenleg, M. and Van Bockern, S. (2002). *Reclaiming youth at risk: Our hope for the future* (Rev Ed.), Bloomington, Solution Tree.

Brennan, M. (2008). Conceptualizing Resiliency: An Interactional Perspective for Community and Youth Development, *Child Care in Practice*, 14, 1, 55-64.

Bridges, W. (2004). *Transitions: Making Sense of Life's Changes*, Cambridge, Da Capo Press.

Brien, A. (1999). Professional Ethics and The Culture of Trust, *Journal of Business Ethics*, 17, 391-409.

Briner, R. (1999). The Neglect and Importance of Emotion at Work, *European Journal of Work and Organizational Psychology*, 8, 3, 323-346.

Broad, R. (2006). *Care Leavers in Transition*, Leicester, De Montfort University. http://www.academia.edu/997813/Care_leavers_in_transition

Brod, M., Tesler, L. and Christensen, T. (2009). Qualitative research and context validity: developing best practices based on science and expertise, *Quality of Life Research*, 18, 1263-1278.

Brodie, I., Melrose, M., Pearce, J. and Warrington, C. (2011). *Providing safe and supported accommodation for young people who are in the care system and who are at risk of, or experiencing, sexual exploitation or trafficking for sexual exploitation*, Luton, University of Bedfordshire. http://www.beds.ac.uk/__data/assets/pdf_file/0008/120788/SafeAccommodationreport_finalOct2011IB_1.pdf

Bronfenbrenner, U. (1979). *The ecology of human development: experiments by nature and design*, Cambridge, Harvard University Press.

Brooker, M. (2011). *Youth Mentoring as an Intervention with Disengaged Young People: A Literature Review*, Department of Communities Western Australia. http://www.communities.wa.gov.au/Documents/Youth/Literature%20Review%20on%20Youth%20Mentoring%20Final%20Report%2025%20October%202011.pdf

Brown, P. (2010). Qualitative method and compromise in Applied Social Research, *Qualitative Research*, 10, 2, 229-248.

Bryan, K., Freer, J. and Furlong, C. (2007). Language and communication difficulties among juvenile offenders, *International Journal of Language and Communication Disorders*, 42, 5, 505-520.

Bryner, J., Elias, P., McKnight, A., Pan, H. and Pierre, G. (2002). *Young People's Changing Routes to Independence*, York, Joseph Rowntree Foundation. http://www.jrf.org.uk/sites/files/jrf/184263108x.pdf

Bullock, R., Courtney, M., Parker, R., Sinclair, I. and Thoburn, J. (2006). Can the corporate state parent? *Adoption and Fostering*, 30, 4, 6-15.

Burchell, G. (1993). Liberal Governments and the techniques of the self, *Economy and Society*, 22, 3, 267-282.

Burns, K. and MacCarthy, J. (2012). An impossible task? Implementing the recommendations of child abuse inquiry reports in a context of 'high' workloads in child protection and welfare, *Irish Journal of Applied Social Studies*, 12, 1, 25-37.

Burck, C. and Cooper, A. (2007). Introduction: dialogues and developments in social work practice: applying systemic and psychoanalytic ideas in the real world, *Journal of Social Work Practice*, 21, 2, 193-196.

Bushman, B. (1984). Perceived Symbols of Authority and Their Influence on Compliance, *Journal of Applied Social Psychology*, 14, 6, 501-508.

Bussey-Jones, J., Bernstein, L., Higgins, S., Malebranche, D., Paranjape, A., Genao, I., Bennett, L. and Branch, W. (2006). Repaving the Road to Academic Success: The IMeRGE Approach to Peer Mentoring, *Academic Medicine*, 81, 7, 674-679.

Butler, E. (2013). Emotional Coregulation in close relationships, *Journal of Social and Personal Relationships*, 30, 1072-1095.`

Butler, L., Little, L. and Grimard, A. (2009). Research Challenges: Implementing Standardized Outcome Measures in a Decentralized, Community-based Residential Treatement Program, *Child and Youth Care Forum*, 38, 2, 75-90.

Bibliography

Bynner, J. (2005). Rethinking the Youth Phase of the Life-course: The Case for Emerging Adulthood? *Journal of Youth Studies*, 8, 4, 367–84.

Cairns, K. (2002). *Attachment, Trauma and Resilience: Therapeutic Caring for Children*, London, British Association for Adoption and Fostering.

Caldwell, L. (2011). Mirroring and Attunement: Self-Realization in Psychoanalysis and Art, *The International Journal of Psychoanalysis*, 92, 4, 1077-1080.

Call, C. and Mortimer, J. (2001). *Arenas of Comfort in Adolescence: A Study of Adjustment in Context*, Mahwah, Lawrence Erlbaum.

Cambridge Dictionaries Online, http://dictionary.cambridge.org/dictionary/british/independence

Cameron, C. and Moss, P. (Eds.) (2011). *Social Pedagogy and Working with Children and Young People: Where Care and Education Meet*, London, Jessica Kingsley

Cameron, C. (2004). Social Pedagogy and Care: Danish and German Practice in Young People's Residential Care, *Journal of Social Work*, 4, 2, 133-151.

Cameron, C. (2013). Cross-National Understandings of the Purpose of Professional-Child Relationships: Towards a Social Pedagogical Approach, *Journal of Social Pedagogy*, 2, 1, 3-16.

Canavan, J. (2008). Resilience: Cautiously Welcoming a Contested Concept, *Child Care in Practice*, 14, 1, 1-7.

Carr, N. (2014). Invisible from View: Leaving and Aftercare Provision in the Republic of Ireland, *Australian Social Work*, 67, 1, 88-101.

Cashmore, J. and Paxman, M. (2006). *Predicting aftercare outcomes: the importance of 'felt' security, Child and Family Social Work*, 11, 3, 232-241.

Castel, R. (1991). From dangerousness to risk. In Burchell, G. Gordon, C. and Miller, P. (Eds.), *The Foucault Effect: Studies in Governmentality*, London, Harvester/Wheatsheaf.

Ceglowski, D., Bacigalupa, C. and Peck, E. (2011). Aced out: Censorship of qualitative research in the age of "scientifically" based research, *Qualitative Inquiry*, 17, 8, 679-686.

Celcis, (2013). Challenge by Choice? Social Pedagogy in Practice, Why, What and How. http://www.celcis.org/media/events/celcis-2013-session-7-social-pedagogy-web-1.pdf

Central Statistics Office, (2014). Survey on Income and Living Conditions (SILC). http://www.cso.ie/en/media/csoie/releasespublications/documents/silc/2012/silc_2012.pdf

Centre for Excellence in Child and Family Welfare Inc. (2006). *Residential Care Monograph*, 13. http://www.cfecfw.asn.au/sites/default/files/Monograph%2013%20Residential%20Care%20Web.pdf

Centre for Youth Wellness, (2014). *New White Paper Outlines Impact of Adverse*

Childhood Experiences, Toxic Stress on Children's Health and Development. http://www.centerforyouthwellness.org/about/our-news/details/?id=285

Chaffin, M., Hanson, R., Saunders, B., Nichols, T., Barnett, D., Zeanah, C., Berliner, L., Egeland, B., Newman, E., Lyon, T. and Miller-Perrin, C. (2006). Report of the APSAC Task Force on Attachment Therapy, Reactive Attachment Disorder, and Attachment Problems, *Child Maltreatment*, 11, 1, 76-89.

Chamberlain, L. (2008). *The Amazing Brain: Trauma and the Potential For Healing,* Philadelphia. http://www.instituteforsafefamilies.org/sites/default/files/isfFiles/The_Amazing_Brain-2.pdf

Charles, K. (2009). *Separated children living in Ireland: A report by the Ombudsman for Children's Office,* Dublin, Office of the Ombudsman for Children.

Child Care Act, 1991, Ireland, http://www.irishstatutebook.ie/1991/en/act/pub/0017/index.html

Child Care Law reporting Project (2015). Publications: Case Histories 2015 Volume 1. http://www.childlawproject.ie/publications/

Children Act 1989, United Kingdom, http://www.legislation.gov.uk/ukpga/1989/41/contents

Children (Leaving Care) Act, 2002, Northern Ireland. http://www.legislation.gov.uk/nia/2002/11/notes/contents

Children and Young Persons (Care and Protection) Act, 1998, New South Wales. http://www.legislation.nsw.gov.au/fullhtml/inforce/act+157+1998+FIRST+0+N

Children and Young People (Scotland) Act, 2014. http://www.legislation.gov.uk/asp/2014/8/pdfs/asp_20140008_en.pdf

Children's Act Advisory Board (CAAB), (2003). Definition and Usage of High Support in Ireland, Report to The Special Residential Services Board. http://www.caab.ie/getdoc/1853e740-ccc7-4084-a226-32e3b22ed9f0/Definition-and-Usage-of-High-Support-in-Ireland.aspx

Children's Mental Health Coalition (2015). *Meeting the mental health support needs of children and adolescents: A Children's Mental Health Coalition View,* Dublin. http://www.childrensmentalhealth.ie/wp-content/uploads/2015/03/Childrens-Mental-Health-Coalition-report-final.pdf

Children's Rights Alliance (2010). *Alliance Response to HSE Figures on Child Deaths*: Press Statement. http://www.childrensrights.ie/index.php?q=knowledgebase/child-protection/alliance-response-hse-figures-child-deaths

Children's Rights Alliance (2010a). http://www.childrensrights.ie/resources/joint-press-statement-ifca-iaypic-and-children%E2%80%99s-rights-alliance

Children's Rights Alliance (2012). Short Guide to the Children's Referendum. http://www.childrensrights.ie/sites/default/files/submissions_reports/files/ShortGuideChildrenReferendum1012.pdf

Clapton, G., Cree, V. and Smith, M. (2013). Moral Panics and Social Work: Towards

Bibliography

a Sceptical View of UK Child Protection, *Critical Social Policy*, 33, 2, 197-217.

Clarke, J., Gewirtz, S. and McLaughlin, E. (2000). *Reinventing the welfare state.* In Clarke, J. Gewirtz, S. and McLaughlin, E. (Eds.), *New Managerialism, New Welfare?*, Buckingham, Open University Press.

Clarke, J. and Newman, J. (1997). *The Managerial State; Power, politics and ideology in the remaking of social welfare*, London, Sage.

Clarke, J. (2008). What's the Problem? Precarious Youth: Marginalisation, Criminalisation and Racialisation, *Social Work and Society*, 6, 2. http://www.socwork.net/sws/article/view/62/364See

Clarke, M. (2015). *Joint Committee on Health and Children. General Scheme of Aftercare Bill: Discussion*. https://www.kildarestreet.com/committees/?id=2014-04-01a.296&s=General+scheme+of+aftercare+bill#g318

Clayden, J. and Stein, M. (2005). *Mentoring for young people leaving care: Someone for me*, Joseph Rowntree Foundation, http://www.jrf.org.uk/system/files/1859354025.pdf

Clough, R., Bullock, R. and Ward, A. (2006). *What works in residential child care: A review of research evidence and the practical considerations*, London, National Children's Bureau.

Clutterbuck, D. (2002). *Learning Alliances: Tapping Into Talent*, London, CIPD.

Coffey, M., Dugdill, M. and Tattersall, A. (2004). Stress in Social Services: Mental Wellbeing, Constraints and Job Satisfaction, *British Journal of Social Work*, 34, 5, 735-746.

Coffield, F., Borrill, C. and Marshall, S. (1986). *Growing Up at the Margins*, Milton Keynes, Open University Press.

Cohen, S. (2002). *Folks Devils and Moral Panics*, 3rd Ed., Abingdon, Routledge.

Coleman, J. and Hendry, L. (1999). *The Nature of Adolescence*, 3rd Ed., London, Routledge.

Coleman, J. (2000). Young People in Britain at the beginning of the new century, *Children and Society*, 14, 230-242.

Coleman, J. (2011). *The Nature of Adolescence*, Fourth Edition, London, Routledge.

College of Social Work, (2012). Briefing for Lord Listowel. http://www.tcsw.org.uk/uploadedFiles/TheCollege/_CollegeLibrary/Policy/HouseofLordsDebateLookedAfterChildren.pdf

Colley, H. (2003). *Mentoring for social inclusion: a critical approach to nurturing mentor relationships*, London, Routledge Falmer.

Collins, J. and Collins, M. (1981). *Achieving Change in Social Work*, London, Heinemann.

Collins, M. and Pinkerton, J. (2008). The policy context of leaving care services: A case study of Northern Ireland, *Children and Youth Services Review*, 30, 1279-1288.

Collins, H. and Evans, R. (2007). *Rethinking Expertise*, Chicago, University of Chicago Press.

Collins, P. (1994). Does mentorship among social workers make a difference? An empirical investigation of career outcomes, *Social Work*, 39, 413–419.

Commissioner for Human Rights, (2008). *Report by the Commissioner for Human Rights, Mr. Thomas Hammarberg on his visit to Ireland.* Council of Europe, Brussels. https://wcd.coe.int/wcd/ViewDoc.jsp?id=1283555

Community Care: Inspiring Excellence in Social Care, (2015). *Social workers to face five years in prison for failing to protect children from sexual abuse, warns Cameron*.http://www.communitycare.co.uk/2015/03/03/social-workers-face-five-years-prison-failing-protect-children-sexual-abuse-warns-cameron/

Cook, R. (1994). Are we helping foster youth prepare for their future,? *Children and Youth Services Review*, 16, 213-229.

Cooper, J. (2007). *Cognitive dissonance: Fifty years of a classic theory*, London, Sage Publications.

Cooper, B. (2011). *Criticality and reflexivity: best practice in uncertain environments*. In Seden, J. Matthews, S. McCormick, M. and Morgan, A. (Eds.), *Professional development in social work: Complex issues in practice* (p. 17–23), New York, Routledge.

Corbett, M. (2008). Hidden children: The story of state care for separated children, *Working Note*, 59, 18-24.

Cordingley, P. (2004). *Teachers using evidence: Using what we know about teaching and learning to reconceptualize evidence-based practice*. In Thomas, G. and Pring, R. (Eds.), *Evidence-based practice in education*, 77-90, New York, Open University Press.

Corsaro, W. (2005). *The Sociology of Childhood*, 2nd Ed., Thousand Oaks, Pine Forge.

Corby, B., Doig, A. and Roberts, V. (2001). *Public Inquiries Into Residential Abuse of Children*, London, Jessica Kingsley.

Côte, J. and Bynner, M. (2008). Changes in the transition to adulthood in the UK and Canada: the role of structure and agency in emerging adulthood, *Journal of Youth Studies*, 11, 3, 251-268.

Côte, J. (2000). *Arrested Adulthood: The Changing Nature of Maturity and Identity*, New York, University Press.

Courtney, M., Dworsky, A., Ruth, G., Keller, T., Havelicek, J. and Bost, N. (2005). *Midwest evaluation of the adult functioning of former foster youth: Outcomes ages 19*, Chapin Hall Centre for Children at the University of Chicago. http://www.chapinhall.org/sites/default/files/ChapinHallDocument_1.pdf

Courtois, C. and Ford, J. (2009). *Treating Complex Traumatic Stress Disorders: An Evidence-Based Guide*, New York, Guildford Press.

Bibliography

Crabtree, B. and Miller, W. (1999). *Doing qualitative research*, Thousand Oaks, Sage.

Craig, G. (2002). Poverty, social work and social justice, *British Journal of Social Work*, 32, 2, 669–682.

Crossman, V. and Gray, P. (Eds.) (2011). *Policy and Welfare in Ireland: 1838-1948*, Sallins, Irish Academic Press.

Cunliffe, A. (2009). Reflexivity, learning and reflexive Practice. In Armstrong, S. Fukami, C. (Eds.), *The Sage Handbook of Management Learning, Education and Development*, London, Sage, (405-418).

Cúram, (2014). *Irish Association of Social Care Workers Magazine*, No. 48.

Curtis, L. (2012). Unit Costs of Health and Social Care, 2012. http://kar.kent.ac.uk/32408/1/full-with-covers.pdf

Cusick, L. (2002). Youth Prostitution: A Literature Review, *Child Abuse Review*, 11, 4, 230-251.

Cuskelly, K. (2013). Tools for Self-Care: Developing Your Own Self-Care Action Plan, Irish Association of Social Workers. http://www.iasw.ie/attachments/2141a435-9a0b-44e0-8806-c6a92a6a9b27.PDF

Dáil Debates, Written Answers. https://www.kildarestreet.com/

Dáil Debates, (2013). Topical Issue Debate: Children in Care. http://www.kildarestreet.com/debates/?id=2013-05-08a.153&s=aftercare#g155

Dáil Debates, (2013). Topical Issue Debate: Foster Care Supports. http://www.kildarestreet.com/debates/?id=2013-07-16a.487&s=residential+child+care#g488

Daining, C, and DePanfilis, D. (2007). Resilience of youth in transition from out-of-home care to adulthood, *Children and Youth Services Review*, 29(9), 1158-1178.

Daly, F. (2012). What do Young People Need When They Leave Care? Views of Care leavers and Aftercare Workers in North Dublin, *Child Care in Practice*, 18, 4, 390-324.

Daniel, B. and Wassell, S. (2002). *Adolescence: Assessing and Promoting Resilience in Vulnerable Children 3*, London, Jessica Kingsley Publishers.

Daniels, H. and Livingstone, M. (2011). *Hackney Child: The True Story of a Neglected but Resourceful Child Surviving Poverty and the Care System*, United Kingdom, Livingstone Photos.

Darmody, M., McMahon, L., Banks, J. and Gilligan, R. (2013). *Education of Children in Care in Ireland: An Exploratory Study*, Dublin, Office of the Ombudsman for Children. http://www.oco.ie/wp-content/uploads/2014/03/11873_Education_Care_SP1.pdf

Davis, M. and Vander Stoep, A. (1997). The transition to adulthood for youth who have serious emotional disturbance: developmental transition and young adult outcomes, *Journal of Mental Health Administration*, 24, 4, 400-427.

Davis, C. and Ward, H. (2011). *Safeguarding Children Across Services: Messages from Research*, London, Jessica Kingsley.

Davis, S. (Ed.) (2000). *The Blackwell Companion to Social Work*, Oxford, Blackwell Publishing.

D'Cruz, H. Gillingham, P. and Melendez, S. (2007). Reflexivity, its Meaning and Relevance for Social Work: A Critical Review of the Literature, *British Journal of Social Work*, 37, 1, 73-90.

D'Cruz, H. Gillingham, P. and Melendez, S. (2009). Exploring the Possibilities of an Expanded Practice Repertoire in Child Protection, *Journal of Social Work*, 9, 1, 61-85.

de RÓsite, À, (2013). Psychological theories of child development. In Lalor, K. and Share, P. *Applied Social Care*, Dublin, Gill and Macmillan.

De Swart, J. Van den Broek, H. Stams, G. Asscher, J. Van der Laan, P. Holsbrink-Engels, G. *et al.*, (2012). The effectiveness of institutional youth care over the past three decades: A meta-analysis, *Child and Youth Services Review*, 34, 1818–1824.

Declaration of the Rights of the Child (1959). http://www.unicef.org/malaysia/1959-Declaration-of-the-Rights-of-the-Child.pdf

Deephouse, D. (1996). Does Isomorphism Legitimate, *Academy of Management Journal*, 39, 4, 1024-1039.

Dekker, J. (2002). In Knorth, E. Bergh, P. and Verheij, F. (Eds.), *Professionalisation and Participation in Child and Youth Care*, Aldershot, Ashgate.

Dekker, S. (2007). *Just Culture, Balancing Safety and Accountability*, Aldershot, Ashgate.

del Valle, J. Bravo, A. Alverez, E. and Fernanz, A. (2008). Adult self-sufficiency and social adjustment in care leavers from children's homes: a long-term assessment, *Child and Family Social Work*, 13, 1, 12-22.

Denzin, N. and Giardina, M. (2006). *Qualitative Inquiry and the conservative challenge*, Walnut Creek, CA, Left Coast Press.

Department of Education and Skills (2014). https://www.education.ie/en/The-Department/Management-Organisation/High-Support-Special-Schools

Department of Health Social Services and Public Safety (2007). *Care Matters in Northern Ireland – A Bridge to a Better Future*, DHSSPSNI, Belfast.

Department of Children and Youth Affairs (DCYA) (2012). *State of the Nations Children*, Dublin, Government Publications. http://www.dcya.gov.ie/documents/research/StateoftheNationsChildren2012.pdf

Department of Children and Youth Affairs (DCYA), (2013). *RIGHT FROM THE START: Report of the Expert Advisory Group on the Early Years Strategy*, Dublin, Government Publications. http://www.dcya.gov.ie/documents/policy/RightFromTheStart.pdf

Department of Children and Youth Affairs (DCYA) (2014). Residential Care. http://www.dcya.gov.ie/viewdoc.asp?fn=/documents/Child_Welfare_Protection/

ResidentialCare.htm

Department of Children and Youth Affairs (DCYA) (2014a). General Scheme and Heads of Aftercare Bill 2014. http://www.dcya.gov.ie/documents/ HeadsAftercarBill2014.pdf

Department of Children and Youth Affairs (DCYA), (2014b). *Better Outcomes Brighter Futures: National Policy Framework for Children and Young People 2014-2020*, Dublin, Government Publications. http://www.dcya.gov.ie/documents/ cypp_framework/BetterOutcomesBetterFutureReport.pdf

Department of Children and Youth Affairs (DCYA) (2014c). Cabinet Approves Heads of Bill for Aftercare Bill 2014 - Minister Frances Fitzgerald. http://www. dcya.gov.ie/viewdoc.asp?DocID=3104

Department of Children and Youth Affairs (DCYA) (2014d). The Children's Referendum. http://www.dcya.gov.ie/viewdoc.asp?fn=/documents/Child_ Welfare_Protection/ChildrensReferendum.htm

Department of Education (2012). *Children's Homes in England Data Pack*, March 2012. http://media.education.gov.uk/assets/files/pdf/c/childrens%20homes%20 data%20pack%20march%202012.pdf

Department of Education (2012a). Care Leavers in England Data Pack. http:// www.crin.org/docs/care%20leavers%20data%20pack%20final%2029%20oct.pdf

Department of Education (2013). *Statistical First Release.* https://www.gov. uk/government/uploads/system/uploads/attachment_data/file/244872/ SFR36_2013.pdf

Department of Education and Skills (2014). https://www.education.ie/en/The-Department/Management-Organisation/High-Support-Special-Schools

Department of Health and Children (DoHC) (2009). *Report of the Commission to Inquire into Child Abuse, 2009. Implementation Plan,* Dublin, Department of Health and Children. http://www.dcya.gov.ie/documents/publications/ implementation_plan_from_ryan_commission_report.pdf

Department of Health Social Services and Public Safety, DHSSPSNI (2013). http:// www.dhsspsni.gov.uk/northern_ireland_care_leavers_aged_19_2012_13.pdf

Department of Health Social Services and Public Safety, DHSSPSNI (2014). Northern Ireland Care Leavers Aged 19; Statistical Bulletin 2012/13. http://www. dhsspsni.gov.uk/northern_ireland_care_leavers_aged_19_2012_13.pdf

Department of Public Expenditure and Reform. *Public Private Partnerships.* (http://www.per.gov.ie/public-private-partnerships/)

Devaney, J. and Coman, W. (2011). Reflecting on Outcomes for Looked-After Children: An Ecological Perspective, *Child Care in Practice*, 17, 1, 37-53.

Devlin, M. (2005). 'Teenage Traumas': The Discursive Construction of Young People as a 'Problem' in an Irish Radio Documentary', *Young: Nordic Journal of Youth Research*, 13, 167-184.

Devlin, M. (2006). *Inequality and the Stereotyping of Young People*, Dublin, The Equality Authority. http://eprints.nuim.ie/1185/1/Inequality.pdf

Devlin, M. (2009). *Youth and Community Work in Ireland: Critical Perspectives: Theorising 'Youth'*, Dublin, Blackhall Publishing. http://eprints.nuim.ie/3526/1/MD_Theorising.pdf

DHSSPSNI (2007). Former Care Leavers in Northern Ireland: Statistical Bulletin. http://www.dhsspsni.gov.uk/stats-cib-oc32006.pdf

DHSSPSNI (2013). Children's Social Care Statistics for Northern Ireland 2012/2013. http://www.dhsspsni.gov.uk/microsoft_word_-_childrens_social_care_stats_201213-2.pdf

DHSSPSNI (2014). Northern Ireland Care Leavers Aged 19; Statistical Bulletin 2012/13. http://www.dhsspsni.gov.uk/northern_ireland_care_leavers_aged_19_2012_13.pdf

Digney, J. and Smart, M. (2104). On Being Stuck: Stalling, restarting and something different, *CYC-Online*, 184. http://www.cyc-net.org/cyc-online/jun2014.pdf

Dima, G. and Skehill. C. (2011). Making sense of leaving care: The contribution of Bridges model of transition to understanding the psychosocial process, *Children and Youth Services Review*, 33, 2532-2539.

DiMaggio, P. and Powel, W. (1983). The Iron Cage Revisited: Institutional Isomorphism and Collective Rationality in Organisational Fields, *American Sociological Review*, 48, 2, 147-160.

Dixon, J. and Stein, M. (2005). *Leaving Care, Throughcare and Aftercare in Scotland*, London, Jessiac Kingsley.

Dixon, J., Wade, J., Byford, S., Weatherly, H. and Lee, J. (2006). *Young People Leaving Care: A Study of Costs and Outcomes*; A Report to the Department of Education and Skills. http://www.york.ac.uk/inst/spru/research/pdf/leaving.pdf

Dixon, J. (2008). Young people leaving care: Health, wellbeing and outcomes, *Child and Family Social Work*, 13, 2, 207-217. Do Something Different, www.dsd.me

Dohrenwend, B. and Dohrewend, B. (Eds.) (1974). *Stressful life events, their nature and effects*, New York, John Wiley.

Doolin, B. (2002). Enterprise Discourse, Professional Identity and the Organisational Control of Hospital Clinicians, *Organization Studies*, 23, 3, 369-390.

Downes, C. (1992). *Separation Revisited*, Aldershot, Ashgate.

Doyle, A., Mayock, P. and Burns, K. (2012). Aftercare not afterthought: Supporting the transition to adulthood for children in care. In Lynch, D. and Burns, K. (Eds.), *Children's Rights and Child Protection: Critical times, critical issues in Ireland*, Manchester, Manchester University Press.

Doyle, J. (2007). Child Protection and Child Outcomes: Measuring the Effects of Foster Care, *The American Economic Review*, 1582-1610. http://www.mit.edu/~jjdoyle/fostercare_aer.pdf

DuBois, D., Holloway, B., Valentine, J. and Cooper, H. (2002). Effectiveness of mentoring programs for youth: A meta-analytical review, *American Journal of Community Psychology*, 30, 2, 157-193.

DuBois, D., Portillio, N., Rhodes, J., Silverthorn, N. and Valentine, J. (2011). How Effective Are Mentoring Programs for Youth? A Systematic Assessment of the Evidence, *Psychological Science in the Public Interest*, 12, 2, 57-91.

Du Gay, P. Salaman, G. and Rees, B. (1996). The Conduct of management and the management of conduct: Contemporary managerial discourse and the constitution of the 'competent' manager, *Journal of Management Studies*, 33, 3, 263-282.

Eastern Health Board (1997). *Working Party on Child Prostitution.* http://www.drugsandalcohol.ie/5899/1/EHB_Report_of_working_party_on_children_in_prostitution.pdf

Economic and Social Research Institute (ESRI) (2009). *Policies on Unaccompanied Minors in Ireland.* http://emn.ie/files/p_20100715105236Policies%20on%20unaccompanied%20minors%20in%20Ireland.pdf

Economic and Social Research Institute (ESRI) (2014). *Policies and Practices on Unaccompanied Minors in Ireland.* http://emn.ie/files/p_20141124075808EMN%20Study%20on%20UAMs%20in%20Ireland%20FINAL%20ONLINE%20VERSION.pdf

Economist (2015). Jailhouse Nation. http://www.economist.com/news/leaders/21654619-how-make-americas-penal-system-less-punitive-and-more-effective-jailhouse-nation

Edmond, R. (2004). Rethinking Our Understanding of the Resident In Group Care, *Child and Youth Care Forum*, 33, 3, 193-207)

Edwards v UK (2002). 35 E.H.R.R. 19.

Eichsteller, G. and Holthoff, S. (2011). Conceptual Foundations of Social Pedagogy: A Transnational Perspective from Germany. In Cameron, C. and Moss, P. (Eds.), *Social Pedagogy and Working with Children*, London, Jessica Kingsley.

Eichsteller, G. (2010). The notion of 'Hultung' in social pedagogy. http://www.childrenwebmag.com/articles/social-pedagogy/the-notion-of-%E2%80%98haltung-in-social-pedagogy

Ellett, A. (2008). Intentions to remain employed in child welfare: The role of human caring, self-efficacy beliefs, and professional organisational culture, *Children and Youth Services Review*, 31, 78-88.

Elliott, I. (2012). *Safeguarding children in the Catholic Church in critical times: Some reflections on the Irish experience.* In Lynch, D. and Burns, K. (Eds.). *Children's Rights and Child Protection: Critical times, critical issues in Ireland*, Manchester, Manchester University Press.

Ellison, M. (2007). Contested terrains within the neo-liberal project, *Equal Opportunities International*, 26,4, 331–351.

EPIC (2010). Briefing Document Aftercare. http://www.epiconline.ie/briefing-document-aftercare

EPIC (2011a). http://www.epiconline.ie/hiqa-follow-up-report-on-foster-care-still-damning/

EPIC (2011b). No Room for Complacency in Child Welfare and Protection,:http://www.epiconline.ie/no-room-for-complacency-in-child-welfare-and-protection/

EPIC (2011c). Press Release, Special Care Unit in Crisis. http://www.epiconline.ie/special-care-unit-in-crisis/

EPIC (2012). '*MY VOICE HAS TO BE HEARD' Research on outcomes for young people leaving care in North Dublin,* Dublin, EPIC Publishing Office. http://www.epiconline.ie/research-on-outcomes-for-young-people-leaving-care-in-north-dublin/

EPIC (2012a). Press Release: Ballydowd Special Care Unit. http://www.epiconline.ie/ballydowd-special-care-unit/

EPIC (2014). http://www.epiconline.ie/hiqa-findings-on-high-support-unit-very-concerning/

Esping-Anderson, G. (1990). *The Three Worlds of Welfare Capitalism*, Cambridge, Polity Press.

Erikson, E. (1950). *Childhood and society,* Rev. Ed., 1965, Hardmonsworth, Penguin.

Erikson, E. (1980). *Identity and Life Cycle,* New York, Norton.

Eriksson, H. and Tjelflaat, T. (Eds.) (2004). *Residential Care: Horizons for the New Century*, Aldershot, Ashgate Publishing.

EUROCHILD (2010). *National Surveys, Children in Alternative Care*, 2nd Ed., Brussels. http://www.eurochild.org/fileadmin/public/05_Library/Thematic_priorities/06_Children_in_Alternative_Care/Eurochild/FINAL_EXEC_SUMMARY.pdf

Eurofound (2014). *Social Situation of Young People in Europe*, Publications Office of the European Union, Luxembourg.

European Court of Human Rights (2001). Z and Others v UK, App. No. 29392/95, General Comment: *29392, Strasbourg.*

EUROSTAT (2015). eurostat newsrelease: euroindicators. http://ec.europa.eu/eurostat/documents/2995521/6581668/3-30012015-AP-EN.pdf/9d4fbadd-d7ae-48f8-b071-672f3c4767dd

Evans, S., Hills, S. and Orme, J. (2012). Doing More for Less? Developing Sustainable Systems of Social Care in the Context of Climate Change and Public Spending Cuts, *British Journal of Social Work, 42, 744-764.*

Evans, H. (2014). The impact of organisations representing children and young people in public care in the United Kingdom, *Dialogue in Praxis: A social work international journal*, 2, 15, 1-2, 59-72. http://www.dialogueinpraxis.net/index.php?id=5&a=article&aid=28

Evetts, J. (2003). The Sociological Analysis of Professionalism: Occupational Change in the Modern World, *International Sociology*, 18, 395.

Evetts, J. (2011). Sociological Analysis of Professionalism: Past, Present and Future, *Comparative Sociology*, 10, 1-37.

Fahlberg, V. (1996). *A Child's Journey Through Placement*, London, British Association of Adoption and Fostering.

Farrelly, R. (1994). The special care needs of adolescents in hospital, *Nursing Times*, 90, 38, 30-33.

Faulkner, K. (2009). Representation and Representation: Youth Participation in ongoing public decision-making projects, *Childhood*, 16 (1), 89-104.

Fenton, M. (2015). Doing the Right thing for Children in Care and Support Seekers. http://www.goodenoughcaring.com/the-journal/doing-the-right-thing-for-children-in-care-and-support-seekers/

Ferguson, I. and Woodward, R. (2009). *Radical social work in practice: Making a difference*, Bristol, The Policy Press.

Festinger, L. (1962). Cognitive dissonance, *Scientific American*, 207, 4, 93–107.

Figley, C. (2002). Compassion Fatigue: Psychotherapists' Chronic Lack of Self Care, *Psychotherapy in Practice*, 58, 11, 1433–1441.

Fitzgibbon, D. (2007). Risk analysis and the new practitioner: myth or reality, *Punishment and Society*, 9, 1, 87-97.

Flatau, P., James, I., Watson, R., Wood, G. and Hendershott, P. (2007). Leaving the parental home in Australia over the generations: Evidence from the Household, Income and Labour Dynamics in Australia (HILDA) survey, *Journal of Population Research*, 24, 51-57.

Focus Ireland (2014). Press Release April 1st. and July 17th.http://www.focusireland.ie/about-homelessness/resource-centre/press/press-releases/892-press-statement-17-07-14   http://focusireland.ie/about-homelessness/resource-centre/press/press-releases/876-pr-02apr

Foley, P. (1998). In Foley, P. Roche, J. and Tucker, S. (Eds.), *Children in Society: Contemporary Theory, Policy and Practice*, Basingstoke, Palgrave.

Foltz, R. (2004). The efficacy of residential treatment: An overview of the evidence, *Residential Treatment for Children and Youth*, 22, 2, 1-19.

Forbes, C. and Inder, B. (2006). *Measuring the cost of leaving care in Victoria*, Department of Econometrics and Business Statistics, Monash University.http://webdoc.sub.gwdg.de/ebook/serien/e/monash_univ/wp18-06.pdf

Ford, J. and Harding, N. (2007). Move over management: We are all leaders now, *Management Learning*, 38, 475-493.

Forster, M. (2001). Financial "Rules" for Child and Youth Care Managers, *Child and Youth Care Forum*, 30, 4, 193-207.

Fortin, J. (2005). 2nd Ed., *Children's rights and the developing law*, Cambridge, University Press.

Foucault, M. (1969). *The Archaeology of Knowledge*, Trans. Smith, S. (2002), London and New York, Routledge.

Foucault, M. (1977). *Discipline and Punishment*, London, Allen Lane.

Foucault, M. (1978). Lecture 29, March 1978. http://www.azioni.nl/platform/wp-content/uploads/2013/04/Foucault-Security-Territory-Population.pdf

Foucault, M. (1980). *Power/Knowledge: Selected Interviews and other Writings 1972-1977*, Brighton, Harvester Press.

Foucault. M. (2006). *History of Madness*. Khalfa J, (Ed.), Murphy J, (trans.), London, Routledge.

Fournier, V. (1999). The appeal to professionalism' as a disciplinary mechanism, *The Sociological Review*, 47, 2, 280-307.

France, A., Freiberg, K. and Homel, R. (2010). Beyond Risk Factors: Towards a Holistic Prevention Paradigm for Children and Young People, *British Journal of Social Work*, 40, 4, 1192-1210.

Francis, P. and Dugger, S. (2014). Professionalism, Ethics, and Value-Based Conflicts in Counselling: An Introduction to the Special Edition, *Journal of Counselling and Development*, 92, 131-134.

Fraser, M. (Ed.) (2004). *Risk and resilience in childhood: An ecological perspective*, Washington, NASW.

Frazer, H. and Devlin, M. (2011). *An Assessment of Ireland's Approach to Combating Poverty and Social Exclusion among Children from European and Local Perspectives*, Maynooth, NUI Maynooth. http://www.combatpoverty.ie/publications/workingpapers/2011-03 AnAssessmentOfIrelandsApproachToCombatingPovertyAndSocialExclusion AmongChildrenFromEuropeanAndLocalPerspectives.pdf

Freeman, M. (1983). *The Rights and Wrongs of Children*, London, Francis Pinter.

Freeman, M. (2000). The Future of Children's Rights, *Children and Society*, 14, 277-293.

Freeman, M. (2007). *A Commentary on the United Nations Convention on the Rights of the Child: Article 3, The Best Interest of the Child*, Leiden, Martinus Nijhoff Publishers.

Freeman, M. (2010). The Human Rights of Children, *Current Legal Problems*, 63, 1, 1-44.

Freeman, M. (2011). 1st Ed., *Human rights; an interdisciplinary approach*, Cambridge, Polity Press.

Bibliography

Freud, A. (1958). *Adolescence: The Psychoanalytic Study of the Child*, New York, International Universities Press, 13, 255–278.

Fu, Q. (2004). *Trust, Social Capital and Organisational Effectiveness*, Major paper submitted to the Faculty of the Virginia Polytechnic Institute and State University in partial fulfilment of the requirements for the degree of Master of Public and International Affairs. http://www.ipg.vt.edu/papers/qhfumajorpaper.pdf

Fulcher, L. and Garfat, T. (2012). Outcomes That Matter for Children and Young People in Out of Home Care, *Reclaiming Children and Youth*, 20, 4, 52-58.http://reclaimingjournal.com/sites/default/files/journal-article-pdfs/20_4_Fulcher_Garfat.pdf

Furedi, F. (2006). *Culture of Fear Revisited*, London, Continuum.

Furedi, F. (2007). *The only thing we have to fear is the 'culture of fear' itself.* NEW ESSAY: *How human thought and action are being stifled by a regime of uncertainty.* http://www.spiked-online.com/newsite/article/3053#.U0Ox1blOXL8

Furlong, A. and Cartmel. F. (1997). *Young people and social change: Individualization and risk in modernity*, Buckingham, Open University Press.

Furnivall, J. (2011). *Attachment informed practice with looked after children and young people*, Institute for Research and Innovation in Social Services. http://www.iriss.org.uk/sites/default/files/iriss_insight10.pdf

Furnivall, J., McKenna, M., McFarlane, S. and Grant, E. (2012). *Attachment Matters for All – An Attachment Mapping Exercise for Children's Services in Scotland*, Scotland, CELCIS. http://www.celcis.org/media/resources/publications/Attachment-Matters-For-All.pdf

Fusco, D. (2013). Is Youth Work being Courted by the Appropriate Suitor?, *Child and Youth Services*, 32, 3, 196-209.

Gambrill, E. and Paquin, G. (1992). Neighours: A neglected resource, *Children and Youth Services Review*, 14, 3-4, 253-272.

Gambrill, E. (2013). *Social Work Practice: A Critical Thinkers Guide*, 3rd Ed., New York, Oxford University Press.

Garfat, T. (1998). The effective child and youth care intervention: A phenomenological inquiry. *Journal of Child and Youth Care*, 12, 1, 21-23.

Garfat, T., Fulcher, L. and Digney, J. (2013). *Making Moments Meaningful in Child and Youth Care Practice*, Cape Town, Pretext Publishing.

Gaskell, C. (2010). "If the Social Worker Had Called at Least it Would Show they Cared": Young Care Leavers' Perspectives on the Importance of Care, *Children and Society*, 24, 136–47.

Gast, L. and Bailey, M. (2013). *Mastering Communication in Social Work: From Understanding to Doing*, London, Jessica Kingsley Publishers.

Gawronski, B. and Strack, F. (Eds.) (2012). *Cognitive consistency: A fundamental principle in social cognition*, New York, Guilford Press.

Gibbons, C. (2007). Aspects of Child Care in the District Court: Appendices, *Judicial Services Institute Journal,* 169. http://www.jsijournal.ie/html/Volume%207 %20No. %202/Judge %20Gibbons_Aspects %20of %20Childcare_Appendices.pdf

Gibbs, L. and Gambrill, E. (1999). *Critical Thinking for Social Workers: Exercises for the Helping Professions,* Thousand Oaks, Pine Forge Press.

Giddens, A. (1991). *Modernity and self-identity: Self and society in the late modern age,* Cambridge, Polity Press.

Gilbert, T. and Powell, J. (2010). Power and Social Work in the United Kingdom: A Foucauldian Excursion, *Journal of Social Work,* 10, 1, 3-22.

Gilligan, R. (1993). The Child Care Act 1991: An Examination of its Scope and Resource Implications, *Administration,* 40, 345-70.

Gilligan, R. (2005). Resilience and Residential Care and Young People. In Crimmes, D. and Milligan, I. (Eds.), *Facing Forward – Residential Child Care in the 21st Century,* Lyme Regis, Russell House Publishing.

Gilligan, R. (2008). Ireland. In Stein, M. Munro, E. (Eds.), *Young people's Transitions from Care to Adulthood: International Research and Practice,* London, Jessica Kingsley Publishers.

Gilligan, R. (2008a). Promoting Resilience in Young People in Long-Term Care: The Relevance of Roles and Relationships in the Domains of Recreation and Work, *Journal of Social Work Practice: Psychotherapeutic Approaches in Health, Welfare and the Community,* 22, 1, 37-50.

Gilligan, R. (2009). Positive turning points in the dynamics of change over the life course. In Mancini, J. and Roberts, K. (Eds.), *Pathways of human development: Explorations of change,* Lanham, Lexington Books.

Gilligan, R. (2009a). The "Public Child" and the Reluctant State, *Éire-Ireland,* 44, 1and2, 265-290.

Gillingham, P. (2006). Risk assessment in child protection: Problem rather than solution? *Australian Social Work,* 59, 1, 86-98.

Giluiani, M. (2003). Theory of Attachment and Place Attachment. In Bonnes, M. Bonaiuto, M. and Lee, T. (Eds.), *Psychological Theories for Environmental Issues,* Aldershot, Ashgate.

Glantz, M. and Sloboda, Z. (1999). Analysis and reconcepualisation resilience. In Glantz, M. and Johnson, J. (Eds.), *Resilience and development: Positive life adaptations,* New York, Kluwer Academic.

Goddard, J. and Barrett, S. (2008). Guidance, policy and practice and the health needs of young people leaving care, *Journal of Social Welfare and Family Law,* 30, 1, 31-47.

Goffman, E. (1968). *Asylums,* Harmondsworth, Penguin.

Goldson, B. (2006). Damage, Harm and Death in Child Prisons in England and Wales: Questions of Abuse and Accountability, *The Howard Journal of Criminal Justice,* 45, 5, 449-467.

Bibliography

Goldson, B. (2009). COUNTERBLAST: Difficult to Understand or Defend: A Reasoned Case for Raising the Age of Criminal Responsibility, *The Howard Journal*, 48, 5, 514-521.

Goossens, L. (2006). Theories of adolescence. In Jackson, S. and Goossens, L. *Handbook of Adolescent Development*, 11- 29, Hove, Psychology Press.

Gordon, E. and Song, L. (1994). Variations in the experience of resilience. In Wang, M and Gordon E. (Eds.), *Educational resilience in inner city America: Challenges and prospects*, Hillsdale, Laurence Earlbaum Associate.

Graber, J. and Brooks-Gunn, J. (1996). Transitions and Turning Points: Navigating the Passage From Childhood Through Adolescence, *Developmental Psychology*, 32, 4, 768-776.

Green, J., Kroll, L., Imrie, D., Francis, F., Begum, K., Harrison, L. *et al.*, (2001). Health gain and outcome predictors during inpatient and related day treatment in child and adolescent psychiatry, *Journal of the American Academy of Child and Adolescent Psychiatry*, 40, 325–332.

Gregory, M. and Holloway, M. (2005). Language and the Shaping of Social Work, *British Journal of Social Work*, 35, 1, 37-53.

Guardian (2009). *Children in care: How Britain is failing its most vulnerable.* http://www.theguardian.com/society/2009/apr/20/care-system-failures

Guardian (2013). *Calls for an inquiry into deaths of four men at psychiatric hospital.* http://www.theguardian.com/society/2013/jul/07/call-inquiry-deaths-psychiatric-hospital

Guilfoyle, M. (2006). Using power to question the dialogical self and its therapeutic application, *Counselling Psychology Quarterly*, 19, 1, 89-104.

Haggerty, R., Sherrod, L., Garmezy, M. and Rutter, M. (Eds.) (1997). *Stress, Risk and Resilience in Children and Adolescents: Processes, Mechanisms and Interventions*, Cambridge, Cambridge University Press.

Hair, H. (2005). Outcomes for children and adolescents after residential treatment. A review of research from 1993–2003, *Journal of Child and Family Studies*, 14,551-575.

Hall, C. (2003). *Mentoring and Young People: A literature Review*, Glasgow, SCRE. http://www.educationandemployers.org/wp-content/uploads/2014/06/mentoring-and-young-people-hall.pdf

Hall, P. (2005). Interprofessional team work: Professional cultures as barriers, *Journal of Interprofessional Care*, 1, 188-196.

Halpern, D. and Misosz (Eds.) (1998). *The Third Way: Summary of the NEXUS On-line Debate*, London, Nexus.

Hanlon, G. and Fleming, P. (2009). Updating the Critical Perspective on Corporate Social Responsibility, *Sociology Compass*, 2/6, 2-12.

Hanlon, G. (1994). *The commercialisation of accountancy*, Basingstoke, Macmillan.

Hanlon, G. (1998). Professionalism as Enterprise: Service Class Politics and the Redefinition of Professionalism, *Sociology*, 32, 1, 43-66.

Hanlon, G. (1999). *Lawyers, the State and the Market: Professionalism Revisited*, Basingstoke, Macmillan.

Hannon, C., Wood, C. and Bazalgette, L. (2010). *In loco parentis*, London, Demos.

Harder, A., Kalverboer, M., Knorth, E. and Zandberg, T. (2008). Pedagogical qualities of institutions for residential youth care. In Minnaert, A. Lutje Spelberg, H. and Amsing, H. (Eds.), *The Pedagogical Quotient*, (103–122), Houten, Bohn Stafleu van Loghum.

Harder, A., Kongeter, S., Zeller, M., Knorth, E. and Knot-Dickscheit, J. (2011). Instruments for Research on transition: Applied methods and approaches for exploring the transitions of young care leavers to adulthood, *Children and Youth Services Review*, 33, 2431-2441.

Harder, A., Kalverboer, M. and Knorth, E. (2011). They have left the building: A review on aftercare services' outcomes for adolescents following residential youth care, *International Journal of Child and Family Welfare*, 14, 86–104.

Harris, L. (1983). The State, capital, and liberal democracy. In Held, D. (Ed.), *States and Societies*, Oxford, Blackwell.

Harris, J. (1998). Scientific management, bureau-professionalism, new managerialism: the labour process of state social work, *British Journal of Social Work*, 28, 839-862.

Harris, J. (2002). Caring for Citizenship, *British Journal of Social Work*, 32, 3, 267-281.

Hartman, A. (1991). Words Create Worlds: Editorial, *Social Work*, 36, 4, 275-276.

Harvey, B. (2014). *Are you paying for that?*, Dublin, The Advocacy Initiative.

Hatfield, E., Cacioppo, J. and Rapson, R. (1994). *Emotional Contagion*, Cambridge, Cambridge University Press.

Hawkins, L., Fook, J. and Ryan, M. (2001). Social workers' use of the language of social justice, *British Journal of Social Work*, 31, 1, 1–13.

Hawkley, L. and Cacioppo, J. (2007). Aging and Loneliness: Downhill Quickly, *Current Direction in Psychological Science*, 19, 58-62.

Hawkley, L. and Cacioppo, J. (2010). Loneliness Matters: A Theoretical and Empirical Review of Consequences and Mechanisms, *Annals of Behavioural Medicine*, 40, 218-227.

Health Information and Quality Authority (HIQA) (2011). http://www.hiqa.ie/social-care/find-a-centre/childrens-centre/oberstown-campus

Health Information and Quality Authority (HIQA) (2011a). http://www.hiqa.ie/social-care/find-a-centre/childrens-special-care

Health Information and Quality Authority (HIQA) (2013b). *Overview of findings of 2012 children's inspection activity: foster care and children's residential services.* www.hiqa.ie/system/files/Analysis-2012-Childrens-Inspections.pdf

Health Information and Quality Authority (HIQA) (2013). http://www.rte.ie/news/2013/0221/368944-hiqa-inspectors-not-assured-children-were-safe/

Health Information and Quality Authority (HIQA) (2013a). *Children's Special Care Units: Inspection Reports.* http://www.hiqa.ie/social-care/find-a-centre/childrens-special-care

Health Information and Quality Authority (HIQA) (2013b). *Inspection Report 636, Oberstown Campus.* http://www.hiqa.ie/inspection-reports/inspection-report-id-636-children-detention-school-oberstown-campus-18-20-june-20

Health Information and Quality Authority (HIQA) (2014). *Inspection (ID 687) of Foster Care Service in Dublin South West/Kildare/West Wicklow.* http://hiqa.ie/social-care/find-a-centre/childrens-foster-care

Health Service Executive (HSE) (2007). *Analysis of Child Care Dataset.* http://www.hse.ie/eng/services/Publications/Children/dataset07.pdf

Health Service Executive (HSE) (2008). *Review of Adequacy for Services for Children and Families 2008.* http://hse.ie/eng/services/Publications/Children/Review%20of%20Adequacy%202008.pdf

Health Service Executive (HSE) (2008a). *Public Health Status Report: Section 3.* http://www.hse.ie/eng/services/publications/HealthProtection/Public_Health_/Health_Status_Report_section_3_and_4.pdf

Health Service Executive (HSE) (2009). *Policies and Procedures for Children's Residential Centres.* http://lenus.ie/hse/bitstream/10147/87082/1/PoliciesProcdsChildResCentres.pdf

Health Service Executive (HSE) (2010). *Child in Care Death Report,* http://www.Tusla.ie/uploads/content/Publication_Report_on_the_deaths_of_young_people_in_care.pdf

Health Service Executive (HSE) (2010a). *Monthly Performance Reports, November.* http://www.hse.ie/eng/services/publications/corporate/performancereports/2010performancereports.html

Health Service Executive (HSE) (2011). *Review of Adequacy for HSE Child and Family Services.* http://www.tusla.ie/uploads/content/Publications_reviewofadequacy2011.pdf

Health Service Executive (HSE) (2011a). *Risk Assessment and Risk Register Process.* http://www.hse.ie/eng/about/Who/qualityandpatientsafety/resourcesintelligence/Quality_and_Patient_Safety_Documents/riskoctober.pdf

Health Service Executive (HSE) (2011b). *Risk Management in the HSE: A Handbook.* http://www.hse.ie/eng/about/Who/qualityandpatientsafety/resourcesintelligence/Quality_and_Patient_Safety_Documents/handbook.pdf

Health Service Executive (HSE) (2012). *Review of Adequacy for HSE Children and Family Services 2010,* http://www.Tusla.ie/uploads/content/Publications_

reviewofadequacy2010.pdf

Health Service Executive (HSE) (2013). *Annual Report and Financial Statements.* http://www.hse.ie/eng/services/publications/corporate/

Heath, A., Colton, M. and Aldgate, J. (1994). Failure to Escape: A Longitudinal Study of Foster Children's Educational Attainment, *British Journal of Social Work*, 24, 3, 241-260.

Hendrick, H. (2009). The Evolution of Childhood in Western Europe c.1400-c.1750. In Qvortrup, J. Corsaro, W. and Honig, M. (Eds.). *The Palgrave Handbook of Childhood Studies*, Basingstoke, Palgrave Macmillan.

Hendry, L., Shucksmith, J., Love, J. and Glendinning, A. (1993). *Young People's Leisure and Lifestyles*, London, Routledge.

Hendry, L., Glendinning, A. and Shucksmith, J. (1996). Adolescent focal theories: age trends in developmental transitions, *Journal of Adolescence*, 19, 4, 307-320.

Hepworth, D., Rooney, R. and Larsen, J. (1997). *Direct Social Work Practice*, 5th Ed., California, Brooks/Cole.

Hernández, P., Gangsel, D. and Engstrom, D. (2007). Vicarious Resilience: A New Concept in Work With Those Who Survive Trauma, *Family Process*, 46, 2, 229-241.

Herrenkohl, T. (2013). Person–Environment Interactions and the Shaping of Resilience, *Trauma, Violence and Abuse*, 14, 3, 191-194.

Hesse-Biber, S. (2010). Qualitative Approaches to Mixed-methods Practice, *Qualitative Inquiry*, 16, 6, 455-468.

Hester, R. (2012). The perfect storm – a moment for decarceration, *Dialogue in praxis: A social work international journal*, 1, 14, 1-2, 27-39.

Higgins, N., Watts, D., Bindman, J., Slade, M. and Thornicroft, G. (2005). Assessing violence risk in general adult psychiatry, *Psychiatric Bulletin*, 29, 131-133.

Hiles, D., Moss, D., Wright, J. and Dallos, R. (2013). Young people's experience of social support during the process of leaving care: A review of the literature, *Children and Youth Services Review*, 35, 2059-2071.

Hiles Howard, A., Call, D., Brooks McKenzie, L., Hurst, J., Cross and Purvis, K. (2013). An examination of attachment representations among child welfare professionals, *Children and Youth Services Review*, 35, 9, 1587-1591.

Hill, M., Davis, J., Prout, A. and Tisdall, K. (2004). Moving the Participation Agenda Forward, *Children and Society*, 18, 77-96.

Hillan, L. (2005). *Reclaiming Residential Care: A Positive Choice for Children and Young People in Care*, The Winston Churchill Memorial Trust of Australia. http://www.acwa.asn.au/cafwaa/Churchill_Report_Lisa_Hillan_2006.pdf

Hinshelwood, R. (2012). On being objective about the subjective: Clinical aspects if intersubjectivity in contemporary psychoanalysis, *International Forum of Psychoanalysis*, 21, 136-145.

Bibliography

HM Treasury (2007). *Policy Review of Children and Young People: A Discussion Paper.* http://dera.ioe.ac.uk/6553/1/cyp_policyreview090107.pdf

Hoffman, D. (2010). Risky Investments: Parenting and the Production of the 'Resilient Child', *Health, Risk and Society*, 12, 4, 385-394.

Holland, S., Renold, E., Ross, N. and Hillman, A. (2008). The Everyday Lives of Children in Care: Using a Sociological Perspective to Inform Social Work Practice. In Lubock, B. and Lefevre, M. (Eds.). *Direct Work: Social Work with Children and Young People in Care*, London, BAAF.

Holland, S. and Crowley, A. (2013). Looked-after children and their birth families: using sociology to explore changing relationships, hidden histories and nomadic childhoods, *Child and Family Social Work*, 18, 57-66.

Hollingworth, K. (2012). Participation in social, leisure and informal learning activities among care leavers in England: positive outcomes for educational participation, *Child and Family Social Work*, 17, 438-447.

Holmes, L. and McDermid, S. (2012). *Understanding Costs and outcomes in Child Welfare Services*, London, Jessica Kingsley.

Holmes, L. (2014). *Supporting children and families returning home from care: Counting the Costs*, NSPCC. http://www.lboro.ac.uk/media/wwwlboroacuk/content/ccfr/publications/Supporting%20children%20and%20families%20returning%20home%20from%20care.pdf

Holohan, C. (2011). *In Plain Sight: Responding to the Ferns, Ryan, Murphy and Cloyne Reports*, Dublin, Amnsety International. http://www.amnesty.ie/sites/default/files/INPLAINSIGHT%20(WEB_VERSION).pdf

Holt, S. and Kirwan, G. (2012). The "Key" to successful transitions for young people leaving residential child care: The role of the key worker, *Child Care in Practice*, 18, 371-392.

Holthoff, S. and Eichsteller, G. (2009). Social Pedagogy: The Practice, *Every Child Journal*, 1, 1.

Horgan, A. (2011). Immigration Policy versus Welfare Policy: Separation Issues facing Separated Children on Arrival in destination Countries, *Critical Social Thinking*, 207-223.

Horton, T. and Wallander, J. (2001). Hope and Social Support as Resilience Factors Against Psychological Distress of Mothers Who Care for Children With Chronic Physical Conditions, *Rehabilitation Psychology*, 46, 4, 382-399.

House of Commons (2014). Residential Children's Homes. http://www.publications.parliament.uk/pa/cm201314/cmselect/cmeduc/716/716.pdf

Houston, S. (2010). Building resilience in a children's home: Results from an action research project, *Child and Family Social Work*, 15, 357-368.

Howard League for Penal Reform (2015). *Weekly Prison Watch*. http://www.howardleague.org/weekly-prison-watch/

Howe, D. (1996). Surface and Depth in Social Work Practice. In Parton, N. (Ed.), *Social Theory, Social Work and Social Change*, London, Routledge.

Howe, D. (1997). Psychosocial and relationship-based theories for child and family social work: political philosophy, psychology and welfare practice, *Child and Family Social Work*, 2, 161-169.

Howe, D. (1998). Relationship based thinking and practice in social work, *Journal of Social Work Practice*, 12, 45-56.

Howe, D. (2005). *Child Abuse and Neglect: Attachment, Development and Intervention*, Basingstoke, Palgrave Macmillan.

Howe, D. (2011). *Attachment across the Lifecourse: A Brief Introduction*, Basingstoke, Palgrave Macmillan.

Hughes, D. (2006). *Building the Bonds of Attachment: Awakening Love in Deeply Troubled Children*, New York, Aronson.

Ietto-Gillies, G. (2006). Is New Labour's 'Third Way' new or just hot air in old bottles? *Post-Autistic Economic Review*, 39, 1, 1-13.

Independent Children's Homes Association (ICHA) (2014). Home Truths: The State of Independent Residential Child Care 2014. http://icha.org.uk/uploads/files/icha_report_final_v3_1.pdf

International Federation of Social Workers: Statement of Ethical Principles: http://ifsw.org/policies/statement-of-ethical-principles/

International Federation of Social Workers: Global Definition of Social Work: http://ifsw.org/get-involved/global-definition-of-social-work/

Irish Association of Social Care Workers (IASCW) 2013. http://www.iasw.ie/news-post.aspx?contentid=900

Irish Association of Social Workers: Code of Ethics: http://www.iasw.ie/attachments/8b37e75a-26f6-4d94-9313-f61a86785414.PDF

Irish Association of Social Workers (IASW) (2014). http://www.iasw.ie/news-post.aspx?contentid=1606

Irish Examiner (2012). http://www.irishexaminer.com/ireland/suicide-levels-among-children-in-care-nearly-10-times-average-198946.html

Irish Examiner (2013). http://www.irishexaminer.com/archives/2013/0302/ireland/17m-care-bill-for-27-troubled-children-224322.html

Irish Examiner (2013a). http://www.irishexaminer.com/ireland/unnatural-deaths-of-children-in-care-double-226052.html

Irish Examiner (2013b). http://www.irishexaminer.com/ireland/hse-paid-uk-firm-288m-for-fostering-service-236289.html

Irish Examiner (2014). http://www.irishexaminer.com/ireland/justice-and-child-welfare-should-not-operate-as-adversarial-interests-258966.html

Irish Examiner (2014a). http://www.irishexaminer.com/ireland/teens-at-care-centre-involved-in-sex-acts-265765.html

Irish Examiner (2014b). http://www.irishexaminer.com/ireland/hse-locking-up-innocent-teens-puts-them-at-risk-254860.html

Irish Independent (2012). http://www.independent.ie/irish-news/the-governments-34m-team-of-special-advisers-26862915.html

Irish Independent (2013). http://www.independent.ie/irish-news/fostered-teen-found-sleeping-rough-48-hours-after-going-into-hse-care-29841023.html

Irish Independent (2014). http://www.independent.ie/irish-news/unit-for-troubled-youths-criticised-29903036.html

Irish Refugee Council, Arnold. S., Sarsfield Collins. L. (2011). *Closing a protection gap: National Report, 2010-11,* Dublin, The Irish Refugee Council. http://www.irishrefugeecouncil.ie/wp-content/uploads/2011/08/Closing-a-Protection-Gap.pdf

Irish Times (2014). http://www.irishtimes.com/business/sectors/energy-and-resources/where-the-irish-water-consultancy-fees-are-going-1.1655358

Irish Times (2014a). http://www.irishtimes.com/news/social-affairs/vacant-beds-for-children-in-care-cost-taxpayer-20m-1.1769338

Irish Times (2014b). http://www.irishtimes.com/news/social-affairs/more-than-200-children-in-unsuitable-care-placements-1.1773201?utm_source=dlvr.it&utm_medium=twitterr

Irish Times (2014c). http://www.irishtimes.com/business/sectors/financial-services/mandatory-system-required-to-deal-with-pensions-time-bomb-1.1946630

Issroff, J. (2005). *Donald Winnicott and John Bowlby: Personal and Professional Perspectives,* London, Karnac Books.

Iwaniec, D. (2006). *Introduction: An overview of children in public care.* In Iwaniec. D. (Ed.), *The Child's Journey Through Care: Placement Stability, Care-Planning, and Achieving Permanency,* Chichester, John Wiley and Sons.

Jackson, S. (2001). The Wounded Healer, *Bulletin of Historical Medicine,* 75, 1, 1-36.

James, C., Stams, G., Asscher, J., De Roo, A. and Van der Laan, P. (2013). *Aftercare programs for reducing recidivism among juvenile and young adult offenders: A meta analytic review, Clinical Psychology Review,* 33, 2, 263-274.

Jarausch, K. (1990). *The Unfree Professions. German Lawyers, Teachers and Engineers 1900-1950,* Oxford, Oxford University Press.

Jennings, M. (2009). *Positive Action in Politics – Lessons and Challenges from Employment Equality Law.*

Jessop, B. (1994). The Transition to Post-Fordism and the Schumpeterian Workfare State, 13-37. In Roger, B. and Brian, L. (Eds.), *Towards a Post Fordist Welfare State?* London, Routledge.

367

Jeyes, G. (2014). Keynote address at Social Care Ireland Conference, Moran Hotel, Cork, 1.4.2014.

Jeyes, G. (2014a). Joint Committee on Health and Children Debate, Vol 2, No 139. http://oireachtasdebates.oireachtas.ie/Debates%20Authoring/DebatesWebPack. nsf/committeetakes/HEJ2014092500002?opendocument

Jeyes, G. (2015). Joint Oireachtas Committee on Health and Children. https:// www.kildarestreet.com/committees/?id=2015-07-17a.7&s=aftercare+bill#g12

Joint Committee on Health and Children (2013). Question 4. http://www. oireachtas.ie/parliament/media/committees/healthandchildren/Questions-and-Replies-composite.pdf

Joint Committee on Public Services Oversight and Commissions (2015). https:// static.rasset.ie/documents/news/directprovisionreport07052015.pdf

Jones, L. and Landsverk, J. (2006). Residential education: Examining a new approach for improving outcomes for foster youth, *Children and youth Services Review*, 28, 1152-1168.

Jones, R., Everson-Hock, E., Papaioannou, D. *et al.*, (2011). Factors associated with outcomes for looked after children and young people; a correlates review of the literature, *Child: Care, Health and Development*, 37, 5, 613-622.

Jordan, B. and Parton, N. (2000). Politics and Social Work in Davies, M. (Ed.), *Blackwell Encyclopedia of Social Work*, Oxford, Oxford University Press.

Joseph, M., O'Connor, T., Briskman, J., Maughan, B. and Scott, S. (2014). The formation of secure new attachments by children who are maltreated: An observational study of adolescents in foster care, *Development and Psychopathology*, 26, 67-80.

Jude, J. and Regan, S. (2010). *An exploration of reflective practice in a social care team*, Children's Workforce Development Council. http://dera.ioe.ac.uk/2764/1/ Microsoft_Word_-_PLR0910013Jude_Regan_proofed.pdf

Kanieski, M. (2010). Securing attachment: The shifting medicalisation of attachment and attachment disorders, *Health, Risk and Society*, 12, 4, 335-344.

Kaplan, B. (1999). *Towards an Understanding of Resilience: A Critical Review of Definitions and Models*. In Glantz, D. and Johnson, L. (Eds.) *Resilience and Development*, 17-83, New York, Kluwer Academic/Plenum.

Kegan, R. and Lahey, L. (2009). *Immunity to Change*, Boston, Harvard Business Press.

Kelleher, P., Kelleher, C. and Corbett, M. (2000). *Left Out On Their Own – Young People Leaving Care in Ireland*, Dublin, Focus Ireland.

Kelliher, F. (2005). Interpretivism and the pursuit of research legitimisation: An integrated approach to single case design, *The Electronic Journal of Business Research Methodology*, 3, 2, 123-132, available online at www.ejbrm.com.

Kemshall, H. (2002). *Risk, social policy and welfare*, Buckingham, Open University Press.

Bibliography

Keenan, T. and Evans, S. (2009). *An Introduction to Child Development*, London, Sage.

Kendrick, A. (2012). What research tells us about residential child care. In *Social Work with Children and Families*, Davies, M., (Ed.), 287-303, Basingstoke, Palgrave Macmillan.

Kendrick, A. (2013). Relations, relationships and relatedness: residential child care and the family metaphor, *Child and Family Social Work*, 18, 77-86.

Kennedy Report (1970). *Reformatory and Industrial Schools Systems Report*, Dublin, Government Publications.

Kennedy, S. (2014). *Right Relationships for Our Children*, Closing Address at Unity Through Relationship Conference, Regency Hotel, November 11th 2014. www.unitythroughrelationship.com

Keyes, C. (2004). Risk and Resilience in Human Development: An Introduction, *Research in Human Development*, 1, 4, 223-227.

Kilkelly, U. (2001). The best of both worlds for children's rights? Interpreting the European Convention on Human Rights in the light of the UN Convention on the Rights of the Child, *Human Rights Quarterly*, 23, 308-326.

Kilkelly, U. (2008). 1st Ed., *Children's rights in Ireland; Law, Policy and Practice*, Dublin, Totell Publishing.

Kilkelly, U. (2011). *A children's rights analysis of investigations*, Ombudsman for Children's Office. http://www.oco.ie/wp-content/uploads/2014/03/10712_oco_audit_report_web1.pdf

Kirkpatrick, I., Ackroyd, S. and Walker, R. (2005). *The New Managerialism and Public Service Professions*, Basingstoke, Palgrave Macmillan.

Klein, N. (2007). *The Shock Doctrine: The Rise of Disaster Capitalism*, London, Penguin Books.

Kleipoedszus, S. (2011). Communication and Conflict: An Important Part of Social Pedagogic Practice. In Cameron, C. and Moss, P. (Eds.) (2011). *Social Pedagogy and Working with Children and Young People: Where Care and Education Meet*, London, Jessica Kingsley Publishers.

Kloep, M. (1999). Love is all you need: Focusing on adolescents' life concerns from an ecological point of view, *Journal of Adolescence*, 22, 49-63.

Knorth, E., Van Den Bergh, P. and Verheij, F. (2002). *Professionalisation and Participation in Child and Youth Care: Challenging Understandings in Theory and Practice*, Aldershot, Ashgate Publishing.

Knorth, E., Harder, A., Zandberg, T. and Kendrick, A. (2008). Under one roof: A review and selective meta-analysis on the outcomes of residential child and youth care, *Children and Youth Services Review*, 30, 123–140.

Koch, J. and Sievers, B. (2012). *What happens after out-of-home care? Models of good practice for Care Leavers in Germany*. www.uni-hildesheim.de/careleaver

Kohn, A. (1993). *Punished by Rewards: The trouble with Gold Stars, Incentive Plans, A's, Praise and Other Bribes*, New York, Houghton Mifflin.

Köngeter, S., Schröer, W. and Zeller, M. (2013). Germany. Presentation at International Expert Workshop: What happens after out-of-home care? Models of good practice for care leavers in Germany. http://www.igfh.de/cms/sites/default/files/Reader%20International%20Expert%20Workshop%281%29.pdf

Kratcoski, P. (2012). *Juvenile Justice Administration*, Boca Raton, CRC Press.

Krinsky, M. (2010). A not so happy birthday; the foster youth transition from adolescence into adulthood, *Family Court Review*, 48, 2, 250-254.

Krinsky, C. (Ed.) (2013). *The Ashgate Research Companion to Moral Panic*, Farnham, Ashgate.

Lalor, K. and Share, P. (Eds.) (2013). *Applied Socail Care: An Introduction for Students in Ireland*, 3rd Ed., Dublin, Gill and Macmillan.

Lansdown, G. (1995). Taking part: Children's participation in decision making, *Journal of Children's Rights*, 8, 243-259.

Lansdown, G. (2009). 1st Ed., *See me hear me; a guide to using the UN convention on the rights of persons*, Save the Children, http://www.derechosinfancia.org.mx/Documentos/see_me_hear_me.pdf

Laser, J. and Nicotera, N. (2011). *Working with adolescents: A guide for practitioners*, New York, Guilford Press.

Lather, P. (2004). This is your father's paradigm: Government intrusion and the case of Qualitative research in education, *Qualitative Inquiry*, 10, 15-34.

Leddin, A. and Walsh, B. (2003). *The Macroeconomy of the Eurozone: An Irish Perspective*, Dublin, Gill and Macmillan.

Lee, N. (1998). Towards an Immature Sociology, *The Sociological Review*, 46, 3, 458-482.

Lee, B., Bright, C., Svoboda, D., Fakunmojo, S. and Barth, R. (2011). Outcomes of group care for youth: A review of comparative studies, *Research on Social Work Practice*, 21, 177–189.

Leeson, C. (2010). The emotional Labour of caring about looked-after children, *Child and Family Social Work*, 15, 483-191.

Lefcourt, H. (2014). *Locus of Control: Current trends in Theory and Research*, New York, Psychology Press.

Lemon, K., Hines, A. and Merdinger, J. (2005). From foster care to young adulthood: The role of independent living programs in supporting successful transitions, *Children and Youth Services Review*, 27, 251-270.

Lerner, R. (2006). Resilience as an attribute of the developmental system. In, Lester, B. Masters, A and McEwen, B. (Eds.), *Resilience in Children*, (40–51), Boston, Blackwell.

Bibliography

Li, J. and Julian, M. (2012). Developmental Relationships as the Active Ingredient: A Unifying Working Hypothesis of "What Works" Across Intervention Settings, *American Journal of Orthopsychiatry*, 82, 2, 157-166.

Liebenberg, L. and Ungar, M. (Eds.) (2009). *Researching Resilience*, Toronto, University of Toronto Press.

Lin, C. (2010). Modelling Corporate Citizenship, Organizational Trust, and Work Engagement Based on Attachment Theory, *Journal of Business Ethics*, 94, 4, 517-534.

Lindsay, M. (2000). Mary. *Journal of Child and Youth Care*, 13, 2, 55-59. http://www.cyc-net.org/cyc-online/cycol-0800-mary.html

Lincoln, Y. and Cannella, G. (2004). *Dangerous Discourses: Methodological Conservatism and Government Regimes of Truth*, Qualitative Inquiry, 10, 1, 5-14.

Lister, R. (1998). Citizenship on the margins: Citizenship, social work and social action, *European Journal of Social Work*, 1, 5-18.

Little, M., Kohm, A. and Thompson, R. (2005). The impact of residential placement on child development: research and policy implications, *International Journal of Social Welfare*, 14, 200-209.

Littlechild, B. (2008). Child Protection Social Work: Risks, of Fears and Fears of Risks – Impossible Tasks from Impossible Goals, *Social Policy and Administration*, 42, 6, 662-675.

Livingston, M. (2001). *Vulnerable Moments: Deepening the Therapeutic Process*, New York, Jason, Aronson.

Lloyd, C. King, R, and Chenoweth, L. (2002). Social Work Stress and Burnout: A Review, *Journal of Mental Health*, 11, 3, 255-265.

Luthar, S., Cicchetti, D. and Becker, B. (2000). The Construct of Resilience: A Critical Evaluation and Guidelines for Further Work, *Child Development*, 71, 3, 5443-5462.

Luthar, S. and Zelazo, L. (2003). Research on resilience: An integrative view. In Luthar, S. (Ed.), *Resilience and vulnerability*, Cambridge, Cambridge University Press.

Luthar, S. (1991). Vulnerability and Resilience: A Study of High-Risk Adolescents, *Child Development*, 62, 3, 600-616.

Lynch, D. and Burns, K. (Eds.) (2012). *Children's Rights and Child Protection: Critical times, critical issues in Ireland*, Manchester, Manchester University Press.

Lyon, M. (2007). Interrogating the Concentration on the UNCRC Instead of the ECHR in the Development of Children's Rights in England?, *Children and Society*, 21, 147-153.

MacDonald, R. (1997). *Youth, the 'Underclass' and Social Exclusion*, London, Routledge.

MacDonald, R. (1998). Youth, Transitions and Social Exclusion: Some Issues for Youth Research in the UK, *Journal of Youth Studies*, 1, 2, 163-176.

MacDonald, R. (2007). Social exclusion, risk and young adulthood. In Coleman, J. and Hagell, A. (Eds.), *Adolescence, risk and resilience*, Chichester, John Wiley.

McAslan, A. (2010). *The Concept of Resilience: Understanding its Origins, Meaning and Utility*, Adelaide, Torrens Research Institute. http://torrensresilience.org/origins-of-the-term

McBride, F. (2014). *Joint Committee on Health and Children. General Scheme of Aftercare Bill: Discussion*. https://www.kildarestreet.com/committees/?id=2014-04-01a.296&s=General+scheme+of+aftercare+bill#g318

McBride, F. (2014a). *Joint Committee on Health and Children Debates. Update on Child and Family Services: Child and Family Agency, Vol. 2, No. 139*. http://oireachtasdebates.oireachtas.ie/Debates%20Authoring/DebatesWebPack.nsf/committeetakes/HEJ2014092500002?opendocument

McCarter, A. (2007). The Impact of Hopelessness and Hope on the Social Work Profession, *Journal of Human Behaviour in the Social Environment*, 15, 4, 107-123.

McCarthy, T. (1989). *The Politics of the Ineffable: Derrida's Deconstructionism in Hermeneutics in Ethics and Social Theory*, London, Wiley.

McCluskey, U. and Hooper, C. (Eds.) (2000). *Psychodynamic Perspectives on Abuse: The Cost of Fear*, London, Jessica Kingsley.

McCrystal, P. and McAloney, K. (2010). Assessing the mental health needs of young people living in State care using the Strengths and Difficulties Questionnaire, *Child Care in Practice*, 3, 6, 215-225.

McHarg, A. and Nicolson, D. (2006). Justifying Affirmative Action: Perception and Reality, *Journal of Law and Society*, 33, 1, 1-23.

McLaughlin, K. (2005). From Ridicule to Institutionalization: Anti-oppression, the State and Social Work, *Critical Social Policy*, 25, 3, 283-305.

McLeigh, J. and O'Neill Briddell, L. (2011). Where have all the children gone? The effects of the justice system on America's children and youth, *The Community*, 1, 334–341.

McSherry, D. Larkin, E. Fargas, M. Kelly, G. Robinson, C. MacDonald, G. Schubotz, D. and Kilpatrick, R. (2008). *From Care to Where? A Care Pathways and Outcomes Report for Practitioners*, Institute of Child Care Research, Queen's University Belfast.

Madonna House Report (1996). http://www.lenus.ie/hse/handle/10147/46317

Magill, M. (2006). The Future of Evidence in Evidence-Based Practice: Who Will Answer the Call for Clinical Relevance?, *Journal of Social Work*, 6, 2, 101-105.

Maguire, M., Ball, S. and Macrae, S. (2001). Post-Adolescence, Dependence and the Refusal of Adulthood, *Discourse: Studies in the Cultural Politics of Education*, 22, 197-211.

Malin, N. (2000). *Professionalism, Boundaries and the Workplace*, London, Routledge.

Margalit, M. and Idan, O. (2004). Resilience and hope theory: An expanded paradigm for learning disabilities research, *Thalamus*, 22 ,1, 58-64.

Marshall, T. (1939). The Recent History of Professionalism, *Canadian Journal of Economics and Political Science*, 5, 325-340.

Martin, P. and Jackson, S. (2002). Educational success for children in public care: advice from a group of high achievers, *Child and Family Social Work*, 7, 121-130.

Maslow, A. (1962). *Toward a Psychology of Being*, New York, Van Nostrand.

Masten, A. and Obradovic, J. (2006). *Competence and resilience in development, Annals of the New York Academy of Science, 1094, 13-27.*

Masten, A. (2001). Ordinary magic: Resilience processes in development, *American Psychologist*, 56, 3, 227-238.

Mayall, B. (2000). The sociology of childhood in relation to children's rights, *The International Journal of Children's Rights*, 8, 243-259.

Mayall, B. (2002). *Towards a Sociology of Childhood*, Buckingham, Open University Press.

Mayall, B. (2009). Generational Relations at Family Level. In Qvortrup, J. Corsaro, W. and Honig, M. (Eds.), *The Palgrave Handbook of Childhood Studies*, Basingstoke, Palgrave Macmillan.

Mayock, P. and O'Sullivan, E. (2007). *Lives in Crisis: Homeless Young People in Dublin*, Dublin, The Liffey Press.

Mayock, P. and Carr, N. (2008). *Not Just Homeless... A Study of 'Out of Home' Young People in Cork City*, Cork, Health Service Executive.

Mayock, P., Corr, M. and O'Sullivan, E. (2008). *Young People's Homeless Pathways*, Dublin, Homeless Agency. http://www.tcd.ie/childrensresearchcentre/assets/pdf/Publications/Homeless_Pathways.pdf

Meade, G. (1934). *Mind, self and society*, Chicago, University of Chicago Press.

Meade, R. (2012). Government and Community Development in Ireland: The Contested Subjects of Professionalism and Expertise, *Antipode*, 44, 3, 889-910.

Mellor, N. (2005). Attention Seeking: The Paradoxes of an Under-Researched Concept, *Educational and Clinical Psychology*, 22, 4, 94-107.

Melrose, M. (2013). Twenty-First Century Party People: Young People and Sexual Exploitation in the New Millennium, *Child Abuse Review*, 22, 155-168.

Melton, G, Lyons, P. and Spalding, W. (1998). *No place to go: the civil commitment of minors*, Lincoln, University of Nebraska Press.

Meltzer, H., Gatward, R., Goodman, R. and Ford, T. (2003). *The mental health of young people looked after by local authorities in England*, London, Stationery Office.

Mendes, P. and Moslehuddin, B. (2006). From Dependence to Interdependence: Towards Better Outcomes for Young People Leaving State Care, *Child Abuse Review*, 15, 2, 110-126.

Mendes, P. Pinkerton, J. and Munro, E. (2014). Young People Transitioning from Out-of-home Care: An Issue of Social Justice, *Australian Social Work*, 67, 1, 1-4.

Mendes, P. (2008). *Australian Welfare Wars Revisited*, Sydney, UNSW Press.

Mennen, F. and O'Keefe, M. (2005). Informed decisions in child welfare: The use of attachment theory, *Child and Youth Services Review*, 27, 577-593.

Mercer, J. and Pignotti, M. (2007). Holding therapy and Dyadic Developmental Psychotherapy are not supported and acceptable social work interventions: a systemic research synthesis revisited, *Research on Social Work Practice*, 17, 513-519.

Miller, T. (1993). *The Well-Tempered Self: Citizenship, Culture and the Postmodern*, Baltimore, John Hopkins University.

Miller, P. and Rose, N. (1995). Production, identity, and democracy, *Theory and Society*, 24, 427-467.

Milligan, I. and Stevens, I. (2006). *Residential Child Care: Collaborative Practice*, London, Sage.

Milligan, J. (1943). Principles for Democracy in Life and Education, *The Elementary School Journal*, 44, 2, 76-85.

Miliband, D. (1994). From Welfare to Wealthfare, *Renewal*, 2, 87–90.

Milner, J. and O'Byrne, P. (2002). *Assessment in Social Work*, Basingstoke, Palgrave.

Ministry of Justice (2014). *Youth Justice Statisics 2012/13: England and Wales.* https://www.gov.uk/government/uploads/system/uploads/attachment_data/file/278549/youth-justice-stats-2013.pdf

Mitchell, T. and Lee, T. (2001). The unfolding model of voluntary turnover and job embeddedness: Foundations for a comprehensive theory of attachment, *Research in Organisational Behaviour*, 23, 189-246.

Molloy, J. (2014). *The Good Manager: Moral Discernment and Courage*. In Howard, N. and Lyons, D. *Social Care: Learning from Practice*, Dublin, Gill and Macmillan.

Monaghan, L. O'Flynn, M. and Power, M. (2013). *Scapegoating in Post 'Celtic Tiger' Ireland: Framing Blame in Crisis Times*, University of Limerick, department of Sociology Working Paper Series, WP 2013-06. http://www3.ul.ie/sociology/pubs/wp2013-06.pdf

Montgomery-Devlin, J. (2008). The Sexual Exploitation of Children and Young People in Northern Ireland: Overview from the Barnardo's Over the Shadows Service, *Child Care in Practice*, 14, 4, 381-400.

Moran, J. (2010). From Catholic Church dominance to social partnership promise and now economic crisis, little changes in Irish social policy, *Irish Journal of Public Policy*, 2, 1. http://publish.ucc.ie/ijpp/2010/01/moran/01/en

Morgan, C. and Murgatroyd, S. (1994). *Total Quality Management in the Public Sector*, Buckingham, Open University Press.

Mullan, C. McAlister, S. Rollock, F. and Fitzsimons, L. (2007). 'Care Just Changes Your Life': Factors Impacting upon Mental Health of Children and Young People with Experiences of Care in Northern Ireland, *Child Care in Practice*, 13, 4, 417-434.

Munro, E. Pinkerton, J. Mendes, P. Hyde-Dryden, G, Herczog, M. and Benbenishty, R. (2011). The contribution to the United Nations Convention on the Rights of the Child to understanding and promoting the interests of young people making the transition from care to adulthood, *Child and Youth Services Review*, 33, 2417-2423.

Munro, C. (2004). *Scratching the Surface: What We Know about the Abuse and Sexual Exploitation of Young People by Adults Targeting Residential and Supported Accommodation Units*, Barnardos. http://www.barnardos.org.uk/ scratching_the_surface.pdf

Munro, E. (2011). *The Munro Review of Child Protection: Final Report. A child-centred system*. London, Department of Education. www.education.gov.uk/ publications/eOrderingDownload/Munro-Review.pdf

Murphy, S. and Shelvin, M. (2012). Loneliness in Northern Ireland, Research Update, 81, June 2012. http://www.ark.ac.uk/publications/updates/

Murphy, D. Duggan, M. and Josephs, S. (2013). Relationship-Based Social Work and its Compatibility with the Person-Centred Approach: Principled versus Instrumental Perspectives, *British Journal of Social Work*, 43, 4, 703-719.

Murphy, G. (2010). Framing Propaganda: Print Media Coverage of Irish Public Service Workers, *Socheolas: Limerick Student Journal of Sociology*, 3, 1, 3-24. http://www3.ul.ie/sociology/pubs/wp2013-06.pdf

Murphy, G. (2014). *The Accidential Entreprenneur*, Dublin, Orpen Press.

Mythen, G. (2004). *Ulrich Beck: a critical introduction to the risk society*, London, Pluto Press.

Nadjiwan, H. (2010). Restorative Justice in Education: Monthly Dialogue, 1, 8, 1-2. http://shalemnetwork.org/wp-content/uploads/2011/12/RJ-MONTHLY-June-10.pdf

Narco (2005). *A Better Alternative: Reducing Child Imprisonment*, London, Narco.

National Children's Strategy (2000). Ireland. http://www.dohc.ie/publications/ national_childrens_strategy.html

National Youth Council of Ireland (NYCI), (2010). *Youth Unemployment in Ireland: The Forgotten Generation. The experience of young jobseekers and their interaction and engagement with key State support services.* http://www.youth.ie/ sites/youth.ie/files/Youth_Unemployment_in_Ireland_web.pdf

Neal, M. and Morgan, J. (2000). The Professionalization of Everyone? A Comparative Study of the Development of the Professions in the United Kingdom and Germany, *European Sociological Review*, 16, 1, 9-26.

Nelson, D. and Quick, J. (1991). Social support and newcomer adjustment in organizations: Attachment theory at work?, *Journal of Organizational Behavior*, 12, 6, 543-555.

Nelson, C. and St. Cyr, K. (2015). What Factors are Associated with Vicarious Resilience? In Quitangon, G and Evces, M. (Eds.), *Vicarious Trauma and Disaster Mental Health: Understanding Risks and Promoting Resilience*, New York, Routledge.

Nevo, I. and Slonim-Nevo, V. (2011). The Myth of Evidence-Based Practice: Towards Evidence-Informed Practice, *British Journal of Social work*, 47, 1176-1197.

New York Times (2011). *A World in Denial of What It knows.* http://www.nytimes.com/2012/01/01/opinion/sunday/unknown-knowns-avoiding-the-truth.html?_r=0

Newell, J. and MacNeil, G. (2010). Professional Burnout, Vicarious Trauma, Secondary Traumatic Stress, and Compassion Fatigue: A Review of Theoretical Terms, Risk Factors, and Preventive Methods for Clinicians and Researchers, *Best Practices in Mental Health*, 6, 2, 57-68. http://www.iupui.edu/~mswd/S501/multimedia/word_doc/burnoutarticle.pdf

Newburn, T. and Shiner, M. (2005). *Dealing with Disaffection: Young people, mentoring and social inclusion*, Cullompton, Willan Publishing.

Newman, J. and Vidler, E. (2006). Discriminating Customers, Responsible Patients, Empowered Users: Consumerism and the Modernisation of Health Care, *Journal of Social Policy*, 35, 2, 193-209.

Newman, T. (2002). *Promoting Resilience: A Review of Effective Strategies for Child Care Services*, Barnardos. http://www.barnardos.org.uk/resources/researchpublications/documents/RESILSUM.PDF

Ní Raghallaigh, M. (2013). *Foster Care and Supported Lodgings for Separated Asylum Seeking Young People in Ireland: The views of young people, carers and stakeholders*, Dublin, Barnardos and HSE. http://www.barnardos.ie/assets/files/Advocacy/2013SeparatedChildren/Report%20into%20separated%20chidren%20in%20foster%20care.pdf

Noddings, N. (1996). *Caring: A Feminine Approach to Ethics and Moral Education*, Berkeley, University of California.

Noe, R., Wang, S. and Tomlinson, E. (2010). The Role of Mentor Trust and Protege Internal Locus of Control in Formal Mentoring Relationships, *Journal of Applied Psychology*, 95, 2, 358-367.

Nolan, K. and Downs, C. (Eds.) (2001). *Preparing youth for long term success: Proceedings from the Casey family program national independent living program*, Washington, CWLA Press.

Noordegraff, M. and Schinkel, W. (2011). Professional Capital Contested: A Bourdieusian Analysis of Conflicts between Professionals and Managers, *Comparative Sociology*, 10, 97-125.

O'Brien, C. (2012). Social Work and the Media in Ireland: A Journalists Perspective. In Lynch, D. and Burns, K. (Eds.) (2012). *Children's Rights and Child Protection: Critical times, critical issues in Ireland*, Manchester, Manchester University Press.

Bibliography

O'Brien, C. (2014). Irish Times. *Vacant beds for children in care cost taxpayer €20 million.* http://www.irishtimes.com/news/social-affairs/vacant-beds-for-children-in-care-cost-taxpayer-20m-1.1769338

O'Brien, M. (2010). Social Justice: Alive and well (partly) in social work practice, *International Social Work*, 54, 2, 174-190.

O'Brien, M. (2011). Equality and Fairness: Linking social justice and social work practice, *Journal of Social Work*, 11, 2, 143-158.

O'Kane, C. (2000). The Development of Participatory Techniques: Facilitating Children's Views about Decision Which Affect Them. In Christensen, P. James, A. (Eds.), *Research with Children Perspectives and Practice*, Abingdon, Routledge.

O'Leary, P., Tsui, M. and Ruch, G. (2013). The Boundaries of the Social Work Relationship Revisited: Towards a Connected, Inclusive and Dynamic Conceptualisation, *British Journal of Social Work*, 43, 1, 135-153.

O'Malley, P. (2008). Experiments in Risk and Criminal Justice, *Theoretical Criminology*, 12, 4, 435-469.

O'Sullivan, E. and Breen, J. (2008). Children in Care in Ireland: 1970-2006, *Social Work Now*, 41, 28-34. http://www.cyf.govt.nz/documents/about-us/publications/social-work-now/social-work-now-41-dec08.pdf

O'Sullivan, E. (2009). *Commission of Inquiry into Child Abuse, Volume IV.* http://www.childabusecommission.com/rpt/04-04.php#ftn.id1

O'Toole, F. (2009). *Ship of Fools: How Stupidity and Corruption Sank the Celtic Tiger,* London, Faber and Faber.

Oakley, A. (1999). Paradigm Wars: some thoughts on a personal and public trajectory, *International Journal of Social Research Methodology*, 2, 3, 247-254.

Olafson, E. (2002). Attachment Theory and Child Abuse: Some Cautions, *Journal of Child Sexual Abuse*, 11, 1, 125-129.

Olsson, C., Bond, L., Burns, J., Vella-Broderick, D. and Sawyer, S. (2003). Adolescent resilience: a concept analysis, *Journal of Adolescence*, 26, 1-11.

Ombudsman for Children (OCO) (2012). *Statement on the examination and proposed investigation of HSE Homelessness Service provision to children who are homeless and accommodated under Section 5 of the Child Care Act and those in the Care of the HSE accessing homeless services.* http://www.oco.ie/wp-content/uploads/2014/03/OCOInvestigationintoHSEHomelessnessprovision.pdf

Ombudsman for Children (OCO) (2013). *A Meta Analysis of Repetitive Root Cause Issues Regarding the Provision of Services for Children in Care.* http://www.oco.ie/wp-content/uploads/2014/03/OCOMeta-analysisofservicesforchildrenincare.pdf

Oireachtas Library and Reserch Centre (2013). Responding to Youth Unemployment in Europe:4. http://www.oireachtas.ie/parliament/media/housesoftheoireachtas/libraryresearch/spotlights/Responding_to_Youth_Unemployment_in_Europe.pdf

Organization for Economic Cooperation and Development (OECD) (2013). *Getting youth on the job track*. In: OECD, *Economic Surveys: Ireland 2013*, Paris, Organization for Economic Co-operation and Development. http://www. keepeek.com/Digital-Asset-Management/oecd/economics/oecd-economic-surveys-ireland-2013_eco_surveys-irl-2013-en#page1

Osterling, K. and Hines, M. (2006). Mentoring adolescent foster youth: promoting resilience during developmental transitions, *Child and Family Social Work*, 11, 242-253.

Opie, I. and Opie, P. (1969). In West, E. and Petrick, P. (Eds.) (1992), *Small Worlds*, Lawrence, University Press of Kansas.

Owens, L. (2008). The Child Welfare Profession's Perception of Residential Care for Children, *Residential Treatment for Children and Youth*, 25, 1, 17-37.

Pais, J. (2003). The multiple faces of the future in the labyrinth of life, *Journal of Youth Studies*, 6, 115-126.

Partington, P. and Brown, G. (1997). Quality assessment, staff development and cultural change, *Quality Assurance in Education*, 5, 4, 208-217.

Parrot, L. and Maddoc-Jones, I. (2008). Reclaiming Information and Communication Technologies for Empowerment in Social Work Practice, *Journal of Social Work*, 8, 2, 181-197.

Perry, B. (2009). Examining child maltreatment through a neurodevelopmental lens: clinical application of the Neurosequential Model of Therapeutics, *Journal of Loss and Trauma*, 14, 240-255.

Perry, M. (2000). Reflections on intitution and expertise, *Journal of Clinical Nursing*, 9, 137-145.

Peters, G. and Savoie, D. (1996). Managing Incoherence: The Coordination and Empowerment Conundrum, *Public Administration Review*, 56, 2, 281-290.

Petrie, P. (2007). Foster Care: A Role for Social Pedagogy?, *Adoption and Fostering*, 31, 1, 73-80

Petrie, P. (2011). Interpersonal Communication: The Medium for Social Pedagogic Practice. In Cameron, C. and Moss, P. (Eds.), *Social Pedagogy and Working with Children and Young People: Where Care and Education Meet*, London, Jessica Kingsley.

Phares, E. (1976). *Locus of control and personality*, New Jersey, Gilver Burdett.

Phoenix, J. and Kelly, L. (2013). 'You Have To Do It For Yourself': Responsibilization in Youth Justice and Young People's Situated Knowledge of Youth Justice Practice, *British Journal of Criminology*, 53, 419-437.

Philip, K. and Hendry, L. (2000). Making sense of mentoring or mentoring making sense? Reflections on the mentoring process by adult mentors with young people, *Journal of Community and Applied Social Psychology*, 10, 211–223.

Bibliography

Phillips, G. (2008). Resilience in Practice Interventions, *Child Care in Practice*, 14, 1, 45-54.

Piaget, J. (1936). *Origins of intelligence of the child*, London, Routledge and Kegan Paul.

Pietroni, M. (1995). The nature and aims of professional education for social workers: A post modern perspective. In Yelloly, M. and Henkkel, M. (Eds.), *Learning and Teaching in Social Work: Towards reflective Practice*, London, Jessica Kingsley.

Pinkerton, J. and Coyle, D. (2012). Leaving Care: The Need to Make Connections, *Child Care in Practice*, 18, 4, 297-308.

Pinkerton, J. and McCrae, R. (1999). *Meeting the challenge? Young People Leaving care in Northern Ireland*, Aldershot, Ashgate.

Pinkerton, J. and Stein, M. (1995). Responding to the Needs of Young People Leaving State Care: Law, Practice and Policy in England and Northern Ireland, *Children and Youth Services Review*, 17, 5-6, 697-709.

Pinkerton, J. (2004). Children's Participation in the Policy Process: Some Thoughts on Policy Evaluation Based on the Irish National Children's Strategy, *Children and Society*, 18, 119-130.

Pinkerton, J. (2006). Developing a global approach to the theory and practice of young people leaving State care, *Child and Family Social Work*, 11, 191-198.

Pinkerton, J. (2011). Constructing a global understanding of the social-ecology of leaving out of home care, *Children and Youth Services Review*, 33, 2412, 2416.

Pinkerton, J. (2012). Understanding Young People's Transitions from State Care: The Need for Connections, *Diskurs Kindheits-und Jugendforschung Heft*, 3, 309-319. http://www.ssoar.info/ssoar/handle/document/39055

Pithers, D. (2013). *Attachment Theory in Practice*, Keynote Address, Social Care Ireland Annual Conference, Strand Hotel Limerick.

Pizzigati, S. (1992). *The Maximum Wage: A Common-Sense Prescription for Revitalizing America - By Taxing the Very Rich*, New York, Apex Press.

Pizzigati, S. (2012). *The Rich Don't Always Win: The Forgotten Triumph over Plutocracy that Created the American Middle Class, 1900-1970*, New York, Seven Stories Press.

Plug, W. and DuBois, R. (2006). Transition patterns between structure and agency. In Walther, A. DuBois, R, and Biggart, A. (Eds.), Participation in Transition, Frankfurt am Main, Peter Lang, 107–26.

Pole, C. Mizen, P. and Bolton, A. (1999). Realising children's agency in research: partners and participants?, *Social Research Methodology*, 2, 1, 39-54.

Polit, F. and Beck, T. (2008). *Nursing research: Generating and assessing evidence for nursing practice*, Philadelphia, Lippincott, Williams and Wilkins.

Pollock, L. (1984). *Forgotten Children*, Cambridge, Cambridge University Press.

Pollack, S. (2010). Labelling Clients 'Risky': Social Work and the Neo-liberal Welfare State, *British Journal of Social Work*, 40, 4, 1263-1278.

Power, M. (1997). *The audit society: rituals of verification*, New York, Oxford University Press.

Princes Trust (2004). *Looking Beyond the Label.* http://www.princes-trust. org.uk/PDF/Princes%20Trust%20Research%20Look%20Beyond%20the%20 Label%20feb04..pdf

Propp, J., Ortega, D. and NewHeart, F. (2003). Independence or Interdependence: Rethinking the Transition from "Ward of Court" to Adulthood, *Families in Society: The Journal of Contemporary Human Sciences*, 84, 2, 259-266.

Prout, A. and James, A. (Eds.) (1997). *Constructing and Reconstructing Childhood: Contemporary Issues in the Sociological Study of Children*, London, Falmer Press.

Prout, A. (2005). *The Future of Childhood: Towards the Interdisciplinary Study of Children*, London, RoutledgeFalmer.

Pryce, J., Shackelford, K. and Pryce, D. (2007). *Secondary traumatic stress and the child welfare professional*, Chicago, Lyceum Books. http://www.lyceumbooks. com/pdf/stsch3.pdf

Raidió Teilifís Éireann (RTE) (2013-8-10). *HSE plans to close children's high-support unit in Monaghan after HIQA report.* http://www.rte.ie/ news/2013/1008/479075-hiqa-rath-na-nog/

Raidió Teilifís Éireann (RTE) (2014-18-10). http://www.rte.ie/news/2014/0918/644761-social-care-workers/

Raffo, C. and Reeves, M. (2000). Youth Transitions and Social Exclusion: Developments in Social Capital Theory, *Journal of Youth Studies*, 3, 147-166.

Raman, S. Inder B. and Forbes, C. (2005). Investing for success: The economics of supporting young people leaving care, Centre for Excellence, *Child and Family Welfare, Monograph 5*

Redmond, G. (2010). Children's agency and the welfare State: Policy priorities and contradictions in Australia and the UK, *Childhood*, 17, 4, 470-484.

Rees, G., Stein, M., Hick, L. and Gorin, S. (2011). *Adolescent Neglect: Research, Policy and Practice*, London, Jessica Kingsley.

Rees, P. (2010). State Dilemmas in the Provision of Alternative Care for Children: Relative Efficacy of Public Sector and Independent Sector Foster Placements, *International Journal of Public Administration*, 33, 6, 325-334.

Reeves, E. (2013). *Public-Private Partnerships in Ireland: A Review of the Experience*, Paper presented to the Nevin Economic Research Institute, Dublin. http://www.nerinstitute.net/download/pdf/reeves_neri_2013_ppp.pdf

Regehr, C., Stalker, C., Jacob, M. and Pelech, W. (2001). The Gatekeeper and the Wounded Healer, *The Clinical Supervisor*, 20, 1, 127-143.

Remen, R. http://www.awaken.com/2013/06/quotes-by-rachel-naomi-remen/

Bibliography

Reynolds, S. (2000). Evidence Based Practice and Psychotherapy Research, *Journal of Mental Health*, 9, 3, 257–266.

Rhule, D. (2005). Take Care to Do No Harm: Harmful Interventions for Youth Problem Behavior, *Professional Psychology: Research and Practice*, 36, 6, 618-625.

Richards, S., Ruch, G. and Trevithick, P. (2005). Communication Skills Training for Practice: the Ethical Dilemma for Social Work, *Social Work Education*, 24, 2, 409-422.

Riccucci, N. and Meyers, M. (2008). Comparing welfare service delivery among public, non-profit and for-profit work agencies, *International Journal of Public Administration*, 12, 31, 1441–1454.

Ridely, J., Larkins, C., Farrelly, N., Hussein, S., Austerberry, H., Manthorpe, J. and Stanley, N. (2013). Investing in the relationship: practitioners' relationships with looked-after children and care leavers in Social Work Practices, *Child and Family Social Work*, 1-10.

Rizq, R. and Target, M. (2010). 'We had a constant battle'. The role of attachment status in counselling psychologists' experiences of personal therapy: Some results from a mixed-methods study, *Counselling Psychology Quarterly*, 23, 4, 343-369.

Roder, O., Eisen, L and Bowling, J. (2015). *What Caused the Crime Decline*, New York, Brennan Centre for Justice. https://www.brennancenter.org/sites/default/files/publications/What_Caused_The_Crime_Decline.pdf

Rogers, C. (1961). *On Becoming a Person*, Boston, Houghton Mifflin.

Rogers, C. (1963). The actualizing tendency in relation to "motives" and to consciousness. In Jones, M. (Ed.), *Nebraska Symposium on Motivation*, 11, 1-24, Lincoln, NE, University of Nebraska Press.

Rogers, C. (1980). *A Way of Being*, Boston, Houghton Mifflin.

Rogers, R. (2011). I remember thinking, why isn't there someone to help me? Why isn't there someone who can help me make sense of what I'm going through? 'Instant adulthood' and the transition of young people out of state care, *Journal of Sociology*, 47, 4, 411-426.

Rogers, W. (2001). Constructing Childhood, Constructing Child Concern. In Foley, P. Roche, J. and Tucker, S. (Eds.), *Children in Society: Contemporary Theory, Policy and Practice*, Basingstoke, Palgrave.

Rolfe, G. (1999). Insufficient evidence: The problems of evidence-based nursing, *Nurse Education Today*, 19, 433-442.

Roper vs Simmons (2005). http://www.law.cornell.edu/supct/html/03-633.ZS.html

Roscommon Report (2010). Roscommon Child Care Case. http://www.hse.ie/eng/services/news/newsarchive/2010archive/oct2010/roscommonchildcarecase.html

Rose, N. (1996). The Death of the Social? Refiguring the Territory of Government, *Economy and Society*, 25, 3, 327-356.

Rose, N. (1999). *Powers of Freedom: reframing Political Thought*, Cambridge, Cambridge University Press.

Ruch, G., Turney, D. and Ward, A. (Eds.) (2010). *Relationship-Based Social Work: Getting to the Heart of Practice*, London, Jessica Kingsley Publications

Ruch, G. (2005). Relationship-based practice and reflective practice: holistic approaches to contemporary child care social work, *Child and Family Social Work*, 10, 111-123.

Ruch, G. (2007). Reflective practice in contemporary childcare social work: the role of containment, *British Journal of Social Work*, 37, 2, 659-680.

Ruch, G. (2009). Identifying 'the critical' in a relationship-based model of reflection, *European Journal of Social Work*, 12, 3, 349-362.

Ruch, G. (2011). Anxiety, defences and the primary task in integrated children's services: enhancing inter-professional practice, *Journal of Social Work Practice*, 25, 4, 433-449.

Ruch, G. (2012). Where Have All the Feelings Gone? Developing Reflective and Relationship-Based Management in Child-Care Social Work, *British Journal of Social Work*, 42, 1315-1332.

Russell, W. (2012). I get such a feeling out of.... those moments: playwork, passion, politics and space, *International Journal of Play*, 1, 1, 51-63.

Rutter, M., Giller, H. and Hagell, A. (1998). *Antisocial Behavior by Young People*, Cambridge, Cambridge University Press.

Rutter, M. (1987). Psychosocial resilience and protective Mechanisms, *The American Journal of Orthopsychiatry*, 57, 316–331.

Rutter, M. (1990). Psychosocial resilience and protective mechanisms. In Rolf, J. Masten, A. Cicchetti, D. Nuechterlein, K. and Weintraub, S. (Eds.), *Risk and protective factors in the development of psychopathology*, (181–214), Cambridge, Cambridge University Press.

Rutter, M. (1994). Continuities, transitions and turning points in development. In Rutter, M. and Hay, F. (Eds.), *Development through life: A handbook for clinicians*, (1-25), London, Blackwell Scientific.

Rutter, M. (2006). Implications for Resilience Concepts for Scientific Understanding, *Annals of the New York Academy of Sciences*, 1094, 1-12.

Rutter, M. (2007). Resilience, competence, and coping, *Child Abuse and Neglect*, 31, 205–209.

Ryan, A. (2006). Post-Positivist Approaches to Research. In *Researching and Writing your thesis: a guide for postgraduate students*, MACE, Maynooth Adult and Community Education, 12-26. http://eprints.nuim.ie/874/

Ryan Report (2009). Commission of Inquiry into Child Abuse. http://www.childabusecommission.ie/rpt/pdfs/

Ryzin, M., Mills, D., Kelban, S., Vars, M. and Chamberlain, P. (2011). Using the bridges transition framework for youth in foster care: Measurement development and preliminary outcomes, *Children and Youth Services Review*, 33, 2267-2272.

Šabić, A. (2013). Young people and risky lifestyles: the dilemma of individualisation and institutionalisation of risk, *Dialogue in Praxis: A social work international journal*, 2, 15, 1-2, 24-25, 73-91.

Sabin-Farrell, T. and Turpin, G. (2003). Vicarious traumatization: Implications for the mental health of health workers, *Clinical Psychology Review*, 23, 449-480.

Saleeby, D. (Ed.) (1997). *The strengths perspective in social work*, New York, Longman.

Samuels, G. and Pryce, J. (2008). 'What doesn't kill you makes you stronger': Survivalist self-reliance as resilience and risk among young adults aging out of foster care, *Children and Youth Services Review*, 30, 10, 1198-1120.

Saunders, L. and Broad, B. (1997). *The health needs of young people leaving care*, Leicester, De Montfort University.

Scannell, L. and Gifford, R, (2010). Defining place attachment: A tripartite organizing framework, *Journal of Environmental Psychology*, 30, 1, 1–10.

Schein, E. (2004). *Organisational culture and leadership*, San Francisco, Jossey-Bass.

Schinkel, W. and Noordegraff, M. (2011). Professionalism as Symbolic Capital: Materials for a Bourdieusian Theory of Professionalism, *Comparative Sociology*, 10, 67-96.

Schofield, G. (2001). Resilience and family placement: a lifespan perspective', *Adoption and Fostering*, 25, 3, 6–19.

Schofield, G. (2002). The significance of a secure base: a psychosocial model of long-term foster care, *Child and Family Social Work*, 7, 259-272.

Scottish Throughcare and Aftercare Forum. *Pathways Handbook*. http://www.scottishthroughcare.org.uk/wp-content/uploads/2012/10/Pathways-Handbook.pdf

Scraton, P. and McCulloch, J. (2009). *The Violence of Incarceration*, Abingdon, Routledge.

Scraton, P. (2004). Streets of Terror: Marginalization, Criminalization and Authoritarian Renewal, *Social Justice*, 31, 1-2, 130-158.

Scraton, P. (2007). *Power, Conflict and Criminalisation*, Abingdon, Routledge.

Seligman, M. (1975). *Helplessness: On depression, development and death*, San Francisco, Freeman.

Shannon, G. and Gibbons, N. (2012). *Report of the Independent Child Death Review Group*, Dublin, Government Publications. http://www.dcya.gov.ie/documents/publications/Report_ICDRG.pdf

Shannon, G. (2010). Fourth Report of the Special Rapporteur on Child Protection:

A Report Submitted to the Oireachtas. http://www.dcya.gov.ie/documents/publications/Rapporteur-Report-2010.pdf

Sharpe, C. (2008). Residential Child Care Can Do With All the Assistance It Can Get, *Irish Journal of Applied Social Studies*, 8, 1, 30-50.

Shill, M. (2011). Intersubjectivity and the Ego, *Psychoanalytical Social Work*, 18, 1, 1-22.

Shonkoff, J., Andrews, S., Garner, M. *et al.*, (2012). The Lifelong Effects of Early Childhood Adversity and Toxic Stress: Technical Report, American Academy of Pediatrics. http://pediatrics.aappublications.org/content/129/1/e232.full.pdf

Shulman, L. (1999). *The Skills of Helping: Individuals and groups*, Illinois, Peacock.

Siegel, A. (2000). *Heinz Kohut and the psychology of the Self*, London, Routledge.

Siegel, D. (2007). *The Mindful Brain: Reflection and Attunement in the Cultivation of Wellbeing*, New York, Norton.

Silveira, F. and Boyer, W. (2015). Vicarious Resilience in Counselors of Child and Youth Victims of Interpersonal Trauma, *Qualitative Health Research*, 25, 4, 513-526.

Simmons, R., Burgeson, R., Carlton-Ford, S. and Blyth, D. (1987). The Impact of Cumulative Change in Early Adolescence, *Child Development*, 58, 5, 1220-1234.

Simms, M., Dubowitz, H. and Szilagyi, M. (2000). Health care needs of children in the foster care system, *Pediatrics*, 106, 4, 909-918.

Sinclair, I. and Gibbs, I. (1998). *Children's Homes: A Study in Diversity*, London, Wiley.

Sinclair, R. (2004). Participation in Practice: Making it Meaningful, Effective and Sustainable, *Children and Society*, 18, 106-118.

Sinuff, T., Cook, D. and Giocomini, M. (2007). How qualitative research can contribute to research in the intensive care unit, *Journal of Critical Care*, 22, 104-111.

Skuse, T. and Ward, H. (2003). *Outcomes for looked after children: Children's views of care and accommodation. A draft interim report for the department of health*, Loughborough, Centre for Child and Family Research: Loughborough University.

Smeaton, E. (2013). *Running from hate to what you think is love: The relationship between running away and child sexual exploitation*, Ilford, Barnardos.

Smith, M., Fulcher, L. and Doran, P. (2013). *Residential child care in practice: Making a difference*, Bristol, Polity Press.

Smith, M. (2003). Towards a Professional identity and knowledge Base: Is Residential Child Care Still Social Work?, *Journal of Social Work*, 3, 2, 235-252.

Smith, M. (2009). *Rethinking Residential Childcare: Positive Perspectives*, Bristol, Policy Press.

Smith, M. (2014). Presentation to the Unity through Relationship Conference,

Bibliography

Dublin. http://unitythroughrelationship.com/wp-content/uploads/2015/07/Dublin-Conference-Mark-Smith.pdf

Social Work Action Network (SWAN), (2014). http://socialworkactionnetworkireland.wordpress.com/

Söderfeldt, M., Söderfeldt, B. and Warg, L. (1995). Burnout in Social Work, *Social Work*, 40, 5, 638-646.

Solberg, A. (1996). The Challenge in Childhood Research: From 'Doing' to 'Being'. In Brannen, J. and O'Brien, M. (Eds.), *Children and Families: Research and Policy*, London, Falmer Press.

Spratt, T. (2001). The Influence of Child Protection Orientation on Child Welfare Practice, *British Journal of Social Work*, 31, 6, 933-954.

Staller, K. (2013). Railroads, Runaways and Researchers: Returning evidence rhetoric to its practice base, *Qualitative Inquiry*, 12, 3, 503-522.

Stanley, J. and Rome, A. (2013). Unit Costs of Health and Social Care 2013. http://www.pssru.ac.uk/project-pages/unit-costs/2013/

Stein, M., Pinkerton, J. and Kelleher, P. (2000). Young people leaving care in England, Northern Ireland and Ireland, *European Journal of Social Work*, 3, 3, 235-246.

Stein, M. and Wade, J. (2000). *Helping Care Leavers: Problems and Strategic Responses*, http://www.york.ac.uk/inst/spru/pubs/pdf/helpingCL.pdf

Stein, M, and Munro, E. (Eds.) (2008). *Young People's Transitions from Care to Adulthood: International Research and Practice*, London, Jessica Kingsley Publishers.

Stein, M. and Frost, N. (2009). Editorial: Outcomes of Integrated Working with Children and Young People, *Children and Society*, 23, 315-319.

Stein, M. (1994). Leaving care, Education and Career Trajectory, *Oxford Review of Education*, 20, 3, 349-360.

Stein, M. (1999). Leaving Care: reflections and challenges. In Stevenson, O. (Ed.), *Child Welfare in the UK*, Oxford, Blackwell.

Stein, M. (2004). *What works for young people leaving care?* Barkingside, Barnardos.

Stein, M. (2005a). *Mentoring for young people leaving care: 'Someone for me'*, York, Joseph Rowntree Foundation.

Stein, M. (2005b). *Resilience and young people leaving care, overcoming the odds*, York, Joseph Rowntree Foundation. http://www.jrf.org.uk/sites/files/jrf/185935369x.pdf

Stein, M. (2006a). Research Review: Young people leaving care, *Child and Family Social Work*, 11, 3, 273-279.

Stein, M. (2006b). Young people aging out of care: The poverty of theory, *Children and Youth Services Review*, 28, 422-434.

Stein, M. (2008). In Stein, M, and Munro, E. (Eds.), *Young People's Transitions from Care to Adulthood: International Research and Practice*, London, Jessica Kingsley Publishers.

Stein, M. (2008a). Resilience and Young People Leaving Care, *Child Care in Practice*, 14, 1, 35-44.

Stein, M. (2012). *Young People Leaving Care: Supporting Pathways to Adulthood*, London, Jessica Kingsley.

Stein, M. (2014). How does care leavers support in the UK compare to the rest of the world? http://www.communitycare.co.uk/2014/10/23/care-leaver-support-uk-compare-rest-world/

Stein, M. (2015). Supportive Pathways for Young People Leaving Care: Lessons Learned from Four Decades of Research. In Whittaker, J. del Valle, J. and Holmes, L. *Therapeutic Care for Children and Young People: Developing Evidence-Based International Best Practice*, London, Jessica Kingsley Publication.

Steinberg, L. (2007). Risk-taking in adolescence: new perspectives from brain and behavioural science, *Current Direction in Psychological Science*, 16, 55-59.

Stephen, D. and Squires, P. (2003). "Adults don't Realise how Sheltered They Are": A Contribution to the Debate on Youth Transitions from some Voices on the Margins, *Journal of Youth Studies*, 6, 2, 145–64.

Stevens, M., Moriarty, J., Manthorpe, J., Hussein, S., Sharpe, E., Orme, J., Mcyntyre, G., Cavanagh, K., Green-Lister, P. and Crisp, R. (2010). Helping other or a rewarding career? Investigating student motivations to train as social workers in England, *Journal of Social Work*, 12, 1, 16-36.

Stevens, J. (2008). The Impact of the National Care Standards in Scotland: putting Article 20 into practice?, *International Journal of Children's Rights*, 16, 263-279.

Stivers, R. (2001). *Technology as Magic: The Triumph of the Irrational*, New York, Continuum.

Storø, J. (2013). *Practical Social Pedagogy*, Bristol, Polity Press.

Strangleman, T. (2012). Work Identity in Crisis? Rethinking the Problem of Attachment and Loss at Work, *Sociology*, 46, 3, 411-425.

Strauss, A. and Corbin, J. (1998). *Basics of qualitative research: Grounded theory procedures and techniques*, London, Sage.

Streeter, C. (1992). Redundancy in Organizational Systems, *Social Service Review*, 66, 1, 97-111.

Stuck, E., Small, R. and Ainsworth, F. (2000). Questioning the continuum of care: Towards a reconceptualization of child welfare services, *Residential Treatment for Children and Youth*, 17, 3, 79-92.

Sunseri, P. (2005). Children Referred to Residential Care: Reducing Multiple

Placements, Managing Costs and Improving Treatment Outcomes, *Residential Treatment for Children and Youth*, 22, 3, 55-66.

Sutton-Smith, B. (1997). *The ambiguity of play*, Cambridge, MA, Harvard University Press.

Tam, H. (1998). *Communitarianism: A New Agenda for Politics and Citizenship*, Basingstoke, Macmillan Press.

Tanner, J. and Arnett, G. (2009). The emergence of 'emerging adulthood': the new life stage between adolescence and adulthood. In Furlong, A. (Ed.), *Handbook of youth and young adulthood*, London, Routledge.

Tarren-Sweeney, M. and Hazell, P. (2006). Mental health of children in foster and kinship care in New South Wales, Australia, *Journal of Paediatrics and Child Health*, 42, 3, 89-97.

Tarren-Sweeney, M. (2010). It's time to re-think mental health services for children in care, and those adopted from care, *Clinical Child Psychology and Psychiatry*, 15, 4, 613-626.

Task Force on Child Care Services (1980). *Final Report*, Dublin, The Stationery Office.

Taylor, D. and Balloch, S. (Eds.) (2005). *The Politics of Evaluation*, London, The Policy Press.

Taylor, M. (1994). Gender and Power in Counselling Supervision, *British Journal of Guidance and Counselling*, 22, 3, 319-326.

Taylor, M. (2007). Professional Dissonance, *Smith College Studies on Social Work*, 77, 1, 89-99.

Taylor, M. (2009). In *Contemporary Social Evils*, David Utting (Ed.), Jospeh Rowntreee Foundation, Bristol, Policy Press.

Teicher, M. Anderson, S. Polcari, A. Anderson, C. and Navalta, C. (2002). Developmental Neurobiology of Childhood Stress and Trauma, *Psychiatr Clin North Am*, 25, 2, 397-426.

Tham, P. and Meagher, G. (2009). Working in Human Services: How Do Experiences and Working Conditions in Child Welfare Social Work Compare?, *British Journal of Social Work*, 39, 5, 807-827.

The Centre for Social Justice (2014). *Survival of the Fittest: Improving Life Chances for Care Leavers*. http://www.centreforsocialjustice.org.uk/UserStorage/pdf/Pdf%20reports/CSJ_Care_Report_28.01.14_web.pdf

The Joint Committee on Social Care Professionals (2002). *Final Report of the Joint Committee on Social Care Professionals*. http://www.lenus.ie/hse/bitstream/10147/46110/1/10672.pdf

The Report of the Independent Child Death Review Group (ICDRG) (2012). http://www.dcya.gov.ie/documents/publications/Report_ICDRG.pdf

The Scottish Government (2014). Children's Social Work Statistics Scotland. http://www.scotland.gov.uk/Publications/2014/03/8922/downloads

Thomas, N. (2007). Towards a Theory of Children's Participation, *International Journal of Children's Rights*, 15, 2, 199-218.

Thorne, B. (2008). What's in an age name?, *Childhood*, 15, 435-439.

Thornton, L. (2005). *Discretion and Law in the British and Irish Social Welfare Systems*, Cork, Cork Online Law Review. http://corkonlinelawreview.com/editions/2005/2005x.pdf

Tomlinson, P. (2008). The Experience of Breakdown and the Breakdown that Can't be Experienced:Implications for Work with Traumatised Children, *Journal of Social Work Practice: Psychotherapeutic Approaches in Health, Welfare and the Community*, 22, 1, 15-25.

Trevithick, P. (2003). Effective relationship-based practice: a theoretical exploration, *Journal of Social Work Practice*, 17, 2, 163-176.

Trevithick, P. (2008). Revisiting the Knowledge Base of Social Work: A Framework for Practice, *British Journal of Social Work*, 38, 1212-1237.

Trevithick, P. (2011). *Social Work Skills and Knowledge: A Practice Handbook*, 3rd Ed., Maidenhead, Open University Press.

Trinder, L. and Reynolds, S. (2000). *Evidence-Based Practice: A Critical Appraisal*, Oxford, Blackwell-Science.

Trowell, J. (1995). Key Psychoanalytical Concepts. In Trowell, J. and Bower, M. (Eds.), *The Emotional Needs of Young Children and their Families: Using Psychoanalytical Ideas in the Community*, London, Routledge.

Turner, B. (1997). From Governmentality to Risk: Some Reflections on Foucault's Contribution to Medical Sociology. In Petersen, A. and Bunton, R. (Eds.), *Foucault: Health and Medicine*, ix-xxii, London, Routledge.

Turney, D. (2012). A relationship-based approach to engaging involuntary clients: the contribution of recognition theory, *Child and Family Social Work*, 17, 149-159.

Tusla (2014). *Monthly National Performance Activity Report, February*. http://www.Tusla.ie/uploads/content/Monthly_National_Performance_Activity_Report_February_2014_final.pdf

Tusla (2014a). *Aftercare Service DNE Review Report*, Tusla.

Tusla (2014b). *Review of Adequacy for HSE Children and Family Services 2012*. http://www.Tusla.ie/uploads/news/Publications_REVIEW_OF_ADEQUACY_2012_FINAL.pdf

Tusla (2014c). *Monthly National Performance Activity Report, June*. http://www.Tusla.ie/uploads/content/Monthly_National_Performance_Activity_Report_June_2014_(2).pdf

Tusla (2014d). *Monthly National Performance Activity Report, August*. http://www.tusla.ie/uploads/content/Monthly_National_Performance_Activity_

Report_August_final.pdf

Tusla (2014e). *Monthly National Performance Activity Report, September.* http://www.tusla.ie/uploads/content/Monthly_National_Performance_Activity_Report_September2014_final.pdf

Tusla (2014f). *Monthly Management Data Activity Report, October.* http://www.tusla.ie/uploads/content/Tusla_Management_Data_Report_October_2014_v1.pdf

Tusla (2014g). *Alternative Care: Practice Handbook,* Tusla.

Tusla (2014h). National Performance Activity Report, Quarter 4, 2014. http://www.tusla.ie/uploads/content/National_Performance_Activity_Report_Quarter_4_2014_Final.pdf

Twardosz, S. and Lutzker, J. (2010). Child maltreatment and the developing brain: A review of neuroscience perspectives, *Aggression and Violent Behavior,* 15, 59-68.

Tweddle, A. (2007). Youth leaving care: How do they fare? *New Directions for Youth Development,* 113, 15-31.

Ungar, M. (2004). *Nurturing Hidden Resilience in Troubled Youth,* Toronto, University of Toronto Press.

Ungar, M. (2008). Resilience across cultures, *British Journal of Social Work,* 38, 218–235.

Ungar, M. (2010). What is resilience across cultures and contexts? Advances to the theory of positive development among individuals and families under stress, *Journal of Family Psychotherapy,* 21, 1, 1–16.

Ungar, M. (2011). The Social Ecology of Resilience: Addressing Contextual and Cultural Ambiguity of a Nascent Construct, *American Journal of Orthopsychiatry,* 81, 1, 1-17.

Ungar, M. (Ed.) (2012). *The Social Ecology of Resilience: A Handbook,* New York, Springer.

Ungar, M. (2013). Resilience, Trauma, Context and Culture, *Trauma, Violence and Abuse,* 14, 3, 255-266.

UNICEF (2006). *Report of the Independent Expert for the United Nations Study on Violence Against Children, http://www.unviolencestudy.org/*

UNICEF (2007). *Implementation Handbook for the Convention on the Rights of the Child,* 3rd Ed., Geneva, Atar Roto Presse.

United Nations Committee on the Rights of the Child (2001). General Guidelines regarding the Form and Content of Initial Reports to be Submitted by States Parties under Article 44, paragraph 1(a), of the Convention, CRC/C/5.

United Nations Committee on the Rights of the Child (2002). *Concluding observations on the Committee on Economic, Social and Cultural Rights: Ireland,* Geneva: E/C.12/1/Add.77

United Nations Committee on the Rights of the Child (2006). *Concluding observations of the Committee of the Rights of the Child: Ireland*, Geneva: CRC/C/IRL/CO/2.

United Nations Committee on the Rights of the Child (2006). *Summary record of the 1182nd meeting (Chamber B) of the UN Committee on the Rights of the Child*, para. 65: Geneva. CRC/C/SR.1182.

United Nations Committee on the Rights of the Child (2006). Forty-third Session, Geneva, 11-29 September 2006, CRC/C/43/3.

United Nations Guidelines on Alternative Care, http://www.iss-ssi.org/2009/index.php?id=25

van Breda, A. Marx, P. and Kadder, K. (2012). *Journey into independent living: A grounded theory*, Johannesburg, University of Johannesburg and Girls and Boys Town South Africa. http://www.girlsandboystown.org.za/images/Journey_Towards_Independent_Living.pdf

van de Kolk, B. (2003). The neurobiology of childhood trauma and abuse, *Child Adolesc Psychiatric Clin N Am*, 12, 293– 317.

van der Kolk, B. (2005). Developmental Trauma Disorder: Toward a rational diagnosis for children with complex trauma histories, *Psychiatric Annals*, 35, 5, 401-408.

Veerman, P. (2010). The Ageing of the UN Convention on the Rights of the Child, *International Journal of Children's Rights*, 18, 585-618.

Vojak, C. (2009). Choosing Language: Social Service Framing and Social Justice, *British Journal of Social Work*, 39, 5, 935-949.

Vostanis, P., Bassi, G., Meltzer, H., Ford, T. and Goodman, R. (2008). Service use by looked after children with behavioural problems: Findings from the England survey, *Adoption and Fostering*, 32, 22-31.

Wade, J. (2003). *Leaving Care, Quality Protects Research Briefing*, No 7, Research in Practice, Darlington.

Wade, J. (2008). The ties that bind: support from birth families and substitute families for young people leaving care, *British Journal of Social Work*, 38, 1, 39-54.

Walker, J. (2008). Communication and Social Work form an Attachment Perspective, *Journal of Social Work Practice: Psychotherapeutic Approaches in Health, Welfare and the Community*, 22, 1, 5-13.

Ward, H., Holmes, L. and Soper, J. (2008). *Costs and Consequences of Placing Children in Care*, London, Jessica Kinglsey Publishers.

Ward, A. (1993). *Working in group care: Social work in residential and day care setting*, Birmingham, Venture Press.

Ward, A. (2002). Opportunity led work: the concept, *Therapeutic Communities*, 23, 2, 111-124.

Bibliography

Ward, H. (2004). Working with managers to improve services: Changes in the role of research in Social Care, *Child and Family Social Work*, 9, 13-25.

Ward, H. (2009). Patterns of insatbility: Moves within the care system, their reasons, contexts and consequences, *Children and Youth Services Review*, 33, 1113-1118.

Ward, H. (2011). Continuities and discontinuities: Issues concerning the establishment of a persistent sense of self amongst care leavers, *Children and Youth Services Review*, 33, 2512-2518.

Watts, B. (2014). Homelessness, empowerment and self-reliance in Scotland and Ireland: the impact of legal rights to housing for homeless people, *Journal of Social Policy*, 43, 4, 793-810.

Webb, S. (2006). *Social Work in a Risk Society: Social and Political Services*, Basingstoke, Palgrave Macmillan.

Weingarten, K. (2010). Reasonable Hope: Construct, Clinical Applications, and Supports, *Family Process*, 49, 1, 5-25.

Whittaker, J. (2004). The re-invention of residential treatment: An agenda for research and practice, *Child and Youth Adolescent Psychiatric Clinics of North America*, 13, 2, 267-279.

Wilberforce, M. Jacobs, S. Challis, D. Manthrope, J. Stephens, M. Jasper, R. Fernandez, J. Glendinning, C. Jones, K. Knapp, M. Moran, N. and Netten, A. (2014). Revisiting the Causes of Stress in Social Work: Sources of Job Demands, Control and Support in Personalised Adult Social Care, *British Journal of Social Work*, 44, 812-830.

Wilson, K. (2000). *Therapeutic intervention* in Davies, M. (Ed.), *Encyclopaedia of Social Work*, Oxford, Oxford University Press.

Winnicott, C. Sheppard, R. and Davis, M. (Eds.) (2013). *Deprivation and Delinquency: D.W. Winnicott*, Abingdon, Routledge.

Winnicott, D. (1956). *The Antisocial Tendency*. In Winnicott, D. (1984). Deprivation *and Delinquency*, London, Tavistock Publications.

Winnicott, D. (1960). *Ego Distortion in Terms of True and False Self*. In The Maturational Processes and the Facilitating Environment, *International Universities Press*, 1987, 140-152.

Winnicott, D. (1973). Delinquency as a sign of hope, *Adolescent Psychiatry*, 2, 364–371.

Winnicott, D. (1975). Primitive Emotional Development. In *Through Paediatrics to Psycho-Analysis: Collected Papers*, New York, Basic Books.

Winnicott, D. (1986). *Home is Where We Start From: Essays by a psychoanalyst*, Harmondsworth, Penguin.

Winter, K. (2006). Widening our knowledge concerning young looked after children: the case for research using sociological models of childhood, *Child and Family Social Work*, 11, 55-64.

Wolfensberger, W. (1972). *The Principle of Normalization in Human Services*, Toronto, National Institute on Mental Retardation.

Woodhead, M. and Faulkner, D. (2000). Subjects, objects or participants? Dilemmas of psychological research with children. In Christensen, P. and James, A. (Eds.), *Research with Children, Perspectives and Practice*, New York, Falmer Press.

Wyness, M. (2009). Children Representing Children: Participation and the problem of diversity in UK youth councils, *Childhood*, 4, 535-552.

Yalloway, M., Hargarden, M. and MacNab, E. (2012). Making 'new connections': The development of a differential response to child protection and welfare. In Lynch, D. and Burns, K. (Eds.), *Children's Rights and Child Protection: Critical times, critical issues in Ireland*, Manchester, Manchester University Press.

Yalom, I. (1995). *The theory and practice of group psychotherapy*, 4th Ed., New York, Basic Books.

Yates, D. (2001). Sink or Swim: Leaving Care in New Zealand, *Social Policy Journal of New Zealand*, 16, 155-174.

Yeo, S. (2003). Bonding and attachment of Australian Aboriginal Children, *Child Abuse Review*, 12, 5, 292–304.

Young, R. (1995). *Colonial Desire: hybridity in theory, culture and race*, London, Routledge.

Youth Homelessness Strategy (2001). http://www.dohc.ie/publications/youth_homelessness_strategy.html

Zolkoski, S. and Bullock, L. (2012). Resilience in children and youth: A review, *Children and Youth Services Review*, 34, 12, 2295-2303.

INDEX

accountability, 273

actualising tendency, 27

Adult Attachment Interview
(AAI), 134

aftercare, 1, 3–8, 16–19, 57, 77,
92, 94, 117, 136, 191–96,
198–202, 206–315
positive outcomes and, 322
research, 218, 230, 225, 239,
241–44
statutory entitlement to, 53,
279, 327–9
economic case for, 330–39
support, 53, 55, 101, 177, 190,
207, 261–64, 280, 284–6

Aftercare Bill (2014), 192, 304,
310–18

Aftercare Service Review Report,
259, 261, 263–4

alcoholism, 10–12, 20–1, 23, 27

Allen, Jon, 30

*Alternative Care: Practice
Handbook*, 262

Anglin, James, 115, 290, 325

Anti-Social Behaviour Order
(ABSO), 188

appliance of science model, 141,
238

Applied Social Studies in Social
Care course, 268

Association of Resident
Managers of Reformatories and
Industrial Schools, 76

Asylums, 62

attachment theory, 7, 43, 61,
119–40, 293
behavioural perspective and,
131
definition of, 120
mentoring and, 176
misapplication of, 138
residential care and, 133–4
trauma, 30

attachments
internalised, 132
multiple, 130
workers', 134, 138

attunement, 41

Ballydowd, 78

Barnardos, 300, 328

Berne, Eric, 47

Bettleheim, Bruno, 291

Bourdieu, Pierre, 47, 119

boundaries, 48, 313

Bowlby, John, 61

Boys Town (USA), 91

burnout, 5, 37

capitalism, 203, 269
"care at the edge", 56–7
care leavers, 7, 52, 55, 122, 143,
    185, 190–94, 206–10, 274, 280,
    297, 304, 312, 316
  deaths of, 298–300
  disabled, 159
  invisible from view, 206, 286
  labelling of, 206, 308
  mentoring and, 146, 173–77,
    286
  number in Ireland, 219, 282–83
  outcomes for, 71, 114, 134, 201,
    218, 233, 236, 309
  poverty and, 54
  research on, 219–21, 282
  stress and, 122, 154
  suicide and, 298
Centre for Excellence in Child and
  Family Welfare, 205
Centre for Social Justice, 220
Child and Family Services (HSE),
  105, 205, 248, 259–60
Child Care Act 1991, 93, 183,
  190–1, 311, 318, 328
child sexual abuse, 67, 152, 222
Children First Bill 2014, 211
Children and Young People Act
  (Scotland), 307
Children's Detention Schools,
  79–80, 103
Children's Referendum (2012), 183
children's rights, 7, 166, 181–202
  risk and, 185–6
children's voices, 197–8
Child Rights Information Network
  (CRIN), 186–7
Commission of Inquiry in Child
  Abuse (2009), 328

compassion fatigue, 37–8
Coovagh House, 78
corporate parenting, 300–10
corporatism, 254
cost/benefit analysis, 8, 330–39
Crannóg Nua, 83, 85, 103

Department for Children and
  Youth Affairs (DCYA), 211, 330
Department of Social Protection,
  290
Diamond Model, 168
Direct Provision, 93–4
doli incapax, 188
Eastern Health Board, 222
empowerment, 283–4
Erikson, Erik, 179
Eurochild, 74
European Charter of Human
  Rights (ECHR), 189, 193, 201–2
evidence-based practice, 137,
  230–33, 237, 242

Featherstone, Brigid, 274
Fitzgerald, Frances, 90, 206, 208,
  281, 284–85, 299, 310, 321
Flanagan, Charles, 84, 285, 310,
  333
focal theory, 7, 149–58
  criticisms of, 157
Focus Ireland, 283, 328
foster care, 60, 62–4, 68, 74, 114,
  130–32, 136, 170, 183, 192,
  242, 307, 311
  failings of, 68–70
  private provision of, 89–91
Foucault, Michel, 266
Four Sides Model of
  Communication, 161–2
Freire, Paulo, 169

Gambrill, Eileen, 326

Gilligan, Robbie, 191, 193, 203, 219, 223, 322, 328

Gleann Álainn, 78

haltung, 165–6

Health Information and Quality Authority (HIQA), 76–80, 95, 106, 211, 231, 287, 322
  Inspection Reports, 69, 76, 78, 323

hierarchy of needs, 153

High Support Units, 77–81, 83, 85, 107
  cost of, 81

in loco parentis, 45, 235, 301

independence, 53–7

independent living, 1, 51, 55, 133, 177, 226, 322

individualisation, 142, 145, 184, 187, 202–3, 205, 255, 301

individualism, 205

International Federation of Social Workers, 6
  Global Definition of Social Work, 271
  Statement of Ethical Principles, 277

Investigation in Deaths in Care (2012), 328

Irish Association of Social Workers Code of Ethics, 271

Irish National Policy for Leaving and Aftercare, 7

Jeyes, Gordon, 189, 307–8, 317–18

Joint Committte on Social Care Professionals, 5

Jung, Carl, 36

Kennedy Report (1970), 65, 76, 190, 210

Kennedy, Sr. Stanislaus, 248

key performance indicators, 250, 255

key worker, 18, 21–2, 25, 128
  role of 49–51

key working, 42, 45

Kohn, Alfie, 259

language, 287–91

leaving care, 4, 55, 123, 143, 152, 156, 159, 198, 200, 284, 289, 298, 311, 322
  numbers each year, 101
  preparation for, 4, 51, 92, 133, 190, 193, 201–2, 209–10, 214, 222, 262, 280, 327

Left Out on Their Own, 137, 223, 328

liberalism, 229

listening, 158–63

loneliness, 13, 18, 50–2, 57, 122

Madonna House Report (1996), 190, 328

Malmo Declaration, 65

managerialism, 230, 250
  new, 251

Maslow, Abraham, 153

maximum wage, 258

McBride, Fred, 282–3

McVerry, Fr Peter. 248

mentoring, 146, 173–8
  engagement, 174

Mentoring for Care Leavers, 174

mentors, 128, 133, 146, 148, 173, 175, 175–78, 286

Munro Report, 2

National Policy for Leaving and Aftercare, 194, 196, 210, 214, 285

National Policy Framework for
  Children and Young People
  2014–2020, 194, 196, 210, 214
neoliberalism, 143, 203, 207, 229–
  30, 237, 252–53, 265
neuroscience, 29, 138
Noddings, Nel, 46

Oberstown Girls and Boys
  Centres, 79, 84–5, 103
O'Brien, Carl, 259–60, 321
Ombudsman for Children, 75,
  200, 328
out-of-state care, 91–2

Pathways Handbook, 4
Piaget, Jean, 123, 194
Pinkerton, John, 4, 208, 219, 235,
  241, 322
Pizzigati, Sam, 258
poverty, 292
professionalisation, 3, 5, 7, 26, 177,
  250–68
professionalism, 5, 7, 256265, 268
Public Private Partnerships, 253
Punished by Rewards, 259

random control testing, 231, 233,
  238
Rath na nÓg, 83, 85
Reilly, James, 307, 310, 316
relationship
  formation, 35
  model of 128
relationship-based practice, 122,
  170–3
relationships, 127–30, 136, 288
  meaningful, 132, 149, 249
  importance of, 42–8, 130
research
  alternative construct, 240–46
  qualitative, 7, 224–31, 237–45

quantitative, 7, 227–36
residential care, 3, 17, 24, 27,
  73–116
  myths around, 60–72
  private provision of, 82–9
  unaccompanied minors and,
  92–4
residential centres, 46, 65, 84–6,
  99, 103, 108, 111, 114, 125–7
  for-profit, 104, 106
  location of, 66, 110–11
  opportunities for meaningful
  relationships in, 132–4
resilience, 7, 44, 111, 140–9, 279
  mentoring and, 146, 174, 176
  risk and, 140–1, 292–4
  social-ecology model of, 158
  vicarious, 38–9
*Resilience and Young People
  Leaving Care*, 148
Review of Adequacy for Children
  and Family Services (HSE), 95
"Right from the Start: Report of
  the Expert Advisory Group on
  the Early Years Strategy", 321
risk, 46, 56, 94, 109, 141–43,172,
  230, 291–300
  assessment, 112, 294–5
Risk Assessment Tool and
  Guidance (HSE), 295
risk society, 186, 232, 306
Rogers, Carl, 27, 46, 165, 187
Ruch, Gillian, 170, 205, 236, 277
Ryan Report (2009), 55, 101, 190,
  210–12, 221

Save the Children (Scotland), 70
Scottish Throughcare and
  Aftercare Forum, 4
self-compassion, 39
Service Level Agreements, 76, 248

sex trade, 221–22

Smith, Mark, 26, 275

Social Care Ireland, 247, 268

social justice, 3, 5, 166, 169, 207–9, 216, 226–7, 229, 270–72, 274

social pedagogy, 4, 164–70

Common Third and, 168

differences between models of, 169–70

social policy, 203–16

SOLER technique, 162

Special Care Units, 77–81, 84–5, 107

cost of, 81

statistics, 108, 192, 219, 227, 230, 260, 278–83

Stein, Mike, 140, 148, 235, 261–63, 307

Stivers, Richard, 261

Stockholm Agreement, 63

Stockholm Declaration, The, 62, 64, 75

strengths-based perspective, 48, 137, 144, 151, 250, 296

stress, 5, 56, 122–23, 151–3

secondary traumatic, 35, 37

and workers, 291, 293

supported lodgings, 94–6

SWOT analysis, 255

system of care, 1, 56–7, 62, 71, 75, 85, 103, 106–7, 114, 278, 290

Task Force Report on Child Care Services (1980), 65, 190

Taylor, Mathew, 205

Technology as Magic: The Triumph of the Irrational, 260

Total Quality Management in the Public Sector, 109

transitions, 52–3, 151–4, 286

non-linear, 124

trauma, 29, 36, 38, 122, 143, 152, 297

system, 278

vicarious, 37–87, 278

Trinity House School, 79

Tusla – Child and Family Agency, 76, 82, 84, 89, 91, 93, 102–5, 189, 191, 211, 260–64, 278–82, 295, 304, 307–8, 310–12, 315–19, 322, 328, 330

UK Children (Leaving Care) Act (Northern Ireland) 2002, 193

unconditional positive regard, 46, 165

United Nations Convention on the Rights of the Child (UNCRC), 7, 101, 182, 189, 193–200, 202, 215–6

Guidelines for Alternative Care of Children, 190, 193

vulnerability, 32–3, 36, 40, 211, 298

Watzlawick's Five Axioms of Communication, 160–1

Winnicott, Donald, 33, 43

wounded healers, 36–7

youth incarceration, 184–5, 187

Youth Crime Action Plan (UK), 185

Youth Homeless Strategy (2001), 190

Z and Others v UK, 202